Career Development Policy & Practice:

The
TONY WATTS READER

ISBN: 978-0-9955511-07

Published by NICEC Ltd 2016
© NICEC Ltd 2016
Reprint 2016
First published by Highflyers Resources Ltd 2015

All rights reserved. No part of this book may be reprinted or reproduced or utilised in any form or by any electronic, mechanical, or other means, now known or hereafter invented, including photocopying and recording, or in any information storage or retrieval system, without permission in writing from the publishers. For a table showing the original copyright for each chapter see pages 379 and 380.

Ⓐ NICEC Ltd
Holmwood House
Farnham Road
Godalming
Surrey
GU8 6DB

Ⓦ www.nicec.org

Edited by Tristram Hooley and Lyn Barham

Tristram Hooley is Professor of Career Education at the University of Derby. He has been the Head of the International Centre for Guidance Studies for five years during which time he worked closely with Tony Watts, co-authoring a number of papers and articles and learning an enormous amount.

His research interests include career development policy, the evidence base in career development and the use of new technologies in education, research and career development.

He believes strongly in Isaac Newton's maxim that academic research is able to see further by standing on the shoulders of giants. It is this that has led him to try and re-present Tony Watts' writings in this volume to enable the career development field to continue to learn from its past.

Tristram has also authored numerous papers, articles and books on career development and related issues and writes the Adventures in Career Development blog.

Dr Lyn Barham is a Fellow of NICEC, where she has been a colleague of Tony Watts for almost 20 years.

Lyn has conducted research into various career development areas including the training and competence frameworks for career practitioners, careers in later working life, and advocacy skills. Lyn shares with Tony Watts a great commitment to international co-operation in career development activity, and served for ten years on the Executive of the International Association for Educational and Vocational Guidance (IAEVG).

Following a 'late career' doctorate, Lyn's research interests now focus on the older workforce and on 'green guidance', career guidance for a sustainable future; on both topics she has written articles and book chapters, and presented at international and national conferences. Lyn is a Legacy Fellow of the Career Development Institute, and co-ordinates CDI's Community of Interest on career development research.

Contents

Acknowledgements
Introduction   1

Section One: Conceptualising Career Development   11

1. Education and Employment: the Traditional Bonds   15
2. Reshaping Career Development for the 21st Century   29
3. Careers Education and the Informal Economies   43
4. The Economic and Social Benefits of Career Guidance   55

Section Two: Models for Practice   67

5. Careers Education   71
6. Power in Careers Guidance Work   79
7. The Concept of Work Experience   85
8. A Conceptual Framework for Work Simulation   111
9. Career Development Learning and Employability   127
10. The Role of Information and Communication Technologies in Integrated Career Information and Guidance Systems   151

Section Three: The Politics of Career Development   167

11. Socio-Political Ideologies in Guidance   171
12. The Implications of School-Leaver Unemployment for Careers Education in Schools   187
13. The Impact of the 'New Right': Policy Challenges Confronting Careers Guidance in England and Wales   205

14. Career Guidance and Social Exclusion: A Cautionary Tale	221
15. The New Career and Public Policy	241

Section Four: International Career Development   257

16. The Role of Career Guidance in Societies in Transition	261
17. Career Guidance: An International Perspective	271
18. Policy Challenges for Career Guidance	285
19. Career Guidance Policies in 37 Countries: Contrasts and Common Themes	295

Section Five: Looking Forward   313

20. Unemployment and the Future of Work	317
21. Career Development: Looking Back; Moving Forward	329
Abbreviated Bibliography	341
References	350
Index	381

Acknowledgements

We are thankful to all the publishers of the original versions of the chapters contained in this book. Further detail about the original publishers and place of publication are included as a footnote to each chapter. We would also like to thank Tony's co-authors (Ian Jamieson, Andy Miller, Bill Law, Richard Sweet and Ronald Sultana) for their agreement to re-publishing the papers that they co-authored with Tony.

Thank you to everyone who provided the input and insights that guided the selection of material in this reader. The editors have benefited from the suggestions of colleagues in a multitude of countries. It is impossible to thank all of them individually, but we would particularly like to mention the support that has been given by the National Institute for Career Education and Counselling (NICEC), the International Association for Educational and Vocational Guidance (IAEVG), the International Centre for Career Development and Public Policy (ICCDPP) and the European Lifelong Guidance Policy Network (ELGPN).

Warm thanks are due to Mike Shaw from Highflyers Resources for his patience, support and persistence which have enabled this book to be published. Thanks also to Vanessa Dodd for creating the index and for sterling work with the OCR machine. Thanks also to Beth Cutts for help with the index.

Our final, and greatest, thanks go to Tony Watts for writing this book over the course of fifty years.

Introduction

> I have written quite a lot on all these matters. My main reason for writing is simple: I do not know what I think until I have written it. In conversation one can get away with loose, exploratory thinking, but in writing it down one has to weigh up the arguments and the evidence, and decide what it all means and where one stands. It is hard work, but important; and if published, it adds to the body of knowledge on which others can draw. I commend it to you as a professional practice.
> (Tony Watts – see chapter 22)

Professor Tony Watts retired in November 2014 after fifty years in the career development field. He became the pre-eminent UK scholar in the field of career development and has written on nearly every subject of relevance to the field. His work spans career theory, practice, policy and questions about efficacy and the evidence base and is unique in its strongly international perspective.

Much valedictory discussion of Tony Watts' contribution has focused on his role as a builder of institutions within the career development field, his generous mentoring of researchers and his pivotal role as a lobbyist and political activist. All these plaudits, and more, are well deserved, but it is also important that the multiplicity of his contributions is not allowed to mask his primary contribution as a researcher, writer and theorist.

The current volume was therefore conceived to draw together the most important of Tony Watts' writings. Steered by the National Institute for Career Education and Counselling (NICEC) the contents of the present volume were identified through a process of consultation with friends and colleagues from across the world. Selection proved difficult as everyone proposed their favourites, with many offering personal anecdotes about how a particular article had introduced them to career development, expanded their thinking, or first engaged them in serious scholarship in the field.

Through a careful process of discussion, re-reading and consulting with academics, practitioners, policy makers and other "Wattsians" the editors gradually managed to whittle the 601 items in Tony's bibliography down to 22. Inevitably sacrifices have had to be made and undoubtedly there will be objections that something vital has been missed. However, we believe that the current volume offers a coherent and powerful introduction to the writing of Tony Watts. We hope that it focuses on the most enduring papers, making many of them available in print for the first time since their original publication.

About Tony Watts

Very few people will be coming to this reader unaware of Tony Watts' contribution to the field. However, it is worth briefly reflecting on his career and providing some biography for those encountering his work for the first time.

Tony Watts graduated in history from Cambridge in 1964 and went to work for Cornmarket Press, a publishing company with interests in careers and higher education. With Adrian Bridgewater, he resolved to establish a non-profit organisation with the aim of shaking up the world of careers and doing something interesting to move the field forward.

> Then Adrian [Bridgewater] and I started talking, saying that this was an interesting and important field in which much more needed to be done. So we started talking about setting up a non-profit organisation, which is what became CRAC. (Watts quoted in Hooley, 2014)

The Careers Research and Advisory Centre (CRAC) quickly established itself as a focus for innovation in the career development field and as an organization which was capable of fortifying practice and engaging policy makers (Smith, 2010). However, Tony was picking up on the beginning of a paradigm change in the way career development was being thought about:

> Then I started reading and to realise that this was actually quite complicated. I read Donald Super's (1957) *Psychology of Careers*, Peter Daws' (1968) *A Good Start in Life*, Martin Katz' (1963) *Decisions and Values* and others, and I thought: this is really intellectually interesting. So I started to think that I wanted to do something that was more serious, for which I needed additional intellectual tools. So I thought: I've got to go back to university. (Watts quoted in Hooley, 2014)

Along with people like Barrie Hopson, John Hayes and Bill Law, Tony Watts would go on to deepen the intellectual base of the field, helping to shift the conceptual framing of career development from a "medical" model to a learning model. He pursued an MPhil in sociology at the University York on career choice and higher education (later published as Watts, 1972). He then returned to CRAC in a research and development role and began to write a mix of practitioner-focused and more academic books, articles and papers.

By the early 1970s Tony was dedicated to the creation of an intellectual base for the career development field. This ambition was pursued through his writing, but also through the initiation of the *British Journal of Guidance and Counselling* in 1973 (Watts, 2014a) and the National Institute for Career Education and Counselling in 1975 (Watts, 2014b). These institutions proved to be enormously important for the field and it is from their early years that we draw much of Tony's most important writing. NICEC in particular proved to be a fertile context from which Tony could engage with the shifts in the political economy that emerged as the post-war consensus gave way to Thatcherism and then to New Labour.

During the period of Conservative Government, Tony Watts and NICEC found themselves in the interesting position of having access to and influence on career development issues with a government of which they were frequently critical. The creative tension of influence and critique stimulated some of Tony's most interesting work including papers on informal economies, unemployment, the New Right and the intersection between the politics and pedagogy of career guidance. The publication of *Rethinking Careers Education and Guidance* (Watts et al., 1996) in many ways marked the culmination of this period, synthesising many of the key ideas that Tony and his colleagues in NICEC had been addressing throughout the period of Conservative Government.

The election of a Labour Government in 1997 seemed to promise new opportunities for the careers sector. However, shifting policy priorities led to the development of the Connexions service (as discussed in chapter 14). The accompanying shift in the policy making process, with a growing focus on special advisers and consultants from professional services companies, increasingly pushed NICEC into the role of critique rather than government-supported research and development. During this period Tony also founded the Centre for Guidance Studies (later renamed as the International Centre for Guidance Studies) at the University of Derby (Hyde, 2014), providing another base for his research work and for the development of the evidence base in the career development field.

Tony became respected as a tireless advocate for the careers sector through the twists and turns of policy under the New Labour and Coalition Governments as he continued to write and publish, with an increasing focus on policy and systems. One of the important roles that he played in the UK was in analysing and critiquing government policy (or the lack of it).[1] His critiques attempt to understand the rationale of government policies (even when he disagreed with them) and to scrutinise incoherence, inconsistency and hypocrisy. Unfortunately this has proved to be a very rich seam.

A committed European and global citizen, Tony is fond of recalling early international influences on his own life, including the story of being wheeled along in a pram during the Second World War following the bombing of the family home. Later he attended a German kindergarten while his father was serving in the army in Germany. These early memories clearly informed his concern to foster international co-operation and to support the transfer of policy and practice from one context to another through collaborative institutions like the European Lifelong Guidance Policy Network and the International Centre for Career Development and Public Policy (Watts, Bezanson & McCarthy, 2014). An enduring feature of his work has been its global perspective and the ability to draw on experiences from a wide range of contexts whilst continuing to attend to the specific cultural and political systems of the countries in which he has worked. In 2001-02 he was recruited to the OECD to work on an international review of career guidance initially covering 14 countries. This ushered in a new phase of his career and contributed to an intensification of his international focus.

Through subsequent work variously with the Council of Europe, the European Commission, the International Labour Organisation, UNESCO and the World Bank, Tony and a close group of colleagues have conducted comparative studies of career guidance systems, extending the initial 14 country study to at least 55 countries (Watts, 2014c). Tony has lectured in more than sixty countries, continuing to undertake research, consultancy and lectures across the globe right up to his retirement; final projects in South Africa and Saudi Arabia showed his enduring engagement with the geographical, political and cultural limits of career guidance.

Tony Watts practises what he preaches. His writings tell us that career development is a lifelong process and that individuals have the agency to manage their careers more or less effectively even within the constraints of the opportunity structure. Tony's management of his own retirement proved to be a case study in effective career management. Over 18 months he documented key developments and initiatives to which he had contributed, handed on batons and conducted what his NICEC colleague David Andrews referred to jokingly as his "farewell tour": delivering lectures, saying goodbye to colleague and friends and sharing final encouragement and warnings with the next generations of researchers and policy makers respectively.

---

[1] Perhaps most notably in a series of almost 30 policy commentaries that he produced for Careers England between 2005 – 2014. These are available from www.careersengland.org.uk.

As Tony settles down to the next phase of his career it is an opportune time for the career development field to reflect on his contribution. The current volume will facilitate that reflection.

Drawing together the Reader

The selection of material for the Reader was challenging. The volume of Tony's output meant that identifying the best and most enduring examples of his writing was bound to be difficult. The editors tackled the task through an extensive consultation with NICEC Fellows and other key individuals from the career development world. While no selection is perfect, we feel that the present volume captures the essence of Tony's writing and re-presents it in a way that will inspire future generations of scholars.

The principles that guided the selection were threefold: (1) quality: we wanted to choose the best and most innovative of Tony's work; (2) relevance: we wanted to select material which remained fresh and which spoke to the contemporary debates in the field; and (3) uniqueness and diversity: we wanted to showcase the breadth of Tony's ideas rather than focusing on a single theme. The editors read widely through Tony's bibliography, drew on the wider consultative group and discussed the selection with Tony Watts himself.

Once chapters had been identified they were organised into five thematic sections and texts were sourced. Where digital versions did not exist, they were created; in other cases digital versions were available, but in a variety of forms. The aspiration was to create a volume which presented Tony Watts' writing in a clean and accessible format, as close to the original text as possible. However the creation of a coherent volume has required a number of editorial decisions; significant actions include the following.

- The excision of passages for reasons of length or relevance. This was done sparingly, and where possible the original text has been preserved. However, in some of the longer chapters the decision has been taken to focus on the conceptual or theoretical elements of the source material (e.g. Chapter 6) with some of the more dated examples being removed (e.g. Chapter 8).

- The removal of minor passages that relate to the original context within which the chapter was found e.g. abstracts from journal articles, final paragraphs in book chapters which link to the next chapter.

- The addition of footnotes to explain acronyms and contextual references that are not explained within the text.

- The standardisation of style, punctuation and referencing across all of the chapters.

- Making minor amendments where typological errors were found in the original.

In addition, this introduction has been created for the volume and a series of short discussions created for each of the thematic sections.

Finally a shortened version of Tony's bibliography has been included to allow those inspired by this volume to seek out his further work.

Reflecting on the themes

In a webinar at the end of his active career in the career development field, Tony Watts described this field as structurally marginal (IAEVG, 2014) – not marginal in the sense of being insignificant, but as operating at the margins between different societal structures. At its best, this can create a situation where career development work is a point of articulation between major structures in our societies: between education, employment, training, communities and – crucially – the individuals shaping and shaped by them. At its worst, when policies are generally related to the major structures in society, it can mean that career development is lost in the interstices. It is to this nebulous, slippery inter-structural field that Tony Watts has devoted his working life.

The inter-structural nature of careers work is mirrored by the interdisciplinary nature of the academic field of career studies, with links to psychology, education, sociology, economics and labour market studies, to name just the most obvious. The danger for theory development in careers work has typically been that it is subsumed into the specific concerns of one academic field without regard to others, or has been disregarded as merely the cracks between these significant, structural paving stones. Conversely, we can argue that 'the topic of career is not so much concerned with parts as with how parts are related and brought to a point in living' (Cochran, 1990, p71).

A great strength of Tony Watts' contribution has been his consistent and persistent effort to address the broad articulation of these larger parts whilst never losing sight of the end purpose of career development as a field that is substantially concerned with the individual. His work addresses a wide range of themes and disciplines as they relate to his central concerns of career and career development. His writing always seeks to offer a conceptual clarity to the unstable and boundary-crossing complexity of careers. It is this ability to identify patterns and develop frameworks for thinking about complex issues that means that his work continues to be vital and relevant many years after it was first published.

For the purpose of this book we have identified five organising themes in Tony's work: (1) conceptualising and framing the field; (2) exploring practice; (3) interrogating policies and politics; (4) international and comparative studies; and (5) providing vision for the future. We believe that this has provided a useful organizing framework for the book, but also concede that there are some major themes in Tony's work that have been missed or only addressed tangentially. Notable omissions include much of his work on new technologies (in which the detail has dated more than in other work), his early work on higher education, and his detailed work on policies, services and interventions where the context which he is writing about is no longer in existence. It is hoped that this Reader can whet the appetites of both new and confirmed Wattsians and stimulate further interest in his wider writings.

The first section addresses the nature of the field of career development. How does the concept of career development fit into the education and employment system? It argues that in the dynamic and fragmented landscape of late industrial capitalism the concept of career can offer individuals a way to forge a pathway across the crazy paving of the social, political and economic structures. To enable this we need to redefine career as each individual's passage through life, learning and work, eschewing elitist ideas that linked career to hierarchical progression. Career takes place as much in the informal economy and the household as it does in the factory and the boardroom. We also need to recognise that there is a range of interventions, and associated pedagogies and professionalisms, which can support individuals to exercise their agency and effectively manage their careers. Tony Watts usually refers to these as career guidance, but in his later writing increasingly came to use the term career development. Career development is both the individual's management of their career and the interventions that are developed to support them. Consequently career development and lifelong learning should be seen as irrevocably interlinked, with both having the potential to serve individual and societal goals.

The second section explores what this looks like in practice. How can educators, counsellors and those involved in managing human resources actively support individuals to develop their careers? Watts has much to say about how the aspiration to support career development can and should be operationalised, emphasising an empowering, educative paradigm in which individuals are supported to develop their career management skills. He conceives career development pluralistically, highlighting counselling, career education, work simulation and work experience as key features of provision. He is constantly enthusiastic about the possibilities of new technologies, embracing their potential both to enhance existing practice and to provide alternative routes for the delivery of service.

Section three examines the political landscapes within which careers unfold and career development is enacted. Tony interrogates the political nature of career development, highlighting its capacity to serve a range of masters and objectives. On one hand, career development interventions can be wielded as a tool by the state and capital to manage the populace and foster quiescence; on the other hand, they can be adopted by radicals seeking to engage people in thinking about alternative futures. These tensions around the approaches to guidance emerged centre-stage in the ideologically-charged political context of growing unemployment in the 1980s. Acknowledging that in its present manifestation career development is primarily a tool of public policy, Tony Watts consequently argues that it is vital to attend to developments in public policy such as the growth of the New Right or New Labour's concern about "social exclusion"; those active in the career development field must build a meaningful response to these concerns.

Section four moves on to examine career development as an international phenomenon. We noted earlier Tony's commitment to international and comparative studies, and this section highlights the value of this perspective. Career guidance as an international practice has coordinating institutions and a global community of practice. However, it is rooted in local delivery, enmeshed in the policies, cultures, education and employment contexts of each country. The realization of the value both of context and of policy borrowing raises key questions about the adaptability of career development outside the English speaking world, in developing countries and even in countries with fundamentally different political economies and civil societies to those in which the concept has so far developed.

And what of the future? A strong strand of utopianism runs through Tony Watts' work, as he repeatedly defines and envisions a world in which individuals' lives and careers can be better. In the final section we see two examples, separated by some three decades, of Tony considering what we have learnt from the past, and where the future might take us.

Final thoughts

This introductory chapter provides an introduction to the life and work of Tony Watts. We hope that it conveys some of the excitement that we ourselves have experienced in revisiting his key works and re-presenting them for a new generation. Now we will leave it to Tony to make the case for the importance of career development, and therefore the significance of his own thinking and writing.

> Within a democratic society, it can be argued, guidance is an important means of making the structure of society work, by linking individual needs to societal needs on a voluntaristic basis. It is not by chance that the growth of formal guidance services has been linked not only to industrialisation but

also to democratisation, to social mobility, and to cultural individualism. In these senses, guidance is a significant lubricant of social development.
(Watts, see chapter 4)

Section One:
Conceptualising Career Development

Section Introduction

Career development sits at the crossroads of disciplines. The field is rooted in psychology and in the discourse of the individual but increasingly encompasses a wide range of other disciplines. Education, sociology, business and management, politics, philosophy and economics have all shaped the field as it has grappled with the way in which individuals pursue their learning and work lives within the context of organisations and society.

In this section Tony Watts addresses this disciplinary complexity. In Education and Employment: The Traditional Bonds he discusses how the field fits into the wider education and employment system by examining the socio-political basis of this system. In this paper and in Reshaping Career Development for the 21st Century he advances the concept of "career" as being the primary means through which individuals interact with this system and argues that this concept offers the potential for individual empowerment within the context of a bureaucratised and marketised society. To achieve this, he notes, the concept of career needs to be democratised and made available to all as an instrument of individual agency.

Tony Watts' conception of career development is expansive and progressive. Career development is broadly framed as being about the individual's pursuit of the good life through a range of spheres: work; learning; family; community; hobbies and interests. In Career Education and the Informal Economies he makes the argument that career development practice needs to understand work and career in far broader terms in order to connect with the realities of people's lives. He purposefully moves away from viewing career development as being about matching individuals to jobs. For Watts, career is a lifelong endeavour and one which requires ongoing purposeful agency from the individual as well as access to help and support.

The importance of offering individuals access to help and support with their careers is the central theme of this book. In The Economic and Social Benefits of Career Guidance, Watts sets out the rationale for public policy engagement in career development. Career development is not only an individual good through which people advance their own interests, but also a social good which contributes to the effective working of the education system, the labour market and to social equity. Watts notes that most career development services are funded, directly or indirectly, by government and that while there is a vibrant and influential private sector it is generally small and only able to impact on the careers of a minority of the population. Given this, it is vital that we take the public policy aspects of the career development field seriously. Career development is political and its past and future are bound up with public policy decisions.

As these chapters demonstrate Tony Watts has been hugely influential in moving the career development field on to an interdisciplinary basis. His contribution has been to conceptualise career development as a progressive and lifelong activity which connects learning, work and other aspects of life. This conception of career and career development is empowering to the individual and relevant to a wide range of public policy goals.

1. Education and Employment: the Traditional Bonds[2]

Ideals and realities

Education has of course much loftier ideals than those of preparation for employment. At its best, it is concerned with the development of the individual's full range of abilities and aptitudes, with the cultivation of spiritual and moral values, with the nurturing of imagination and sensibility, with the transmission and reinterpretation of culture. Indeed, there is a strong tradition within education which derides the instrumental or utilitarian, and which regards vocational matters as being improper educational concerns. As Peterson (1975) puts it:

> Education is, by tradition and in theory, a leisure activity. The word school is etymologically associated with leisure and the belief that "study" and "scholarship" and "learning" should be undertaken for their own sake and arise from the individual pupil's interest is a cliche of the educational theorist and of the prize-giving address. (p.93)

Nonetheless, education has a close relationship with the world of work. Societies expect schools to develop in young people the knowledge, attitudes and skills which will enable them to contribute to the economy. Young people and their parents, too, expect schools to help them enter a worthwhile job. In a survey carried out by Morton-Williams and Finch (1968), 87 per cent of 15-year-old school-leavers thought that schools should 'teach you things which will help you to get as good a job or career as possible' (p. 4) and 89 per cent of parents agreed with them (p. 19). Only 47 per cent of teachers and 28 per cent of heads at that time considered this objective as very important for schools (p. 42). Teachers frequently, however, find it useful to invoke the claim 'If you work hard, you will get a good job'.

Historically, the vocational connections of education in Britain are strong and pervasive. As Williams (1961) points out, the first English schools, from the late sixth century, had a primarily vocational intention: that of training intending priests and monks to conduct and understand the services of the Church, and to read the Bible and the writings of the Christian Fathers (p. 127-8). As education grew during the Middle Ages, it 'was organised in general relation to a firm structure of inherited and destined status and condition: the craft apprentices, the future knights, the future clerisy' (p. 131). This remained true through to the eighteenth century, which was

---

[2] **Editorial footnote:** Reprinted, by permission of the publisher, from Dale, R. (ed.): Education, Training and Employment: Towards a New Vocationalism? Oxford: Pergamon, 1985.

remarkable for the growth of a number of new vocational academies, serving commerce, engineering, the arts, and the armed services (p. 134): in these academies, young people were prepared for the occupation they were to assume and the place in society it implied. The old classical education was still focused towards the old professions for which it had a vocational appropriateness – the church, the law (and later, as it grew, towards the Civil Service).

It was only really during the Industrial Revolution that, as Williams puts it, 'the old humanists muddled the issue by claiming a fundamental distinction between their traditional learning and that of the new disciplines' – notably science and technical education:

> ... it was from this kind of thinking that there developed the absurd defensive reaction that all real learning was undertaken without thought of practical advantage. In fact, as the educational history shows, the classical linguistic disciplines were primarily vocational, but these particular vocations had acquired a separate traditional dignity, which was refused to vocations now of equal human relevance'. (p. 142)

The result was that elite educational institutions from the Victorian era tended to propagate a particular academic and cultural heritage which was associated with a gentlemanly disdain for vocational application, and particularly for industrial manufacture. The seductive social advantages attached to these strategies helped to produce a gentrification of the industrialist, which – it has been influentially argued – has contributed significantly to Britain's economic decline (Wiener, 1981).

At the same time, however, the Industrial Revolution also saw the gradual extension of schooling from select and usually privileged groups to the mass of the population. Again, vocational motives were present. The new factories required large numbers of skilled and semi-skilled employees. Workers recruited for the land were notoriously ill-adapted to factory disciplines, and the schools were seen as one way in which they could be socialised into such disciplines. The aim was explicitly expressed by William Temple, when advocating in 1770 that poor children should be sent at the age of four to workhouses where they should be employed in manufactures and given two hours' schooling a day:

> 'There is considerable use in their being, somehow or other, constantly employed at least twelve hours a day, whether they earn their living or not; for by these means, we hope that the rising generations will be so habituated to constant employment that it would at length prove agreeable and entertaining to them ... ' (quoted in Thompson, 1967. p.84)

Factories required time-discipline, they required obedience, and they required a capacity to engage in rote, repetitive work. The new elementary schools were structured to develop all three, as well as to develop the basic skills of reading and counting that would equip workers to understand and implement simple instructions.

During the nineteenth century, such schooling was extended to all. In 1816 about 58 per cent of children attended a school of some kind for some period; by 1835 the figure had risen to 83 per cent, though the average duration of school attendance was still only one year; by 1851 the average duration had been raised to two years; and in 1870 universal elementary schooling became compulsory (Williams, 1961, pp. 136-7). The notion of compulsory schooling owed much to the 'public educators', who argued that men had a natural right to be educated, and that any good society depended on governments accepting this principle as their duty (ibid, p. 141). It also owed much to those who argued that a limited education in appropriate attitudes and habits – diligence, thrift, sobriety, deference to superiors, etc. – was necessary for social and political stability (see Simon, 1960, chapter three). On the whole, it was the links between the concerns of the latter group and the focus of the 'industrial trainers' on the social character required by the industrial work-place which tended to be predominant in determining the content of the elementary school curriculum. They were even more influential on the method of pedagogy, with its emphasis on formal instruction requiring pupils to perform specified tasks within set periods of time determined by their teachers.

The battle between the 'public educators', the 'industrial trainers' and the 'old humanists' – as Williams (ibid) terms them – continued through the nineteenth and into the twentieth centuries. Gradually scientific and technical education became established in the schools and universities, though still subject to the snobberies of the 'old humanists'. Gradually, too, the school-leaving age was raised, partly in response to arguments about the upgrading of the skill requirements of jobs and the need for the country to utilise more fully its human resources and talents. In 1944 secondary education for all was established on a tripartite basis – grammar, technical, and secondary modern. The divisions were intended to be broadly related to likely occupational destinations. Technical schools, designed largely to prepare for technician-level occupations, were never established on any very extensive scale; the grammar schools, however, led clearly to 'white-collar' occupations; while the secondary modern led to 'blue-collar' occupations (Swift, 1973). The tripartite structure accordingly produced a system of what Turner (1960) termed 'sponsored' mobility, in which students were selected early for their occupational and social level, and thereafter were prepared for this status in terms partly of appropriate skills, but also of appropriate expectations, standards of behaviour, and values.

The rigidities of this system attracted increasing criticism during the 1950s and 1960s. It was pointed out that early selection meant decisions about the level of pupils' occupational destinations were being made prematurely before their abilities and aptitudes were evident, and that this had the effect of reinforcing the advantages stemming from their home background (Floud et al., 1956). The ideological concern for greater equality of opportunity, together with the demands for a more highly skilled work-force from a then prospering economy, provided a climate in which the decision was made to merge the three forms of school into comprehensive schools catering for the full range of ability. The system of 'sponsored' mobility was accordingly replaced to some extent by a system of 'contest' mobility. This Turner (1960) likened to a race or other sporting event, in which all compete on equal terms for a limited number of prizes, and in which premature judgements on the results of the race are avoided.

In the event, this change was never fully implemented. Some areas continued to maintain selective schooling, in practice and even sometimes in name. The differences between catchment areas meant that comprehensive schools in some areas were very like grammar schools, whereas in others they were virtually indistinguishable from secondary moderns. Again, the retention of rigid streaming in many comprehensive schools permitted curricular divisions to survive institutional integration. Finally, the continued existence of elite forms of education outside the state educational system, in the independent schools, meant that some parents continued to be able to purchase advantageous positions in the 'race'.

The incomplete implementation of the comprehensive school reforms meant that the socialisation processes within schools preparing pupils for their levels of occupational destination continued to operate (Ashton and Field, 1976), but that they were increasingly concealed within a curriculum structure and examination system which permitted all pupils to take part in the 'race' instead of prematurely excluding large numbers from it. Whereas in 1961-62 73 per cent of pupils in England and Wales had left school without even attempting a public school-leaving examination (Ministry of Education, 1964, table B), the growth of comprehensive schools – along with the advent of the CSE, and the raising of the school-leaving age to 16 – meant that by 1973-74 only 20 per cent of pupils left school in England without a graded GCE/CSE result, and by 1980-81 this figure had fallen to 11 per cent (DES, 1982b, table 3). Since the main prizes were perceived as being associated with 'white-collar' work, almost all pupils became subjected to a more academic curriculum, with increased emphasis on the acquisition of knowledge and the ability to reproduce it on paper for the benefit of examination assessors (Dore, 1976). While the content of the curriculum thus became less relevant to the occupations which many pupils would come to perform, its connections with the world of employment grew no less. Its basic rationale was that it provided a meritocratic foundation on which selection for occupational destinations could be based. If secondary schools in particular no longer prepared pupils for particular forms of employment in such an overt and direct way as hitherto, what they did continued to be influenced and justified by the extent to which it determined access to employment.

The bonds

It will be evident from this brief historical outline that links with employment have been, and continue to be, a powerful influence on the development of education in Britain. In broad terms, four functions which educational institutions can play in relation to employment can be distinguished: those of selection, socialisation, orientation, and preparation. Each will now be briefly examined in turn.

Selection

Over the past century or so, there has been a steady movement from the ascription of status by birth to the achievement of status through education. As a result, the educational process has ceased to be concerned simply with the transmission of skills and values: increasingly it has taken on the functions of allocating and selecting as well as training individuals for their adult roles (Banks, 1976, p.5). Particular educational qualifications are now necessary prerequisites for entry to many occupations, and are used in selection by many employers. The case for credentialism of this kind is partly based on a utilitarian principle of efficiency, recognising the importance of developing the society's talents to the full and deploying them to maximum effect, so that the most able people can find their way into the most important and demanding jobs. In part, too, it is concerned with equity, making it possible for the social status of individuals to be determined by their talents and their efforts rather than by the accidents of birth.

It is important to recognise that in practice credentialism seems to satisfy neither of these principles very satisfactorily. In terms of efficiency, the relationship between educational qualifications and degree of success in an occupation is often very low (for American evidence on this, see Hoyt, 1965; Collins, 1979). This may be partly because professional associations, in the search for reduced supply and increased status, are constantly upgrading the educational qualifications required for entry (Dore, 1976; Watts, 1973b); the same process is used by employers seeking convenient ways of restricting the number of job applicants to a manageable size. As Berg (1970) has shown in the USA, this process of meritocratic inflation can proceed to a point where, far from adding to workers' productivity and satisfaction, it reduces them because the workers are over-qualified and their skills are not being utilised. Moreover, many of the attributes which are most important in determining occupational success – social skills, for example – are not measured by educational qualifications. Such qualifications are thus often used as criteria for occupational entry not because they are relevant but because they are administratively convenient and publicly defensible.

Their defensibility is largely due to the appearance they give of being socially equitable. But here, too, there is room for scepticism. Bourdieu and Passeron (1977) argue that schools trade in exclusive forms of 'cultural capital' based on the symbols, language forms, structure and meanings of bourgeois culture, and that students with access to such cultural capital – primarily through their families – do well in school because educational achievement is measured in terms of the skills and knowledge which the cultural capital provides. Certainly it is the case that upper-middle-class children born in the period 1930-49 were three times as likely as lower-middle-class children to reach a university, and nearly 12 times as likely as lower-working-class children to do so (Halsey, 1975). Admittedly these differentials were lower than for children born during the period 1910-29, suggesting some reduction of social class inequalities of access to educational opportunities. Westergaard and Resler (1975), however, have suggested that this moderate widening of education as an avenue of ability has been counteracted by a concomitant contraction of other channels of mobility – notably independent entrepreneurial activity and mid-career promotion up the rungs of bureaucratic hierarchies – resulting from, among other things, increased attention to educational qualifications in schools and colleges. As a result, they argue, credentialism and the expansion of educational provision are likely to have had little or no net impact on social mobility. Even if one does not argue such an extreme case, it is clear that credentialism does not remove inequalities, and that even if it diminishes them to some extent, it adds apparent legitimacy to those that remain.

Moreover, the extent of the use made of educational qualifications should not be exaggerated. As Maguire and Ashton (1981) demonstrate, employers do not in practice place such emphasis on educational qualifications as schools often imagine they do. At the higher levels of the occupational hierarchy, qualifications are often necessary but not sufficient: employers use them as a convenient pre-selection device when deciding which applicants to consider more closely, but thereafter pay little attention to them. At the lower occupational levels, qualifications are frequently used simply as crude measures not of cognitive abilities but of such normative qualities as perseverance and capacity for hard work, or are ignored altogether.

Nonetheless, the process of credentialism has had a powerful effect on education. It has increased the demand for education; it has also affected its nature. In surveys conducted in Ireland, Raven (1977) found that the goals to which primacy was attached by pupils, ex-pupils, parents, teachers and employers – for example, the fostering of personal qualities and capabilities like initiative, self-confidence, and the ability to deal with others – received scant attention in schools and, as a result, were poorly attained. Teachers and pupils worked not towards the goals which they believed to be the most important from an educational point of view, but towards goals that could be assessed in a manner acceptable for the award of educational qualifications. The result was to restrict what went on in schools to activities that were narrowly utilitarian and instrumental in scope. The available evidence indicates that much the same is true in Britain.

This process contains many ironic contradictions. Intrinsic educational values are subordinated to the extrinsic need to provide tickets to employment. Yet the content of these 'tickets' has very little direct vocational relevance, and its indirect relevance is much more pertinent to white-collar than to other occupations. The content is controlled not by employers but, ultimately by the universities. For at each stage of the educational system, the content of the curriculum tends to be determined by the needs not of those who will 'drop out' at that stage, but of those who will go on to the next; and at the apex of this structure stand the universities, which in addition exert a powerful influence on school examination boards. Their control protects the school curriculum from vocational influence, in line with the heritage of Williams' 'old humanists'. The status of subjects tends to be measured by the extent to which they have moved away from utilitarian or pedagogic traditions and have become 'academic' (Goodson, 1983).

The result is an extension to almost all school pupils of an academic curriculum very like that previously offered only to the few in the grammar schools. This curriculum is experienced by many young people as irrelevant to their immediate and future interests. The notion that the traditional liberal curriculum has some particular intrinsic virtue which work-oriented subjects do not, as a medium through which spiritual, intellectual and aesthetic powers can be developed, is itself open to question (Peterson, 1975). But even if it were true, the chances of achieving these ends with pupils suspicious of such a curriculum are greatly diminished by the examination system, which means that these pupils see the curriculum chiefly as a means of labelling them as failures through an opaque process based on restricted academic criteria. They are aware that the applicability of these criteria outside the educational world is highly disputable, particularly in the non-professional and non-clerical jobs for which many of them are destined. Moreover, although the whole process is justified to them by the supposed need to perform a sorting and pre-selection function for employers, this service in reality is not as widely used by employers as is commonly supposed; and because of their limited vantage point, pupils tend to underestimate even the extent to which it is used (see Gray et al., 1983).

Thus although the examination system provides an effective motivational spur for some, it is counter-productive for others, and can indeed alienate them permanently from formal learning. It also more generally develops an instrumental attitude to learning and work in which intrinsic motives such as actual enjoyment of working hard are rejected and regarded as socially unacceptable (Turner, 1983). Indeed, Flude and Parroll (1979, pp. 67-8) consider that 'it is the attitudes and values engendered by public examinations, and the image of education which this adolescent, academic steeplechase provokes in parents, teachers and pupils, which represent the main barrier to the development of recurrent education'.

Socialisation

The second function which educational institutions can play in relation to employment is that of influencing students' attitudes to the world of work, and to their own function within it, through the formal and informal organisation of educational institutions and the social relations within them. In the USA, Bowles and Gintis (1976) have argued that in many key respects the structure and social relations of education accurately reflect and reproduce the structure and social relations of the work-place. Both are organised hierarchically; in both, alienated workers are motivated by extrinsic rewards (examination marks in school, pay at work); and in both, work tasks are fragmented. This close correspondence between the social relationships which govern personal interaction in the workplace and the social relationships of the educational system (ibid, p. 12) means that schools nurture, within young people of different types, attitudes and behaviour consonant with their likely future levels of participation in the labour force. Those destined for managerial and professional occupations are presented during their educational careers with situations in which they are asked to be autonomous, independent and creative; those destined for the shop-floor are subjected to custodial regimes which stress obedience to rules, passivity and conformity.

In the British context, Ashton and Field (1976) have described how the identities of pupils destined for different occupational levels are established or reinforced by the identities created within their schools. Thus those destined for 'extended careers' – characterised by long training and the continuing prospect of advancement – come to see themselves as possessing superior abilities, to see the successful performance of their allotted school tasks in the light of the long-term rewards associated with the entry into a 'good career', and to understand the importance both of personal advancement and of loyalty to the organisation. The importance of 'getting on' and of 'making something of themselves' is also transmitted to those destined for 'short-term careers' – in skilled manual trades, technical occupations. and some forms of clerical and secretarial work – which again are characterised by formal training but which offer little chance of advancement beyond a certain level. Here, though, the organisational structure of the school, including streaming and more informal channelling mechanisms, restricts their access to the certification required for entry to extended careers.

Finally, those destined for 'careerless occupations' which require little training and offer no prospects of promotion and little or no intrinsic job satisfaction receive derogatory messages which, as we have seen, teach them to see themselves as 'failures'. Their realisation that academic subjects have no rewards to offer them persuades them instead to seek some alternative sources of reward or satisfaction in the here and now, for example through persistent rule-breaking and 'messing about'. Not only are these young people committed to semi-skilled and unskilled work by their educational experience, but their self-image of being academically inferior, their concern with obtaining extrinsic rewards as immediately as they can, and their desire to leave school as soon as possible, all mean that jobs of this kind have certain attractions. As Willis (1977) points out, this means that the very forms of resistance used within a school counter-culture by alienated groups of working-class boys lead them to make a largely willing entry into unskilled forms of labour, in which they are subsequently trapped – a powerful, even poignant, form of 'self-induction'. They even presage the forms of resistance – skiving etc. – which will enable them to cope with the monotony of such jobs.

Such analyses can evidently be applied too rigidly, to a point where they become mechanistic and deterministic. Clearly there are many respects in which schools do not reproduce the values and social relations of the workplace. Indeed, some influential commentators in recent years have argued that schools do not mirror the world of work well enough, but instead encourage patterns of dependency and immaturity which inhibit the process of transition to adulthood and to employment (Bazalgette, 1978a; Scharff, 1976). Clearly, too, the divisions between the groups distinguished by Ashton and Field are not as rigidly marked as the description above might suggest. The movement from a 'sponsored' to a 'contest' system – however incomplete it may have been – means that the forces of socialisation have been weakened somewhat, because the point of differentiation has been postponed, and its rigidity relaxed to some extent. Teachers have become more resistant to the notion that they should be performing a 'sorting' function, and adapting pupils to accept low-level jobs which make little use of their potential. Such resistance has indeed proceeded to a point where numbers of employers have grown concerned about the discrepancies between the expectations and attitudes that school-leavers have been encouraged to develop and the demands that will realistically be made of them (for a useful analysis of these and other differences of view between teachers and employers, see Bridges, 1981). Nonetheless, the changes that have taken place in opening up opportunities within educational institutions are often more apparent than real: for example, secondary school pupils continue to be sifted by teachers in terms of their perceived aptitudes, despite the rhetoric of pupils making their own subject 'choices' (Woods, 1979, especially chapter 2). The process of socialisation into employment remains a strong feature of the educational system – all the stronger because it is often implicit rather than explicit, and hidden even to the teachers who promote it.

Orientation

The third function is concerned with deliberate curricular interventions designed to help students to understand the world of employment, and to prepare for the choices and transitions they will have to make on entering it. To some extent it can be seen as an attempt to reinforce the process of socialisation where it is not proving sufficiently effective. Alternatively, it can also be seen as being designed to make the process more visible and therefore open to question and deliberation – to make it a learning process rather than merely a conditioning process.

This orientation function has two distinguishable facets. One is careers education, which is concerned with helping students to prepare for their individual career choices and transitions. From its traditionally peripheral position within education, based on narrow concepts of information-giving and individual interviewing, careers guidance in the early 1970s increasingly came to be incorporated into the curriculum itself (Schools Council, 1972; DES, 1973; Watts, 1973a). Many schools and other educational institutions now have curricular programmes focused around four broad aims: 'opportunity awareness', covering awareness of the range of alternatives open in and around the world of work, the demands they make, and the rewards and satisfactions they offer; 'self awareness', covering awareness of the distinct abilities, interests, values, etc. that define the kind of person one is and/or wishes to become; 'decision learning', covering development of decision-making skills; and 'transition learning', covering development of skills to cope with the transition to work and subsequent career transitions (see chapter 5). Some schools establish careers education as a separate 'subject'; some integrate it into a broader programme of social and personal education; and some seek to 'infuse' it across the traditional areas of the curriculum. A survey conducted in 1975-8 by Her Majesty's Inspectorate (DES, 1979) found that half of secondary schools had a programme of this kind in the fourth and fifth years[3] for all their pupils, and a further 12-15 per cent a programme for some of their pupils. Careers education programmes have also been introduced in higher education (Watts, 1977a) and for adults (Watts, 1980a). The notion that careers education programmes can help people to participate actively in the decisions that determine their lives has been questioned by Roberts (1977; 1981), who argues that in reality people's lives are largely determined by the opportunity structure, and that many people have to accept what they can get. This has been disputed by other writers (e.g. Daws, 1977; 1981; Law, 1981a; 1981b), who have argued that there remains sufficient scope for such programmes to have an impact.

---

3 Editorial footnote: For pupils aged 14-16. Equivalent to year/grades 10 and 11.

The second facet of the orientation function is learning about work, as part of social and political education within (in particular) schools. The central concept here is that all school pupils – regardless of when and where they are to work themselves, and as part of the preparation for their role not of worker but of citizen – should be taught to understand the place of work in society. Various approaches have been developed, including curriculum courses on 'industry' and related topics, and infusion of such topics into traditional subjects across the curriculum. There has also been emphasis on experiential methods, including work experience, work simulation, and the use of 'adults other than teachers' (including employers and trade unionists) in the classroom (see Jamieson and Lightfoot, 1982; Watts, 1983c).

A particular concern behind many such programmes has been the notion that young people should understand the process of wealth generation in general and the role of manufacturing industry in particular. Discussion of such matters is in principle welcomed not only by the political right but also by the left, so long as it is possible to regard the status quo as open to challenge and question (see e.g. Edgley, 1977). In practice, however, the boundaries set by government statements and the like tend to be narrow, and to avoid any suggestions that the matters under discussion are disputable or politically controversial. Some teachers thus fear that if they engage in such issues, they will be compelled to engage in a form of indoctrination. Accordingly, they sometimes prefer to evade the issues altogether (Beck, 1981, p.89). Significantly, the most effective project in this area – the Schools Council Industry Project – has disarmed such suspicions by having the support of the Trades Union Congress as well as the Confederation of British Industry, and has adopted a low-profile approach in which emphasis has been placed not on centrally-produced policy statements and curriculum materials, but on encouraging local curriculum development which is experience-based and in which the teachers' role is shared to a much greater extent than is usual with employers, unionists and other members of the community (see chapter 7; also Jamieson and Lightfoot, 1982).

Preparation

The fourth and final function is that of promoting the acquisition of specific skills and knowledge which students will be able to apply in a direct way after entering employment. As we have seen, this function was strongly evident in the practice of education up to the Industrial Revolution, if only in relation to certain occupations. Subsequently it has diminished in prominence, certainly within schools and universities. The general view has come to be that such preparation should properly be left to employers and to other post-school institutions like colleges of further education and polytechnics. It is argued, for example, that introducing significant vocational training into schools would require resources, equipment and expertise which schools rarely possess. It would also run the danger of limiting pupils' occupational horizons prematurely, and – unless great care was taken – it might develop knowledge and skills which would be inappropriate to, or would rapidly become outdated in, a changing labour market. Further, it is pointed out that many of the skills that are most important at work are generic skills like numeracy and literacy: if schools concentrate on these, then they are providing a form of preparation but without closing options unnecessarily.

On the other hand, it is recognised that what the Brunton Report in Scotland felicitously termed the 'vocational impulse' (SED, 1953, p. 24) can be a powerful incentive to learning. Also, unless steps are taken to introduce a wider range of vocational skills into the school curriculum, the effects of schooling may be to establish a bias in favour of the white-collar occupations to which, as was suggested earlier, the academic forms of learning used in schools tend to be most relevant. The result may be to raise aspirations which cannot be met, and to develop attitudes that impede occupational flexibility.

On the whole, however, the tendency until recently has been to limit the extent to which schools have been involved in vocational preparation. The vocational courses set up in many secondary-modern schools in the 1950s to yield the motivational advantages of the 'vocational impulse' largely disappeared with comprehensive reorganisation, and teachers became resistant to them, for reasons already mentioned. Even employers tended on the whole to bear out the findings of the Carr Committee (National Joint Advisory Council, 1958. p. 23) that 'the overwhelming majority of industries are of the opinion that education given at school before the minimum school-leaving age is reached should be general rather than vocational in character' and should not engage in offering 'some sort of vocational instruction which industry itself is much better qualified to give'. Trade unions, too, consistently opposed vocational education in schools, on the grounds that it would operate to the disadvantage of working-class children, who would be bound to be pressurised into forms of work which were more appropriate to their social station than to their innate aptitudes and abilities (Jamieson and Lightfoot, 1982). Certainly the evidence from such programmes in the USA indicates that, narrowly defined, they are almost invariably limited to low-attaining students and lower-level occupations, that they restrict access to higher-status and better-paid jobs, and that they accordingly acquire a stigma which limits and in time discredits their appeal (Grubb and Lazerson, 1981). In short. the irony of vocational-preparation programmes is that they tend to deprive their students of access to what in terms of status and income must be regarded as the real vocational prizes.

Concluding comments

It will be evident that there are some tensions and conflicts between the four functions of education in relation to employment, and that the balance between them has shifted over the years. In broad terms, the brief historical outline presented earlier in the chapter can be analysed as a process within which the socialisation and preparation functions on the whole were weakened over time, while the selection and orientation functions in general grew stronger.

To understand this, it is helpful to return to Turner's (1960) distinction between 'sponsored' and 'contest' systems of social mobility. In a 'sponsored' system, in which young people are prepared from an early age for their different occupational and social destinations, any selection function will be performed so early that it will not unduly influence the content of the curriculum: instead, the curriculum will be dominated by the socialisation and preparation functions, with the orientation function being largely redundant. On the other hand, in a true 'contest' system, in which a common curriculum is offered to all young people and allocation to destinations is postponed until towards the end of the process, the curriculum will tend to be dominated by the demands of the selection function: there will thus be little or no room for the preparation function except in the most general sense, and the socialisation function will be sufficiently weakened that there will be demands for it to be bolstered (or further undermined?) by a more deliberate orientation function.

Of course, Britain has never had a true 'contest' system of social mobility. Nonetheless, the three decades following the Second World War saw a significant shift of will in that direction, and as a result the examination system came to dominate the work of secondary schools. Within a growing economy capable of offering employment of some kind to all who wanted it, it had some credibility. The number of prizes seemed sufficient to sustain motivation on the part of a sufficient number of pupils, and there was something to offer even to the losers. In the 1970s and 1980s, however, the economic climate changed drastically, and growing unemployment threatened to undermine the rules of the race.

2. Reshaping Career Development for the 21st Century[4]

Introduction

The symbolism of the new millennium is particularly portentous for the career guidance profession. The profession is essentially a twentieth-century creation. It was at the turn of this century that the first vocational guidance bureaux began to appear both in the USA and in Europe, and that the first major book in the field – Frank Parsons' posthumous classic, *Choosing a Vocation* (Parsons, 1909) – was published. In historical terms, if one looks at it from a detached viewpoint, career guidance was a classic product of the late industrial era. It was at that point, where the traditional mechanisms of role allocation within social classes ceased to be sufficient to cope with the pace of economic and industrial change, that formal guidance services began to be developed to supplement them. The role of such services was to provide more formal and more flexible role allocation. Their methods reflected this role.

Within the industrial era, the field has been only weakly professionalised. Both here and in other countries, many of its practitioners are members of other professional groups – teachers, psychologists, labour-market administrators. It is only a fairly small residual group who define themselves primarily as careers advisers or career counsellors. They include many worthy and dedicated individuals, but their work on the whole has remained undervalued. This is partly because the shape of people's careers has been largely dictated by selective organisational processes within the education and employment systems. The role of guidance has been to supplement and to lubricate these processes.

Now, however, we are not only at the turn of the century, but at the turn of a millennium, and in the middle of a major historical transformation to a new era. The language used to describe the new era varies: a post-industrial era, a post-modern era, a new information age. Robert Reich[5] has called it "the second great crossing", comparable to the move from the land to the factory. The question this poses is whether the career guidance profession has a role in this new era, and if so, what that role is. Is it a profession whose time is passing, or a profession whose time has come?

---

4 Editorial footnote: Paper given as the Inaugural Professorial Lecture, University of Derby. Reprinted, by permission of the author and the University of Derby, from a CeGS Occasional Paper. Derby: Centre for Guidance Studies, University of Derby, 1999.
5 Editorial footnote: Robert Reich is a writer and academic who served as the Secretary of Labor in the first Clinton Administration.

The traditional concept of career

The traditional concept of career has been concerned with progression up an ordered hierarchy within an organisation or profession. If you ask most people what they understand by career, this is still the conception they hold. It is an essentially bureaucratic conception: neat and orderly. It is not without virtue. It provides order for individuals, giving them a secure basis for their lives. It provides order for society, because it ties individuals into social structures, rewarding them for their investment in those structures. It is meritocratic, allowing individuals to be promoted according to their abilities and achievements rather than the accidents of birth. It permits individual choice, particularly in choosing the particular ladder which the individual seeks to climb. It therefore requires careers advisers to help individuals in making these initial choices. Thereafter, however, the system requires little further lubrication from such advisers: it works of its own accord.

Our educational system, we should note, is still based on this model. It is heavily front-loaded. It is expected to select out and process young people, so that they emerge ready to set foot on their appointed ladder. The apparatus of course choices is part of this process. Careers advisers and teachers involved in guidance roles are its technicians. They may not like to think of themselves in this way, but in structural terms that is what they are: technicians, lubricating the system.

But this model is fragmenting – fast. It less and less describes the real world. There are fewer ladders around, and those that survive look less and less secure. The reason is the pace of change. Bureaucracies work well in a relatively static world, but they struggle to cope with change. And change is now endemic: particularly economic change, stemming from the globalisation of markets; and technological change, stemming from the pervasive impact of information and communication technologies. The result is that all organisations have to be prepared to change much more regularly and much more rapidly than ever before. They are therefore seeking more compact, more fluid and more flexible forms. Accordingly, they are less and less prepared to make long-term commitments to individuals. The orderly pathways are disappearing: as Robin Linnecar[6] graphically put it, it's now more like crazy paving, which individuals are having to lay for themselves.

The effect can feel like anarchy, as the familiar landmarks disappear. Rifkin (1995) talks about the end of work; Bridges (1995) talks about the end of jobs. It is easy, too, to find people who talk about the end of career. But I believe they are wrong to adopt such apocalyptic tones, much as millennial musing may tempt them to do so. That is why I have chosen the more transformative metaphor of "careerquake"

---

6 Editorial footnote: Robin Linnecar is a prominent business man, speaker and coach. His metaphor likening career to crazy paving was extensively cited in a range of publications in the 1990s.

(Watts, 1996): a shaking of the foundations of traditional conceptions, but with the opportunity to build new and more robust structures in its wake. It is also why Audrey Collin and I have used the alternative Christian metaphor of death and transfiguration (Collin & Watts, 1996). Work has a critical role within all religions, as a way of making sense of our time on earth. But the structures through which it is organised are made by people, and they change. They took very different forms in pre-industrial eras than in the industrial era, and they are clearly going to take very different forms again in the post-industrial era into which we are now moving. These new forms could be much creative, offering much more scope for the realisation of untapped human potential, than the models we have had hitherto. But only if we can find the concepts and the structures which will release this potential. I believe that a re-cast concept of career has a critical role to play in this respect.

The new concept of career

"Career", in my view, now needs to be redefined. Like many good words in the English language, it is richly ambiguous. It can describe neat progression up a hierarchy; but we also refer to "careering about". We need to redefine it as the individual's lifelong progression in learning and in work. Learning embraces all forms of learning: not only formal education, but training, and informal learning too. Work embraces all forms of work: not only employment, but self-employment, and unpaid work within the home and community as well. The challenge is the notion of "progression". Progression can take place laterally as well as vertically: it can incorporate elements of "careering about". But it retains the sense of development, of moving forward: career is more than mere biography. Learning is the key to progression in work. Our task is to help all individuals to interweave the two, on a lifelong basis.

This task is big business: indeed, it lies at the heart of the challenges with which governments are grappling as we approach the new millennium. The public debates are conducted largely in code. The key phrases used are three-fold: the need for labour-market flexibility, for a skills revolution, and for avoiding social exclusion. We need labour-market flexibility in order to respond to change. We need a skills revolution – a raising of the skills of all our people – in order to be competitive in world markets. And we need to avoid social exclusion – marginalising particular groups of people – both because it is morally wrong and because it is enormously expensive in terms of its impact on drug usage, crime, and violence, which reduce the quality of life for all of us. The trouble is that the three goals tend to drive in different directions. Flexibility easily means increasing gaps between the work-rich and the work-poor: between those who can make it big, and those who are left to fight for survival. This increases social exclusion; it also means that many of those trying to make out on the edge of the labour market have no opportunity to enhance their skills.

In the UK, we have emerged from a long period of "new right" government, which believed that the free flow and flexibility of markets would deliver trickle-down solutions to these problems. This was decisively rejected at our General Election last year. The new Labour Government does not worship unreservedly at the altar of markets. But nor does it believe that we can return to a planned economy, or the rigid bureaucracy of an old-style welfare state. It is seeking a "third way": a way of working with the grain of markets, but filtering them, supporting them, supplementing them, in ways which ensure that we avoid social exclusion and achieve the skills upgrading we need (Blair, 1998; Giddens, 1998).

It is my firm belief that the concept of "careers for all", based on the new definition I have offered, is one of the keys to the third way. "Lifelong learning" is now a widely-heard mantra. What the use of the word "career" does is to link lifelong learning to work, to add the element of progression, and to ground both firmly in the individual. But for people to understand the new concept, and to see it as applying to all, requires major changes in their mind-set. Certainly in the UK, many people are locked into the old concept, seeing "career" as describing the past rather than the future, as applying to "them" rather than to "us". Those involved in career guidance need to be at the forefront of efforts to change the mind-set. And that requires, I believe, an active involvement in public policy.

Policy used to be about structures and systems: about setting up government interventions administered by government bureaucracies. Now, increasingly, it is about enabling processes: about working with, and seeking to influence, the enterprise and energies of many other people and organisations. It is about ensuring that public interests are met, as far as possible, through private actions, but influencing these actions to ensure that they collectively meet the long-term interests of all, rather than the short-term interests of the few. That is why words like "partnerships" are nowadays rife in public-policy documents. Career guidance services need to be parts of these partnerships, bringing their distinctive expertise to the table.

One of the powerful elements careers advisers bring with them is their understanding of the importance of so-called "soft" interventions which work through people rather than on them. All their professional activities are interventions of this kind. Just as employers are becoming increasingly aware of the importance of soft process skills alongside hard technical skills, so policy-makers need to become more aware of the power and significance of soft policy interventions. Most policy-makers still find it difficult to get hold of them: they tend to be locked into structural mind-sets, into system-think rather than person-think. The career guidance profession can help them to adapt to the softer ways of thinking. And in doing so, it can help them to understand the importance of its own work as soft policy interventions.

This is critical for the profession, because without policy attention and support, its work looks vulnerable. Viewed from a distance, much of it seems very much like a relic from the late industrial era. In all countries, career guidance systems are still heavily concentrated around the exit point from full-time education into the world of work. Their information systems, whatever they call them, still tend to be occupational systems rather than career systems. They describe a world of work ordered neatly into occupations and organisations, with neatly-defined entry points framed in terms of educational qualifications. We all know that the world of work is much more complex and dynamic than this – more messy, in fact – but in seeking to tidy it up to make it comprehensible, the profession tends to fall back on the old models.

The risk is that what it is left with is a fading role within a fading structure. Schools, in particular, look more and more like industrial-era remnants. We still herd pupils into schools, just as we used to herd workers into factories. Attendance is mandatory: no "hot desks" here. Information is transmitted by teacher to pupil, rather than building systems around the power of information technology. Motivation is based extrinsically on gaining access to pieces of paper which provide passports to enter the world of work. Careers advisers are gatekeepers, checking the visas.

I exaggerate, of course, but I do worry that what the career guidance profession is left with is shoring up an outdated school structure, plus a marginal role in labour-market management, and a few services in the private sector to which only a small minority of adults have access. If this is all it is, it could get stripped out quite quickly – particularly as non-professional services which seem to offer what it can offer are more and more freely available on the Internet.

The profession needs therefore to get serious about promoting what it can offer, and to ensure that it is based on a cutting-edge understanding of the transformations that are taking place in the world of work. In my view, it has a critical role to play in helping both individuals and organisations to adapt to the transformations. In this sense, it is an agent of change – not in a naively radical 1960s sense but in dancing with the rhythms of historical change. In schools, for example, it should be at the forefront of helping schools to think through the implications of the new world of work for their structures and their curriculum (see Bayliss, 1998). It also needs to ensure that young people when they emerge from schools are equipped with the career management skills which will enable them to construct their careers. This is a far more demanding role than just slotting them into university or college courses. It needs to start in primary school, not at the end of secondary school. It is essentially about learning, and learning accordingly now needs to be at the heart of career development theories.

Implications for career theory

My NICEC colleague Bill Law (1996) has recently developed a career learning theory in which he suggests that career-development learning can be built in cycles, which develop progressively through four stages: the sensing stage, in which a person is able to sense career-related information and impressions; a sifting stage, in which they are able to sift this material into recognisable patterns that become the basis of action; a focusing stage, in which they are able to focus the material more tightly; and an understanding stage, in which they are able to identify causes and effects in specific scenarios. Increasingly, people need the more advanced capacities in order to manage their careers effectively. But these more advanced capacities cannot be developed unless the more basic capacities have been built to support them.

There are links between Bill Law's work and John Krumboltz's (1994) social learning theory. John Krumboltz, too, focuses on career counsellors as facilitators of continuous learning: learning new skills, challenging self-defeating beliefs. These need to be adapted to the new concept of career. Krumboltz has suggested, for example, that instead of emphasising decision-making, we should be emphasising the wisdom of open-mindedness. He has also suggested that unplanned events should be seen not just as an inevitable but also as a desirable aspect of everyone's career. I agree, but I want to have it both ways. That is why I like oxymorons. H.B. Gelatt (1989) has talked about "positive uncertainty": a phrase to conjure with. Krumboltz and his colleagues (Mitchell et al., 1999) are working with the concept of "planned happenstance". I favour "planful serendipity". "Serendipity" is one of the joyous words in the English language: the Oxford dictionary describes it as "the faculty of making happy and unexpected discoveries by accident". We need it. But if that is all we have, the risk is that we are simply being reactive, waiting for something to turn up. We also need a sense of direction: a flexible plan which we are ready to adapt when unexpected events occur, and which will probably help us to spot and make sense of these events.

There is a link here with constructivist theories, which also have much to offer for the new millennium. Constructivist approaches focus on helping individuals to be authors of their career narratives: to tell the story so far; to shape the themes and tensions in the story line; and to start drafting the next chapter (Savickas, 1993). Such narratives need to incorporate planful serendipity. I like the technique adopted in one research study (Bateson, 1994) of asking people to interpret their own life history twice: first on the basis of smooth continuity ("Everything I have ever done has been heading me for where I am today"), and then on the basis of serendipitous discontinuity ("I've only arrived here as a result of series of accidents and interruptions"). We could all, I suspect, write both stories, using the same material.

I also contend, however, that our theories need to have a stronger sociological frame than they tend to do. The power of "career" derives from its capacity to link the private work of the individual to the social and economic structure. There is a danger that if we over-psychologise the concept of "career", we allow it to become, in a literal sense, privatised. That means that we lose sight of all the inequalities in opportunity structures and cultural capital which for many people constrain not only the narratives they can construct, but the lives they can lead. If we want to support "careers for all", we cannot afford to base our work on psychologised naivety.

Implications for policy and practice

So much for theory. What about policy and practice? The key issue is how we can reconstruct our career guidance provision so that it is accessible to individuals not just at the start of their working lives but throughout their working and learning lives. Careers can no longer be foretold: they are forged through a series of decisions we all make throughout our life-span. Guidance needs to be available at all these decision points. What is more, it needs to be available to help us to review regularly whether and when we need to make new decisions: to invest in new skills, to scan new possibilities. In the USA, Jane Goodman (1992) has suggested the analogy of dental check-ups: going not only when we are in pain, as if to have a tooth pulled, but for regular checks to maintain our career health. How do we do this? How do we ensure this kind of access?

This is a policy question as well as a question of practice. Career guidance is not only a private good: it is a public good too. It reduces drop-outs from education and training, and mismatches in the labour market. It offers benefits to education and training providers, increasing the effectiveness of their provision by linking learners to programmes which meet their needs. It offers benefits to employers, by helping employees to come forward whose talents and motivations meet the employer's requirements. And it offers benefits to governments, in two ways: by fostering efficiency in the allocation and use of human resources, and by fostering social equity in access to educational and vocational opportunities – the balance between these will depend on the political hue of the government in question. It is a soft policy instrument, but – as I argued earlier – soft instruments are likely to be more effective in the new millennium than the more macho instruments of the past.

So how, in the public interest, are we to ensure access for all to career guidance throughout their lives? Is this an impossible dream? Or could we make the dream come true? I want to suggest five alternative models of delivery.

The first is to see the formal education system as the natural home for lifelong access to career guidance. This is on the basis that people will increasingly be returning to formal education at various stages throughout their lives, when they want to reorientate themselves or to develop new skills. Tom Bentley (1998) has recently suggested that schools and colleges should become neighbourhood learning centres, welcoming learners of all ages, and becoming the focus for career as well as social and health services alongside their educational programmes. Since the education system is the base for most career guidance at present, this would allow organic development of current provision. But it assumes that the education system is the sole and exclusive base for learning: a proposition which is becoming less and less tenable, particularly now that some work organisations are conceiving themselves as learning organisations.

This leads to the second model, which is to see career guidance as being provided by the primary work and/or learning base where individuals are located, which in most cases will be either an educational institution or an employer. The merit of this model is to validate employers as deliverers of career counselling. A growing number of organisations are introducing systems to support career self-management: career planning workshops, assessment centres, career resource centres, mentoring systems, and the like. More and more organisations, too, are setting up systems of regular development reviews, sometimes as part of appraisal systems but sometimes separate from them. The growth of such systems has been strongly encouraged by the voluntary Investors in People programme, in which employers can be kitemarked if they meet certain specifications – including opportunities for development reviews. These strongly parallel the systems of recording achievement and action planning which are now becoming established within educational institutions. Together, they provide much of the structure for the kind of regular check-ups which Jane Goodman is advocating. Their limitation, however, is that they miss out significant groups of people who are not engaged in formal education or employment. They also tend to be more knowledgeable about, and sometimes strongly biased towards, opportunities within the organisation as opposed to those outside. And they are much more evident in large than in the small and medium-sized organisations where employment is increasingly concentrated.

The concern about impartiality leads towards a third model, which is to base career guidance in intermediary structures between individuals and employers – trade unions and professional associations, for example. NICEC has recently done some work with the Trades Union Congress, looking at the extent to which trade unions can act not only as advocates of such guidance in the workplace, within their collective bargaining role, but also as deliverers of such guidance (Ford & Watts, 1998). We found some fascinating examples of practice, as we have with professional associations. They are however limited at present, and at a fairly modest level of professional skill. And, of course, many people are not members of such an organisation. There are also other kinds of intermediary structures – deployers like Manpower, brokerage organisations, networks of various kinds – which offer potential as bases for career guidance. But at present they are uneven in density and in the extent to which guidance gets subsumed beneath other agendas.

The concern for greater universality of independent provision leads to a fourth model, which is to view lifelong career guidance as a separate public service. The problem here is the cost. So far, no country has committed itself to providing such a service at a scale commensurate with the need. Where services exist, they are often little more than tokenistic: hidden away within government buildings, with minimal marketing, to ensure that demand can be met with minimal supply. Or they are limited mainly to information and placement services. Often, too, these services are part of employment services which also have the role of policing access to unemployment benefits: this can limit and distort their guidance potential. It thus leaves open the question of where a wider range of career guidance services is to be found, and who is to pay for them.

This leads to the fifth model, which is to view career guidance as a stand-alone profession. Perhaps in the future, just as many of us have our doctor, our dentist, our solicitor, our accountant, so we will also have our careers adviser, to whom we will go when we have a problem, but also when we want a check-up. Is this a viable model? Are we likely to be willing to pay for such a service? Or perhaps are we more likely to do so if the professional base is wider? In the USA, for example, the career guidance profession has traditionally been part of the counselling profession, though with periodic inclinations to separate development. The counselling links sustain a strong holistic view of the individual, which embraces the spiritual dimension in which there is growing interest (Handy, 1997). They are also helpful in supporting two sets of links which are likely to become increasingly important in the new millennium: with relationship counselling, because careers increasingly have to be negotiated between partners and within family systems; and with stress counselling, because of the stress likely to be caused by more discontinuous career patterns. The links with counselling tend however to devalue the informational base which is such an important part of career guidance. Other models may be worth exploring.

For example, I am constantly struck at present by the links between career guidance and financial guidance. Individuals are having to take more and more responsibility for their pensions and social insurance, just as they are having to take more responsibility for their careers. Financial planning is as important as career planning. Indeed, the two are increasingly intertwined. Might the two come closer together, perhaps through distinct professionals working together in partnership, or perhaps through a stronger process of symbiosis – or even cross-breeding? I am currently doing some work with Brian Stevens of Finance and Education Services (FEdS) exploring these possibilities.[7]

Cross-cutting all of these issues is the impact of information and communication technologies. Their key effect is to remove the constraints of time and place from both learning and work – and from career guidance. The extent to which we will seek in future to meet each other face-to-face in physical locations to conduct these activities, or to have more sustained interactions using the growing array of communication systems now becoming available to us, is likely to have a significant impact on the nature of, and the balance between, the five models I have outlined. We are still all working out our own rules about when it is best to use the telephone, the fax, the email, snail mail, or face-to-face meetings. The key take-off point is likely to be when the currently separate hardware of the computer, the telephone and the television become integrated in the home and elsewhere. At that point – not far away now – our rules may undergo a more radical shift. Will in future people want instant videoconferencing access to a career counsellor when they are working on the Internet at home, rather like telephone banking? How will we respond to the flexible access this will require? Will we form consortia, so that calls can be referred on to someone who is prepared to work on the nightshift? Or will people want to build a continuous relationship with a particular counsellor? And will people still want to come to the careers service or consulting room, partly because of the direct personal interaction but also perhaps because of the more intense focus which a change of territory provides?

My own view is that we need to look at all these issues much more closely and more strategically than we do at present. At their core is the question of whether a market is likely to develop which will expand provision, or whether it is difficult – and undesirable – to commodify career guidance in the way this would require. As a recent market-research project carried out by Marketry and NICEC for the Guidance Council (Wilson & Jackson, 1998) has indicated, marketing guidance is problematic, for a number of reasons: it is a process not a product, a means not an end; at its heart is not meeting people's immediate wants, but helping them to clarify their longer-term needs. On the other hand, the development of the market in career guidance could be one of the ways of meeting the public interest without making strong demands on the public purse. It is interesting that even in Germany, where the *Bundesanstalt für Arbeit* formerly had a state monopoly in the provision of career guidance and placement services, the monopoly has now been broken.

What is happening in the United States is of interest in this respect. I tried to persuade our last Government to fund a study of the development of a career guidance industry there, on the grounds that if it was possible to develop such

---

7 Editorial footnote: This work was later published in a number of articles including Watts & Stevens (1999).

an industry, the States – and particularly perhaps California – is the place where it was most likely to have happened. The Government was voted out of office before it was able to commission the study, but my initial explorations suggested five propositions. First, it seems that the only area where a significant market has developed for career guidance services is outplacement counselling, where the employer pays, is prepared to pay real money, has an interest in a positive outcome, but has no interest in what that outcome should be; outplacement firms seeking to diversify tend to move into areas like career coaching where, again, the employer pays. Second, there are a fair number of career counsellors who offer a private practice where the user pays, but many do so as a sideline to other forms of other professional practice: there are, as yet, few signs of this provision developing as a real market. This is linked to the third point, which is that whilst some individuals seem prepared to pay for career counselling, they only in general appear willing to do so at levels which cover marginal costs rather than full costs. Fourth, again linked to this, there has been significant growth of non-profit "third-sector" organisations where the user may be charged a fee but this is subsidised and (often) means-tested in some way. And fifth, while some fee-paying counselling and psychotherapy services are covered to some extent by insurance policies, this is in general not true of career counselling, except in the very limited number of cases where it can be linked to mental health disorders of some kind.

These findings confirm what seems to be happening in the UK too. What then can we conclude about the extent to which the market can deliver the public interest in ensuring lifelong access to career guidance? The evidence available to date suggests that the market is likely to have a significant role to play, but that it will not of itself deliver what is needed. There is still an important role for government: partly to ensure that there are appropriate regulatory and quality-assurance procedures in place to protect the interests of the individual customer or client; and partly to provide for market failure, especially in the case of those who are unlikely to be able to afford, or willing to pay for, the guidance services they need.

On the first of these, the National Advisory Council for Careers and Educational Guidance – which brings together all the relevant professional bodies and stakeholders in the career guidance field – has developed, with government support, quality standards for all sectors of career guidance provision.[8] The Government has now approved in principle the Council's proposals for an accreditation body to implement these standards in the adult guidance sector, and ways are being sought of achieving coherence with standards in other sectors.

On market failure, a possible solution could be the concept of Individual Learning Accounts. The Government's current commitment to ILAs is fairly modest, limited

8 Editorial footnote: These standards later evolved into the Matrix standard. See http://matrixstandard.com/ for further information on this.

to pump-priming a million accounts. ILAs could however be one of the "big ideas" which the Government will need if it is to achieve a second term. The key is whether significant elements of current public funding for further and higher education are rechannelled through such accounts. If so, ILAs will become the main means through which post-compulsory education training will be funded in the new millennium. The key principles are two-fold: that individuals are best placed to choose what and how they want to learn; but that responsibility for investing in learning needs to be shared between the state, employers and the individual. It is a way of breaking out of the current impasse where each of these three parties has an interest in lifelong learning, but expects the others to pay. Career guidance would seem essential as the means of reconciling the two principles: reassuring the state and employers that while decisions about the use of their contributions will be made by individuals, these decisions will be well-informed and well-thought-through. But potentially, too, Individual Learning Accounts could be a way of breaking out of the marginal-costs barrier to the expansion of guidance provision itself, enabling the guidance to be paid for on a full-cost basis by getting employers and the state to supplement what individuals are prepared to pay. It is also compatible with the state paying most or all costs in the case of particularly disadvantaged groups.

Implications for practice

I am conscious that I have said less about practice than about theory and policy. I think it is important, however, to review the extent to which career guidance practices relates to the world of the present and the future, or of the past. NICEC has recently reviewed the constructs of work used in career guidance, in the light of the move towards more flexible organisational structures and more flexible labour markets (Hirsh, Kidd & Watts, 1998). One of the intriguing questions is whether occupation, which is still one of our dominant constructs, is likely to become more or less significant in this new world. On the one hand, it could be argued that the decline of organisational careers means that occupation is likely to grow in importance as a way of mapping careers that span movement across different organisations and different forms of work contract.

This is the view taken, for example, in Arthur & Rousseau's book *The Boundaryless Career* (Arthur & Rousseau, 1996). On the other hand, it could be argued that the key in future, reflecting the shift of focus from employment to employability, is not "what I do" (i.e. current occupation) but "what I can do" (in terms of capabilities and competencies) – which will require a new language. This is the kind of issue which we need to address and resolve if we are to be ready for the new millennium.

Conclusion

I fervently believe that the career guidance profession has a future. Not only that: I believe it is a better future. It ceases to be technicians of systems: it becomes what it has always wanted to be – facilitators of the individuals who will make the systems work. Indeed, I believe it has a critical role to play if the new post-industrial era is to offer more fulfilling lives for more people than the industrial era has.
The old model has served some of us well. But for many it has limited the extent of the opportunities they have had for fulfilling their potential. We all have more possibilities within us than we ever realise. If people can move not only flexibly but also progressively within the world of learning and of work, they are more likely to lead rich and fulfilling lives. The help of the career guidance profession is crucial in this respect. But only if we can develop the theories, the policies and the practices that we need for a new era. That is the challenge – and it is one that should inspire and empower us.

3. Careers Education and the Informal Economies[9]

Careers guidance has developed as a by-product of bureaucratisation. The traditional 'matching' approach has required that broad categories of jobs be described in ways which make it possible to match individual attributes to them. Perhaps inevitably, therefore, careers guidance has been drawn towards the bureaucratised sector of the labour market where jobs are formalised in groups and (often) defined and protected by professional-bodies or trade union structures, with formal entry channels defined in terms of educational qualifications. This sector is relatively easy to describe, not least because there are ready-made mechanisms through which information can be collected.

Moreover, although different, educational approaches to careers guidance have begun to develop and to be implemented more widely (see Watts and Ferreira Marques, 1979, chapters 1-2), they too have tended to rest heavily on the informational resources developed under the traditional approach. The picture of the world presented by careers education therefore tends to be one of a static series of well-defined and preformed occupational holes into which individual pegs are to be fitted on the basis of readily identifiable attributes – notably educational credentials.

In reality, the labour market is much more complex, more dynamic, and more responsive to individual initiatives than this picture suggests. Moreover, much economic activity takes place outside the formal economy altogether. As those involved in careers education struggle to respond to the new challenges posed to them by high rates of unemployment (see chapter 12), it is increasingly important that more attention be addressed to alternatives outside the bureaucratised sector of the formal economy. The aim of this paper is to provide a conceptual framework for viewing these alternatives, and to examine their implications for the practice of careers education.

The 'free' sector of the formal economy

The emphasis placed on the bureaucratised sector of the formal labour market in careers education programmes is hardly surprising. Such programmes are located in educational institutions, which are legitimated largely through the system of

---

[9] Reprinted, by permission of the publisher, from *British Journal of Guidance and Counselling*, Volume 9 No. 1, January 1981, 24-35. DOI: 10.1080/03069888108258198.

credentialism which they support. In secondary schools, in particular, the chief basis for the organisation's control of its pupils is the promise that 'If you work hard and pass your exams, you'll get a good job'. Where careers education programmes emphasise the sector of the labour market in which this promise is valid, it is serving the interests not only of the labour-market sector, but also of the school itself.

Patently, however, there are important sectors of the labour market where the promise is invalid. Ashton and Maguire (1980) point out that the pure credentialist model, in which applicants with the highest educational qualifications are selected, is used by hardly any employers; that employers tend at most to use such qualifications for screening purposes (i.e. as a form of preselection) or for focussing purposes (i.e. merely directing the recruitment drive at students with a given level of ability); and that for a lot of jobs (including many in the middle as well as the lower ranges of the occupational hierarchy) such qualifications are totally functionless.

Cherry (1980) accordingly distinguishes the bureaucratic sector of the labour market from what she calls the 'free' sector, in which young people are seen not as finding their way on the basis of formal qualifications, but as kicking and fighting their way through the labour market to obtain or create a job which can just accommodate the abilities they have to offer. In a large longitudinal study of males followed up at the age of 26, she found that the level of occupational functioning among the more highly qualified young people was determined instrumentally by qualifications rather than directly by measured ability, whereas the unqualified leavers achieved a relationship between ability and functioning through methods other than qualifications – notably through the effects of ambition. This latter group was not confined to lower-level occupations. Indeed, Cherry discovered that as many as 17% of intermediate non-manual (mainly managerial) jobs held within the sample were held by men who had never passed a public examination. One would anticipate that as the sample progresses in age and in occupational experience, this figure is likely to rise even higher.

The precise nature of the 'free' sector is not defined very clearly by Cherry, but it seems likely to be composed in particular of small firms where credentials tend to be less significant (see Ashton and Maguire, 1980a; Curran and Stanworth, 1979b; also Collins, 1974). The Bolton Committee (1971) defined a 'small firm' in different ways: for example, in some cases it was based on annual sales turnover, in others on the work-force being 200 employees or less (in the case of manufacturing) or 25 or less (in the case of two other industries). Using these definitions, it estimated that approximately 4.4 million people were working in small firms in the industries covered by its enquiry, and that this represented over 30% of the total employment in those industries (ibid, pp.33-34). Moreover, an American study found that firms of 20 or fewer employees generated 66% of all new jobs in the USA between 1960 and 1976 (Birch, 1979, table 3). Although the more romantic views of social relations in small firms have recently been questioned (Curran and Stanworth, 1979a), such firms merit more attention from careers education than they often receive.

The difficulties which careers guidance services in general have in communicating with small firms have been analysed in a study by Hedges (1978) of employment and the small firm in Covent Garden. The small firms in his sample tended to be reluctant to use public services (including the Careers Service) for placement purposes, preferring to use private agencies or other means. Moreover, Hedges points out that careers programmes within local schools tended to ignore small companies, which were less forthcoming, less well prepared with material, and less easy to visit to the benefit of large numbers of students. To this list might be added the point that, particularly in working-class areas, teachers often live outside the area, and are ignorant of the structure of the local labour market. Yet, as Sawdon et al. (1980) demonstrate, the job-entry patterns of young people tend to be highly localised. Sawdon et al. accordingly recommend that careers education should be area-specific, aiming to familiarise students with the workings of the local economy, rather than being based solely on general materials broadcast or published nationally; similar recommendations in relation to the role of the Careers Service have been made by Ashton and Maguire (1980b).

A further area of the 'free' sector which tends to be neglected in careers education programmes is that of self-employment. Such programmes are inclined to assume that their task is to adapt youngsters to jobs that already exist. They accordingly teach a passive, reactive stance to job-creation, and tend to ignore entrepreneurial activities. Yet out of the total UK labour force of 26.3 million, 1.9 million are self-employed (Department of Employment, 1980). Moreover, the self-employed tend to have much higher levels of job satisfaction than those who are working for other people (Consumers Association, 1977). Some self-employment, of course, requires capital as well as highly-developed skills, qualifications, etc., but a number of options are realistically and immediately open to young school-leavers, including window-cleaning, car-cleaning, painting and decorating, and gardening. The Careers and Occupational Information Centre have produced a leaflet called Working for Yourself that gives tips and advice, and a number of popular books on self-employment are also available. Careers education programmes could well make more use of these published resources, as well as of personal contacts with the self-employed (e.g. among students' parents).

The informal economies

Beyond this, however, there is the intriguing question of whether careers education programmes need to broaden their definition of work to encompass forms of economic activity which take place outside the formal economy altogether.

Gershuny and Pahl (1979/80; 1980; also Gershuny, 1979) have pointed out that a considerable and probably increasing amount of work is carried out in three informal economies.

The first is the 'black' economy, otherwise known as the 'underground' or 'hidden' economy. This covers work conducted wholly or partly for money which is concealed from taxation or regulatory authorities: it ranges from undeclared criminal and immoral earnings (e.g. prostitution, drug-trafficking), through office pilfering and perks, to undeclared income earned in particular by the self-employed, by 'moonlighters', and by the unemployed. A recent estimate by Macafee (1980), based on the national accounts, suggests that the hidden economy accounted for 3.3% of the national income in 1978, as opposed to 1.4% in 1972; an estimate from the rather different perspective of the Inland Revenue, using different definitions of the term 'black economy', put the figure at 7.5% (quoted in ibid, p.86). In Italy the proportion has been estimated as being as high as 40%, and parts of the black economy seem to be officially tolerated as a matter of policy (Hansen, 1979); in Third World countries, too, official attitudes have been changing, following the report of the International Labour Organisation (1972, chapter 13) on Kenya, which suggested that parts of the urban informal economy there should be supported and promoted rather than being ignored or harassed. Similar arguments are now being advanced in Britain: the Outer Policy Research Circle (1979) points out that among the arguments put forward are that the hidden economy 'provides a safety valve, a means of anticipating official recognition of anomalies, or recognising individual merit, and a channel for "unqualified ability", the opportunity for personal control of the work situation, and the sheer pleasure of beating the system'. Clearly some activities within the black economy would be regarded by most people as being immoral; with many others, however, the moral boundaries are much less clear. Indeed, Henry (1978, chapter 8) has documented the strong and spontaneously-evolved normative controls which operate among participants in the hidden economy, and has suggested that policing is best left to such controls.

The black economy is closely related to the formal economy, in the sense that it is still focused around a cash nexus. This is not however true of the other two informal economies. One of these is the communal economy, which involves the production of goods or services that are consumed by people other than the producers, but are not sold on a monetary basis. This ranges from baby-sitting circles or car pools which operate on a formal exchange of tokens or credits, to exchanges of skills or equipment which are part of a relationship of generalised reciprocity. The boundary with the hidden economy is often blurred: Henry (1978) points out that what is important in hidden economy trading is often not the monetary benefits it produces, but the relational ties and bonds of friendship which it generates and reinforces; payments are often made in kind rather than in money and for many of the participants such trading is more moral than most legitimate business, because it is concerned with helping other people (ibid, p.78). Certainly most stable working-class communities contain rich networks of reciprocal support which not only help to bind the community together but also mean that less recourse has to be made to the formal economy outside. The economic as well as social importance of such networks to the individual (see Pahl, 1980; Wallace, 1980) needs for example to be borne closely in mind if the possibility of leaving the network and moving to a new area in search of paid employment is being considered.

The third informal economy is the household economy, which covers work within the home involving the production for internal consumption of goods or services for which approximate substitutes might otherwise be purchased for money. This includes cooking, decorating, laundry, child care, home repairs, garden produce, etc. In the USA, Burns (1975) estimated that if all the work done within the household by men and women were converted into monetary form, the total would be equal to the entire amount paid out in wages and salaries by every corporation in the country; in Britain, Gershuny (1979) calculated on the basis of time-budget figures that by 1974/75 the total time devoted to household production (i.e. domestic work) in the UK amounted to about four-fifths of that devoted to formal economic activities.

To illustrate the distinctions between these different economies, Pahl (1980, pp.4-5) points to the various options open to someone wanting particular job done – repairing a broken window, for example. He could

(a) hire a glazier through the formal economy, paying the full cost including value-added taxes;

(b) find someone nearby who is known to be able to mend windows and pay cash for the job, possibly thereby entering the black economy because he would not know whether such a person was declaring all his or her income, paying all his or her taxes, or working in time already paid for by another employer;

(c) ask a neighbour to do it within the communal economy, either in exchange for specific goods or services now or in the future, or as part of a broader ongoing relationship;

(d) do the job himself in his own time with his own tools, within the household economy.

The key argument being developed by Gershuny and Pahl (see ibid, p.3; also Gershuny, 1978) is that an increasing amount of work is now being carried out in the informal economies rather than the formal economy, for sound economic reasons.

Manpower productivity in manufacturing industry rises much faster than in the formal services sector, yet various institutional forces (e.g. government incomes policies) tend to maintain or even to narrow wage differentials between sectors. Therefore costs of service outputs tend to rise faster than those of manufacturing industry. At the same time, the declining cost of tools (especially power tools) and appliances, and the development of new materials whose use requires lower levels of skill, make informal production of certain services cheaper and more viable. The result is the substitution of informal production of services for the purchase of service from the formal economy: examples include the increasing popularity of 'do-it-yourself', and of household construction work paid for in cash; and also the purchase of cars and TV sets as a substitute for purchase of transport and entertainment services.

The implications of these arguments are profound. They suggest that, barring government intervention, employment within the formal economy is likely to decline still further as a source of goods and services. They also suggest that the livelihood of many people will depend less on formal bureaucratised employment and more on the skills they have to deploy in their own households and communities.

Whether these trends are socially desirable is open to question. Certainly the informal economies offer a considerable degree of personal autonomy, and this seems to be a powerful attraction for those who participate in them (Gershuny and Pahl, 1979/80). Producing services for oneself or in reciprocal exchange with others is likely to be personally more satisfying and rewarding, reducing the alienation which results from the division and formalisation of labour (see Pahl, 1980). Moreover, from the consumer's point-of-view, the informal economies offer the possibility of making available personal services which, because they are not widely traded, are not constrained by the need to be hyper-efficient in their use of labour (Gershuny, 1979).

On the other hand, political and economic power remain vested in the formal economy, and the growth of the informal economy could readily permit the development of a split society like that in many Third World countries, where policies of social protection are only extended to a small section of the economically active population, and the rest are too busy 'making out' to challenge the distribution of social protection (Bromley and Gerry, 1979). Moreover, those who are outside formal employment are often those least well-equipped with the skills necessary for productive and rewarding informal activities; similarly, the areas with the highest levels of unemployment are frequently those with poor social infrastructure and limited markets for black economy products (Gershuny and Pahl, 1979/80). The dangers and difficulties, in short, would be especially acute if the encouragement of the informal economies were used as an excuse to erode the basis of the welfare state, and/or if partial or total dependence on such economies were forced upon weak sections of the community rather than being freely chosen by relatively capable individuals.

With these caveats, it seems that the informal economies may offer a fruitful direction for policy responses to the acute unemployment problems which seem likely to continue to face Britain for the foreseeable future. In an earlier paper (Watts, 1978a), it was suggested that if society was to maintain a concern for social equity[10], it had to choose between two broad policy directions: a 'right to work' model, in which work in the form of paid employment was regarded as intrinsically good, and the state intervened to make it available to all; and a 'leisure society' model, in which such work was kept to a minimum, and individuals were given a basic 'economic floor' and were then permitted a free choice between whether to work or not. It may be that the informal economies offer a compromise between these two scenarios, retaining and extending the work ethic, but without imposing a rigid bureaucratic structure to implement it. Certainly there seems to be little sign at present of a social tolerance of the higher levels of taxation and bureaucratic intervention which would be required to extend formal employment: indeed, the political and social trends seem currently to be in the reverse direction. Moreover, the pressures for efficiency within the formal economy continue. At the same time, there is little sign of willingness on the part of unions and professional bodies to allow wage and salary levels in the formal economy as a whole to fall to a point where substantial work-sharing could take place, or to allow those in the service sector to fall in relative terms to a point where this sector could expand. For these and other reasons, the informal economies seem likely to continue to grow. The issue for governments is whether to attempt to repress them, to ignore them, or to acknowledge their existence and – within defined limits – encourage them.

A similar issue confronts schools, and especially those involved in careers education: do they ignore the informal economies, or do they acknowledge their existence and help individuals to understand and use them more effectively? Issues about desirability intrude here too, and clearly need to be argued out in depth. In addition, however, schools have a more pragmatic responsibility to help youngsters to cope with society as it is emerging. If therefore the informal economies are an increasingly important part of that society, schools which ignore them are doing their pupils a disservice.

The implications of this for careers education are considerable. In the past, careers education has tended to focus on paid employment, on the grounds that it is central to individuals' survival and fulfilment. These assumptions now need to be questioned. If the key focus is on the individual's fulfillment, then it has already been

---

10 The term used in the paper was 'equality', but on reflection 'equity' seems more appropriate.

argued elsewhere (Watts and Herr, 1976) that many people even in times of full employment draw their main satisfactions from outside their paid work, regarding it simply as the means to implement their aspirations in their family, their community, and their leisure activities (see e.g. Dubin, 1956; Goldthorpe et al., 1968). The analyses in this paper now suggest that in terms of survival, too, paid employment needs to be examined alongside self-employment and alongside work within the informal economies. Pahl (1980) has begun to document a 'new kind of rationality' (Gershuny and Pahl, 1980, p.8), which uses a subtle calculus to allocate time and energy between paid employment, for which one gains money and perhaps social satisfaction, and work with one's own tools in one's own time, for which one gets much satisfaction and perhaps some money (or, at least, saving of money) as well. Arguably, the development of this form of rationality is an important task for careers education, enabling it to form a valuable and potentially synergetic alliance with consumer education.

It is important not to overstate the argument here. Formal employment will continue for a long time yet to consume the energies; and to determine the income and life-style, of a large proportion of the population. It will also continue to be the central feature of the economy, and – not least – to determine significantly the resources that are available within the informal economies.

But by focussing too exclusively on formal employment and traditional economic models, we may find it impossible at a societal level to find adequate and creative responses to the new situations in which we now find themselves, or at an individual level to help people to cope with and surmount the problems that confront them.

Concluding comments

The key issue underlying this paper is the definition of 'work' which is used by those responsible for careers education programmes. At least six definitions, of increasing breadth, can be offered

1. Formal paid employment within that sector of the economy which is directly concerned with wealth-generation.
2. Formal paid employment within large bureaucratic organisations.
3. Formal paid employment within an organisation of any size (including small businesses).
4. Economic activity within the formal economy.
5. Economic activity rewarded by cash, whether within the formal economy or outside it.

6. Any application of productive effort.

At present, careers education tends to be concerned mainly with (2), and there have been recent pressures to narrow its focus towards (1) (referred to by some as 'real work'). The aim of this paper has been progressively to extend the definition towards (6).

To implement such a redefinition, it may be useful to use with students some of the conceptual framework which has been suggested in this paper, and to question, consolidate and (where necessary) extend the students' own definitions of 'work'. Beyond this, there are implications for the techniques and resources that are used in careers education, placing less exclusive emphasis on centralised data banks like those represented in the traditional careers literature, and more emphasis on exploratory techniques and on using and extending the students' own contacts and experiences. Part-time jobs, for example, tend often to be ignored in careers education programmes, yet they provide a valuable concrete introduction to the informal economies – of which they are, of course, part.

The difficulties of confronting the challenge imposed by the informal economies must not however be underestimated. Schools do not readily provide a neutral framework within which alternative realities – and the ethical and political issues related to them – can be juxtaposed and explored. Instead, they tend to reflect and present a formalised and publicly-acceptable view of the world. They are themselves formal institutions, and in attempting to deal with the informal, are liable to formalise and distort it, translating it into 'official' terms. Moreover, as was pointed out earlier, it meets their own organisational needs to present a view of the world which is highly bureaucratised, points of entry being rigidly determined by educational qualifications. To bring this view of the world into question, even by exposing its partial quality, is to challenge the basic control mechanism within the school.

It must also be questionable whether students will regard teachers as having any legitimate place, or anything to offer, in relation to the informal economies. Teachers are themselves the epitome of the bureaucratised, credentialised world: reared by it, achieving their position by virtue of their success according to its dictates, and now firmly institutionalised within it. To expect them to move with confidence outside that world is asking a lot: to expect youngsters to respect their expertise outside that world is asking even more. Indeed, it may be that students in general accept the demands of schools (if at times with some ritualistic friction) precisely because they are partial and restricted, and therefore leave space for students to develop more total views of reality in their own individual, autonomous ways: for schools to attempt to enlarge their area of concern might well be interpreted by at least some youngsters as a form of totalitarian expansionism which should be strenuously resisted.

Yet at the same time it is also clear that the partial, 'official' view of the world presented by schools is only likely to continue to be accepted if it continues to bear some resemblance to at least part of the youngsters' own conceptions of the world in which they live. If the gulf between the two widens, school will be perceived as being more and more irrelevant. To make the point simply, schools which focus on educational qualifications rather than on directly usable skills are unlikely to command the conformity or even the physical presence of youngsters who feel they have nothing to hope for from such qualifications.

Ultimately, of course, the educational implications of the issues posed in this paper go a long way beyond the particular concerns of careers education. Schools which wish to confront these issues in a total and direct way are likely to have to engage in some very radical re-thinking indeed, focusing their primary attention no longer on educational qualifications but on the development of skills and knowledge within contexts which demonstrate and encourage their ready applicability to practical tasks in the home and the community. Some vivid and creative ideas of what such a school might look like have been outlined by Ward and Fyson (1973). A number of similar ideas have been implemented in an interesting way in the Tvind schools in Denmark, in which theoretical education is linked with practical skills which enable the students to develop immediate working roles of direct use to the school community: printers to produce school materials, car mechanics to repair and suitably equip the school buses, food technologists to secure the economic foundations of communal life, builders for the school buildings, and so on. Pupils have to decide in the light of comparative figures whether, for instance, it would be more profitable and cheaper to purchase more cows and pigs than to buy meat. Wrong decisions mean a rise in living costs which reduce other possibilities and cause irritation: students experience directly, and have to live with, the consequences of their decisions.

By contrast, the school systems in most countries at present tend to develop a kind of dependency, based on the notion that so long as students learn certain bodies of knowldge and are able to reproduce them in examinations, they will have appropriate opportunities open to them. Such a framework, however limited, is viable so long as it operates within a system of full employment which delivers the opportunities. If however the system fails to deliver, then youngsters are left feeling betrayed and impotent. One alternative, as outlined briefly above, is a school system which is concerned with producing youngsters who have the skills and the confidence and self-reliance to take responsibility for their own survival and fulfilment – whether in the formal economy or outside it. Such an alternative is worth examining even at a time of full employment; at a time of high unemployment, it becomes all the more cogent.

Radical responses of this kind, however, pose fresh problems of their own unless they are implemented throughout the system. While so many elite jobs remain firmly entrenched within the bureaucratised sector, accessible only to those who acquire the appropriate credentials, there is a danger that those who are educated according to an alternative model will be rigidly excluded from such jobs. The continuing dilemma is that a 'contest' system (Turner, 1960) which aims to give all youngsters a chance to enter these jobs is likely to adopt a curriculum that is at best relevant only to the future needs of the 'winners', and leaves the 'losers' high and dry; whereas a 'sponsored' system which attempts to serve the future needs of different groups tends to further entrench the existing socio-economic divisions within society. Uneasy compromises between the two models seem likely to continue. In this situation, careers education has a particular responsibility to ensure that at least some response is made to the curricular challenge posed by the informal economies.

4. The Economic and Social Benefits of Career Guidance[11]

Introduction

For most career guidance practitioners, the individual is the central focus of their attention. Most such practitioners are drawn to the work by their interest in people. Whatever the nature of their interventions, the concern is to help individuals in making decisions and transitions that will bring satisfaction and fulfilment to them.

For many practitioners, therefore, reviewing the economic and social benefits of career guidance is extraneous to their frame of reference. Nonetheless, it is critical that such reviews take place: that the case for such benefits is examined, the evidence marshalled. The reason is that most career guidance services around the globe are funded, directly or indirectly, by government – whether it be local, regional or national government. In other words, they are available free of charge to the user, and resourced through the tax system. In some countries there is a private sector in the guidance field, but on the whole it is small and of marginal importance in volume terms.

The rationale for including career guidance as part of social-welfare provision is in principle two-fold. The first is that guidance is a "worthy good" (Savas, 1987) which is so intrinsically desirable that individuals should have a civic right to have access to it regardless of the resources at their private disposal. The problem with this argument is that it is difficult to define clear criteria for including and excluding particular goods or services from the list of such "worthy goods". The list tends to expand inexorably, fuelled by the self-interest of professional groups for maximising the budgets at their disposal, and by the pressures on politicians to promise goods and services to voters in order to secure election (Niskanen, 1971). The result over the last 20 years or so has been a strong backlash against what was seen as the reckless expansion of the welfare state, and a concern to restore market principles to social and economic activities wherever it has been possible to do so. It was argued that the disciplines of the market would ensure that the scale of provision responded to consumer demand rather than to the interests of the producers.

---

[11] **Editorial footnote:** Reprinted, by permission of the author and International Association for Educational and Vocational Guidance, from *Educational and Vocational Guidance Bulletin*, No. 63, 1999.

This leaves open, however, the second argument for public provision of career guidance, which is that it is not only a worthy private good, but also a public good. If this is the case, and if the social and economic benefits of guidance in these terms can be demonstrated, then there remains a strong argument for continued public investment in guidance, or at least for public intervention in the case of market failure.

It is chiefly for this reason that I and my colleagues at NICEC have given considerable attention over the last few years to looking at the arguments and the evidence for such benefits. In this paper, I will draw on four main pieces of work. Two were conducted earlier in the decade: reviews of the learning outcomes of guidance (Killeen & Kidd, 1991) and of its economic benefits (Killeen, White & Watts, 1992), both subsequently summarised by Killeen (1996). The other two have recently been completed: a review of the relationship of careers education and guidance to school effectiveness (Killeen, Sammons & Watts, 1999) and an exploratory review of the social benefits of guidance (Killeen, Watts & Kidd, 1998). The main author in all these pieces of work has been my NICEC colleague John Killeen, and I gratefully acknowledge my debt to him.

The focus of attention of the four reviews is mapped in figure 1 both in temporal terms (immediate, intermediate, ultimate) and in terms of the frame of reference (individual, organisational, societal). Like most maps, it over-simplifies the reality. But it provides a useful framework for the rest of this paper.

Figure 1: Outcomes of guidance

	Individual	Organisational	Societal
Immediate	Learning outcomes		
Intermediate	→	School effectiveness (e.g.)	
Ultimate		→	Economic benefits Social benefits

Learning outcomes

I want first to say a little more about what we call "learning outcomes". These have represented, and are likely to continue to represent, the core of any attempts to evaluate the impact of guidance. There are two main reasons for this. The first is appropriateness: the fact that they directly represent the aims of guidance interventions. Most such interventions are concerned not to prescribe what individuals should do but to help them require knowledge, skills and attitudes which will help them to make more effective decisions and transitions: in short, to acquire learning outcomes. The second is practicability. Since learning outcomes are immediate, they can be measured reasonably simply and cheaply; studies of longer-term outcomes are more expensive to mount. Moreover, the longer-term outcomes are more subject to contamination from extraneous factors. Effect sizes inevitably decline over time.

Learning outcomes can be analysed in relation to the four broad aims of the "DOTS" framework: self awareness; opportunity awareness; decision learning; and transition learning (see chapter 5). There are a few other relevant variables which do not fit into this framework, notably "precursors": attitudinal factors like attitudes to decision-making, reduced decision anxiety, and internal locus of control for career decision-making (Killeen & Kidd, 1991).

Evidence on the learning outcomes of guidance is substantial and convincing. Repeatedly the studies conclude that positive findings far outweigh null results. Negative findings – that guidance does the reverse of what is intended – are virtually unknown. Our NICEC review of forty studies found that only four reported no gains in the categories we identified, that thirty reported wholly positive results, and that gains were reported in each outcome category more often than null results. Moreover, positive results were reported for each main type of guidance intervention: classes and courses, workshops and groups, individual guidance, test interpretation and feedback, experience-based interventions, and multi-method interventions. Broadly similar conclusions have been found in American meta-analyses of good-quality controlled studies by Spokane & Oliver (1983) (see also Oliver & Spokane, 1988). Spokane & Oliver also concluded that individual guidance has the biggest impact per counsellor hour; that classroom (i.e. careers education) interventions have the biggest overall effects, due to the extent of their "time on task"; but that workshop (i.e. group guidance) interventions are the most cost-effective.

There is much more that could be said about learning outcomes, but for present purposes they are less relevant in their own right than as a potential building-block in addressing the issue of longer-term social and economic benefits. Since the longer-term studies are much more expensive and difficult to mount, there are likely to continue to be fewer of them. If however a few strong studies could be mounted of the relationship between immediate learning outcomes and the longer-term social and economic outcomes, and if positive connections between them could be established, then the learning outcomes could thereafter be regarded not only as of value in their own right but also as proxies for the longer-term outcomes (Killeen,

White & Watts, 1992). To date, such studies have not been conducted.

Impact on school effectiveness

The second body of evidence I want to examine is less exhaustive than the others: it is an exemplar of a wider field. While the immediate beneficiary of guidance is the individual, there are also a range of organisational beneficiaries. These include education and training providers: guidance can increase the effectiveness of their provision by linking learners to programmes which meet their needs and inspire their motivations, so improving learning performance. They also include employers: guidance can filter employees whose talents and motivations are suited to the employers' requirements. In each of these cases, guidance can produce such benefits both prior to entry – the filtering effects of guidance provision can reduce the costs of recruitment and enhance its efficacy – and on an ongoing basis within the organisation.

Our review of impact on school effectiveness is a sub-set of this cluster of potential effects. Since most schools are publicly funded, it is in a sense more closely linked to economic and social benefits than learning outcomes are. From a professional perspective, our review was motivated by a belief that the attention given to career education and guidance programmes in schools is likely to be significantly determined by the attitudes of headteachers and of senior management within schools, and that such attitudes are likely to be strongly influenced by their view of the relationship between such programmes and the wider aims of the school. Within the UK context, senior managers in schools are currently under much pressure to raise achievement as measured by attainment targets and examination passes. A NICEC enquiry identified three perspectives on the relationship of careers programmes to this aim. The positively supportive view was that careers work was not only of value to pupils in its own right but also made a positive contribution to raising achievement. The neutral view was it had little or no impact on the achievement agenda. The distractive view was that, while it might be worthwhile in itself, it diverted attention from this agenda. Where the positively supportive view was held, careers work was likely to be seen as a whole-school responsibility; where the neutral view was adopted, it was likely to be segmented as a separate activity; where the distractive view was held, it was likely to be marginalised (Andrews et al., 1998).

The distractive view, it is worth noting, has in the past exerted some influence not only on senior management in schools but also on policy-makers at national level. When in the UK the National Curriculum was first launched, careers education and guidance was defined as one of five cross-curricular themes. These themes, however, came to be regarded by government ministers not as a strengthening of the curriculum but as a "dangerous distraction" (Graham & Tytler, 1993). Indeed, in due course the themes became so marginalised by ministers that they became the element of the curriculum that dare not speak its name – chiefly on the grounds that they would distract pupils from the core business of achieving their attainment targets and examination passes.

In view of this, perhaps the most important conclusion to draw from our careful review of the research on the effects of career education and guidance programmes on school effectiveness (Killeen & Sammons, 1998) is that we have found no evidence at all that it has negative effects. The research is admittedly limited. Much of it relates to the US concept of career education, which embraces stronger elements of vocational education, including the development of specific vocational skills, than its UK counterpart (Watts & Herr, 1976). Such programmes show some evidence of modest but positive effects on various measures of academic achievement (see e.g. Evans & Burck, 1992). Similarly, an important study by Lapan, Gysbers & Sun (1997) of the effects of comprehensive guidance programmes shows that they had a modest but significantly additive effect on self-reported grades as well as on the perceived value of education as a preparation for the future.

The balance between the two findings of the Lapan et al. study is important. As noted earlier, the direct aims of career education and guidance are concerned with learning outcomes related to preparation for the future, particularly the ability to make and implement career decisions and more generally to manage one's career. In seeking effects on such matters as academic motivation and attainment, we are seeking evidence on what are, in a strict sense, side-effects: on matters which are not directly part of its purpose. Also, such matters are already the direct object of much effort and investment, so that when we look at the effects of career education and guidance here, we are likely to be working at the margin (Killeen & Sammons, 1998). This means that the absence of negative effects should be regarded as quite sufficient to justify the place of such programmes in schools. Any evidence of positive effects should be regarded as a bonus.

There is indeed an argument that too much evidence of this latter kind could be dangerous, leading to justifications for such programmes being mounted in terms of their indirect rather than their direct benefits: in other words, in terms of their effects on academic motivation and attainment rather than on preparation for career self-management. This might tempt the unwary to distort the nature of such programmes, or to demean their intrinsic value by viewing them purely as a means rather than as a valid end in themselves.

Nonetheless, there is a strong theoretical case for supposing that career education and guidance programmes are likely to have a positive effect on educational motivation and hence on academic attainment. The rationale can be framed in terms of motivation theory (Killeen, Sammons & Watts, 1999). This suggests, for example, that motivation depends in part on people's estimates of the extent to which expenditure of effort will lead to "success" outcomes. Willingness to participate in education, and to expend effort and persistence in pursuit of performance goals, are partly determined by these effort-performance expectancies. Careers programmes should thus enhance motivation by enabling students to see the relevance of educational performance to success in working life, to identify the rewards which they value and which they will obtain as a result of educational performance, and to see how effort and persistence can lead to such success outcomes. Similar propositions can be framed in terms of other aspects of motivation theory, such as self-efficacy theory, achievement motivation theory, and attribution theory.

On balance, the limited evidence gathered so far seems to support this rationale. Certainly there is no evidence that careers programmes have negative effects on motivation and attainment: the limited evidence we have suggests that they have modest but positive effects on these variables. This is helpful in advancing the case for time and resources being devoted to these programmes, indicating that we are in the fortunate position here of being not in a "zero-sum game" but in a "win-win" situation. In the UK we do however need more studies of this kind, gathered in relation to our own career education and guidance programmes, before we can be totally confident in this regard.

Economic benefits

I want now to move on to the third body of evidence: that on economic outcomes. In economic terms, career guidance can assist the efficient operation of the labour market in three main ways: by supporting the individual decisions through which the labour market operates; by reducing some of its market failures; and by contributing to institutional reforms designed to improve the functioning of the labour market.

In relation to the first of these, supporting individual decisions, three main kinds of decision are generally identified in economic analyses of the labour market. One is labour supply decisions: about whether to offer one's labour, and if so, for how many hours of work. In principle, the better informed individuals are, the more there is likely to be an effective balance between supply and demand. The second is human capital decisions: about how much education and training to invest in, and of which sorts. In principle, the better informed individuals are about the likely future returns from investment in education and training, the more effective their investment decisions will be. The third is job search decisions: about which jobs to apply for and accept, and the extent and length of their search. In principle, again, career guidance should increase the efficiency of job search by reducing both the search costs of finding a particular kind of job and the extent to which – as a result of imperfect information or limited search – individuals take jobs which are significantly below their abilities: this in turn should produce higher productivity.

The second potential economic benefit – reducing market failure – focuses on the aggregate effect of improperly informed choices, and again has three sub-categories. One is reducing drop-outs from education and training. This has immediate costs in terms of wasted investment in the education and training itself: in the UK, the Audit Commission and HMI (1993) estimated the public costs of educational courses for 16-19-year-olds alone taken by students who did not achieve their intended outcomes as being about £500 million – to say nothing of the substantial wastage of students' own time. In addition to this, we calculated the benefit costs of excess unemployment related to non-qualification as being around £350 million per annum: if guidance encouraged only 10% of current drop-outs to attend qualifications at a higher level, this could save £35 million per annum as well as having other social – as well as personal – returns (Killeen, White & Watts, 1992).

Guidance can also reduce mismatch. It seems possible that about one-third of unemployment may be attributable to mismatches between supply and demand in terms of occupational levels, industrial sectors, and other factors, and that about half of this might be attributable to occupational mismatch. On this basis, every 1% impact on occupational mismatch could save £10 million for the Exchequer in unemployment costs.

In addition, guidance can remotivate discouraged workers: in other words, those who are no longer looking for work, but would be interested in a job if they thought they had a chance of securing one. The costs of such discouraged workers are considerable, not only in terms of benefits and income support, but also in terms of loss of output, and reduced competition in the labour market. Guidance could lead to reductions of such costs by extending the awareness of opportunities and addressing individuals' attentions to possibilities previously overlooked.

The third and final potential economic benefit of guidance is that it can support institutional reforms designed to improve the normal functioning of the labour market. Reforms of the education and training system, for example, all require effective guidance in order for individuals to be aware of such changes and to attend to them in their career decision-making. Unless they do so, the reforms are unlikely to be effective.

On many of these issues, little or no direct evidence is available. The main reason is the methodological difficulties mentioned earlier: that many of the effects are not likely to be visible for some time; and that the longer the time that elapses, the more other factors come into play. Controlled trials are particularly difficult to sustain over long periods: control cannot be indefinitely extended, nor guidance indefinitely denied. There is also a more fundamental difficulty: that if the purpose of guidance is to help individuals to clarify and implement their own goals, this makes it difficult to find appropriate standardised criteria against which to evaluate the outcomes.

It is though worth noting a series of UK studies, mainly conducted in the 1920s and 1930s, which examined the effectiveness of so-called "scientific" guidance based on a matching model and particularly on the use of psychometric tests. These studies demonstrated that those who entered jobs in line with the recommendations based on such guidance were more satisfied with, and more stable in, their jobs, than those in jobs differing from the recommendation. They also showed that in controlled trials, the effect of the guidance was to raise individuals' perceptions of the suitability of their jobs and to reduce job turnover. Since in other studies, mainly in the USA, positive if weak relationships have been found between job satisfaction and job performance, it is plausible to suppose that at least some of the effects demonstrated in these studies represented economic benefits (for a review of these various studies, see Watts & Kidd, 1978; Killeen, White & Watts, 1992).

The only direct published evidence to date relating the economic benefits of career guidance service to their economic costs was a series of US studies on the effectiveness of Job Clubs as opposed to conventional employment counselling. The cost per placement was $167 (excluding premises); at six months, mean monthly welfare payments had reduced by 48% ($100) for Job Club participants but only by 15% for controls. This appeared to indicate a net saving (Azrin et al., 1980; 1981). It represents strong positive evidence, though related to a particular form of guidance intervention: the extent to which it is transferable to other guidance interventions is unclear.

Social benefits

NICEC's work on the economic benefits of guidance was conducted under the Conservative Government led by Margaret Thatcher, who famously declared that "there is no such thing as society; there are only individuals and families" (quoted in Gilmour, 1992, p.111). It was politically sensible, therefore, for our work to be framed in narrow economic terms, and indeed our work was – I believe – influential in ensuring that public budgets for career guidance were protected and even, in some cases, increased in real-money terms. Many of us were, however, concerned that framing the case in such terms could be dangerous in the longer term, leading to a limited understanding of the role of guidance, and leaving the field dangerously exposed if political whims changed.

And change they have. With the election with a massive majority of the Labour

Government under Tony Blair in May 1997, a different political agenda has emerged in which more attention is being given to social issues – in particular, avoiding social exclusion. It is accordingly now important for the case for public investment in guidance to be framed in social as well as economic terms. NICEC has thus recently been commissioned by the UK Careers Services National Association to conduct a small exploratory study to identify what social benefits guidance might yield, and to make proposals for possible further work in this area (Killeen et al., 1999). Our main proposal is for a limited literature review, but this review has not yet been conducted. Our work to date has focused around a workshop attended by a number of senior managers of guidance services where we brainstormed the social benefits of guidance, using the nominal group technique to do so; our initial report (Killeen, Watts & Kidd, 1998) comprised our distillation of, and subsequent reflections on, the issues raised at the workshop.

The case for guidance having a role in reducing social exclusion is not difficult to make. Social exclusion is commonly defined as exclusion from the formal institutions of education, training and employment. In these terms, guidance services have both a preventive role, enabling individuals to avoid such exclusion, and a reintegrative role, enabling individuals to escape such exclusion. To some extent they perform these roles routinely. After all, they operate generally to support participation in education and training and to incorporate individuals into the labour market. If their routine provision is effective in these respects, this is likely of itself to reduce social exclusion.

There is indeed some evidence in the UK that the routine provision is used disproportionately by some groups at particular risk of social exclusion. For example, there is evidence that black youngsters of Afro-Caribbean or Asian descent tend to be more dependent on formal guidance services than do white youngsters. They are less likely to be able to obtain from their family or friends the informed help they need in order to gain access to opportunities. They are accordingly more likely to have recourse to careers officers and careers teachers (e.g. Sillitoe & Meltzer, 1985; Verma & Darby, 1987).

Beyond this, however, there are possibilities for targeting guidance provision more directly and more specifically at those who are at risk of, or already experiencing, social exclusion. A number of initiatives have for instance been developed in the UK and other parts of Europe through which formal guidance services are working closely with other community agencies to reintegrate young people who have dropped out of the formal education, training and employment system (Ford, 1998; Watts & McCarthy, 1996). The UK Government is also now encouraging careers services to target significant parts of its work in schools on disaffected young people, to help to prevent them from dropping out of the system.

There is a delicate balance to be struck here. Clearly there is a need for targeted strategies. On the other hand, this can easily suck in substantial resources: work with disengaged young people, in particular, is notoriously labour-intensive and time-consuming. This can seriously reduce the resources available to the population at large. Moreover, there is a danger that career guidance then becomes stigmatised as a remedial activity for those unable to cope for themselves, rather than as a developmental activity that needs to be available to all.

This suggests that it is also important to develop a case based on the role of guidance not just in avoiding social exclusion but in enhancing social development. In a sense, the view of the Blair Government that labour market flexibility is a necessary facilitator of economic growth provides an opening for such a case. Such flexibility requires increased help for individuals to manage their own careers in uncertain conditions by enhancing their sense of "control" or "ownership", and helping them to adopt an active approach to self-development and the maintenance of employability. This is a universal requirement for all, not a targeted injunction for a few.

Beyond this, however, an even broader social rationale can be developed. Within a democratic society, it can be argued, guidance is an important means of making the structure of society work, by linking individual needs to societal needs on a voluntaristic basis. It is not by chance that the growth of formal guidance services has been linked not only to industrialisation but also to democratisation, to social mobility, and to cultural individualism (Watts, 1996e). In these senses, guidance is a significant lubricant of social development.

Operationalising claimed social benefits in a way which enables them to be tested is not likely to be easy. Many of the variables we have looked at in our reviews of economic benefits and of impact on school effectiveness are relevant here too: social benefits overlap with educational, psychological and economic benefits, rather than being a separate watertight category of their own. But the notion of social benefits encourages us to look at a wider range of outcomes than any one of the others are likely to encompass – including, for example, "quality of life" variables. It is also possible that social benefits are not simply aggregates of individual benefits, but also include additional interaction effects: for instance, that the benefits of guidance may be transmitted from parents to children, or vice-versa, or along peer networks.

Conclusion

In this paper, I have argued that there are strong a priori grounds for claiming that career guidance has economic and social benefits. It is important that we do not overstate the case. It is easy to exaggerate the scale of effects which might reasonably be anticipated. Only very limited benefits would be sufficient to justify the modest level of public investment that is currently made in guidance services. But this presents a considerable methodological problem if we wish to test the claims: large samples and sensitive instruments are needed to reveal gains which are small in absolute terms, if also large returns on small investments (Killeen, Watts & Kidd, 1998).

There are further methodological difficulties. One is the problem of defining the intervention whose impact we are seeking to measure. In this paper I have ranged from careers interviews through curriculum programmes to Job Clubs. Are we seeking to measure the effect of a particular intervention at a single point in time: a single counselling interview, for example? If so, this is comparable to seeking to measure the impact of a single school lesson: the effects are likely to be minute. Or are we looking at the effect of a series of interventions over a long period of time? If so, the problems of defining and controlling these interventions, and of finding control groups which have access to no such interventions, become far more difficult to solve.

There is a need for further research on all these matters. However, research is expensive, and research resources need to be deployed where they are most likely to be fruitful. My personal view is that such resources would be much better used on helping us to understand the processes of guidance and how to provide it more effectively than on further "black box" research which ignores the intervention itself and is interested only in demonstrating outcomes as a way of judging whether the activity is worthwhile.

This is not to say that the reviews we have undertaken have not been worthwhile. As I said at the outset, I believe they are vital if we are to argue the case for public investment in guidance. On both economic and social benefits, we can conclude that there is strong case on a priori grounds, that the direct evidence available to date is limited but positive, but that much more extensive research needs to be mounted if definitive evidence is required. In the meantime, in the absence of such definitive evidence, the a priori arguments and the limited positive evidence stand: the burden of proof rests on those who wish to dispute the arguments.

Section Two:
Models for Practice

Section Introduction

The first section of this book explored concepts of career and underlined that many individuals will benefit from access to professional help and support as they progress through their career. This section focuses on the nature of such support. Throughout his own career, Tony Watts has examined the form and nature of career development interventions, bringing to this task the capacity to analyse and develop taxonomies which offer both insight and structure for career practitioners, their managers and those who train them.

In the extracts from Schools, Careers and Community, co-authored with Bill Law, are two examples of such taxonomies. First is the original articulation of the DOTS schema (chapter 5) which became a pervasive, influential and enduring analysis of the purpose and tasks of career education. The second extract from this book (chapter 6) explores 'power' in careers guidance work, a topic which has received scant treatment by other writers on careers. Power flows through the structures and dynamics of institutions and their stakeholders. Watts and Law examine the nature and impact of such power flows, addressing questions as relevant now as in the 1970s when this was written.

The following two sections address aspects of career development work in schools. Engagement and experience are key themes in the extract from Rethinking Work Experience (chapter 7), teasing out how learning experience and 'work' in this partial sense contribute to career development. For the school, the aims, curriculum links and potential forms of work experience tasks are examined and categorised. Employer engagement is also a theme within the following extract, from Mirrors of Work: Work Simulations in Schools (chapter 8). Here, concepts about the nature of work and the purposes of education, as outlined earlier in this volume, inform discussion of ways to design activities which effectively harness employers' interests in education and meet shared learning objectives. Again the emphasis is on the value of active engagement of pupils rather than passive listening.

Attention then turns to higher education. In Career Development Learning and Employability Learning Tony Watts draws on his explorations of practice in order to offer typologies of curriculum and institutional activities for developing the employability skills of undergraduates. The analysis of current and possible ways of working is presented as a tool for evaluating current work and planning provision.

As technologies developed, Tony Watts explored their impact on careers work in The Role of Information and Communication Technologies in Integrated Career Information and Guidance Systems. Again focused on clients, their needs, and the ways that practitioners seek to help them, this section looks at modes and levels of integration of ICT into existing models of professional practice.

Throughout all these examples, Tony's eye is fixed firmly on the end beneficiary: the school or university student, the adult in trouble or in transition. Pervasive in these writings is the belief that – with necessary, timely and appropriate support – individuals have the capacity and commitment to engage and to flourish. However, as the following section will explore, economic and political conditions can cause extreme headwinds which limit progress.

5. Careers Education[12]

'Careers education' is a relatively new addition to educational jargon. It is sometimes used as a new synonym for 'careers work' and 'careers guidance' – terms which have been in use for some time, even though the activities they describe have always tended to be rather peripheral concerns in most schools. But 'careers education' potentially describes a new approach to careers guidance work, one which brings it much closer to the centre of the school. For it ceases to see the school's task as being simply that of providing diagnostic advisory services which will help to make better decisions for students on the societal positions (in terms of education or employment) they should enter on leaving school. Instead it sees the school's central task as being that of helping students to develop the skills, and acquire the concepts and information, that will help them to make such decisions for themselves. This is not only a much more ambitious task: it is also a much more essentially educational one. For it focuses attention not on the diagnostic skill of the careers adviser, but on student learning. Perhaps the most clear sign of the change is that careers guidance is beginning to be seen as an activity which takes place not only in interview rooms – suggesting a form of interaction which most schools are neither staffed nor built to provide in any profusion – but also in the heart of the school: the classroom. A further sign is the complementary emergence of approaches to interviewing which are based not on advice-giving but on counselling, with the interviewer focusing his skill not on helping the student to make wise decisions (with the assumption that he knows what these should be), but on helping him to make decisions wisely (Katz, 1969). In many ways, indeed, the changing approach to careers guidance can be characterised as one in which the processes of information and advice have begun to be supplemented and to some extent overtaken by the more complex processes of careers education and counselling (Watts, 1973a). In this report we will be concerned with careers guidance in general, but with careers education in particular.

The official approbation given to careers education has been marked in recent years by two documents. The first was the report of the Schools Council working party on the transition from school to work, which significantly was entitled *Careers Education in the 1970s* (Schools Council, 1972), and which gave rise to the Schools Council Careers Education and Guidance Project. The second was the report of the Department of Education and Science on *Careers Education in Secondary Schools* (DES, 1973), which reported the results of a statistical survey of the provision schools made for careers guidance, which gave a prominent place to the issue of curriculum time for careers education, and which also made some strong recommendations

---

12 Editorial footnote: Co-authored with Bill Law. Reprinted with permission of the authors from *Schools, Careers and Community*. London: Church Information Office, 1977.

about the centrality of careers education and about the need for schools to pay more attention to it. But little effort has been devoted so far to conceptualising the objectives of careers education in a clear and satisfactory way (see Watts and Herr, 1976), and little research has been conducted into the form it takes.

Assumptions

We approached our task[13] with certain assumptions. The first is about the importance of guidance: we take the view that the provision of certain kinds of careers guidance facilities, incorporating careers education, is a necessary step in the development of a society in which people can be more fully autonomous. The second assumption is about the tasks of careers education, which we take to be concerned with helping people become aware of the opportunities open to them, aware of the individual personalities which they can implement in relation to those opportunities, skilled in the kind of decision-making tasks which confront all who need to reconcile who they are with where they are, and able sensibly to anticipate and cope with the transitions to each succeeding phase in their individual careers. The third assumption is about the diffuseness of careers education in particular and of careers guidance in general: we take it to be too subtle and too complex an undertaking to be left solely to the specialists and professionals, but rather a task which inevitably is shared by the total community, and should be planned to take account of this fact. Since these assumptions underpin much of what we have to say in this report, we will attempt to elaborate them and to explain the bases on which they rest.

The importance of careers education

The growing attention paid in recent years to careers guidance – and now to careers education – is explicable in terms of its having begun to perform essential functions for our society which were formerly performed in other ways. Among these perhaps the most important is that of deploying people to the variety of roles that are open in our society and thus of deploying life-chances – both occupational and non-occupational. In the past, such functions have been performed by a variety of formal and informal, public and private, selection procedures. There was a time, not so very long ago, when it was possible to predict within quite tight limits the kind of roles a person would have by knowing three pieces of information – where, to whom, and with what sex he or she was born. Life-chances are no longer commonly deployed

13 Editorial footnote: The research on which this report was based originated in the concern of the Church of England Board of Education about careers education in Church schools. The project was in two parts, one involving descriptive surveys of careers education provision in six schools, and the other based on two consultations, referred to as Nutford and Britewell.

on quite so crude a basis. By stages, more rational and more egalitarian methods have begun to emerge.

Turner's (1960) distinction between sponsored and contest mobility represents two of the stages in this development. In a pattern of sponsored mobility the acquisition of improved life-chances depends upon gaining acceptance by those in power, who select on undeclared criteria (including e.g. nepotism). In a pattern of contest mobility, on the other hand, the acquisition of improved life-chances depends upon earning them by successfully competing for selection on the basis of publicly-declared criteria. In particular, the public examination system represents a more accountable and more objective basis than sponsorship for deploying education-chances and (ultimately) life-chances. But the examination system has now itself come under attack, partly because of doubts about its technical efficiency, and partly because of more basic doubts about its impersonal and manipulative character. And it is at the point in social development where it is felt that people should no longer be selected for life-chances, but should be invited – at least to some extent – to self-select themselves, that careers guidance becomes socially important. Initially, such guidance may be based on advice-giving. Eventually, however, it is coming to be realised that while advice at times may be useful, it does not ultimately foster autonomy. If people are really in any genuine sense to self-select themselves, they must not be told what to do, but rather helped through careers education and counselling to acquire the skills, concepts and information they need to make their own decisions.

The importance of careers education is augmented by the increasing multiplicity and complexity of choices and transitions now open to students in school. There has been an enormous diversification in the structure of the working world – in sources of energy, in manufacturing and distributive processes, in management and organisational structures. Within the volume of work that is available there is much greater variety than a generation or two ago. As a result, young people are confronted with many more job titles than were their parents on leaving school or college. Coupled with this phenomenon of diversification and specialisation, there has also been in recent years a rising level of unemployment, and a general upward shift in the level of education and training required to carry out the work offered. Unemployment is hitting hardest the least qualified.

The overall picture of the world of work, therefore, is one of change. It is notoriously difficult to predict from one five-year period to the next what shifts are going to occur in the demand for labour – as recently graduated chemists, computer programmers and school teachers can affirm. But a changing employment market of decreasing volume, increasing complexity and rising entry standards seems to us to argue for increased rather than decreased guidance provisions, especially if those provisions are concerned not just with resolving the student's immediate problem but rather with equipping him with enduring resources that will help him when facing future problems. For example, intermittent periods of unemployment may in the future be a necessary feature of employment, at least at lower levels of entry and training. It is also increasingly probable that, having entered a particular occupation at whatever level, there will be a variety of subsequent choices and transitions to make concerning training and specialisation, and even mid-career transfer to an entirely different type of work. And that is to say nothing of the wide range of non-educational and non-occupational choices that students at school are faced with. The plurality and flux of the employment market-place is paralleled by plurality and flux in the consumer market-place, the leisure market-place, the morality market-place. The argument that our society needs people who have been prepared to cope with change and choice has never been stronger than it is now. Our assumption is that guidance is about preparing students to cope with – and make fruitful use of – such change and choice.

Let us be more specific. It would still not be too difficult to find a school where admission is determined by 11+ selection, where the opportunity to take chemistry in the third year is contingent upon satisfying the teacher that enough 'scientific ability' has been demonstrated at the end of the second-year general science course, where the pattern of public examination entries is left for teachers to decide on the basis of 'ability' and 'mock' exams, and where certain students are 'encouraged' to stay on for a 'science' sixth (and some quite specifically discouraged from staying for any kind of sixth year at all). In such a school an individual might find himself qualified in mathematics, physics and chemistry to A-level at the end of the eight years of secondary education without ever having had to make a clear decision about the direction his life should take, or in any real sense participate in the formation of that particular destiny. By contrast, it is not at all difficult now to find schools in which parents are invited to apply for admission of their children, where parents and children will be invited to consider whether the students should develop a scientific rather than some other kind of course, where the students will be invited to participate in decisions about examination entries, and where they will be given an opportunity to consider whether the sixth form is an appropriate place for them to continue their education or not.

In this latter kind of school the individual is faced with a number of choice points and transitions over which he has some degree of control. He needs to be prepared to exercise that control in an adequate and appropriate manner; exercising it is likely to prepare him for the further choices and transitions he will meet in his adult future. It is these two forms of preparation – immediate and long-term – with which careers education is concerned. Hence our argument that the less selection takes precedence in such situations, and the more self-selection is allowed to operate, the more important careers education provision becomes.

The tasks of careers education

In our view, there are four careers education tasks to be accomplished with each student, facilitating the development respectively of (i) opportunity awareness, (ii) self awareness, (iii) decision learning, and (iv) transition learning. We shall examine each of these in turn.

By opportunity awareness we mean the help which is given to students to experience and gain some understanding of the general structure of the working world they are going to enter, the range of opportunities which exist within it, the demands that different parts of it may make upon them, and the rewards and satisfactions that these different parts can offer. We mean opportunity awareness also to refer to the exploration of the different paths and strategies which are open (or closed) to particular individuals for gaining entry to those opportunities. And at the level of the individual we take it to refer to the combination of demands, offers and strategies which match (or at least do not mismatch) a particular individual's characteristics. We have argued elsewhere that the opportunities to be covered in careers education should encompass not only educational and occupational opportunities but also leisure, community and family opportunities: in other words, that careers education should be concerned not just with occupational roles but with non-occupational roles too (see Watts and Herr, 1976). Nonetheless, although we attempted to discern how far the schools in our survey regarded careers education in these terms, for purely practical reasons we decided for the purposes of the study to pay primary attention to occupational opportunities: only in this way could we limit our data-collection task to manageable proportions. In general, we have noted attention to non-occupational roles where this is linked to the formal careers guidance provisions, but we have not attempted to identify other activities which are solely concerned with such roles.

By self awareness we mean the help that is given to students to develop their own sense of themselves as unique individuals, with personal characteristics which in some respects are like other people's but in other respects are not. It is to address the question 'what kind of personality is it that I take with me to implement in the world of opportunities that exist for me?' In part it involves an exploration of actual and potential personal strengths – qualifications, abilities, aptitudes, practical skills, personal qualities, and physical strengths. In part it is an exploration of limitations in these various respects. But it is also the exploration of personal needs, involving questions about what kinds of satisfactions are sought, what kind of interests are developing, what personal aspirations are being formulated, and what is most valued in one's experience of the world. Some of the needs expressed by a young person will be deeply internalised and abiding, some will be specific to the situation and transitory. The converse of the exploration of needs is the exploration of frustrations – what is experienced as antipathetic, irritating, dissatisfying. To some extent all of the curriculum and extra-curriculum of the school – and especially perhaps subjects like English, art and music – provide an opportunity for such self-exploration. In this study however we have focused our attention mainly on activities which are concerned with it in a direct way, and which relate to what we have called opportunity awareness. To incorporate a self-awareness component into a careers education programme is to pay attention to the importance of the self-concept in the facilitation of career preferences and choices (Super, 1957).

By decision learning we mean the help that is offered to students to understand the variety of ways in which decisions can be made. That might mean, for example, helping them to understand the various pressures, expectations and cues which are offered to someone in a decision-making situation. It might mean helping them to understand the various styles in which decisions can be made – ranging from impulsive to deeply deliberate – recognising that different people make different decisions in different ways, and that some decision-making styles are more appropriate for some situations than for others. There are also certain skills which students can acquire that will help them to make decisions in a manner more satisfactory to themselves – skills such as those of collating information and ordering priorities. At some point, too, individuals will need to take account of the risks involved in decision-making – balancing the desirability of different outcomes against the probability that they will occur. And it seems to us likely that young people will need some help in learning to take responsibility for decision-making, accepting authority and accountability for the running of their own lives. What we are talking about here, then, are the skills and awareness that students need in order to integrate what they know of themselves with what they know of their opportunities, and in order to convert these two kinds of knowledge into an implementable decision. The skills involved are mainly generic ones for which career decisions are but one area of application: our analyses have made some recognition of this point, but for practical reasons we have attempted comprehensively to log only those activities which are directly concerned with career decision-making.

By transition learning we mean helping students to gain the awareness and skills they need to cope with the transitions consequent upon their growing up and upon the particular decisions they make. It could mean, for example, gaining some understanding of how school life is different from work life – more attractive and manageable in some respects, less so in others. It could mean helping the students relate what they are learning at school to what will happen at later stages in their lives. It could also mean helping them to acquire the skills and information they need to cope with the new situations they will meet – communication skills, interpersonal skills, budgetary skills, information about trade unions, information about supervisory patterns at work, and so on. Transition learning is, therefore, concerned with helping the student to gain a realistic understanding of what will come later in his career development, and to acquire the coping skills he will need to make this transition appropriately and successfully. There may of course be considerable variations in the types of learning that are required by different students: transition to routine work in a factory may present very different problems from transition to undergraduate work in a university. Moreover, different people approach these transitions with different advantages and disadvantages – for some the acquisition of communication skills may be a priority, for others the erosion of naive expectations may be more important. There is a case also for helping students to begin to anticipate the decisions which will need to be made after the initial transition has been made – for instance, whether to stay in the job one has originally selected or to try something else. In general we judge transition learning to be an essential element in careers education, anchoring the processes of opportunity awareness, self awareness and decision learning to future realities, and helping students to prepare not only for making decisions but also for implementing them.

Guidance as a community enterprise

Our final assumption is that the guidance of young people towards future roles is an activity in which representatives of a wide cross-section of the community have both a right and a responsibility to engage. A good many of the studies conducted over the past two decades of how young people arrive at their career decisions have yielded the finding that they lean as much or more upon informal sources of help in the family, the peer group, and the wider community, as upon formal professional sources of help in the school and Careers Service (see e.g. Carter, 1962; Jahoda and Chalmers, 1963; Maizels, 1970). There have been numerous attempts to diagnose what appears at first sight to be a failure on the part of the professionals. They include suggestions that intervention by professionals is often scheduled too late to be of any use, that there are conflicts between the professional role conception and the client's expectation concerning the kind of help that should be offered, that the professionals are not given enough time to do their work, and so on. No doubt such attempts at diagnosis have their validity, but we submit that they may not be as adequate or as necessary as explanations as is sometimes imagined. The process of making an occupational choice is linked to a complex matrix of influences extending well back into the family and neighbourhood life of the individual. Similarly occupational choice is linked to a complex matrix of consequences involving not only the educational-vocational life of the individual but his social, domestic and leisure life, and indeed his personality. It would be surprising if such issues could be resolved to the satisfaction of any client within the limits set by the professional guidance provisions of curricular and extra-curricular work in school and of interviews with the careers officer.

It seems to us inevitable therefore that any individual engaged in the search for his or her future roles will call upon non-specialised, neighbourhood and informal resources, as well as those offered by the professionals. Not only is it inevitable: it is also highly desirable. We agree with Illich (1971) that it is dangerous to allow too much responsibility for the upbringing of our children to fall into the hands of a professional minority. The community has a right to participate in the upbringing of its young.

Such a notion assigns to the professional a harder rather than an easier task, for it means that the guidance role needs to work essentially by transgressing the school's boundary structure – in other words, to become a marginal role in the school. It has to be concerned with the meaning which is given to the student's experience not only by the student himself and by his teachers, but by parents, employers, other education and training institutions, other agencies of guidance outside the school, professional associations, trade unions, and ultimately by consumers and the whole social, economic and political structure in which we all participate. Within such a conception, the professional becomes not merely a source of guidance, but also a facilitator of multifarious other sources, many of which will have important careers education functions to play. Indeed he may need to become more than merely a facilitator.

6. Power in Careers Guidance Work[14]

We have been working with a distinction between the 'structures' and the 'dynamics' of the schools we have been examining. The distinction corresponds to the two sets of questions we have posed ourselves: questions to do with 'how schools do careers guidance' and with 'why schools do careers guidance'. A word which has as yet barely been introduced in the vocabulary of this report, but which seems to us to offer some prospect of expressing a unifying concept in much of what we have observed, is the word 'power'. It rephrases and reverses the order of our two basic questions so that they become: 'What is it that empowers a careers guidance system?' and 'How is that power transmitted through the system?'

The importance of the concept of 'power' has been implicit in much of what we have reported from the two consultations.[15] A lot of the anxiety at the Nutford consultation was expressed in terms of exaggerated claims to power and fear of manipulation by others. Resistance to the use of 'role' was seen as restrictive of personal commitment and autonomy. Again, the use of the terms 'dependency' and 'fight' as model terms for the description of social interaction is, implicitly, to use the syntax of power: dependency is to legitimise the power of another; fight is to dispute it.

It is arguable, of course, that the words 'authority' or 'influence' might prove as useful in articulating such notions. We select the word 'power' because it suggests the more raw psychological and sociological material out of which authority and influence are generated. The word 'energy' would have served almost as well, but connotes only the 'fuel' which drives the system. What we mean by power is broader than that. To use an automotive analogy, the power of an automobile is the product both of the energising fuel it uses and of the mechanics which transmit an explosion into the turning of the wheels. Power, in other words, is the product of dynamics and mechanics: a shortfall in either domain will result in loss of power. We argue that in social systems there is an analogous relationship between, on the one hand, the motivations, commitments and feelings of people that energise the systems, and on the other, the structures, roles and skills through which that energy is transmitted. Even at the level of individual functioning, empathetic feelings are powerless without empathetic technique. At the level of organisational change, innovatory intentions

---

14 Editorial footnote: Co-authored with Bill Law. Reprinted with permission of the authors from *Schools, Careers and Community*. London: Church Information Office, 1977.
15 Editorial footnote: The two consultations, referred to as Nutford and Britewell, each were 2-day facilitated events involving school personnel, parents, employers and other stakeholders. Each involved some 35-40 people, and operated through processes of questioning and feedback.

may be counter-productive without organisational skills. The power of any system or any group within a system is the product both of what is intended and of what there is in terms of skill, technique, structure, to deliver. Power is enhanced, for parents, employers, teachers and the others, where there is both commitment and access to organisational and technical structures through which the commitment can be transmitted. Power is a matter of knowing 'how' as well as knowing 'why'.

Most of the issues identified in the six schools we have studied and the two consultations can, in our view, be articulated in a more general sense in terms of the use and abuse of power. Indeed, this seems to us to offer a way of pulling together the main strands of our study. We therefore set out below some questions for the attention of decision-makers concerned with careers guidance in schools. And, wherever we can, we suggest the kind of answers to those questions which our contacts with our schools have suggested to us.

1. What proportion of the power in the school system should be diverted into careers guidance and its different objectives? We have observed considerable variation between schools in terms of the volume of their investment in careers guidance. In general, it is the larger schools that have invested most. We do not however feel that any of the schools we visited have yet grappled with the full implications of careers guidance in general and of careers education in particular. Notably, we feel that much more attention needs to be paid to the tasks of developing the students' self-awareness, their decision-making skills, and the skills they will need to accomplish the transition from school to work.

2. How much of the power for careers guidance should be generated inside the school and how much outside it? In terms of volume of activity our observation is that most of the schools place very heavy reliance on the skills, information and other resources that are available inside the school. We have argued that this makes neither economic nor social sense.

3. What can be done to implement the potential power of the community to participate in the guidance of its young? The strategy we have suggested is one of developing new roles for parents, etc., and not an attempt to recover and reinstate their traditional roles. In the case of parents, for example, an individual parent can no longer know all that his son or daughter needs in order to cope with his or her particular future, but parents collectively provide an enormously valuable and powerful source of world-knowledge. It seems to us that the school needs to accept some responsibility for harnessing these resources and for making separate deals with each of the elements in its community. Not all are able to contribute everything: there are things for instance that parents can do that employers cannot, and vice versa. The school has high social centrality and is strategically well-placed to act as facilitator and co-ordinator of a regained

communal responsibility for its young, mediated in new and – potentially – less restrictive ways.

4. Why is the Careers Service characterised by such low power in the careers guidance system, and what can be done to make better use of its high centrality in terms of contacts and information? This question represents a special case of the issues raised in question 3. Careers officers are the best-trained group in the guidance systems we observed, and in several of the schools we saw substantial evidence of the quality of their commitment and skill. They also provide some safeguard against careers guidance deteriorating into a power struggle between different schools for preferential positions in the labour market. Moreover, their role is legitimised by other groups in the system – particularly by employers, with whom they have closer contacts than schools are able to have. Yet their power to contribute to the careers guidance system is heavily contingent upon the way in which they are treated by the school. The effective implementation of the careers officer's distinctive skills, training for which has already been paid for by the community, is a priority for any school concerned with careers guidance work, although it is not in any sense an alternative to effective careers education programmes within the school.

5. How far is professionalisation in careers guidance hiving off to specialists power that should be more widely dispersed? This is a further elaboration of question 3. There is evidence that guidance is on the threshold of becoming a recognised specialism within the teaching profession. But at the same time, other teachers for instance are unwilling to relinquish their responsibility for guidance, and generate materials and activities of great usefulness, or potential usefulness, to the guidance of students. It seems to us that ways need to be found of reconciling specialisation and generalisation in guidance provisions. It would be a pity to allow one type of provision to expand at the expense of the other. Specialists should accept responsibility for encouraging and implementing the efforts of their colleagues – both inside and outside the school – in the guidance of the young.

6. How can personal commitment be used to empower organisation development? This question is a further elaboration of question 5. Where personal initiations are taken over by organisational roles and structures, how can we be sure that what is valuable in the former is not lost in the latter? Much of what we have observed reinforces the view that even where organisational provisions are initiated from the top, the way in which those provisions are experienced by students still remains contingent upon the extent to which individual members of staff are motivated and have the skills to implement them. The alternative model of facilitating and legitimising informal initiations made by members of staff themselves seems to us to be a strategy well worth implementing more

widely. Within such a model, the task of decision-makers is to identify, facilitate, legitimise and incorporate into the formal organisation, constructive initiations made informally by members of their staff – and, indeed, by members of the school's community. In other words, not only should the formal careers guidance system continue to harness and foster resources in other parts of the school and community, but ideally it should itself be organic and rooted in the real – rather than merely the hoped-for – potentiality of the organisation.

7. How can powerful counterbalances within a system be counterpoised and made integrative rather than destructive? This question arises inevitably from question 6. Where staff initiations are permitted they tend, as we have seen at Britewell, to conflict with each other. Our observations from the two consultations suggest that where conflicting commitments – antitheses – are brought into communication with each other, rich and useful results can often be achieved in terms of synthesis. People's views are modified by exposure to other people's views. The implication of this is that people talk to each other directly and not solely 'through the chair', the chair being represented by some arbitrating hierarchical group which can easily deprive them of any opportunity of realising their own view of the situation. This is not to say that where such communication can occur all conflicts will be resolved. But our observations of the process in the consultations suggest that boundaries can be established and contracts made between groups so that a real sense is gained of where responsibilities lie. Residual conflict will remain, particularly where the participants in discussion are widely dispersed in terms of their positions in the school and its community. But such conflict – where it can be clearly stated and tolerated – itself becomes a powerful means for challenging and enriching the assumptions and objectives upon which action is based.

8. How far are role definitions the expression of personal power or a curtailment of it? This question arises directly from question 7 because the process of synthesis which we observed in the consultations seemed to lead towards some attempt to define the content and limits of the roles of the various groups represented. The very use of the term 'role' was – as we have seen – experienced as restrictive. Guidance as a notion lends itself very readily to partnership with the notion of 'interpersonal relationship': a great deal of the literature of counselling is given over to a discussion of the facilitative nature of such relationships. But the implication of what we have argued in this context is that the quality of the interpersonal relationship between the careers guidance practitioner and his client is not the only reality in the consulting room. The practitioner is in a contractual relationship with other professionals, with his own employers, with the parents, and with the labour market, and he also has a contractual as well as an interpersonal relationship with his client. 'Contract' implies limits,

responsibilities, accountability, and a route of escape both for the helper and for the student. The notion of a defined role, with defined limits, responsibilities, accountabilities and termination points, seems to us to provide a useful basis for declaring a contract with which all parties are cognisant and from which they know what to expect. On the other hand, it can become a curtailment of personal power where individuals are not free to opt into and out of roles, where they are not able to participate in the formulation of these roles, and where the whole of their activity in the life of the organisation – both informal and formal – is circumscribed by role definitions.

9. How much power do students have to accept or resist careers guidance? There were several hints in our study – and particularly in the two consultations – of the extent to which guidance can become manipulative, and far from furthering the development of individual autonomy, can inhibit it. Care and concern for individual students is an important component of the power in careers guidance systems: unless it is controlled, however, it can easily trap students into dependence. The concept of role may again be helpful here as a way of defining the limits of guidance and so allowing room for the individual to accept or resist it. There are implications too both for the structure of the school and for guidance methods.

10. What kind of power should guidance technology be seeking to harness? In relation to guidance methods, there must be room for the suspicion that psychology and sociology are by stages yielding technologies which are capable of moulding individual personalities and social systems to externally-determined shapes with some precision and power. Knowledge of such means is far from complete, and this study has suggested that what knowledge is extant has not yet much permeated the skills of guidance practitioners in schools. But there is every reason to suppose that the formal, sustained and deliberate application of (say) conditioning techniques to guidance could, within a matter of decades, yield powerful results. Before long teachers could have considerably more potent means to reduce substantially the incidence of serious reading retardation, non-attendance, even anti-social behaviour. The possibility of extending such technologies to problems connected with occupational choice, the acceptance of unemployment and the control of supply to the labour market, should also be taken into account. What decision-makers in the field of careers guidance should perhaps be considering now is what kind of guidance technology we should be attempting to develop: one designed to yield predictable behavioural outcomes, or one designed to facilitate a more open and participative exploration of oneself and one's situation on the part of the student. If, as we have suggested, careers guidance represents part of a social trend from an attributive to a participative means of role-deployment in our society, then the answer to that question will

hopefully be that we will develop a guidance technology which yields power to the individual.

In relation to this last issue, perhaps the over-riding and most profoundly reassuring observation we have made in this study is of the liveliness and resilience of the young people we met. The schools we visited are of very different types and in very different social settings, but we did not have one conversation with the youngsters in them which could not at the very least be characterised as good-humoured and informative: at their best, indeed, our conversations with them were highly stimulating, incisive and perceptive. We encountered some resentment that they were being treated as though they had less maturity than they believed themselves to have. We encountered some criticism of the types of provisions that were made. But we also encountered an impressive ability on the part of the youngsters to understand the problems and conflicts in which the teachers were involved, and a considerable capacity to 'make allowances'. Whatever efforts are made by teachers, at whatever level of skill and sophistication, in the end the individual student selects, internalises and co-ordinates the impressions and information which together form his experience of guidance. Ultimately, every student is his own career co-ordinator.

7. The Concept of Work Experience[16]

The aim of this chapter is to explore the concept of work experience. In doing so, we will look at narrow and broad definitions both of 'work' and of 'experience'. We will examine the various aims which are attached to work-experience schemes, and the extent to which they can be achieved through alternative kinds of experience both inside and outside the work-place. We will then look at some of the different forms which work experience may take in practice. Finally, we will explore the arguments for broadening the concept of 'work', and at their implications for work-experience programmes.

The core concept

'Work experience' is a paradoxical phrase, in that it is firmly distinguished from 'work', and is used to describe schemes in which only part of the full 'experience' of work is available. To be more specific, it is applied to schemes in which people experience work tasks in work environments, but without taking on the full identity of a worker (Watts, 1983c). The key distinction is that the role of students on a work-experience scheme is that not of employee but of learner. Accordingly, they are only attached to the work-place on a short-term basis, and are not normally paid by the 'employer' (apart perhaps from travelling expenses). On the other hand – a further paradox – it is arguable that the learning yield will be substantial and distinctive only if the experience gets as close as possible to that of being an employee. Many of the difficulties and confusions about work experience stem from this role tension.

Our concern in this book is with school-based work-experience programmes, under which school[17] students go out to work-places for periods of, usually, between one and three weeks (though there are other patterns too). It is worth noting, however, that work experience also forms a part of many courses in further and higher education, including 'sandwich' courses in which the workplacement may be much longer – sometimes up to a year.

---

16 Editorial footnote: Reprinted, by permission of the publisher, from Miller, A., Watts, A.G. & Jamieson, I.: *Rethinking Work Experience*. London: Falmer, 1991.

17 'School' in this connection is defined to cover sixth-form colleges and also to cover courses in colleges of further education and tertiary colleges which are also offered in schools: thus it includes A-level courses in FE but excludes FE vocational courses.

In addition to these education-based examples, the term 'work experience' has confusingly also been applied to schemes like the Youth Training Scheme[18] in which participants are work-based: here the work experience is central, and off-the-job education and training is cast in a supportive role. In school-based work-experience programmes, this relationship is reversed: such programmes are designed – in principle, anyway – to support activities within the school curriculum.

Aims and curricular frames

Work-experience schemes have a variety of aims: some declared, and some latent; some highly respectable, and some more dubious in character. We have analysed the aims in a variety of documents at national, local and school level, and we believe that the great majority can be grouped under the ten categories shown in figure 2, which we have labelled enhancing, motivational, maturational, investigative, expansive, sampling, preparatory, anticipatory, placing, and custodial. We will look at each of these in turn.

The enhancing aim is concerned with enabling students to deepen their understanding of concepts learned in classroom settings, and to apply skills learned in such settings. This tends to be specific and planned, and to cover what Fuller (1987) refers to as 'coursework integration'. As the DES guidelines put it:

> Work-related activities offer valuable opportunities for project work which can enhance understanding of the subject(s) concerned. (DES, 1988a)

The most effective examples tend to occur in particular departments like English, Mathematics, Social Studies, or Humanities, where the work experience has been used to conduct research into topics being covered within the classroom (see e.g. Fortune, Jamieson and Street, 1983; Holmes, Jamieson and Perry, 1983). But surveys within TVEI[19], where one would expect this kind of integration to be more common than elsewhere, have suggested that it is rarely achieved to any significant extent (Barnes et al., 1987; Saunders, 1987).

The motivational aim is concerned with making aspects of the school curriculum more meaningful and significant to students, so improving their levels of academic attainment.

---

18 Editorial footnote: The Youth Training Scheme was a UK government initiative providing largely job-based training for unemployed 16-17 year olds; it ran from 1983-89.
19 Editorial footnote: The Technical and Vocational Education Initiative (TVEI) was a curriculum initiative for 14-18 year olds that ran from 1983 to 1997.

This is more general and unplanned than the enhancing aim, and views applicability as a means of increasing motivation for further learning. Here work experience is seen as:

> ... an opportunity for them to relate prior learning to real world applications and begin to understand the need to take care of their own learning, that is, to learn how to learn. (IPM, 1988)

Figure 2: Possible aims of work experience

1. Enhancing – to enable students to deepen their understanding of concepts learned in classroom settings, and to apply skills learned in such settings.

2. Motivational – to make the school curriculum more meaningful and significant to students, so improving their levels of academic attainment.

3. Maturational – to facilitate students' personal and social development.

4. Investigative – to enable students to develop their knowledge and understanding of the world of work.

5. Expansive – to broaden the range of occupations that students are prepared to consider in terms of their personal career planning.

6. Sampling – to enable students to test their vocational preference before committing themselves to it.

7. Preparatory – to help students to acquire skills and knowledge related to a particular occupational area, which they will be able to apply if they wish to enter employment in that area.

8. Anticipatory – to enable students to experience some of the strains of work so that they will be able to manage the transition to work more comfortably.

9. Placing – to enable students to establish a relationship with a particular employer which may lead to the offer of a full-time job.

10. Custodial – to transfer some of the responsibility for particular students for a period.

Source: Adapted with modifications from Watts (1983c). The main changes are the splitting of the 'social-educational' aim into the maturational and investigative aims, the splitting of the 'vocational' aim into the expansive and sampling aims, and the addition of the enhancing and preparatory aims.

The argument is that once students have seen the general applicability of the knowledge and skills they are learning in school, they will be more motivated to acquire them. Even if this is not the case in terms of the 'use value' of the knowledge and skills themselves, it may be so in terms of the 'exchange value' of the examination qualifications to which they lead: the students may recognise more clearly the importance of such qualifications for entering particular occupations at particular levels of the labour market.

The maturational aim is concerned with facilitating students' personal and social development. Holmes, Jamieson and Perry (1983) point out that 'work experience ... provides a unique opportunity for young people both to test and assess their ownership of social skills and develop them further' (p. 16). AMMA develop the point:

> Working alongside adults as colleagues can contribute powerfully to young people's social development. Work experience gives students opportunities to develop self-confidence and social skills, to form relationships outside their peer group and to learn how to make their own decisions in an adult environment. (AMMA, 1988)

Also, students can learn more about themselves and about their own strengths and weaknesses by experiencing how they cope with a new environment in which new and different demands are made of them.

The investigative aim is concerned with enabling students to develop their knowledge and understanding of the world of work. This covers such matters as:

> How different workplaces are organised, what the work processes are, what social relations at work are like, and what part trade unions play at the workplace. (TUC, n.d.)

It may be seen mainly in localised terms:

> Promoting a knowledge of the industrial, commercial and public employers in the area and understanding of how they function. (HMI, 1988a)

It may also be seen in much broader terms:

> To understand what is meant by 'work' is to understand the structure of society and why it is organised as it is, and how the economy operates. (AMMA, 1988)

If it forms part of a course concerned with such world-of-work learning, this could be regarded as a particular application of the enhancing aim: even where it does not form part of such a course, however, work experience may be expected to deliver in these terms. Stronach (1984) notes that this concept of learning about work rather than learning for work opens the door to less normative and more genuinely educational approaches to work experience. Shilling (1987), too, demonstrates that work experience can provide a basis for critical explorations of labour relations and work-place practices rather than performing a purely adaptive role. In practice, though, HMI (1990) report that 'rarely is work experience seen as an opportunity to explore a wider industrial and economic brief' and that 'despite the high quality of experiences many students gain little understanding of the structure and organisation of business or of the nature of the local economy' (p. 20).

The expansive aim is concerned with broadening the range of occupations that students are prepared to consider in terms of their personal career planning. This embraces what Barnes et al. (1987) term 'work testing' – 'testing more than one of the work experiences on offer in order to identify the likes and dislikes associated with different kinds of work experience' (p. 115). In addition, it covers challenges to traditional sex-stereotyping of occupations:

> An important opportunity for girls to gain experience in work traditionally reserved for men and for boys to be placed in traditionally female areas of employment. (TUC, n.d.)

The need to take account of such equal-opportunities considerations is also mentioned in the guidelines from government (DES, 1988a) and employer organisations (IPM, 1988).

The sampling aim is concerned with enabling students to test their vocational preference before committing themselves to it. Official views here are more ambivalent: though approved by HMI (1988a), it is not mentioned in the DES (1988a) guidelines, and the TUC (n.d.) declare that work experience 'should not be used simply as job sampling'. But it is very common in practice: Barnes et al. (1987) noted that 'virtually all the schools [in their sample] appeared to have oriented placements towards pupils' preferred vocational interest whenever this was possible' (p. 115). Indeed, Fuller (1987) found that post-16 'there were extreme cases where we felt that [work-experience programmes] were being used as a substitute for vocational counselling in institutions which appear to make rather perfunctory efforts in that direction for their academic students' (p. 45).

The preparatory aim is concerned with helping students to acquire skills and knowledge related to a particular occupational area, which they will be able to apply if they should subsequently enter employment in that area. It mainly occurs in relation to vocational courses post-16; even in pre-vocational post-16 courses, notably CPVE, it is not very common (FEU, 1985, p. 119), and pre-16 it is very rare indeed. The TUC (n.d.) state firmly that school-based work experience 'should not be part of any training for a particular job', and the DES (1988a) agree that it 'must not be seen as a preparation ... for any particular job or career'.

The anticipatory aim is concerned with enabling students to experience some of the strains of work so that they will be able to manage the transition to work more comfortably. This includes such matters as:

> To understand the expectations that employers and adult workers will have of them, and how they themselves will fit into working patterns and working relations that are very different from those at school. (TUC, n.d.)

The purpose here is clearly adaptive:

> Young people who have had the advantage of well-managed work experience are likely to adapt more quickly to working life, YTS or apprenticeship. (IPM, 1988)

Whereas the expansive and sampling aims were concerned with preparation for choices, this aim is concerned with preparation for transitions.

The placing aim is concerned with enabling students to establish a relationship with a particular employer which may lead to the offer of a full-time job. As with the sampling and preparatory aims, this is regarded by the TUC as an abuse of the concept:

> Work experience should not be ... a means for employers to decide which young people they might like to employ. (TUC, n.d.)

The DES concur:

> Must not be seen as a ... means of entry to any particular job or career. (DES, 1988a)

Employers' bodies tend to take a more benign view:

> A potential means of finding a job ... seems to be a perfectly legitimate sub-aim. (IPM, 1988)

AMMA attempts to steer a middle course:

> Work experience is neither a job sampling exercise for students, nor a recruitment drive for employers. Nonetheless, it would be naive to pretend that many students, teachers, parents and employers view work experience as anything other than a way for young people to find a job. Indeed, this is a perfectly legitimate aim – but only one of very many potential benefits. (AMMA, 1988)

This indeed seems to represent what happened in practice: HMI (1983) in a survey of schools in Wales reported that 'few schools regarded actual entry into employment as a principal aim of work experience schemes but all saw this as a useful side-effect' (p. 3).

Finally, the custodial aim is concerned with transferring some of the responsibility for particular pupils for a period. This is rarely defended as a principle, but Barnes et al. (1987) note that work experience in some instances represents 'a way of filling in the post-examination vacuum in a legitimate sort of way and, in some cases, a way of taming the more truculent pupils' (p. 117). In a survey of 227 area careers officers conducted in the mid-1970s, four quoted instances of school refusers who were persuaded to try work experience, and twenty-two mentioned that in their opinion schemes were being used 'to get rid of disruptive youngsters' (Walton, 1977, p. 9). This still happens, but is becoming less common as work experience is increasingly coming to be viewed as being appropriate for all students rather than only for a few.

Figure 3: Possible curricular frames for work experience

Curricular frame	*Related aim(s)*
A. Academic subject(s)	Enhancing
B. Personal and social education	Maturational
C. World-of-work learning	Investigative
D. Careers education	Expansive; sampling; anticipatory
E. Vocational course	Preparatory

Of these ten aims, seven provide a basis for a curricular frame for work experience (see figure 3). Thus the enhancing aim provides a basis for work experience to be incorporated within one or more academic subjects; the maturational aim for it to be incorporated within personal and social education; the investigative aim for it to be incorporated within world-of-work learning; the expansive, sampling and anticipatory aims for it to be incorporated within careers education; and the preparatory aim for it to be incorporated within a vocational course.

For the present, two points are worth noting. The first is that the five frames occupy different points on what we might call the 'work-experience triangle': the relationship between the student, the world of work, and school subjects (figure

3). Thus a 'personal and social education' frame focuses on the effect of work experience on the personal development of the individual student; a 'world-of-work learning' frame is concerned with its effect on the student's understanding of the world of work; and an 'academic subject(s)' frame is concerned with its effect on the student's understanding of, and motivation for, his or her traditional school subjects. The other two frames are located along two of the sides of the triangle: a 'careers education' frame is concerned with the effect on the student's personal career planning in relation to the world of work; and a 'vocational course' frame with its effect on the student's capacity to relate what he or she is learning in school to the sector of the world of work with which it is linked.

The second point is that all five of these frames make it possible to incorporate work experience as part of the experiential learning cycle developed by Lewin (1951) and Kolb (1984). This views effective learning as occurring in a four-stage cycle of concrete experience, reflective observation, abstract conceptualisation, and active experimentation (figure 4). Work experience can offer opportunities both for concrete experience and for active experimentation. But its learning potential will only be harnessed if it is integrated into a curriculum frame which also provides opportunities for reflective observation and abstract conceptualisation, and for maintaining the momentum of the cycle.

Figure 3: Mapping of possible curricular frames on the 'work experience triangle'

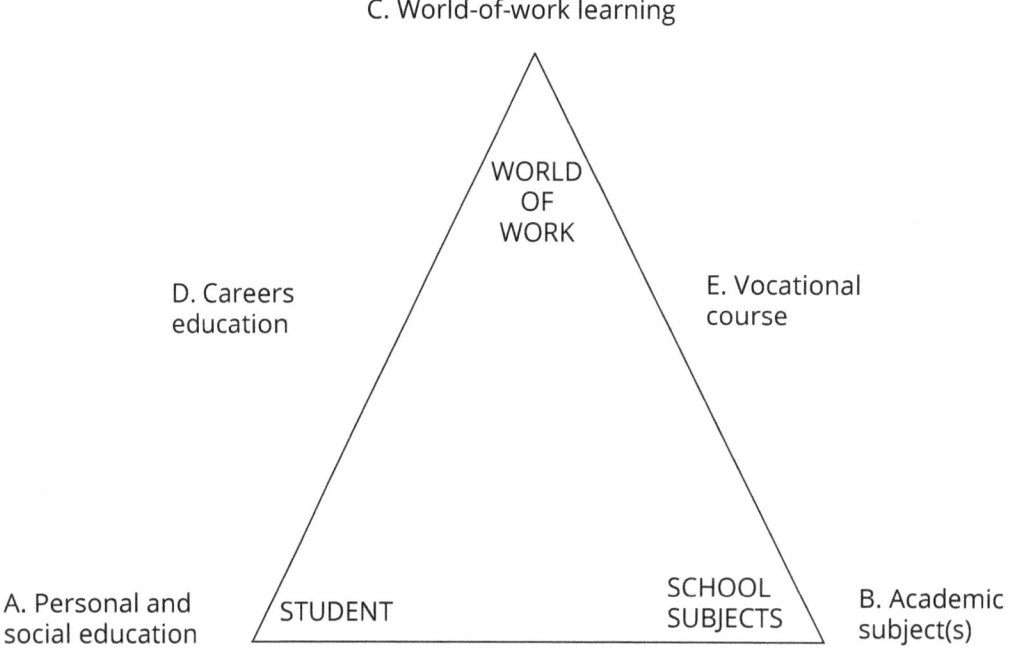

Figure 4: The experiential learning cycle

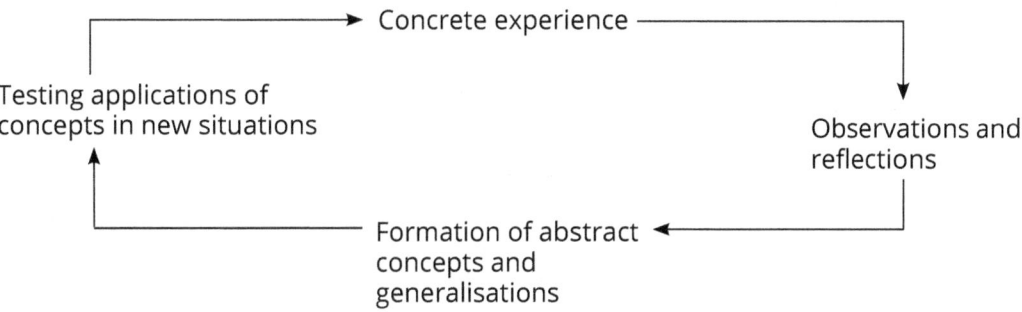

Source: Lewin (1951); subsequently amplified by Kolb (1984).

Related concepts

It is important to recognise that many of the aims attached to work-experience schemes can also be achieved through other forms of experiential learning about work. In seeking to clarify the concept of work experience, it is helpful to relate it to some of these other forms. We earlier defined work experience as describing schemes in which students experience work tasks in work environments, but without taking on the full identity of a worker. This can be contrasted with work observation, in which students experience work environments but not work tasks; and with work simulation, in which students usually experience work tasks but not work environments (figure 5).

Figure 5: Work experience and some related concepts

	Work tasks	Work environments
Work experience	✓	✓
Work observation		✓
Work simulation	✓	

Work observation takes two main different forms. The first is work visits, in which 'individuals or (often) groups of students are guided around workplaces to watch a range of employee activities and work processes. Such visits have been an accepted educational method for longer than work experience, though lack of adequate structure and planning has sometimes meant that they have fallen into disrepute (Bennett, 1983).

The second form of work observation is work shadowing in which an individual student follows a particular worker for a period of time (usually between two days and a week), observing the various tasks in which he or she engages, and doing so within the context of his or her total role (Watts, 1986a). This may involve the student carrying out some tasks for the 'work-guide' (i.e. the person being shadowed), but this is only a subordinate means to the observational end: to understanding what it is like to be in the shoes of the work-guide. In work experience, the reverse is the case: there may be an element of shadowing – particularly in training the student to carry out the tasks which he or she has been allocated – but this is merely a subordinate means to the task-performance end (ibid).

Thus not only are work observation and work shadowing different in their nature from work experience, but they also focus on different aspects of the work-place. Whereas work experience focuses primarily on work tasks, work visits focus primarily on work processes, and work shadowing on worker roles (figure 6). These foci are not of course mutually exclusive: a student on work experience may well also learn about work processes and worker roles. But because the primary focus is different, the nature of the learning yield is likely to vary in character.

Figure 6: Primary foci of different forms of work-based learning

	Work tasks	Work processes	Worker roles	Worker environments
Work experience	✓✓	✓	✓	✓
Work visits	✓	✓✓	✓	✓
Work shadowing	✓	✓	✓✓	✓
✓✓ – primary focus; ✓ – additional focus.				
Source: Watts (1986).				

Work simulations consist of operating representations of work tasks outside real work situations (Jamieson, Miller and Watts, 1988). They can take many different forms, including 'design and make' simulations, production simulations, mini-enterprises, work practice units, business games, and school work tasks. In many cases they may take place within schools, though various devices can be used – including the use of 'adults other than teachers' – to add an element of verisimilitude and to enable students to test the simulation against the reality it is purporting to represent. One of the distinctive virtues of work simulation as a form of work-related learning is that it is easier to organise and control for learning purposes: this makes it easier to secure effective integration into the curriculum (ibid).

All these different approaches have their own strengths and weaknesses. There has been a tendency to regard work observation and work simulation as flawed forms of work experience. We refute this view. Certainly the direct experience offered by work experience is qualitatively different from the constructed experience offered by work visits, the vicarious experience offered by work shadowing, and the simulated experience offered by work simulations. On the other hand, work observation and work shadowing have three distinct advantages over work experience.

The first is that they provide access to work situations and to occupations which do not lend themselves to work experience. Limitations are imposed on work experience by various considerations, notably that of skill requirement: only the simplest operations which can be learned quickly can be undertaken during a short period of work experience, and such experience tends therefore to be confined to unskilled or routine activities (Watts, 1983c). Work observation and work simulation are not subject to such restrictions. It is possible, for example, to observe or simulate highly skilled occupations like those of a doctor or senior manager, for which work experience is inconceivable.

The second is that work observation and work simulation tend to be more economical in terms of time. This may not always be the case: some mini-enterprises and work practice units, for example, may be very demanding in time terms. But it is often possible to mount effective simulations or visits or shadowing schemes within the space of a day or two. This makes them less vulnerable to the most common objection levelled at work-experience schemes: the amount of time they consume and the opportunity costs this involves in terms of classroom learning.

The third advantage is that work observation and work simulation can be used with a much wider age-range. Work experience is limited by the Education (Work Experience) Act 1973 to students in or beyond the final twelve months of compulsory schooling – i.e. from the age of 15. Work observation and work simulation, on the other hand, have been used extensively in the lower years of secondary schools and indeed in primary schools (see Jamieson, Miller and Watts, 1988; Smith, 1988; Watts, 1986a).

It is worth noting, however, that the aims of these different techniques are very similar to those we outlined earlier in this chapter for work experience. There are a few exceptions. The placing and custodial aims apply to work simulations marginally if at all. In addition, the primary foci of the different techniques may imply particular strengths in relation to particular aims: the focus of work shadowing on work roles, for example, may mean that it is particularly appropriate for the sampling aim, whereas the focus of work visits on work processes may make it particularly appropriate for the investigative aim. But these are only differences of degree, and are likely to be less influential than the particular characteristics of a particular scheme.

Forms of work experience

Our discussions so far have implied that work experience is a unitary concept. In practice, however, it can take a number of different forms. We suggest that at least five such forms can be distinguished (figure 7). We will look at each of these in turn.

Figure 7: Forms of work experience

1. Doing an actual job.

2. Providing an 'extra pair of hands'.

3. Helping someone in an actual job.

4. Rotating around different departments.

5. Carrying out specifically constructed tasks.

The first is doing an actual job. This involves being given tasks which are integral to the operations of the work organisation, and which another employee would normally have to carry out if the student were not there. As Hodge (1987) points out, this allows the students to feel a sense of responsibility for the work undertaken, and to develop an impression of being part of the organisation. Since, however, there is little time for training, the tasks tend – as we have seen – to be low-level and to involve little real responsibility: they typically include such activities as filing, checking, simple assembly work, and clerical routines.

The second is providing an 'extra pair of hands'. This is particularly risky from the point of view of student learning and of student satisfaction, because it tends to mean being given tasks which no one else wants to do, and can also mean that there are times when the student is doing nothing. HMI (1983) cites a couple of examples:

> A girl placed in a local primary school expressed resentment at being 'given the dirty jobs'. She was clearing up paint work which pupils had been allowed to leave in a mess but with the promise, which in the event was not fulfilled, that when this was completed she could help a pupil with her painting. She had spent her previous visits cleaning out cupboards. (p. 15)

> A boy from a remedial class was attending for 2 or sometimes 3 days a week a garage mainly concerned with haulage .... He was given no more than unskilled, routine tasks, such as sweeping the floor and operating the push-button steam cleaners, and was occasionally allowed to travel on a lorry. The proprietor was not prepared for him to take any part in work like dismantling or reassembling; in inclement weather he might spend the day sitting by the fire. (p. 17)

Such 'dogsbody' work seems, however, to be mentioned only by a small percentage of students (Sims, 1987, p. 102). More positively, this kind of approach can involve being given a series of well-designed tasks which are drawn from existing jobs but do not currently form a particular job: the current trend towards flexible job structures based on multi-skilling makes this easier to mount, and indeed pushes it closer towards our first form, doing an actual job – with its attendant advantages.

The third is helping someone in an actual job. This incorporates an element of work shadowing, and indeed may sometimes become work shadowing:

> One interviewee was based with an optician for two weeks. His employer introduced him to a wide range of activities opticians are involved in, including clinic and hospital work, methods of lens grinding and contact lens manufacture, and both prophylactic and curative therapeutics. However, the student spent his entire time watching, since there wasn't anything he could actually do. (Fuller, 1987, p. 89)

In other cases, however, the student may genuinely act as a kind of assistant, fully occupied in a series of work tasks. This has the merit of being likely to ensure a high level of supervision.

The fourth is rotating around different departments. Fuller (1987), for example, cites a case of a local authority environmental health department where students spent each half-day with a specific supervisor on a specific task (p. 109). Fuller regards this with approval. Hodge (1987), however, points out that:

> Pupils often enjoy the stimulation and variety of this sort of approach, but during a two-week Work Experience placement, the time available is arguably too short for any lasting impression to be gained and it can be confusing for the pupil. It can also give a false impression about the amount of variety available in a worker's life, since the pupil is unable to discover for himself that work can be both routine and boring at times. (p. 10)

Such an approach incorporates elements of a work visit, and indeed this produces the countervailing advantage cited by Hodge:

> The use of this approach by firms can also provide the analytical pupil with a useful overview of the structure and organisation of the company, leading to a fuller understanding of the concepts involved. (p. 10)

The fifth is carrying out specifically constructed tasks. In this case tasks are thought up which, while of possible use to the work organisation, are extraneous to its normal operations. Such 'work-based projects' were a familiar feature of the Youth Training Scheme (MSC, 1985). When developed for use in school-based work-experience schemes they may in some cases be designed by the employer; in other cases they may be designed jointly by the employer and the school, and may also involve some negotiation with the students themselves. Thus, for example an A-level course in Business Studies included a work-experience research project which was designed by the Business Studies tutor and an employer's representative and was designed to contribute to the company: the written report was presented to the GCE board, but in addition the student had to present a ten/fifteen-minute talk to people at the firm as well as to the tutor (Fuller, 1987). In another example, Ursuline High School in Wimbledon set up a 'Task week' which involved year-l0 students working in groups of four to six on specific tasks designed to be of value to an employer. They were given the format of the task by the employer, but were allowed to plan and organise the week. Examples of the tasks that emerged are shown in Box 2.8. In a sense, such practices are at the boundary of the concept of 'work experience'. The extent to which this term can properly be applied to them is related to the extent to which the student feels accountable to the employer. If such accountability is weak, then the student is in reality carrying out a school project which happens to be linked to a work-place; if it is strong, then the student can genuinely feel that he or she is carrying out a project for an employer, as a form of work experience. In such terms, its merit is that it leaves considerable scope for initiative and responsibility, and may provide opportunities for finding out a lot about the nature and structure of the work organisation; its disadvantage is that the students may be given too little guidance and support, and may be left largely to their own devices, which may tend to make them feel extraneous to the work of the organisation (Hodge, 1987).

Figure 8: Examples of tasks in the Ursuline High School 'Taskweek'

Task employer	Title of task	Activities
Electricity Council	The functions and workings of the Electricity Council's staff training college at Horsley Towers	To investigate the role of Horsley Towers in staff training and produce a video highlighting these activities.
SEGAS	Investigation of staff sports facilities.	Finding out: 1. what facilities are used and how often; 2. factors influencing their use; 3. whether job/status has any bearing on facilities used: 4. improvements/changes which could be made.
British Telecom	Safety campaign.	To look at existing health and safety material and identify areas where health and safety literature is needed. To design health and safety posters.
CAFOD (Catholic Association for Overseas Development)	Investigation into homelessness and child labour.	To interview young people on their views about the reasons why their peers feel the need to leave home. To investigate the extent of child labour in England.

Source: Barry (1985-86)

These five forms of work experience are not necessarily mutually exclusive, and it is possible to combine elements of two or more of them. For example, some element of rotating around different departments might be used in the early stages of a placement, as part of the induction process, before settling down to doing an actual job or helping someone in an actual job. Nonetheless, it is useful to tease out the pros and cons of each form, and indeed such an analysis might be useful in negotiating what form or forms a placement should take. In addition to the points already noted, it is worth pointing out that the later forms in the list leave the student in a 'student' role, whereas the earlier ones move them closer to an 'employee' role involving accountability and responsibility to the employer (rather than the school) for work undertaken. Linked with this, the later forms involve the student in a kind of voyeurism in relation to the work-place, whereas the earlier ones prefer immersion.[20] Both are 'real' but in different ways: immersion feels 'real' in experiential terms, whereas the voyeurism of rotation and of constructed tasks may feel forced and artificial; on the other hand, the latter may provide an experience which is more 'real' in cognitive terms (understanding how the organisation as a whole is structured and operates).

Broadening the concept of 'work'

So far, we have been defining 'work' in conventional terms as referring to 'paid employment'. In recent years, however, some concern has been expressed about the need to broaden this definition. In part this has stemmed from high levels of youth unemployment, and the pressure this has posed to explore alternatives to paid employment (see Watts, 1983a; also, e.g. Smith and Storey, 1988). Stronach (1984) notes how high unemployment paradoxically led to the expansion of vocational preparation, and how 'the paradox was resolved by creating a comprehensive, if vague, definition of "work" as separate from employment and by positing the need for personal development' (p. 54). In part, too, the demand for a broader definition has been related to the linked but separable growth of interest in 'education for enterprise' (Gibb, 1987; Rees, 1988; Watts and Moran, 1984), and in encouraging students to consider the possibility of generating their own work through becoming self-employed or setting up a small business or cooperative.

The link between work experience and this wider concept of work has been established, for example, by HMI (1988):

> Preparation for working life presupposes that pupils will be encouraged to interpret the concept of work in relation to a series of definitions: these range from work seen as paid employment to work viewed as the tasks to which human creative energies can be focused. Work experience helps in this process. (p. 14)

---

[20] We are grateful to Ian Stronach for this observation.

The CPVE[21] 'notes of guidance', too, note that

> It is one of the main aims of CPVE to enable young people to familiarise themselves with a range of occupations including both those associated with paid employment and those associated with work at home or within the community from which no income is derived. (JBPVE, 1985, p. 180)

The CPVE notes go on, however, to view work experience as providing a 'substantial opportunity to concentrate upon work which is associated with employment, often in a particular and limited form' (ibid, p. 180). In what senses could the concept of 'work' in work experience per se be defined more widely?

One possibility is to extend the concept to cover voluntary work of various kinds: in other words, to break down the barrier between work experience and community service. At one school in an area of high unemployment, for example, the concept of work experience was increasingly being integrated with that of community service, with 'work' being defined not just as employment but more broadly as 'corporate activity towards some end' (Watts, 1983a, p. 45). Again, a project in Renfrew was designed 'to analyse work and other community placements and relate them to pupil needs': it found that 'although pupils recognised the differences between community placements and work placements, they approached them in a similar manner' (Clarke, 1985). In all such schemes, however, it is important that the differences between paid work and unpaid work are brought out very clearly, and placed in a political and economic framework which explores their implications for standards of living and for economic independence. There also may be difficulties about allocation of placements, particularly if only a single placement per student is possible: there is a danger that students allocated community rather than work placements may regard themselves as being labelled as unemployable.

A second possibility is to extend the concept of work experience to cover self-employment, and setting up small businesses and cooperatives. This could be done by looking for work-experience placements with sole traders, in cooperatives, etc. It could also be done by enlarging the definition of work experience to embrace mini-enterprises, in which typically a group of students sets up a company or cooperative, develops a product or service, and trades for a period, before winding up the business. We would regard this in strict terms as being a form of work simulation (see Jamieson, Miller and Watts, 1988, ch. 5). In some important senses, however, mini-enterprises are 'real': in particular, they involve real money. Carney and Turner (1987) have suggested a form of progression in which students move from (A) a traditional work-experience placement in a local company, through (B)

---

21 Editorial footnote: The Certificate of Pre-Vocational Education (CPVE) was a qualification developed under the Technical Vocational Education Initiative (TVEI); it ran from 1985 to the early 1990s.

forming work-experience project teams that undertake a task set by the teacher (in consultation with local employers) which enables them to examine various aspects of employment, to (C) designing an enterprise which provides goods and services to the community. This is shown diagrammatically in figure 9, which also shows what Carney and Turner term 'line X ... Y', which shows how young people who participate in this range of activities can become increasingly involved in the design and management of their learning through work experience.

Figure 9: A progression model for work experience

Source: Carney and Turner (1987).

Harnessing students' existing experience of work

In considering such wider concepts of work, it is important to recognise the experiences of work which students may already have had both inside and, more particularly, outside school. Dewey (1963) pointed out how 'the principle of continuity of experience means that every experience both takes up something from those which have gone before and modifies in some way the quality of those which come after' (p. 35). If part of the function of work experience is to develop students' concepts of work, it is important that it should not be seen in a vacuum.

There is for example a considerable research literature on the ways in which children's household work is related to the development of helping behaviour, the growth of independence, and induction into work. As Goodnow (1988) points out in a review of this literature, such work 'calls for effort, it is regarded by most other people as useful, and it usually involves relationships with other people, often in the form of proceeding toward their goals or requiring their cooperation in order to proceed towards one's own' (p. 7). Zelizer (1985) notes that two rationales or justifications tend to be put forward for children's household activities: parents' need for children's work; and the developmental value of tasks (their capacity to develop 'body, mind and character' [p. 98]). She also notes the evolution of a third rationale: an egalitarian ethos in which all family members share the chores. There is, however, clear evidence that the allocation of tasks to boys and to girls tends to reflect the domestic division of labour: girls tend to be more frequently involved in domestic chores than their male counterparts; and girls tend to be predominantly involved in tasks like washing and laundry work, cooking meals, cleaning about the house, looking after other children, and sewing or mending clothes, whereas boys tend to be involved in gardening, painting, fixing things and washing the car (see, e.g. Finn, 1984). Attitudes towards the gender segregation of work may be strongly formed by such practices.

Secondly, many children engage in various forms of voluntary work in the community. Courtenay (1988), for example, found that 15 per cent of young people in the Youth Cohort Study had done community work during the school day in years 10 and 11. Most such work falls into four main areas: environmental projects, and working with disabled people, elderly people, and young children (CSV, 1987). In addition to such school-based activities, other voluntary-work activities may be based around scouts and similar groups.

Thirdly, it is important to recognise that many students while still at school engage in paid employment in the form of part-time and holiday jobs. In the Youth Cohort Study, Courtenay (1988) found that 56 per cent had had a part-time job during years 10 and 11, as opposed to only 29 per cent who had had work experience organised by the school. Boys were slightly more likely than girls to have had a part-time job (58 per cent compared with 53 per cent). Finn (1984) points out that such work 'represents a learning experience which, whilst the particular kind of work might be rejected, makes for a continuity between pre- and post-school economic life, and ensures an early exposure to the rigours of the labour market' (p. 44). In particular, it differs from school-based work-experience schemes in the sense that the young people involved have a contractual relationship with an employer which is based on payment for services rendered: they receive a wage in return for sustaining certain levels of job performance and if they fall below these levels of performance they may be sacked. Traditionally, many of the jobs involved have been essentially juvenile rather than adult jobs (Roberts, 1967) – newspaper rounds being a classic example – and considerable concern has been expressed both about employers' exploitative practices (MacLennan, Fitz and Sullivan, 1985) and about the links between such part-time jobs and poor attendance, behaviour and academic performance at school (Davies, 1972).

More recently, however, Baxter (1988) and Roberts, Dench and Richardson (1987) have found that students with higher levels of academic attainment are now as or more likely to take spare-time employment. Roberts et al. suggest that this may be because less-able pupils are experiencing a squeeze on their part-time opportunities, whereas aspiring parents may be starting to encourage school-children to supplement their pocket-money with spare-time jobs, and employers – particularly in distribution and in hotels and catering – are looking increasingly to bright students to fill part-time and temporary vacancies. Roberts et al. argue that this may represent a move towards American attitudes and practices, in which part-time employment is regarded as enabling the students to stay-on rather than being an enemy of education. In support of such attitudes and practices, American research has indicated that, while very extensive work involvement amongst some groups is associated with an increase in their rate of dropping out, less extensive work involvement actually appears to lead to increased rates of high-school completion (D'Amico, 1984). There have also been suggestions from other American research that the opportunities provided by spare-time jobs for learning how to interact effectively with others may provide a partial antidote to adolescent egocentrism (Steinberg et al., 1981), though in terms of adolescent psycho-social and moral development there seem to be negative effects as well as positive ones – it can for example lead to the development of cynical attitudes towards work and the acceptance of unethical work practices (Steinberg et al., 1982).

A fourth form of experience of work which merits attention is helping in family businesses. This has traditionally been regarded with some suspicion by teachers and others. But Steinberg (1984) suggests that it may have some clear advantages over other forms of experience of work. In particular, adolescents may be more likely to feel that their labour is important, which may increase their sense of responsibility; parents, because they have a stake in keeping their children involved in the family enterprise, may expose them to more diverse tasks and more of the internal workings of the business than would other employers; and working for one's parents may transform the adolescents' family relationships in positive ways. These are all hypotheses which have not so far been tested by research.

Finally, a small number of students may engage in entrepreneurial activities on their own account. Some, for example, have been very successful in developing and selling software packages. Others have engaged in other entrepreneurial activities. The dilemmas this can impose were illustrated by a report published in the Mail on

Sunday (11 March 1984):

> A schoolboy who swopped log tables for log fires has been told to stop making money and get back to the classroom. Darren Murfet, 15, stopped going to school so he could concentrate on the £12,000-a-year business he had built up, recycling industrial waste wood for domestic use. He told teachers he couldn't return to the John O'Gaunt comprehensive in Hungerford, Berks, because he has orders piling up from his 350 customers. Last week his parents were fined £300 for failing to ensure that he attend school …. Darren, a remedial pupil who is legally entitled to leave school in May, said: 'I worked hard to get the business going. I don't want to end on the dole.' But his headmaster, Mr David Lee, said yesterday he deplored the example Darren had set other pupils.

Steinberg (1984) points out that in general, these various forms of adolescent work differ from adult work in one important respect. Drawing upon Mark Twain's definition 'that Work consists of whatever a body is obliged to do and that Play consists of whatever a body is not obliged to do', Steinberg points out that the distinction falls short in relation to discussions of work – and particularly of paid employment – during adolescence: 'Adolescent work is generally not obligatory, but voluntary. For the typical adolescent, it is school, not work, that "a body is obliged to do" ' (p. 3). It is worth noting that school-based work experience schemes are in an interesting position here: in a sense, it is only by being incorporated into the school that 'work' in its employment-related sense can be incorporated into the realm of obligation.

Steinberg makes a further point which is important in relation to our concerns in this chapter. He defines work as 'any activity in which a young person engages – paid or unpaid, obligatory or voluntary – that places the adolescent, subjectively and objectively, in the role of "worker", adding to or replacing the other primary roles of adolescence, that is, the roles of "family member" and "student"'. But he then goes on to suggest that 'work' is likely to have its most positive developmental impact on the adolescent when the work role itself is merged with another primary adolescent role (that is, with the role of student or family member). Here he draws on Bronfenbrenner's (1979) suggestion regarding the developmental value of connections between the different settings in which children spend time. It is on these grounds that Steinberg explains the hypothesised virtues of children helping in family businesses. More significantly in relation to our main interests in this book, it is also on these grounds that he explains the American evidence that the experiential programmes which show the most consistent impact on students' psycho-social development were those which were more 'school-like' and less 'work-like': 'career intern' programmes in which participants were classed more as students than as workers in their placements, and community-service programmes in which students were learning about community problems. What seemed to make the difference was the level of integration into the curriculum.

These are important findings, which support the case for structured work-experience programmes in the curriculum. Nonetheless, there would seem to be a strong case for such programmes to take account of students' existing experiences of work. At present such experiences tend to remain totally separate from school-based work-experience schemes. Sometimes they penetrate such schemes, in unhelpful ways:

> Many youngsters contented themselves with extending into school time work in which they had been participating at weekends or in school holidays, and some cases were encountered of pupils 'working' in their own family concerns. Much of the value of work experience is lost if it does not extend the perspectives of pupils. (HMI, 1983, p.13)

If, however, such programmes are to extend the students' perspectives, they need to enable students to draw upon and explore the prior experiences upon which these perspectives are based (Varlaam, 1983).

Mapping widening concepts of work

If students' experiences of work are to be drawn upon in this way, it may be helpful to conceptualise the main different forms of work within the formal and informal economies, and then to identify the forms of work experience which seem related to each of these categories. A model for doing this is outlined in figure 10.

For the majority of adults, paid employment provides the main source of their income as well as a prime determinant of their social status and identity. School-based work-experience schemes provide opportunities for exploring paid employment, as do part-time and holiday jobs.

In recent years, however, there has been increasing interest in self-employment, in which people work not for others but for themselves. Such people fall into three main groups: first, those who are self-employed and working on their own; second, those who set up businesses employing other people; and third, those who set up workers' cooperatives which are owned by the workers themselves (Watts, 1983a). Opportunities for exploring such forms of work are provided formally by mini-enterprises and by work experience with sole traders, cooperatives, etc.; more informally, they can be provided by helping in family businesses and by students' own entrepreneurial activities.

Figure 10: A conceptual map of work and related forms of work experience

Form of work	Related forms of work experience	
	Structured by school	Not structured by school
Formal economy		
Paid employment	School-based work experience	Part-time/holiday jobs
Self-employment	Mini-enterprises Work experience with sole traders, co-operatives, etc.	Helping in family businesses Entrepreneurial activities
Informal economies		
Hidden economy	—	Entrepreneurial activities Part-time/holiday jobs
Communal economy	Community-service programmes	Voluntary work
Household economy	—	Household work

In addition to these different forms of work within the formal economy, a considerable amount of work is undertaken within three informal economies (Gershuny and Pahl, 1979/80; 1980; see also Watts, 1983a, ch. 9). The first is the hidden economy, sometimes called the 'black' economy (we prefer to avoid this term, because of its racist overtones). This covers work conducted wholly or partly for money which is concealed from taxation and regulatory authorities: it ranges from undeclared criminal and immoral earnings (e.g. prostitution, drug-trafficking), through office pilfering, to undeclared in-come earned in particular by the self-employed, by moonlighters and by the unemployed. Schools are likely to disapprove of such activities, but it is important that they should acknowledge the existence of the hidden economy, and it may be fruitful to explore some of the ethical and socio-political issues it poses. Since students' entrepreneurial activities and part-time/holiday jobs are often themselves hidden-economy activities, they can provide a base-point for such discussions.

Figure 11: Narrow and broad definitions of 'work' and of 'experience'

	Narrow definition	Broad definition
Work	Only paid employment	Also • self-employment • hidden economy • communal economy • household economy
Experience	Only direct experience	Also • vicarious experience • constructed experience • simulated experience

The second informal economy is the communal economy, which involves the production of goods or services which are consumed by people other than the producers, but are not sold on a monetary basis. This ranges from baby-sitting circles or car-pools which operate on the basis of a formal exchange of tokens or credits, through exchanges of skills or of equipment which are part of a relationship of generalised reciprocity between friends, neighbours, etc., to pure gift activities – including voluntary work, and some acts of friendliness or neighbourliness – for which no reciprocity is expected. School-based community-service programmes and students' own voluntary activities are examples of such communal-economy work.

Finally, there is the household economy, which covers work within the home that involves the production for internal consumption of goods or services for which approximate substitutes might otherwise be sought elsewhere. Examples include cooking, decorating, child care, home repairs, and garden produce. Again, students' own household work provides instances of such activities.

Conclusion

In this chapter we have explored narrow and broad definitions both of 'work' and of 'work experience'. A narrow view of 'work' defines it as 'paid employment'; a broad definition also includes self-employment and the three informal economies. Similarly, a narrow view of 'experience' limits it to direct experience; whereas a broad definition also includes vicarious experience (work shadowing), constructed experience (work visits) and simulated experience (work simulations). These varying definitions are summarised in figure 11. In the remainder of this book[22], we will

---

22 Editorial footnote: Referring to Miller, Watts & Jamieson (1991).

concentrate in the main on the narrow definitions. This is partly to confine our area of study to manageable proportions, and partly because these are the definitions conventionally adopted by schools. We consider it important, however, that 'work experience' defined in this narrow sense be viewed in the broader context of the other areas we have discussed.

8. A Conceptual Framework for Work Simulation[23]

Definitions

Simulations have been defined in different ways by different writers. Schulz and Sullivan (1972, p. 5), for example, define a simulation as 'an operating model of a real system or process'. Tansey and Unwin (1968) define it in greater detail as 'the representation of a situation or environment by some analogue, usually of less complexity and greater convenience, and often with a compressed time scale'. From these and other definitions, two key features of a simulation can be identified (Percival and Ellington, 1980):

- It must represent a real situation of some sort.

- It must be operational, i.e., constituting a working model rather than a static analogue (like a photograph or map).

A simulation is also normally (though not invariably) characterised by two additional features:

- It simplifies reality, concentrating on the essentials of a situation or environment.

- It accelerates reality, unfolding time at a faster rate than in real life.

It is important to distinguish simulations from three related but more limited concepts. The first is case-studies, which comprise descriptions of a situation presented in order to illustrate particular issues or problems. The situations may be fictitious or actual; the presentation may be written or oral. In addition, case-studies may be 'closed', in which case they are 'case-histories'; or they may be more open, encouraging problem-solving. But in all these cases, the students remain 'outside' the material, so that the material is not open to subjective manipulation.

The second related concept is role-plays, which involve inviting individuals to imagine that they are in a particular situation. This may involve being oneself in that situation, or taking on the role of another person, who in turn may be either real or imagined. Usually the role-player plays opposite one or more other people taking various other parts. The aim, however, is not to entertain an audience – as in

---

23 Editorial footnote: Reprinted, by permission of the publisher, from Jamieson, I., Miller, A. & Watts, A.G.: *Mirrors of Work: Work Simulations in Schools.* Lewes, Sussex: Falmer, 1988.

acting – but to express one's own ideas and enhance one's own understanding (van Ments, 1983). An extension of role-playing is sociodrama, where the focus is less on the individual role than on the social grouping which it represents and the social problems it explores. In both cases, the situation is usually outlined in only very general terms – 'from there, the action is free-wheeling' (Greenblat, 1981, p. 114). Such role-play and sociodrama in free-form situations have become common in drama and English classes in schools (see, for example, Rennie et al., 1974).

The third and final related concept is games, which are defined by Abt (1968, p. 67) as 'any contest (play) among adversaries (players) operating under constraints (rules) for an objective (winning victory or playoff)'. This definition needs to be extended to cover one-player games in which the player plays against the game 'system' (as in many computer games, for example). In all these games, chance may or may not play a part, but there will usually be 'right' and 'wrong' answers.

Simulations are, in a sense, a combination of at least the first two of these three related concepts. They involve a case-study element, which provides the 'scenario' for the action (Percival and Ellington, 1980). They also involve a role-play element, which provides the element of active participation. Simulations thus provide more active involvement than do case-studies proper, and more structuring of procedures and relationships than do role-plays proper. In addition, they may or may not involve a game element: when a game is based on a model of a real situation, or when a simulation incorporates an element of competition between the participants, it can be regarded as what Bloomer (1973) terms a 'simulation/game'. Business games, for example, fall into this category. For the purposes of this book, we will extend the term 'simulation' to cover such forms.

Building on these definitions, we define work simulations as operating representations of work tasks outside real work situations. This calls into question, however, our definition of work. Watts (1983a) has distinguished six possible definitions, which gradually enlarge in scope: in other words, each of the later definitions subsumes the ones that precede it. The definitions are:

a) Formal paid employment within that sector of the economy which is directly concerned with wealth-generation – referred to by some as 'real work', and usually identified (not entirely accurately) with private industry and commerce.

b) Formal paid employment within any kind of organisation.

c) Economic activity within the formal economy – including self-employment.

d) Economic activity rewarded by cash, whether within the formal economy or within the so-called 'black' economy.

e) Any application of productive effort on behalf of others – this covers not only economic activity rewarded by cash, but also the production of goods or services that are consumed by people other than the producers but are not sold on a monetary basis (for example, voluntary work).

f) Any application of productive effort – this also covers the production for internal consumption of goods or services for which approximate substitutes might otherwise be purchased for money (for example, household work).

There are however problems with trying to separate society into wealth-creating and wealth-consuming segments (Jamieson, 1986). Moreover, it seems clear that in future fewer people are likely to be employed in manufacturing industry, and it is arguable that fewer people will be in traditional employment at all. This suggests that a strong case could be made for adopting a much wider definition (see Watts, 1983a; 1983c). If it were too wide, though, it would be difficult to manage in practical terms; moreover, there seem as yet to be no simulations which explicitly explore the links between definitions (d)-(f) and the debate about the future of work. For present purposes, therefore, we will pragmatically adopt definition (c).

The six types

Work simulations as used in schools can take many different forms. For our purposes, we have grouped them into six broad categories: 'design and make' simulations, production simulations, mini-enterprises, work practice units, business games, and school work tasks. In the remainder of this chapter, we will introduce each of these briefly in turn, and will then examine some of the similarities and differences between them, before looking at some of the other forms of work simulation which do not fit readily into these categories.

'Design and make' simulations are basically concerned with design and prototype construction. They range from simple problem-solving exercises, such as designing packaging for a product, to more complex simulations involving designing and constructing prototypes of, say, rough-terrain vehicles or fashion jewellery. They are particularly common in CDT[24] teaching, but are found in other areas of the curriculum too. In some cases the emphasis is mainly on the 'design' element; in some cases it is stronger on the 'make' element.

Production simulations are concerned with mass production, and typically attempt to mirror assembly lines in manufacturing industry. Sometimes they use material like Lego bricks to make products which can be dismantled at the end of the exercise; sometimes they produce goods which can be reused. Little attention tends to be given to marketing and sales, and even where it is, any usable products are

24 Editorial footnote: Craft, Design and Technology (CDT) was a school subject until the introduction of the National Curriculum in the late 1980s.

only hypothetically 'sold' before being given to students or made use of in other ways. Such simulations usually provide opportunities for students to take on the roles of managers and workers, and are often developed to cover a wide range of roles. They thus explore issues related to the division of labour, and are frequently also designed to explore industrial relations issues including pay differentials, conditions of work, and the like. Sometimes they are developed into 'factory simulations', where attention is paid to using industrial clothing and reproducing other features of the factory environment.

Mini-enterprises take the process of design and production a stage further by placing them within the context of a total process, in which students set up and run their own business. Typically, a group of students establishes a company or co-operative, develops a product or service, and trades for a period, before winding the business up. Sometimes this process is attenuated somewhat by concentrating on the distribution and marketing of an existing product – establishing a tuck-shop or stationery shop, for example. A still more attenuated version is 'enterprise simulations', where the focus is on the planning of the business rather than its operation. In contrast, mini-enterprises proper are, in important senses, 'real' businesses; in particular, they involve real money. In the end, though, 'earning' is subordinated to 'learning'.

Work practice units are in physical terms the most elaborate forms of work simulation used by schools. Their distinctive feature is that they are designed to resemble industrial premises as closely as possible. Often, indeed, they are based not within schools but in old industrial premises which have been taken over and adapted for educational purposes. Students usually attend on a block-release basis.

Originally the main concern of such units was to give students experience of the disciplines of repetitive work in work environments; in some cases, however, they are now used in more flexible ways, allowing increased student responsibility and autonomy.

Business games are mainly focused on decision-making in the running of business enterprises. In the typical business game, students take the roles of competing teams of managers who have to take various decisions about rival products or services operating within the same market. The emphasis may be mainly on co-operation within the teams between students representing different functions – marketing, personnel, production, finance, etc. – or more on competition between the teams as their decisions interact with one another. In the case of 'company simulations', the focus is totally on the former. There are other distinctions too: 'total enterprise' business games cover most or all of the functional areas of business; 'functional' business games concentrate on decisions in one area only, usually production or marketing. An increasing number of business games are now computer-assisted.

Finally, school work tasks are rather different from the other simulations covered here in the sense that they are not 'constructed' simulations. Instead they are 'real' within the context of the school, in the sense that they produce goods or services which assist or enhance the work of the school. This may include 'teacher' tasks like acting as 'peer tutors'; 'ancillary' tasks like acting as school receptionists; or 'extraneous' tasks like work in school banks. Such tasks can be regarded as work simulations where they are viewed as simulating parallel tasks in the outside world, and where the learning potential which ensues from such parallels is harnessed.

It should be noted that these six types are not in practice wholly discrete categories. Thus the more attention production simulations pay to marketing and sales, the closer they move to mini-enterprises. Again, the growth of elements of student autonomy in some work practice units has allowed strong characteristics of mini-enterprises to be incorporated into them. Other overlaps could be cited. Nonetheless, our contention is that the six types are sufficiently distinguishable from one another, and cover a sufficiently broad range of current practice in the use of work simulations in schools, to provide an adequate framework.

Figure 12: Time demands

	'Design and make' simulations	Production simulations	Mini-enterprises	Work practice units	Business games	School work tasks
Demanding in time			●	●		
More flexible	●	●			●	●
Block basis	●	●	●	●	●	●
Intermittent basis	●		●		●	●

Some similarities and differences

In reviewing these six forms of work simulations, it is clear that they can be distinguished in a number of ways. One is their time demands (figure 12). Work practice units and mini-enterprises tend to be particularly demanding in terms of time; the others are more flexible, covering a range of activities from those which consume a lot of time to those which can be organised within a single class period or two. Work practice units and production simulations tend to be organised on a block basis; the others can be organised on a block basis too, but also more readily lend themselves to being phased at intervals over a longer period. A second distinction is the extent of pre-packaging. Many work simulations are developed by the teachers who use them, often in collaboration with people from industry and business. Production simulations and business games, however, are also published in kit form, sometimes including detailed instructions and materials. 'Design and make' simulations and mini-enterprises are also available in this form. Linked to this, but distinct from it, is the extent to which the key parameters of the simulation – in terms of its rules, roles, interactions, goals, and criteria of success – are 'externally' fixed by the designer, or are left to be determined 'internally' by the participants (Ruben, 1973). Mini-enterprises tend to be internally parametered, and so to a lesser extent do 'design and make' simulations. The other types may allow room for internal parametering, but tend to be more externally parametered.

Figure 13: Extent of pre-packaging

	'Design and make' simulations	Production simulations	Mini-enterprises	Work practice units	Business games	School work tasks
Published packages available	●	●	●		●	
Internally parametered	○	○	●	○		○
Externally parametered	○	●	○	●	●	●

A third distinction is whether the main focus of the simulation is on work roles, on work tasks, on work processes, and/or on work environments (figure 14). Work practice units cover all four, and are particularly concerned with simulating work environments. The others usually focus mainly on work roles, tasks and processes, with 'design and make' simulations and school work tasks tending to have a particular focus on tasks.

Chapter 8 A Conceptual Framework for Work Simulation

Figure 14: Main focus

	'Design and make' simulations	Production simulations	Mini-enterprises	Work practice units	Business games	School work tasks
Work roles	○	●	●	○	●	○
Work tasks	●	●	●	●	●	●
Work processes	○	●	●	●	●	○
Work environments		○		●		

Distinctions can also be drawn within each of these foci. In terms of work roles, for example, the range of roles offered to students varies considerably (figure 15).

Figure 15: Work roles

	'Design and make' simulations	Production simulations	Mini-enterprises	Work practice units	Business games	School work tasks
Manager		○	●		●	
Technical	●	○	●	○		
Operator		●	●	●		●
Trade-union		○	○		○	
External		○	○		○	

Business games tend to concentrate on managerial roles; by contrast, production simulations, work practice units and school work tasks tend to be mainly concerned with operator-level worker roles, though they may offer managerial roles as well. 'Design and make' simulations are more concerned with technical roles related to the design process, and some of the other simulations may offer a wider range of technical roles: some production simulations, for example, may offer roles as quality controller, as store/stock controller, as secretary/typist, as accountant, and so on; similarly, business games may offer such roles as marketing/sales manager, personnel manager, production manager, and financial manager/ accountant. Mini-enterprises can offer a particularly wide range of roles, since they have to encompass all the functions of a business. Trade-union roles are most readily built into production simulations, though they can be introduced into some other types too. Some simulations may also include 'external' roles for students, like roles as journalists, canteen workers, and bank managers: this is particularly true of production simulations. All these roles may differ considerably from one another in the extent to which they are prescribed or include a discretionary element. In addition, simulations like mini-enterprises require roles to be internalised in a stronger and deeper way than is the case in, for example, a business game.

Work tasks vary a great deal too (figure 16). As was evident from our earlier descriptions, 'design and make' simulations concentrate mainly on design and prototype construction, while production simulations – and, to some extent, work practice units – tend to focus on (small-batch) production. Mini-enterprises can embrace both of these, and also tend to add strong attention to finance and to marketing and sales, as well as some attention to personnel matters. Business games may cover most of these functions, but at a decision-making rather than an operational level. School work tasks are limited by definition to tasks which form part of, or can readily be attached to, the normal operations of schools.

Figure 16: Work tasks

	'Design and make' simulations	Production simulations	Mini-enterprises	Work practice units	Business games	School work tasks
Design and prototype construction	●		●			
Production		●	●	●	○	○
Finance			●		○	○
Marketing and sales			●		○	○
Personnel		○	○		○	

So far as work processes are concerned (figure 17), business games tend to concentrate particularly on informal inter-personal processes, whereas the other forms of work simulation focus more on formal processes, including physical operations. Group processes within work teams are likely however to be important not only in business games but also in 'design and make' simulations, in production simulations, and in mini-enterprises. Inter-group processes are particularly prominent in business games and mini-enterprises, both at the level of relations between different functions within the same company and, especially with business games, at the level of relations between different companies competing in the same market. Production simulations often offer experience of inter-group processes in relation to conflicts between managers and shop-floor workers. All these processes are also significantly affected by the outcomes of the simulations. In the case of mini-enterprises and of school work tasks, the outcomes are concerned in a direct way with the delivery of goods or services to real consumers, and are thus exposed to the disciplines this imposes: with mini-enterprises in particular, they are also exposed to a range of financial issues concerned with the handling of cash and distribution of profits, and of legal issues concerned with product liability. The other forms of work simulation are usually not affected by such pressures and problems.

Figure 17: Work processes

	'Design and make' simulations	Production simulations	Mini-enterprises	Work practice units	Business games	School work tasks
Physical processes	●	●	●	●		●
Group processes	●	●	●	○	●	○
Inter-group processes		○	●		●	

In relation to work environments (figure 18) work practice units are distinctive because they are often based in disused industrial premises, with attempts being made to simulate real work contexts as closely as possible. Other forms of work simulation tend to be based in the school, though on occasion they may be located in real work-places or on a neutral site like a teachers' centre. In all these cases, efforts may or may not be made to make use of some of the trappings of work contexts like clocking in and wearing industrial clothing.

Figure 18: Work environments

	'Design and make' simulations	Production simulations	Mini-enterprises	Work practice units	Business games	School work tasks
School	●	●	●		●	○
Neutral		○	○	○	○	
Industrial		○	○	●	○	

All of these similarities and differences reflect similarities and differences in terms of learning objectives (figure 19). These can cover a wide range of motivational, social-educational, vocational and anticipatory objectives. Work practice units have traditionally been more concerned than the others with anticipatory objectives, preparing students for the strains and disciplines of the work-place. In other cases, the tendency is to concentrate on a mix of motivational, social-educational and vocational objectives, though the nature of these objectives, and the balance between them, can vary a great deal.

Figure 19: Learning objectives

	'Design and make' simulations	Production simulations	Mini-enterprises	Work practice units	Business games	School work tasks
Motivational	●	●	●	●	●	●
Social-Educational	●	●	●	●	●	●
Vocational	●	●	●	●	●	●
Anticipatory				●		

Finally, there are a number of other important differences which distinguish different examples of these various forms of work simulation, but which do not systematically distinguish the different types from one another. These issues include:

- What linkages are established between the simulation and the reality it purports to represent, including what use is made of 'adults other than teachers' for this purpose.

- The teaching skills and values which are applied.

- The extent and nature of the preparation, briefing and debriefing that are provided.

- Whether the simulation is part of the curriculum or is extra-curricular, and the extent and nature of the links that are established with other parts of the curriculum.

- Whether any attention is paid to assessment, and if so, how.

- Whether any attention is paid to evaluation, and if so, how.

Some other forms of work simulation

These six forms of work simulation, however, by no means exhaust the range of possibilities. In the first place, if we return to the distinction we drew earlier in this chapter between simulations on the one hand and case-studies, role-plays and games on the other, it is important to recognise that there are work-related forms of each of these latter three categories. While according to our definition they cannot be regarded as full simulations, they nonetheless merit being noted here.

Work-related case-studies comprise descriptions of situations presented in order to illustrate particular work-related issues or problems. They are used extensively in medical education and legal education. They have also been an important element of business and management studies since being introduced at Harvard in the early years of the present century. Their use in Britain was significantly boosted by the establishment in 1973 of the British Case Clearing House at Cranfield Institute of Technology. In recent years many case-studies have been adapted or developed for use in schools. They vary from one another in a number of ways:

- In some cases they are based on real cases; in other cases they are fictitious.
- They may be based on published materials; or they may be locally developed by teachers working with local industrialists.
- Sometimes they are present in written form; sometimes orally.
- They may be presented as closed case-studies, for analysis and discussion; or as open situations, for problem-solving.
- They may be for individual use, in which case they are generally used to illustrate the application of principles; or for group use, to encourage the sharing of ideas and perspectives.

Where presented in open form for group use, a typical recommended method (CRAC, 1986) is to present the case-study, to divide students into small groups of 5-8 to discuss it and provide solutions to the problems defined in it, and to ask the small groups to report back to the large group. Sometimes an element of role-play may be built in by inviting particular individuals or groups to take a particular standpoint within the discussions: at this point the case-study can come close to developing into a full simulation, though normally the role-play element is only developed to a limited degree.

Work-related role-plays involve inviting students to imagine they are in particular work-related situations. This can take a number of different organisational forms, as is illustrated in figure 20. Such role-plays are often used for rehearsal: for testing out some new situation that one has to face, for example, selection interviews, so as to increase one's ability to cope with the stress that may be involved. They are also used to develop sensitivity and awareness by enabling students actively to explore their stereotypes of particular roles, such as industrial managers and trade-union officials, and to deepen their understanding of the point-of-view and feelings of people who occupy these roles. Finally, they can be used to develop skills, including interpersonal skills and group-dynamic skills. Role-players may be invited to imagine themselves in a given situation, or to react as they believe another person, whether real or imagined, would in the situation. Again, the situation may be described in detail or left largely to the imagination of the role-players. The more elaborate the scenario, the nearer the role-play comes to being a simulation. Indeed, one could argue that in all work-related role-plays the scenario will need to be sketched in sufficiently to justify calling it a simulation (for a more detailed discussion of role-play, see Shaw et al., 1980; van Ments, 1983).

Work-related games cover games in which the content is related to work but the process is not. Some concepts and practices are very difficult to represent in simulated form: in such cases, teachers who want to use active forms of learning may find they are able to take advantage of these 'non-simulation games'. Work-related examples include board games, where the game element is designed simply to maintain motivation and interest rather than for simulation purposes.

These three categories, then, come close to work simulations in some respects but not in others. In addition, there are a number of other examples of practice which can be regarded as full work simulations, but which are not covered within the six forms outlined earlier in this chapter. Most can be viewed as work samples, in the sense that they provide opportunities for students to experience particular tasks drawn from the world of work. Many of the work simulations defined earlier also include work samples, but build them into more elaborate and more extensive structures.

Work samples can adopt a variety of different sampling procedures, and be designed for a variety of different purposes. Firstly, they can be designed to sample particular occupations, for purposes of career exploration. Following the pioneering work of Krumboltz and Sheppard (1969) in the USA, CRAC developed a number of Work Experience Projects designed to provide samples of work as transport clerk, receptionist, printer's reader, sales promoter, policeman/woman, and bank cashier. Similar kits have been produced by some professional bodies: the Chartered Insurance Institute, for instance.

Chapter 8 A Conceptual Framework for Work Simulation

Figure 20: Some ways of organising role-play

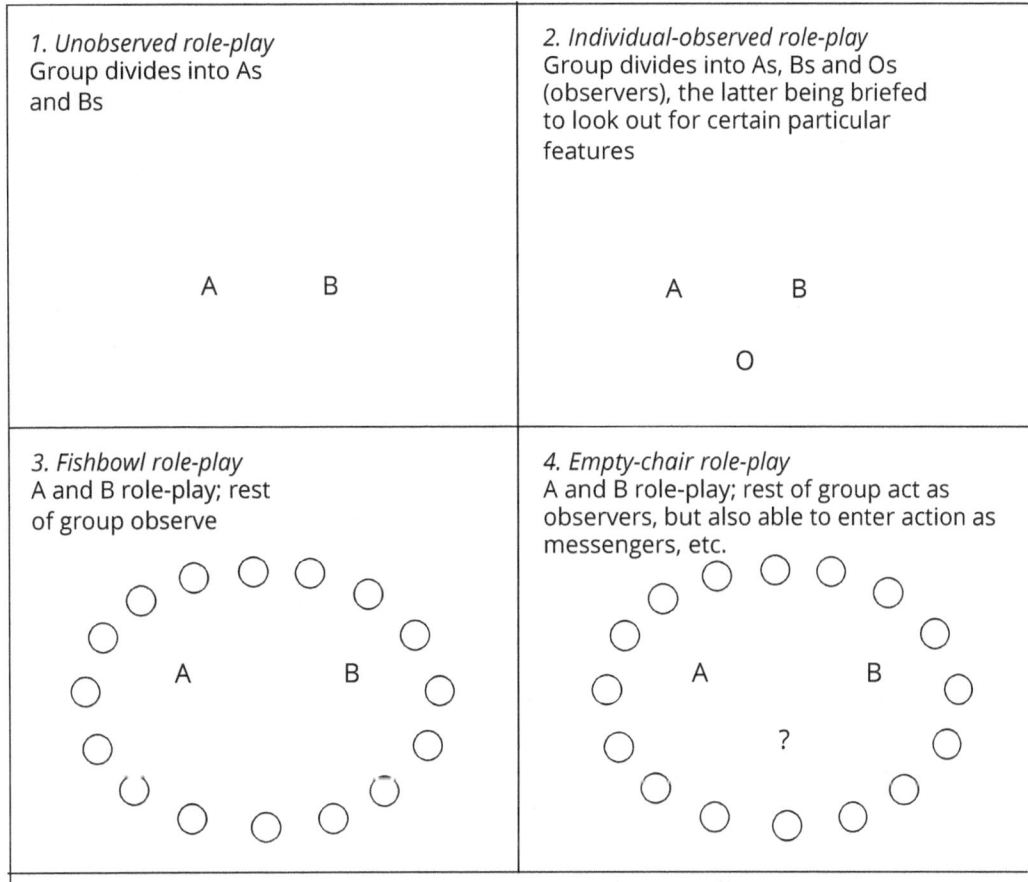

Note: These examples relate to two-player role-plays for illustrative purposes. They can readily be adapted to role-plays involving three or more players.

Secondly, samples can be designed to sample particular traits (finger dexterity, etc.) which cover a number of occupations, for the purposes of vocational self-assessment. A simple example is samples of keyboard skills as used in a number of TVEI[25] schemes. A more elaborate example is the 'skills samples' included in the Occupational Preparation Systems developed by Inter-Action. These comprise an audio-visual instruction tape with slides and a kit of equipment and material needed to complete a series of tasks, along with a framework for self-assessment and for trainer assessment against standardised criteria. They are designed mainly for use in the Youth Training Scheme, though some use has been made of them in schools.

Thirdly, samples can be designed to sample particular work settings, to broaden

25 Editorial footnote: The Technical and Vocational Education Initiative (TVEI) was a curriculum initiative for 14-18 year olds that ran from 1983 to 1997.

students' understanding of such settings and/or to develop skills associated with the settings. For instance, schools not infrequently design office simulations, to enable students to develop clerical and secretarial skills under work-like pressures. Again, some schools have played out court cases to give students an insight into legal procedures. A Hertfordshire school found that the local Magistrates Court would, with careful negotiation, allow students to simulate a court case in situ in the court; this was felt to have 'increased pupil interest and understanding beyond measure' (Clements, 1985).

Finally, samples can be designed to sample particular applications of skills or knowledge acquired within the curriculum. A wide variety of problem-solving tasks, craft tasks and so on, used in various parts of the curriculum, are drawn from work situations and can be regarded as forms of simulation so long as their relationship to their origins is drawn out.

These categories of work samples overlap with one another. Sometimes they are actual work samples, in the sense that they are taken from an actual job situation and involve the use of the actual materials and/or equipment, though in a simulated situation; sometimes they are simulated work samples, in the sense that they are constructed as close representations of reality.

The work samples can also vary from one another in terms of the level of interaction they involve. In this respect it may be worth mentioning two particularly common but contrasting forms of work samples. One is in-tray exercises, which are used a great deal in management training (including training of head teachers) as well as in secretarial training, and can be adapted for use in schools. The typical management-training example is for the student to receive an in-tray of various correspondence, memos and messages: he or she has to place these in order of priority and then to decide what action to take on each of them. Usually decisions have to be made within time limits, and the sense of pressure may be sustained by introducing additional information at intervals during the exercise. Such experiences are basically individual exercises, though they can be run with small groups of two or three; in addition, other group members can be used not only as observers but also as visitors, telephone callers, customers, etc., thus making the exercise into more of an 'oral in-tray'.

A second form is negotiation simulations, in which two or more parties seek to resolve a conflict of interest or to reach agreement on the terms and conditions of an exchange. A common example is collective bargaining between managers and trade-union representatives; a contrasting example is a trading simulation where a salesperson is trying to sell a product or service to customers, and to agree appropriate prices, discounts, delivery dates and so on. Such simulations can take a 'zero-sum' form, in which one party's gain represents another party's loss: this is particularly the case where there is only one bargaining variable, such as pay or price. Where however there is a range of factors which the parties can bargain over, there may be opportunities for compromise and co-operation which will enable both parties to make gains. The classic example of such a 'non-zero-sum' simulation is 'Prisoners Dilemma' (Rapaport and Channah, 1970) in which players who co-operate can avoid the serious consequences of failure.

Negotiation simulations can be set at a number of different levels: negotiations between individuals, between groups, between organisations, between nations. They can also be either formal or informal: formal bargaining occurs commonly in collective bargaining and in international trade negotiations; informal bargaining in negotiations between individuals and between departments within an organisation. In usage within schools, there is merit in structuring simulations of collective bargaining by, for example, keeping the groups apart so that each has to prepare a case and respond to each other's case in a systematic way. This makes the process easier to manage, and enables the spotlight to be focused on the micro-features of the bargaining process, instead of allowing the proceedings to be dominated by the most forceful students.

It will be evident from these examples that work simulations and related techniques can cover many different features of work organisations, ranging from individual work tasks to relations between organisations (and even between nations). These in turn reflect many different levels of behaviour. Some illustrations in ascending order are shown in figure 21.

Figure 21: Some features of work organisations covered by work simulations

Feature of the organisation	Level of behaviour	Form of work simulation (examples)
Individual work tasks	Individual	Work sample
Management priorities	Individual	In-tray exercise
Manager/worker relations	Inter-personal	Role-play
Work team	Group	'Design and make' simulation
Department	Inter-personal and group	Office simulation Functional business game Production simulation Work practice unit
Management/trade-union relations	Inter-group	Negotiation simulation
Interaction between departments	Inter-group	Company simulation
Whole organisation	Inter-group and organisational	Mini-enterprise
Interaction between organisations	Inter-organisational	Business game

Note: These examples are not designed to be rigid or exhaustive.

9. Career Development Learning and Employability[26]

Sustainable employability

Benefits of the focus on employability

The attention within higher education to enhancing students' employability potentially serves a number of important purposes.

First, it responds to students' motivations for entering higher education. A survey of school students found that the most important personal reasons cited for going to university were, alongside 'to study a subject that really suits me', three vocationally-oriented reasons ('to have a professional career', to improve my job prospects', 'to gain entrance to a well-paid career'): each of these four reasons was rated by around four-fifths as extremely or very important (Connor et al., 1999, p.12). Where student tuition fees are payable, such vocational motivations are likely to be strengthened.

Second, it responds to policy concerns, in two respects:

- An important part of the rationale for the large sums which the Government invests in higher education is the contribution which it makes to the development of the country's human capital (e.g. NCIHE, 1997; see Yorke, 2006, p.4). The more employable students are, the greater the economic yield is likely to be from this investment.

- Expanding higher education is also designed to serve social-equity goals by increasing access for disadvantaged groups. To achieve such goals, attention needs to be paid not only to ensuring the participation of these groups in higher education but also to enhancing their subsequent success in the labour market (Morey et al., 2003).

Third, far from undermining wider academic values, it can be interpreted as reinforcing such values, in three respects:

- By emphasising generic competences rather than direct subject relevance, it can help to resist creeping vocationalism in terms of course content, and

---

26 Editorial footnote: Reprinted by permission of the publisher, from *Career Development Learning and Employability* (Learning and Employability Series Two No 5). York: Higher Education Academy, 2006. For additional resources and discussion from the HEA on employability please see www.heacademy.ac.uk/workstreams-research/themes/employability.

to legitimise the continuing value of traditional academic disciplines. Over two-thirds of graduate vacancies in the UK are for graduates in any subject (Graduate Prospects, 2005/6); employers tend to be much more concerned with generic 'graduate attributes' than with subject knowledge (Harvey et al., 1997).

- Because the generic competences valued by employers are developed largely through active teaching and learning processes, a constructive alliance can be forged between the employability agenda and pedagogic reform (Pedagogy for Employability Group, 2006).

- Because these generic competences can also be developed through active extra-curricular activities, the employability agenda can reaffirm the value of the wider student experience, including participation in student-organised activities.

At the same time, it may require organisational change within higher education (Knight & Yorke, 2004). In particular, it may necessitate:

- Concern not just with good academic practices but with promoting the goals of employability through such practices.

- Making such goals transparent to teachers and students.

- Adding supplementary programmes where appropriate to ensure the achievement of these goals.

One of the key processes in achieving such change is auditing the curriculum to determine the extent to which the teaching and learning methods in use meet employability goals, and then reviewing how deficits can be addressed (Harvey, 2001; Knight & Yorke, 2004).

Competing definitions of employability

Definitions of employability can be broadly divided into three groups.

The first are those which focus on immediate employment. Graduate first-employment statistics have for some time been used as a performance indicator in higher education (HEFCE, 2001). It has, however, been widely recognised that they have been a crude measure, in three respects:

- They have been based on data collected six months after graduation. This takes inadequate account of the length of time which many graduates take to manage their transition into a graduate-level job, whether because they have deferred job applications until after their final examinations, or because they choose to travel for a while or to undertake further studies, or because they take short-term jobs to clear some of their student debts before seeking more permanent employment.

- They have taken no account of the level of the jobs entered, and whether these jobs have made significant use of graduate competences.

- Students' success in gaining employment is determined not only by the effects of their higher education but also by their own pre-existing attributes and by the state of the labour market and the ways in which it operates at local, national and international levels (Harvey, 2001).

Some modifications have recently been introduced in an attempt to address these limitations.

The second are definitions which focus on immediate employability. These avoid the limitations of the 'immediate employment' definition. They are commonly defined in terms of students' possession of the attributes to obtain a 'graduate job'. They tend to include a strong focus on students' 'work readiness': in other words, their ability to cope with the demands of the workplace without requiring additional training to do so. Their field of vision is accordingly somewhat restricted.

The third are definitions which focus on sustainable employability. These are concerned with the ability not only to secure a first job but also to remain employable throughout life. As Knight & Yorke (2004, p.46) put it, employability 'does not rest when the first graduate job is achieved' but needs 'to be constantly renewed to be sustainable'. Such definitions accordingly include not only the wider range of attributes required to be successful within jobs; they also include the attributes required to manage one's career development in ways that will sustain one's employability.

Early formulations of the second and third of these definitions focused strongly on skills, variously framed as 'personal transferable skills', 'key skills', 'core skills', 'generic skills' and 'employability skills'. This focus has more recently been widely criticised, chiefly on the grounds that 'skills' is too limited a concept to embrace what employability comprises (Bennett et al., 2000; Holmes, 2001; Knight & Yorke, 2003; 2004). An alternative formulation which has been more widely accepted has been the USEM model (Knight & Yorke, 2004), in which employability is viewed as being influenced by four broad and inter-related components:

- Understanding (viewed as being broader and deeper than 'knowledge').

- Skills (or, preferably, 'skilful practices', which includes the deployment of skills).

- Efficacy beliefs (including students' views of themselves and personal qualities).

- Metacognition (including students' self-awareness regarding, and capacity to reflect on, their learning).

Sustainability and career development

The attention to career development in definitions of sustainable employability has not always been strong:

- Knight & Yorke (2004, p.25) include 'skilful career planning and interview technique' in their list of 'seven meanings of employability', but the specification of interview technique tends to restrict the focus, as does the accompanying note which suggests that its concern is with 'knowing the rules of the job-seeking game'.

- The definition of employability offered by Yorke (2006, p.8) – which focuses on the 'skills, understandings and personal attributes that make graduates more likely to gain employment and be successful in their chosen occupations' – can be read as assuming that graduates will remain within a single occupation, and as not attending to the competences required to manage progression within and possibly across occupations.

Similarly, much of the now-extensive literature on employability in higher education pays little attention to the conceptual work on career development or to the work that has been done on career development learning.

On the other hand:

- The policy-oriented analysis by Hillage & Pollard (1998, pp.12, 17) suggests that one of the four main elements of employability is 'deployment' – the extent to which individuals 'are aware of what they have got and how they choose to use it' – and defines this to comprise career management skills, job search skills, and 'the extent to which they are adaptable to labour market developments and realistic about labour market opportunities'.

- The Universities UK report *Enhancing Employability, Recognising Diversity* (Harvey et al., 2002) states that employability development has three focuses: development of employability attributes; willingness to learn and reflect on learning; and development of self-promotional and career management skills.

- The code of practice issued by the Quality Assurance Agency for Higher Education (2001a) states that higher education institutions should prepare students not only 'for a successful transition to employment' but also 'for effective management of their career thereafter'.

Career development learning

Terminology

The terminology used to describe career development learning in higher education has fluctuated.

For some time, the term used was career(s) education. This term came into common usage in UK schools in the early 1970s (Schools Council, 1972), and began to be applied within higher education later in the same decade (Watts, 1977a). It has retained currency in schools but, partly perhaps for this reason, has lost some ground within higher education – though it is still widely used there (e.g. AGCAS, 2005; QAA, 2001a).

In the 1990s, the term career management skills began to be used fairly extensively within higher education. It was used, for example, to describe a government-funded development programme covering eight institutions (Hustler et al., 1998). The term 'career management' had previously been used in the 1980s to describe policies and practices used by large business organisations to develop the careers of middle and senior management (ibid., p.4); increasingly, however, it has been used to describe 'career self-management' (King, 2004).

The term career development learning is of more recent origin (Watts, 1999a; Patton & McMahon, 1999). The reason for its growing usage within higher education in the UK is linked to the growing reaction against the limitations of the language of 'skills' and of skill-based views of employability. In particular, it can encompass the notion of supplementing attention to career management skills with the use of career development theory as 'a knowledge-based, intellectually rigorous frame' (AGCAS, 2005, p.24) which can be used by students as a tool for self-understanding – 'as researchers of their own lives' (McCash, 2006).

Definitions

Career(s) education was defined by Watts (1977a), following Law & Watts (see chapter 5), as consisting of planned experiences designed to facilitate the development of:

- Self awareness – in terms of interests, abilities, values, etc.

- Opportunity awareness – knowing what work opportunities exist and what their requirements are.

- Decision learning – decision-making skills.

- Transition learning – including job-search and self-presentation skills.

This formulation – widely described as the DOTS model – was also adopted by Hillage & Pollard (1998). A broadly similar model was used in the cognitive processing theory of career development developed in the USA by Peterson et al. (1991), though with more attention to the 'processing' of career development. Law (1996), too, has adapted the model by adding a process dimension to indicate the stages through which learning in these respects can be developed.

AGCAS (2005) reframes the DOTS learning goals somewhat, itemises a series of learning outcomes for each of them (see figure 22), and states that any theoretical model for careers education provision should 'be congruent with, and encompass as a minimum all these four elements, if it is to enable students to implement fully informed and sound career plans' (p.5). McCash (2006), on the other hand, argues that the persistent and hegemonic status of the DOTS model has impeded the adoption of more innovative theories and more creative frameworks. He acknowledges that the model can be stretched to meet some of its limitations, but contends that it would be better to start again from first principles.

In some respects (e.g. the references to 'customer needs' rather than just 'employer needs', and to 'creating' as well as 'exploring' opportunities), the Hawkins & Winter list potentially incorporates options related to self-employment as well as employment. This focus could, however, be made more explicit and extended a great deal further (see Moreland, 2006). Programmes in education for entrepreneurship and enterprise are limited, and to be found in less than a third of higher education institutions (ibid, p.3); where they exist, they are often timetabled separately from career development learning. But the two areas are closely inter-related and can benefit from being combined (AGCAS, 2005, p.28).

Figure 22: Careers education learning outcomes (adapted from AGCAS, 2005)

Self awareness
- Identify knowledge, abilities and transferable skills developed by one's degree
- Identify personal skills and how these can be deployed
- Identify one's interests, values and personality in the context of vocational and life planning
- Identify strengths and weaknesses, and areas requiring further development
- Develop a self-reflective stance to academic work and other activities
- Synthesise one's key strengths, goals and motivations into a rounded personal profile

Opportunity awareness
- Demonstrate knowledge of general trends in graduate employment and opportunities for graduates in one's discipline
- Demonstrate understanding of the requirements of graduate recruiters
- Demonstrate research-based knowledge of typical degree-related career options and options in which one is interested

Decision making
- Identify the key elements of career decision-making, in the context of life planning
- Relate self-awareness to knowledge of different opportunities
- Evaluate how personal priorities may impact upon future career options
- Devise a short/medium-term career development action plan
- Identify tactics for addressing the role of chance in career development
- Review changing plans and ideas on an ongoing basis

Transition learning
- Demonstrate understanding of effective opportunity-search strategies
- Apply understanding of recruitment/selection methods to applications
- Demonstrate ability to use relevant vacancy information, including ways of accessing unadvertised vacancies
- Identify challenges and obstacles to success in obtaining suitable opportunities, and strategies for addressing them
- Demonstrate capacity to vary self-presentation to meet requirements of specific opportunities
- Demonstrate ability to present oneself effectively in selection interviews and other selection processes
- Identify challenges and obstacles to adapting successfully to new environments, and strategies for addressing them
- Demonstrate awareness of attitudes crucial to the achievement of one's goals

Note: In the AGCAS (2005) document, these learning outcomes are set at two levels – 'threshold' and 'exemplary' – to mark low and high points in career development.

Figure 23: Career self-management behaviours (King, 2004)

Positioning behaviours (making sure one has the contacts, skills and experience to achieve one's desired career outcomes)

- Strategic choice of mobility opportunity – initiation of job moves, or acceptance of proposed changes made by another party (e.g. one's employer)
- Strategic investment in human capital – investing in training or educational qualifications
- Active network development
- Job content innovation – development of substantive changes in methods or procedures used to perform job tasks and enlargement of one's effective task environment

Influence behaviours (actively attempting to influence the decisions of key gatekeepers to desired career outcomes)

- Self-promotion
- Ingratiation – making oneself more attractive to others
- Upward influence – increasing gatekeepers' understanding of one's desired outcomes and their sense of obligation to deliver them

Boundary management (balancing the demands of work and non-work domains)

- Boundary maintenance – concerned with the location of the boundary between work and non-work roles
- Role transition – navigating the transition between work and non-work roles.

Career self-management focuses less on learning outcomes than on the behaviours that people can use to eliminate or resolve the thwarting conditions they would otherwise experience in their careers. It has been defined by King (2004) as comprising three groups of behaviours: positioning behaviours; influence behaviours; and boundary management (figure 23). This formulation is focused mainly on adults in mid-career. Many of the behaviours identified by King are in effect merged with elements of the DOTS model in the list of career management skills developed earlier by Hawkins & Winter (1995), who also refer to them as self-reliance and effective learning skills (figure 24). While conceptually eclectic and less parsimoniously elegant than the DOTS and King models, this list has been influential in the development of career development learning programmes within higher education.

Figure 24: Career management/self-reliance/effective learning skills (Hawkins & Winter, 1995)

Self awareness
- Able clearly to identify skills, values, interests and other personal attributes
- Able to pinpoint core strengths and 'differentiating factors'
- Equipped with evidence of abilities (e.g. summary statement, record or 'portfolio')
- Actively willing to seek feedback from others, and able to give constructive feedback
- Able to identify areas for personal, academic and professional development

Self-promotion
- Able to define and promote own agenda
- Can identify 'customer needs' (academic/community/employer) and can promote own strengths in a convincing way, both written and orally, selling 'benefits' to the 'customer', not simply 'features'

Exploring and creating opportunities
- Able to identify, create, investigate and seize opportunities
- Has research skills to identify possible sources of information, help and support

Action planning
- Able to plan a course of action which addresses: 'Where am I now?' 'Where do I want to be?' 'How do I get there?'
- Able to implement an action plan by: organising time effectively; identifying steps needed to reach the goal; preparing contingency plans
- Able to monitor and evaluate progress against specific objectives

Networking
- Aware of the need to develop networks of contacts
- Able to define, develop and maintain a support network for advice and information
- Has good telephone skills

Matching and decision making
- Understands personal priorities and constraints (internal and external), including need for a sustainable balance of work and home life
- Able to match opportunities to core skills, knowledge, values, interests etc.
- Able to make an informed decision based on the available opportunities

Negotiation
- Able to negotiate the psychological contract from a position of powerlessness
- Able to reach 'win/win' agreements

> **Political awareness**
> - Understands the hidden tensions and power struggles within organisations
> - Aware of the location of power and influence within organisations
>
> **Coping with uncertainty**
> - Able to adapt goals in the light of changing circumstances
> - Able to take myriads of tiny risks
>
> **Development focus**
> - Committed to lifelong learning
> - Understands preferred method and style of learning
> - Reflects on learning from experiences, good and bad
> - Able to learn from the mistakes of others
>
> **Transfer skills**
> - Able to apply skills to new contexts

In some respects (e.g. the references to 'customer needs' rather than just 'employer needs', and to 'creating' as well as 'exploring' opportunities), the Hawkins & Winter list potentially incorporates options related to self-employment as well as employment. This focus could, however, be made more explicit and extended a great deal further (see Moreland, 2006). Programmes in education for entrepreneurship and enterprise are limited, and to be found in less than a third of higher education institutions (ibid, p.3); where they exist, they are often timetabled separately from career development learning. But the two areas are closely inter-related and can benefit from being combined (AGCAS, 2005, p.28).

Relevance to employability

According to Watts & Hawthorn (1992, p.15), personal transferable skills and career management skills have some degree of overlap but are essentially different in focus:

- The focus of career management skills is upon competence in making and implementing the decisions that determine one's career.

- The focus of personal transferable skills is on competence within the positions that one enters as a result of these decisions and transitions.

It has subsequently been suggested (Watts, 1997, p.43) that career management skills can be viewed in two ways:

- As a sub-set of employability skills.

- As a related set of meta-skills which enable individuals to develop and use the full range of their other skills.

The case for the latter view is strong. Meta-skills are linked to Butcher & Harvey's (1998, p.75) definition of meta-ability as 'an underlying, learned ability which plays an important role in allowing a wider range of ... knowledge and skills to be used effectively'. They are also linked to metacognition, which Yorke & Knight (2006, p.6) define as subsuming: elements of 'learning how to learn'; of reflection in, of and for practice; and of a capacity for self-regulation. Career development learning would seem to fit well into this definition, focusing as it does on self-management of progression in learning and work, based on reflection on past achievements and what can be learned from and built upon these achievements.

Career development learning is also relevant to what Bridges (1993, p.50) terms 'transferring skills': 'the meta-skills ... which enable one to select, adapt, adjust and apply one's other skills to different situations, across different social contexts and perhaps similarly across different cognitive domains'. Transfer of skills appears clearly to be enhanced by the use of varied learning contexts (see e.g. Wolf et al., 1990): this makes it possible to practise the skills in the different settings, or at least to see their relevance to those settings. This is part of the rationale for the inclusion of work experience within higher education. Beyond this, however, transfer would seem likely to be enhanced by interventions concerned with helping students to explore possible future career directions, particularly if attention is paid to the relevance of the skills to those directions. At the very least, work of this kind would seem likely to increase students' motivation for work on employability, by enabling them to see its relevance and the benefits it may offer them (Watts & Hawthorn, 1992, p.15).

Implementing career development learning within higher education

Delivery strategies

In broad terms, three delivery strategies for promoting career development learning can be distinguished (Hustler et al., 1998):

- Through specific modules.
- Through more general cross-curricular integration.
- Outside the curriculum.

There are three forms of modular approach:

- Generic, where the same module is designed to be available to students in any department or course.

- Customised, where a generic template is adapted to the needs of particular departments or courses.

- Bespoke, where modules are developed for specific purposes within particular departments or courses.

The generic strategy needs more limited development time and can be rooted directly in established notions of what career development learning comprises. The customised strategy tends to lead to more active involvement of academic staff; the bespoke strategy to more ownership by academic staff.

Modules on career development learning were well-established in the USA in the 1970s (Watts, 1977a), and have continued to develop there (Folsom & Reardon, 2003). They developed later in the UK, but were given a significant boost in the late 1980s and 1990s by the Enterprise in Higher Education programme (Ball & Butcher, 1994; Watts & Hawthorn, 1992) and by a subsequent government-funded programme which focused specifically on career management skills (Hustler et al., 1998).

In a survey by Pierce (2002), around a third of institutions reported that career management skills modules were available to students. In most cases, the take-up was tiny compared to the total student population. In one institution, however, 25% of students took advantage of such modules, and in another (the University of Reading) it was compulsory for all students.

Careers modules typically range from 5 credits (half-modules) to 20 credits, though some are larger (AGCAS, 2005). A number extend to 30 or even 60 credits, at which stage they effectively become a degree course pathway (McCash, 2006). They are often located in the second year of degree programmes, though the first and final years are also used (AGCAS, 2005). In some cases, the credits count towards the 360 credits that comprise a first degree and so are taken into account in the degree classification; in others, they are viewed as 'optional extras' which are credit-rated and academically assessed, appear on the student's degree transcript, but do not count towards the 360 credits and degree classification (some universities have developed separate 'awards' or 'skills certificates' for such extra provision).

In addition to or in place of such modules, career development elements can be integrated within programmes by linking them to existing course components, so that the career development learning is 'caught' rather than 'taught' (Hustler et al.,

1998, pp.19-22). This may be done:

- On an opportunistic basis.

- On a systematic basis: for example, as part of a 'module template' providing greater transparency for the skills (including career management skills) embedded within each module.

In these cases, the involvement of academic staff is likely to be even stronger. Finally, career development learning can be promoted through extra-curricular activities (ibid, pp.23-25). These include:

- ICT-based activities – e.g. computer-assisted career development learning programmes on CD-ROM, or the creation and enhancement of websites.

- Non-credit-bearing special events – e.g. careers fairs, one-off sessions on particular career management skills (e.g. self-presentation), or short residential courses.

Links to personal development planning

In a number of institutions, close links have been established between career development learning and the processes of personal development planning (PDP). The introduction of such processes is part of the implementation of the Dearing Report's recommendation that institutions, over the medium term, should develop a Progress File designed to assist students to identify their achievements and to provide information about these achievements to others (NCIHE, 1997). Two means were envisaged:

- A transcript recording achievement (to follow a common format).

- A PDP process through which students could 'monitor, build and reflect upon their personal development'.

All institutions were to have implemented the PDP aspect of the Progress File by 2005/06 (QAA, 2001b) (though in Scotland, the deadline was deferred). A review by Ward et al. (2005) suggested that progress had been made, but that implementation was still variable and uneven.

PDP processes are relevant to, and overlap with, career development learning in at least three major respects:

- They help students to translate learning experiences into the language of employability and to support reflection and the development of self-knowledge.

- The skills of reflection, recording and action planning enhanced by PDP processes lie at the heart of career management skills.

- They develop a bank of evidence that students can 'mine' in presenting themselves effectively to future employers.

Conversely, career development learning helps to ensure that PDP processes are not limited to learning and to the present, but have a future orientation that incorporates work and career too. It thus 'acts as a crucial nexus between the undergraduate "present" and the "future" of life after graduation' (AGCAS, 2005, p.26).

Teaching and learning methods

The teaching and learning methods used in career development learning need to meet at least two major requirements:

- They need to be personally engaging, and therefore based on active involvement of students and use of interactive teaching and learning methods.

- They need to make the world of work 'become "real"' (AGCAS, 2005, p.10), and therefore include active involvement of employers and, where possible, direct experiences of work.

Certainly there is room for traditional instructional methods for some elements of the programme, including teaching the academic elements of career development theory. But such methods are unlikely to be sufficient.

Personally engaging teaching and learning methods mentioned by AGCAS (2005) and by the Pedagogy for Employability Group (2006, p.13) include:

- Facilitative teaching styles that encourage and model an open and honest exploration of the career planning process.

- Using short 'buzz-group' discussions within lecture-group sessions.

- Self-audits (e.g. of personal and career management skills).

- Role-play (e.g. recruitment personnel, mock interviews).

- Peer review (e.g. of CVs or of assignments).

- Card-sort exercises (e.g. devising a sequence of decision-making activities).

- 'Snowballing' activities which begin with pair-based work, progressively combining to produce a larger-group response to the challenge set.

- Problem-based methods.

- Supplementing lectures with on-line peer discussion groups or tutor-managed discussion forums.

- Self-directed learning.

In addition, there is potential for active involvement of students in the design and delivery of programmes. This can include (Hustler et al., 1998, pp.31-34):

- Systematic consultation of students, through surveys or focus-group discussions, in designing programmes.

- Using immediate student feedback in reviewing programmes.

- Contacting former career management module students after graduation to provide longer-term feedback.

- Involving such graduates in the delivery of modules to current students.

Such forms of participation can mean that students feel they have 'more of a say' than in other areas of their higher education studies. This can result in an increased sense of ownership over their personal learning in the career development area.

Similarly, the need for realism in relation to the world of work provides a compelling rationale for the active involvement of employers in the design and delivery of programmes. This can include (ibid, pp.27-31):

- Involvement in planning and development – e.g. contributing to the definition of career management skills, to the production of course materials (including on-line materials), to staff-development programmes, and to course design.

- Making direct contributions to programme delivery – e.g. providing or making inputs to workshops, lectures and seminars, and acting as hosts for project work and placements.

Particularly strong areas for such involvement include activities related to recruitment and selection (e.g. interview simulations; application/CV analysis) and team-building and problem-solving tasks. The involvement of employers can add significantly to the relevance and realism of these activities, and their credibility to students. Employers' motivations for involvement include:

- Conveying a positive image of their company or organisation.
- Access to prospective applicants.
- Company policies encouraging community involvement.

There is however a tendency for employer contributions to come mainly from large rather than small or medium-sized organisations, and for such employers to be more prepared to involve themselves with vocationally-oriented courses and/or in higher-status institutions.

Opportunities for direct experiences of work can contribute strongly to career development learning. The Dearing Report recommended that all institutions should 'identify opportunities to increase the extent to which programmes help students to become familiar with work, and help them to reflect on such experience' (NCIHE, 1997, p.136). Three main categories of such work experience can be distinguished (Harvey et al., 1998; Little et al., 2002; Little & ESECT colleagues, 2005):

- Organised work experience as part of a programme of study. This may include long placements on sandwich courses, short placements on other courses, and clinical or practice programmes on some professional degrees. It ranges from doing an actual job, through shadowing a worker in a job, to carrying out a work-based learning project. Some may be paid; some may not. It may also include credit for year-long placements unconnected to a specific programme; for part-time, term-time or vacation work; or for voluntary (unpaid) work.

- Organised work experience external to a programme of study. This includes national programmes: for example, STEP, which arranges project-based placements in small companies and not-for-profit organisations; and CRAC's InsightPlus, which recognises and accredits skills developed through part-time employment, voluntary work or student activities. It also includes more local schemes of these kinds.

- Ad hoc work experience external to a programme of study. This includes part-time jobs that students set up for themselves, for earning rather than learning purposes. In addition to the vacation work that most students have traditionally undertaken, around 60% of full-time students now work during term-time, and do so for an average of 10-14 hours per week (Harvey et al., 2002).

To these can be added work simulations within higher-education settings, in the form of either simulated environments (e.g. print studio) or simulated techniques (e.g. business game).

Career development learning can use all of these experiences as resources for learning. In particular, it can:

- Help students to prepare for such experiences in ways which harness their career development learning potential.

- Help students to reflect on the career development learning they can draw from such experiences, both during and after the experiences (see Moon, 1999; 2004).

- Help students to develop evidence of work-related experience and possibly proficiency that can be used in future job applications.

Assessment and evaluation

The assessment methods used for career development learning need to reflect the learning goals of the programmes. Methods can include (Hustler et al., 1998, pp.49-53):

- Reflective essays or reports.
- Learning logs and portfolios, including action plans.
- Group or individual projects.
- Group or individual presentations.
- Direct assessment of CVs, applications and interviews.
- Written examinations.

Where the focus is upon personal information, attention is focused not on the content but on the quality of analysis and articulation (AGCAS, 2005, p.11). Some assessments may be for formative purposes only; some may use simple pass/fail classifications; some may use grades or degree classifications.

Evaluations of the effectiveness of career development learning programmes in the UK are still very limited. A review in the USA of 40 evaluation studies of career planning courses within higher education institutions (Folsom & Reardon, 2003) found that:

- In relation to outputs (e.g. career thoughts, career decision-making skills, career decidedness, vocational identity), 88% of the studies reported positive gains, and 12% reported no changes.

- In relation to outcomes (e.g. persistence in college, satisfaction with field of study, job satisfaction), 9 of the 11 studies measuring such outcomes reported positive gains, and two reported no changes.

The Centre for Career Management Skills at the University of Reading, which makes learning outcomes related to career management skills compulsory for all the university's students, is currently conducting a research programme that is examining:

- Subjective outcomes (e.g. self-efficacy, perceived control, adjustment, life satisfaction) before, during and after the transition into employment.

- Impact on vocational preferences.

- Objective outcomes two years after graduation (e.g. entry to graduate-level employment, earnings).

How careers services can help

The changing role of careers services

Yorke & Knight (2006, p.14) suggest that 'in many cases a preferred way of enhancing an institution's contribution to student employability is to strengthen the careers service, although the impact will be muted if the service lacks a curriculum presence'. Similarly, Harvey et al. (2002) comment on the growing recognition by institutions of the need to develop a longer-term integrating strategy for employability that includes closer links between central services and programme-based initiatives.

Careers services within higher education institutions vary considerably in their size, in the roles they carry out, and in their organisational location within the institution. Their traditional core role has been to help students to manage the choices and transitions they need to make on exit from their courses of study. The services' core activities have traditionally comprised (see e.g. UGC, 1964; Watts, 1997):

- Individual and group guidance.

- Information services.

- Employer liaison and placement services.

A criticism of such services has been that they tended to have more to offer to students who already knew how to help themselves, and that, in those groups of students that appeared to be in most need of the service, significantly lower proportions were likely to have used it. The latter included those who achieved poor degrees, mature students, students from lower socio-economic groups, and arts students (Rowley & Purcell, 2001). There has accordingly been growing pressure on careers services to target their services at such groups (Harris Committee, 2001). Overt targeting can however be problematic (Morey et al., 2003). An alternative strategy is to adopt new approaches to service provision to all students.

Certainly the nature of careers services' core work has changed dramatically. In many institutions, individual and group guidance is now increasingly based on short interventions and group activities rather than long guidance interviews. Growing use is made of ICT, including the strategic use of websites and e-guidance to extend access to services (Offer et al., 2001; Offer, 2003; Madahar and Offer, 2004). Greater attention has been paid to quality assurance of services, including accreditation against the Matrix quality standards (Maguire, 2005).

In addition, around the traditional core activities, many services have developed a range of other activities, some of which have the potential for radically changing the nature and structure of the service. A review of strategic directions for higher education careers services (Watts, 1997) identified a number of options, four of which were based on stronger embedding within the institution:

- The integrated guidance model, in which the careers service becomes an integral part of a continuous guidance process available to students pre-entry, on entry, and throughout the student's course, as well as on exit from it.

- The integrated placement model, in which the careers service's concern for placement on graduation becomes part of an integrated placement operation which also includes course-related placements, and placements into part-time and vacation jobs.

- The curriculum model, in which the careers service becomes part of the teaching delivery vehicle for, or of a consultancy service designed to support academic departments in, incorporating into course provision the development of employability and career management skills.

- The learning organisation model, in which the careers service becomes part of a service designed to foster the career development of all members of staff, including contract researchers and other staff, as well as students.

Each has significant structural and resourcing implications. The contention is that these models are not incompatible with one another, but that there are some tensions between them which mean that, beyond a certain level of provision, they may require some degree of structural separation (ibid, p.44).

Of these four models, the curriculum model is particularly relevant to the concerns of this paper. It was implicitly given primacy by the Harris Committee (2001), which redefined the prime function of higher education careers services as being 'to help the institution produce better-informed students who are self-reliant, able to plan and manage their own learning and have sound career management skills' (p.15). It added that careers services 'have key roles in delivering, or helping tutors to deliver, aspects of the curriculum, for example relating to the development of students' career management skills, arranging work experience and encouraging students to reflect on that experience' (p.30).

A follow-up to the Harris Committee's report found that a quarter of institutions argued that 'partnerships with academic departments in contributing to and embedding CMS [career management skills] development' should now be viewed as 'core' rather than 'additional' activities (Universities UK, 2002, p.33). A later survey by Maguire (2005) found that no less than 90% of services reported that they had partnerships with academic departments in contributing to career management skills development, and 76% in embedding career management skills in the curriculum.

The growth of personal development planning has also strengthened the curriculum role of careers services in a number of institutions. The Harris Committee (2001, p.30) stated that 'individual academic departments must have lead responsibility in helping students to compile their Progress Files, but Careers Services have an important role to play in ensuring that the Progress File is viewed not as an end in itself, but as a tool to aid successful planning and progression'. In practice, Little & ESECT colleagues (2005, p.13) report that 'in many higher education institutions, PDP and career development are viewed as an integrated process rather than separate activities, with careers services (or Centres for Career Development, as some are now titled) taking the lead role in delivery'.

The organisational location of careers services remains an important issue. They can be aligned with other student services, with academic services, or with marketing services; or organised on a stand-alone basis (Watts, 1997, pp.26-27). The survey by Maguire (2005) indicated that in 53% of institutions the careers service was located in student services, and only in 14% under teaching and learning. Some institutions, however, had adopted some degree of hybridisation which attached careers services to teaching and learning structures even though they were located elsewhere within the institutional structure.

If, in the longer term, career development learning becomes widely embedded within higher education as part of a 'core curriculum', this could have considerable implications for the structural position of careers services within institutions. Possibilities mentioned by Hustler et al. (1998, p.47) include:

- Providing curriculum consultancy and support within the traditional careers-service model, alongside its traditional functions.

- Restructuring the careers service as an academic service rather than a student service.

- The careers service becoming, or existing alongside, a teaching unit focusing on career management as an academic discipline in which research can be conducted.

Models of partnership with teaching departments

Attitudes within teaching departments to the need for career development learning, and to whose responsibility it is to provide such learning, tend to vary, depending on the nature of the course (see Watts & Hawthorn, 1992):

- Within vocational courses, which are linked to a specific occupation, and are regarded as essential for entry to, and as providing preparatory training for, that occupation (e.g. medicine, architecture), the department is likely to view career development related to that occupation as being its own primary responsibility (though is unlikely to pay any attention to career development outside it).

- Within semi-vocational courses, which lead to a wide range of occupations, but with the expectation that they will be regarded as essential or desirable for entry to many of those fields (e.g. chemistry, psychology), the department is likely to view responsibility for career development learning as being shared with the careers service.

- Within non-vocational courses, from which it is common for students to enter a wide range of occupations, to most of which the subject content of their course is not directly relevant (e.g. history, philosophy), the department is likely to view career development learning as being primarily the responsibility of the careers service.

There are a number of different models for the respective roles of the careers service and teaching departments in delivering career development learning. These include (Hustler et al., 1998, p.41):

- Specialists: delivered solely by careers advisers.

- Consultancy: careers advisers lend support and expertise to work undertaken by departments, including involvement in planning groups, materials development and informal staff development.

- Parallel delivery: academic staff and careers advisers have separate slots in a departmentally-based programme, usually initiated and owned by the department.

- Integrated: academic staff and careers advisers work as a joint course team.

Such models have considerable implications for the staffing of careers services, and for the competences required by their staff. In addition to their traditional advisory, information and brokerage roles, they may now be expected to play roles as teachers and as academic leaders (ibid, pp.39-40). This requires:

- Greater pedagogic knowledge and skills than they have usually had in the past.

- A stronger grounding in career development theory, not only as a theoretical basis for their own professional practice but also as a body of knowledge for them to teach to students as part of the students' career development learning (McCash, 2006).

- 'Academic empathy', in order to work effectively with the distinctive contexts and cultures of different teaching departments and disciplines (Hustler et al., 1998, p.56).

A number of institutions have already taken steps to respond to these changed requirements.

Conclusion

Career development learning offers an additional dimension to institutional strategies designed to foster the employability of students. It makes the value of such strategies transparent to students; it also strengthens the sustainability of their benefits.

Career development learning has not always been as strongly represented in employability strategies as it should have been. The last few years, however, have seen a rapid growth of career development learning programmes within higher education institutions. In most cases, they currently cover only a minority of students; in a few, they have been extended to larger numbers or even made obligatory.

If career development learning programmes are to continue to grow and develop, the nature of careers services within higher education and their relationships with teaching departments need to be further reframed. The intellectual foundations of career development learning also need to be strengthened. It is hoped that this paper will support and contribute to these developments[27].

---

27 Author acknowledgements: The author acknowledged the help of Val Butcher, Margaret Dane, Zella King, Phil McCash, David Stanbury and Rob Ward in commenting on an earlier draft of this paper.

10. The Role of Information and Communication Technologies in Integrated Career Information and Guidance Systems[28]

Introduction

Information and communication technologies (ICT) are transforming career information and guidance services, just as they are transforming service delivery in other sectors (e.g., banking and health services). This poses major issues for policy-makers. To what extent can investment in ICT enhance the cost-effectiveness of services? Should investment in ICT be viewed as an alternative to face-to-face services, or as a means of enhancing the quality of such services? What are the respective roles of government, of career guidance professionals and of the private sector in promoting the application of ICT within this field? This article, based on a paper prepared for the European Commission and the Organisation for Economic Co-operation and Development, addresses these and related issues from a policy perspective.

Evolution

The evolution of the application of ICT in the field of career information and guidance can be divided into four phases. The first was the mainframe phase, from the mid-1960s to the late 1970s. A number of computer-aided guidance systems were developed which demonstrated the potential of ICT. But the costs of direct interaction with the computer meant that the only systems which proved widely practicable in cost terms were based on batch processing. The static nature of this process and the feedback delays limited the implementation of such systems.

The second was the microcomputer phase, from the early 1980s to the mid-1990s. The advent of the microcomputer made interactive usage much more economical, and also made it easier to develop and market limited software packages; its attractiveness grew as more powerful versions of the personal computer were developed. The result was a substantial growth in the number of computer-aided

---

[28] **Editorial footnote:** Reprinted, by permission of the author and the publisher, from *International Journal for Educational and Vocational Guidance*, Volume 2 No.3, 2002. IJEVG is the journal of the International Association for Educational and Vocational Guidance. DOI 10.1023/A:1020669832743. With permission of Springer Science+Business Media.

guidance systems, and in the extent of their usage. By the 1990s it was difficult to find a guidance service in any developed country which did not make use of such systems.

The third was the web phase, in the late 1990s. The advent of the Internet meant that instead of free-standing systems located in career guidance centres, websites could be developed which individuals could access instantly from a wide variety of sites, including their homes. The ease of developing such websites produced a massive increase in their number; the ease of interconnecting them meant that they no longer needed to be viewed as discrete entities. Rather than perceiving ICT solely as a service from external suppliers, guidance services began to develop their own websites.

The fourth is the digital phase, which we are now entering[29]. The hitherto separate analogue streams of the computer, the television and the telephone are merging into an integrated digital river (Cunningham & Fröschl, 1999). Individuals are now able to access the Internet not only through their personal computers but also through their televisions and mobile phones. Greatly enhanced bandwidth will shortly enhance its speed and its capacity for transmitting video and audio as well as text.

Across these four phases, three key trends can be discerned. The first is increased accessibility. Whereas initially ICT-based career guidance and information services were available only at a select number of technically-equipped service locations, they are now available not only in most guidance services but also in a vast range of other locations – homes, workplaces, community locations. The second is increased interactivity. In the early stages, resources were developed as separate systems, offering only limited interactivity with users. Now, they are highly interactive not only with users but also with each other and across inter-media boundaries. The third is much more diffused origination. Whereas the initial computer-aided guidance systems were developed by large organisations with substantial resources at their disposal, anyone can now develop their own website. This has led to much stronger private-sector activity in this area, which in turn has implications for public policy, to be discussed later.

Applications

Existing European ICT-based resources in the field of career information and guidance have been classified by Offer (1997) in relation to the DOTS model

---

[29] **Editorial footnote:** This article was originally published in 2002. Watts subsequently published a number of other papers building on it and exploring the further development of this "digital phase", e.g. *Careering through the Web* written in 2010 with Tristram Hooley and Jo Hutchinson.

developed by Law and Watts (see chapter 5): self awareness, opportunity awareness, decision learning, and transition learning.

Resources concerned with self awareness are designed to help users to assess themselves and to develop a profile in terms which can be related to learning and work opportunities. These resources range from simple self-assessment questionnaires to psychometric tests. They also include more open-ended brainstorming approaches.

Resources concerned with opportunity awareness include databases of learning and/or work opportunities, with a menu of search criteria which enable users to find data relevant to their needs. The databases may cover: education/training institutions or courses; occupations, employers, or job vacancies; voluntary-work opportunities; and information on how to become self-employed. Some include relevant labour-market information on supply and demand. There are also some examples of work simulations which enable users to explore particular occupational areas in an experiential way.

Resources concerned with decision learning include matching systems which enable users to relate their personal profiles to relevant learning or work opportunities. The outcome is a list of the opportunities which match the profile most closely (Offer (1997) lists these matching systems as a separate category). Also included here are content-free decision-making resources designed to help users to explore options in a systematic way, balancing the desirability of particular options against the perceived probability of achieving them.

Finally, resources concerned with transition learning are concerned with helping users to implement their decisions. These may include support in developing action plans, preparing curricula vitae, completing application forms, and preparing for selection interviews; it may also include help in securing funding for learning opportunities or for becoming self-employed.

From a policy perspective, it is important to recognise the range of these applications. Policy interventions, especially in the form of public funding, are often confined to a limited sub-set of this range – databases, for example.

Many separate packages and websites cover only one or two of these features; some, however, cover more. In the days of computer-aided guidance systems on mainframes and microcomputers, there was a debate about the relative merits of mini systems, each addressing particular guidance functions, and of maxi systems which attempted to cover as many as possible of these functions and to facilitate cross-pathing between them (prominent examples of maxi systems included DISCOVER and SIGI in the USA, CHOICES in Canada, and PROSPECT (HE) in the UK).

Some argued that a plurality of mini systems encouraged diversity and choice, enabling users to select the mix of such systems which met their needs; others that maxi systems enabled users to move seamlessly between different functions, avoiding semantic discrepancies and conceptual discontinuities, and modeling the full scope and complexity of the career decision-making process (Jackson, 1993; Watts, 1993). The advent of the Internet reframed this argument, by making it possible for websites to build quasi-maxi systems on what Offer (1997) termed a Lego model – piece by piece, sometimes through links to other sites.

The feasibility of developing ICT-based systems which cover the whole of the guidance process poses the issue of how such resources relate to the role of the guidance counsellor. How far should they be viewed, for some clients at least, as an alternative to the guidance counsellor? To which clients might this be appropriate?

Clients

Traditionally, most guidance services have been built around one-to-one counselling interviews. The models used in such interviews have varied: from diagnostic approaches in which the guidance counsellor has analysed the individual's attributes and made appropriate recommendations, to person-centred approaches in which the guidance counsellor helps clients to explore their perceptions of themselves and of the opportunities open to them, and to reach their own decisions. In more recent years, however, there has been a move in many countries towards a more open professional model, in which the concept of the guidance counsellor working with individual clients in a psychological vacuum is replaced or supplemented by a more diffuse approach, utilising a more varied range of interventions (e.g., curriculum programmes, group work, and use of ICT-based resources), with a greater emphasis on the individual as an active agent rather than a passive recipient within the guidance process (Watts, Guichard, Plant and Rodriguez, 1994). As part of this, some guidance services have moved away from a service centred on long interviews to an open-access model, with information rooms containing ICT and other resources supported by brief informal interviews, and with long interviews being available as a residual resource to those who need them (e.g., Watts, 1997).

To rationalise such a model, Sampson, Peterson, Reardon and Lenz (1999a) and Sampson, Palmer and Watts (1999b) contend that a screening process is required. They distinguish three levels of service delivery. Individuals who are initially judged to have a high level of readiness for decision-making are referred to self-help services: career resource rooms and websites designed to assist them in selecting, locating, sequencing and using needed resources with little or no staff assistance. Those judged to have a moderate level of readiness are referred to brief staff-assisted services: practitioner-guided use of resources, supplemented by group sessions. Those with a low level of readiness are referred to individual case-managed services: individual counselling and longer-term group counselling. Estimates of those requiring case-managed services tend to fall between 10% and 50%, depending on the population, with the remainder being divided between those requiring self-help and brief staff-assisted services. A range of readiness assessment measures, using a variety of constructs (e.g., career certainty/indecision, vocational identity, dysfunctional career thoughts), exist to help in the screening process (Sampson, Palmer & Watts, 1999b); dimensions such as age, socio-economic status, gender and educational level represent administratively convenient but conceptually inadequate proxies for such measures. The choice of these constructs/dimensions is crucial in planning services. A further important policy issue is whether decisions about the extent of staff assistance are to be made by policy-makers or counselling staff on a rationing basis, by counselling staff in negotiation with clients, or by the clients themselves.

Such screening models were initially devised to apply to clients who visit career guidance centres. In addition, however, ICT now has the capacity to take services to individuals who find it difficult to visit such centres – because they live in geographically remote areas, for example, or because they have disabilities or are home-based for other reasons, or because they are occupied during the centre's opening hours. The concept of distance guidance, by telephone or through the Internet, makes it possible to deliver guidance services to remote locations, with or without direct staff assistance.

In addition, some clients may prefer to access services at a distance. Increasingly, in all fields, consumers want a service to be available when they identify a need for it, with minimum delay and minimum effort: they want it here, and they want it now. They may be willing to undertake visits to dedicated physical centres where this is feasible and is perceived as offering added value, but their decision rules in this respect are becoming more and more discriminating. These decision rules may be influenced by their preferred learning style. For example, Sampson, Peterson, Reardon and Lenz (1999a) suggest – using Holland's (1973) personality typology – that an Investigative individual who typically uses independent problem-solving might prefer (and learn more effectively) using the Internet to obtain career resources and services; whereas a Social individual who typically uses interaction with others in problem-solving might prefer (and learn more effectively) by interacting with guidance counsellors and fellow clients in a career centre.

In these various respects, ICT has the potential to significantly increase access to guidance services, freeing it from constraints of time and space. At the same time, however, there may be restrictions on access to the ICT resources themselves. There is widespread concern that the growth of the Internet is exacerbating inequalities between the information-rich and the information-poor: between industrialised and developing countries; between the rich and poor within each nation; and between those who are technically literate and those who are technically inept (OECD, 2000). In the USA, for example, households with incomes of $75,000 and higher are twenty times more likely to have access to the Internet than those at the lowest income levels, and more than nine times as likely to have a computer at home (cited in Lee, 2000). Growing access to the Internet through the television and telephone is likely to reduce these gaps; libraries and other public information points can also have an important role to play. For the present, though, the gaps remain substantial.

Integration

Levels of integration

Most computer-aided guidance systems have been designed so that they are capable of being used on a stand-alone basis, without guidance counsellor support. In general, however, most commentators on the use of such systems advocate the benefits of integrating them into more broadly-based guidance services. There are three models for such integration. The first is the supported model, in which the user is seen – usually for a brief period – before and/or after using the system. The second is the incorporated model, in which the system is used within another guidance intervention – within a classroom session, for example, or within a counselling interview, enabling guidance counsellor and client to work with the system side-by-side. While this latter example can be very fruitful, it also means that, far from reducing the guidance counsellor time required by the client, the system may increase it. The third model is the progressive one, in which the use of the system is preceded and/or followed by other guidance interventions – interviews, group sessions, experience-based approaches like work experience and work shadowing – in a developmental sequence (Watts, 1996a). One of the functions of the screening process proposed by Sampson, Peterson, Reardon and Lenz (1999a) and Sampson, Sampson, Palmer and Watts (1999b) is to prescribe such a sequence, based on the client's needs.

These models can also be applied to websites, but here levels of integration are potentially much stronger. Sampson, Peterson, Reardon and Lenz (1999a) distinguish between independent websites which are free-standing and may be developed by a wide variety of commercial, governmental and other agencies, and integrated websites which are developed by career centres themselves. The integrated websites are of particular strategic significance for career centres because they sit at the interface between, on the one hand, their local face-to-face services and other resources within their centres, and on the other, the independent web-based services – often national or international in nature – which provide a rich range of additional resources but can also be seen as competition. Through their websites, career centres can identify the global resources they wish to utilise (some through simple technical links, but others requiring commercial or non-commercial partnership arrangements), and then intertwine them with their own local provision. In this way, they can fuse high tech with high touch (Offer, Sampson & Watts, 2001).

Roles of integrated websites

Offer and Sampson (1999) suggest that career centres' websites can have at least five different purposes. One is as a funnel into their own existing off-line services, aiming to maximise take-up of these services. The second is to act as a diversion, seeking to take the pressure away from these off-line services by diverting users to other, usually web-based resources where their needs can be met. The third is an enhancement of such diversion, seeking to deliver on-line guidance within the site itself. The final two add further enhancements: providing a forum for putting users in contact with others facing similar issues to their own, or with people who may offer help in relation to these issues (e.g., potential career mentors); and providing a source of distance learning programmes in career management skills and related areas (for examples, see Offer, Sampson & Watts, 2001).

Most of these purposes are not, of course, mutually exclusive, but the choice and balance between them require strategic decisions to be made, as do the choice of partners for any partnership arrangements. Not only this, but the process of making such decisions can be a valuable opportunity to review the strategic development of the centre as a whole. Many career centres clearly start by simply establishing a presence on the Internet: as Offer (1998) puts it, "we're here, because we're here, because we're here". Thereafter, it seems likely that they go through four developmental stages. The first is promotional: promoting what the service offers off-line. The second is adaptive: delivering some of these services in on-line form. The third is innovative: delivering new services on-line which are not possible, or less feasible, off-line – which is where any partnership arrangements may come into play. The fourth is synergistic: to intertwine on-line and off-line services in new ways. The further a career centre moves through these stages, the more it is using its website as an agent of change in relation to its service provision as a whole (Offer, Sampson & Watts, 2001).

Telephone helplines

Alongside websites, there has been growing interest in the use of telephone helplines in delivering career information and guidance services. The largest telephone helpline service in this field is the Learndirect service in the UK, which was launched in February 1998 and by the end of 2000 had responded to 2.4 million calls. Other more limited helplines have been launched in other countries, including Canada and New Zealand. A comparative analysis of these helplines indicates that some have been promoted essentially as information services; others as career counselling services. Some are focused primarily on learning or on work; others on career, embracing the two. Some are aimed at young people or adults; others are all-age. Some are separate services based on callcentres; others are integrated in various ways into more broadly-based services (Watts & Dent, 2002).

The decisions made about the framing of helplines in these various respects are critical. Included in this is the extent to which the service should be offered at national or at local level. With Learndirect, the original idea was that calls should be routed to helplines based as locally as possible. This is the model used, for example, by the UK National Health Service helpline NHS Direct: calls are routed to local callcentres, and are only passed elsewhere when lines are busy; the notion being that, in time, it might become the gateway to all local health services (McLennan, 1999). In the case of Learndirect, by contrast, the helpline is offered largely at a national level. This can result in some loss of quality, in terms of access to local knowledge. Against this needs to be set the consistency of service and of helpline adviser training offered by relatively large-scale operation. Such decisions have a significant influence on the balance between global and local dimensions in guidance provision. This in turn is critical in determining the level of integration that is possible with face-to-face services.

Technological synergy

A further important issue here is technological synergy. Whereas the Learndirect helpline was originally conceived as a separate service, a Learndirect website has now also been introduced, and increasing attention is being focused on integration between the two. The website includes not only courses and occupations databases, but also a diagnostic package which provides an assessment of skills, interests and values, and connects the results to occupational families. Each page of the website includes a call-me button which generates a telephone call from a Learndirect adviser. In principle, it should be possible in future for the adviser to bring up on their screen the caller's work to date – a draft curriculum vitae, for example – and work on it on-line with them. Conversely, more callers could be encouraged to access the website and be supported in doing so. Again, greater use of e-mail should make it possible to sustain contact over a period of time through a mixture of synchronous (e.g., telephone) and asynchronous (e.g., e-mail) communications (Watts & Dent, 2002).

The concept of flexible usage of the telephone, website and e-mail, linked with face-to-face facilities, opens up new opportunities for the delivery of career information and guidance. It means that individuals can initially access help in the form which is convenient to them and with which they feel comfortable. Some feel comfortable visiting a careers centre; some do not. Some are more comfortable on the telephone, or on e-mail; some are not. A further dimension will be added to this by the likely move towards ready domestic access to videophones or interactive digital television. All of these could be regarded not as alternative services but as portals into a wide, flexible and well-harmonised network of services which can enrich the learning pathways available to the individual. Public policy sometimes seems to impede such harmonisation (see e.g., Watts & Dent, 2002); it could, however, proactively promote it.

Resource-centred v. relationship-centred

A key issue in relation to such models is the significance attached to the relationship between the individual and the guidance counsellor. The model could be based on a co-ordinated range of resources, of which the guidance counsellor is seen as one. Or it could place the relationship with the guidance counsellor at the centre, viewing other resources as supports to this relationship. In the latter case, it needs to be recognised that the relationship can now be sustained in a variety of ways: not only face-to-face but also at a distance; and in the latter terms, both through synchronised communications like the videophone, the telephone and Internet "chat", and also through asynchronous communications like e-mail and voice-mail.

The rationale for the relationship model is that career decisions have an important cognitive component, but that they are bound up very closely with people's feelings about themselves, their sense of identity, and their dreams and aspirations. Accordingly, the individual can best be helped by working in a relationship with another individual who has the skills to enable them to address their distinctive identity. This is a strong tradition within the career guidance field, but has come under attack on two linked grounds: that by placing the relationship at the centre, it cedes too much power to the guidance counsellor; and that because it is so labour-intensive and guidance counsellors are costly, it is not practicable or sustainable as an extensively delivered model. This leaves the alternative view that guidance professionals should see themselves primarily not as counsellors but as managers of guidance resources: managing diverse resources in ways which enable individuals to find the means through which their personal needs can best be met (Watts, 1996a).

In relation to these two models, ICT tends to be viewed as leaning towards the resource-based model. But this is not necessarily the case: certainly ICT does not of itself demand a jettisoning of the relationship model. Indeed, there is a risk that contrasting the two models too starkly may implicitly hold frozen the familiar and established practice of the face-to-face one-to-one interview. As Tait (1999) has pointed out, it is important to understand how technology is now transforming the ways in which human relationships are pursued and managed. Instead of assuming that crucial elements are lost when relationships are mediated by technologies, more attention needs to be paid to how technology is enabling such relationships to be developed and sustained in ways which are released from the constraints of space, time and physical presence.

Constantly lurking beneath professional anxieties about the use of ICT in guidance has been the fear of reductionism: that the use of technology will lead to simplistic, quick-fix, information-based approaches, in which the human element is marginalised or eliminated. Increasingly, however, it can be used within an integrated approach not only to supplement but also to extend the range of this human element.

The key distinctions now are not simply between human interventions and ICT-based interventions, but between a more complex range of interventions: direct face-to-face counsellor-client interactions, on either a one-to-one or group basis; technically mediated counsellor-client interactions, on either a synchronous or asynchronous basis; and stand-alone ICT-based services in which standardised services can be repeatedly used by different users without additional human resource cost. An important issue is how these different interventions can be optimally blended in effective service delivery, attending to clients' varied needs and preferred learning styles. This has implications both for the training of guidance counsellors, and for wider public policy.

Policy issues

The potential roles of public policy in relation to career information and guidance services are four-fold: legislation, remuneration (i.e., funding), exhortation and regulation (Watts, 2000a). Legislation is important in some countries in providing the essential base for such services, but is likely to apply to the services as a whole rather than to ICT in particular. The other three roles, however, can apply specifically to the use of ICT in career information and guidance services.

Funding

Many governments have seemed prepared to offer funding for initiatives involving the use of ICT in this field. Indeed, they have not infrequently seemed more willing to provide funding for such initiatives than for extensions of other forms of service delivery, and also less demanding in seeking evidence of effectiveness (Watts, 2001a). In part this is because such funding is often linked to wider policy agendas:

in particular, the interest of many governments in promoting e-learning (OECD, 2001) and in improving the ICT capability of their citizens, as a way of seeking to ensure their nation's future economic competitiveness. It therefore has a kind of face validity which sometimes seems to protect it from close critical scrutiny. Also, it is commonly justified in terms of promising future cost savings in expenditure on face-to-face career guidance services, or – a somewhat different argument – extending access to such services without commensurate increases in costs. Systematic evidence of such effects, and whether they involve any reductions in quality of outcomes, is however currently lacking. Indeed, there is some anecdotal evidence that ICT-based services may increase rather than reduce the demand for face-to-face services – and therefore lead to greater frustration if these services are not available.

It may also be that the notion of evaluating the relative merits of different models of service delivery – face-to-face, by computer, by telephone and so on – as discrete alternatives is now outdated. In the past, these have tended to be viewed as alternative means to the same ends, which should accordingly be evaluated in comparative cost-effectiveness terms. If however – as argued earlier in this paper – effective models of delivery are interweaving human and technical resources in ever denser ways, this may be an inappropriate approach. Instead, it may be that the important question now is how these models can be most effectively combined in a synergistic way, so that they add value to one another, and provide new service-delivery options for clients.

The role of government in funding ICT-based services is though open to question on more basic grounds: that the development of such services can be safely left to the market, and that public intervention is accordingly unnecessary. Certainly the Internet has fostered the growth of an open market in the field of career information and guidance: anyone anywhere can launch such services. For example, web-based recruitment agencies are increasingly offering guidance or careers advice as a loss leader (Offer, Sampson & Watts, 2001).

The role of the market in relation to ICT in particular is closely linked to its role in relation to career information and guidance in general. The core of the case for public investment in such services is that they represent not only a private good but also a public good, in terms of their contribution both to economic efficiency and to social equity. Traditionally, such services have often been perceived as part of social-welfare provision. In recent years, efforts have been made in a number of countries to apply market principles to social and economic activities wherever this is feasible. Under this view, public intervention in relation to public goods should be confined to areas where there is market failure (Watts, 1996b).

Market failure

In relation to career information and guidance, the market would seem to be potentially inadequate in three important respects. The first is impartiality. The market tends to respond to the needs of those with most resources at their disposal. In the field of career information and guidance, therefore, it tends to be drawn to the recruitment interface, and to the needs of employers at that interface (e.g., Offer, Sampson & Watts, 2001). This can both constrain and distort the services that are offered, focusing them around the need to fill the vacancies on offer rather than to meet the individual's needs. This may not be sufficient to fulfil the public interest.

Secondly, there may be market failure in terms of investment. This is particularly true in relation to career information, which is not excludable: individuals are not willing to pay for the collection and provision of information which will subsequently be available to others free of charge. This suggests that career information services should be provided by the state. On the other hand, it is argued by some that guidance services should not be funded in this way, because they are specific to the individual and therefore are excludable (Bartlett, Rees & Watts, 2000). It is significant, however, that in practice the only area where a significant market has developed for career guidance services is outplacement counselling, where the employer pays but has no interest in the nature of the outcome; elsewhere it seems to be difficult to commodify guidance in the way that a market with growth potential would require (Watts, Guichard, Plant and Rodriguez, 1994; see chapter 2).

In relation to ICT, the argument for the public interest in investment in career information is evident in the number of countries where governments have supported the development and maintenance of databases on educational and occupational opportunities. Such databases can either be made directly accessible to clients, or can be made available for private-sector organisations to package and distribute, whether on a fee basis or not, as a means of assuring the quality of non-government information provision. In the USA, for example, federal and state funding have for many years supported a network of career information delivery systems, co-ordinated by the National Occupational Information Co-ordinating Committee (McKinlay, 1989) (though federal funding for NOICC has now ceased).

It is also significant, however, that all of the major maxi computer-aided guidance systems (see earlier) were developed initially with funding from government or from private foundations (Watts, 1993). Similarly, Sampson (1999b) has argued that publicly-supported Internet-based systems allow centralised planning of the resource and service design, increasing the likelihood that different functions will be effectively integrated (e.g., using the output of a transferable skills analysis as input for the creation of a curriculum vitae). Sampson notes that governments and foundations prefer to provide pump-priming funding for innovations which the private sector will then maintain, reinvesting a proportion of the profits into ongoing development. This is the model that was used in the case of North American maxi systems like CHOICES, DISCOVER and SIGI (Watts, 1993).

This is linked to the third potential source of market failure, which relates to ownership. If the aim is to integrate ICT as closely as possible into more broadly-based guidance services, and if these services are publicly-funded, then marketisation of the ICT-based services may impede the extent of the integration that is feasible. This issue underpinned the turbulent history of the UK maxi system – PROSPECT (HE). It is also evident in, for example, current concerns in university career centres in the USA about the extent to which many of their mission-critical activities are now dependent on commercial vendors like Monster.com. These vendors are perceived to be using their position to remove the career centres from the graduate recruitment process and establish a direct customer relationship with the student and employer (Offer, Sampson & Watts, 2001) – an argument that arguably would severely weaken the wider guidance role of these centres.

Such arguments may provide a case for some level of continued public investment in ICT in career information and guidance services. Nonetheless, there is clearly an important role for the market too, harnessing additional resources and encouraging competition that will foster innovation. The balance is likely to vary across countries, depending on their structures and traditions and on the political philosophies of their governments.

Quality assurance

Where the role of the market is extensive, there remain issues about whether governments should retain a residual responsibility for ensuring quality – either by exhortation, through guidelines and the like, or by regulation. These issues are particularly pressing in relation to the Internet. The quality of websites varies massively. Some are well-designed and user-friendly; some are not. Many give no information about the sources of data and when they were last updated. A study of websites offering no-cost career assessment found that almost none included any reference to how instruments had been developed or to underpinning psychometric data on reliability and validity (Oliver & Zack, 1999). There often appears to be no security regarding the confidentiality of client data. Little account is commonly taken of clients with visual disabilities or low vocabulary levels.

A variety of strategies can be adopted in response to such issues. One is to offer guidelines; another is to produce detailed quality standards. These can be linked to a self-assessed kitemarking system based on websites' affirmations that they meet these standards; or to an accredited kitemarking system based on verification by an external body. All these systems can be voluntaristic, or can be made compulsory – for example, for any services used by, or referred to by, guidance services in receipt of public funding.

Three further questions need to be addressed here. First, should such standards relate to the websites alone or to the guidance services in which they are embedded? The fact that some websites are independent and some are integrated (see earlier) suggests that both are needed. Second, should governments that decide to go down these routes seek to develop the necessary tools and mechanisms themselves, or to encourage and support other bodies to do so? The main relevant guidelines produced to date in Canada, the UK and the USA have been produced by professional bodies (NCDA, 1997) or by independent sectoral bodies (Canadian Labour Force Development Board, 1998; Guidance Council, 2000). Third, should standards be developed, set and accredited at national level, at multinational (e.g., European) level, or at a global level? The global nature of the Internet would suggest the latter, but there may be a trade-off here between desirability and feasibility.

Conclusion

The role of ICT in guidance can be seen in three ways: as a tool, as an alternative, or as an agent of change (Watts, 1986b). Policy-makers have often tended to view it in the first two guises: either as a supplement to existing services or a potential substitute for such services. But the wider emergence of websites and helplines as forms of technically mediated service delivery means that the potential of ICT as an agent of change – paralleling the transformations in many other service sectors – is now far greater than before. It is this that now provides the main policy challenge.

Section Three:
The Politics of Career Development

Section Introduction

The field of psychology has exerted a strong influence on career development. Career development is about the individual, their decision making and their interaction with organisations and other individuals. However, as Tony Watts reminds us in this section, this career development takes place within the context of the wider world. More specifically it takes place within economic conditions and public policies that are intensely political.

The section begins with Socio-Political Ideologies in Guidance which sets out Tony Watts' seminal conceptual framework for thinking about the politics of career development. Career development, he argues, can take many stances, seeking to manage the status quo or to deliver change for the individual or society. The categories of conservative, liberal, progressive and radical guidance are both descriptive and thought-provoking, asking both how career development has operated in the political field and how it should operate.

The political nature of guidance is illustrated in The Implications of School-Leaver Unemployment for Careers Education in Schools. In this chapter Tony Watts asks how career development programmes can address sub-optimal economic situations. Should such programmes seek to encourage students to pursue work at any costs, raise the possibilities of alternative life styles or seek to illuminate the reasons for unemployment and catalyse people towards change? Tony Watts' argument highlights the fact that all career development is political and provides a range of ways in which practitioners can seek to operate within this political space.

In The Impact of the 'New Right': Policy Challenges Confronting Careers Guidance in England and Wales and in Career Guidance and Social Exclusion: A Cautionary Tale Tony Watts pulls back and examines how public policy discourses and themes impact on the structures that support career development. He notes that career development has a strong dependence on the public sector either through its embedding in the public education system or through public funding for career development services. Consequently the career development sector needs to be able to understand and orient itself toward contemporary public policy discourses, even where these are not the ones that members of the sector might have chosen. For Tony Watts, career guidance is constantly in a dialogue between idealism and realism. The vision of the universal lifelong career development system buttressed by a range of policy supports which he sets out in The New Career and Public Policy is one to agitate for, but in the meantime the field needs to relate to contemporary political concerns.

These chapters demonstrate the intensely political nature of Tony Watts' contribution to thinking about career development. His writing moves across a range of levels and addresses the politics of the classroom, of the government and of the political or educational theorist. While the individual remains at the heart of career development, these chapters remind us that we forget the societal and political dimension of the field at our peril.

11. Socio-Political Ideologies in Guidance[30]

Introduction

Careers education and guidance is a profoundly political process. It operates at the interface between the individual and society, between self and opportunity, between aspiration and realism. It facilitates the allocation of life chances. Within a society in which such life chances are unequally distributed, it faces the issue of whether it serves to reinforce such inequalities or to reduce them.

In principle, the more choice individuals have, the more scope there is for guidance. This is illustrated in figure 25, which outlines a spectrum of gradually increasing scope for choice and exercise of self-determination (within competitive constraints).

Figure 25: Selection and choice: adapted from Madsen, 1986.

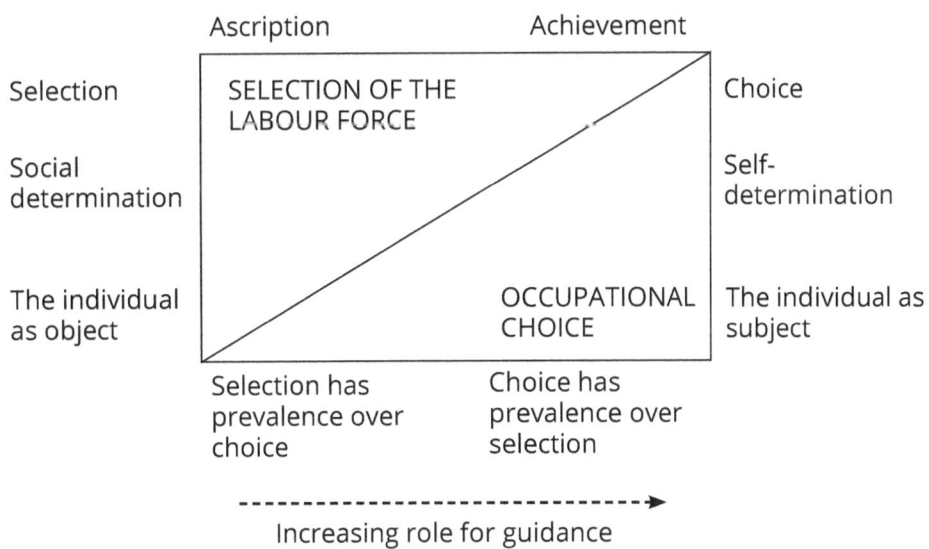

Madsen (1986) suggests that the model can be applied historically, demonstrating the shift from pre-industrial societies with a social order based largely on ascription to industrial societies with a social order based more extensively on achievement.

---

30 Editorial footnote: Reprinted, by permission of the publisher, from Watts, A.G., Law, B., Killeen, J., Kidd, J.M. & Hawthorn, R. (1996): *Rethinking Careers Education and Guidance: Theory, Policy and Practice.* London: Routledge.

This helps to explain why formal guidance services have tended to emerge as a product of industrialisation. Within societies based on achievement rather than ascription, with increasingly complex and volatile occupational structures, the family's capacity to communicate information on opportunities becomes inadequate. Individuals are likely to need guidance from more formal sources in order to make effective use of their increased freedom to choose; conversely, the social structure is more likely to require arrangements which support the free choice of the individual but relate it to social needs.

Madsen also suggests that within industrial societies the model can be applied in social-structural terms, indicating the greater choice available for the middle class than for the working class, to whites than to blacks, to males than to females. This implies that guidance is more relevant to the first group in each of these pairs than to the second. On the other hand, part of the concern of guidance services has often been to maximise the capacity for choice for groups with constrained opportunities.

Indeed, the origins of the vocational guidance movement in the USA were as a process of gradualist social reform, seeking to improve the work conditions of the lower classes (Brewer, 1942). Such reform was designed to restructure society so that 'the human potentialities of all members may be more fully utilised in the interest of each and in the interest of all' (Williamson, 1965, p. 43). It was set within a democratic ideal which respected the rights of individuals to make free choices about their own lives, sanctioning 'neither the exploitation of the individual by society, nor the disregard of the interests of society by the individual' (quoted in Stephens, 1970, p. 112).

Despite these origins, and the complex issues they raise, the socio-political nature of guidance has tended to be given limited attention in the professional literature or in the professional training of guidance counsellors. In part this can be attributed to the way in which guidance services have become institutionalised within schools or other organisations, or within government bureaucracies. In part, too, it can be attributed to the way in which the theoretical basis of professional guidance practice has been dominated by psychologists. Particularly in the USA, but in most other countries as well, the dominant guidance theories – and the theories of career development on which they have been based – have been psychological rather than sociological or economic in nature (see Killeen, 1996a). This is perhaps understandable, since at the point of intervention the focus of attention is the individual. But it means that the social context of the intervention, and the socio-political nature of the intervention itself, tend to be neglected and implicitly regarded as unproblematic.

In reality, the socio-political nature of guidance is highly problematic. Guidance can be a form of social reform; it can also be a form of social control. There are important choices to be made. To clarify the nature of these choices, the present chapter will offer four alternative approaches to guidance from a socio-political perspective. These approaches will then be elaborated in relation to the challenge posed by unemployment, and also in relation to the issues of gender and ethnicity.

Four approaches

Most writers on guidance have tended to view it in liberal[31] terms as a non-directive process concerned with helping individuals to choose the opportunities appropriate not only to their abilities and skills but also to their interests and values. This approach has been strongly influenced by the models of non-directive counselling developed by Carl Rogers (1961): while it recognises the desirability of a wider range of interventions, it holds to the ideal of respecting and valuing the right of individuals to make decisions concerning their own lives. Guidance is seen as facilitating this process, not influencing it in a particular direction (Daws, 1967). Careers education, for example, is viewed as an appropriate complement to counselling, helping individuals to develop the skills, knowledge and understanding they need in order to make their own informed decisions (Watts, 1973a).

Such views tend to be criticised by sociologists, who commonly view guidance as an essentially conservative force, operating as an agent of social control. Its main function is seen as adapting individuals to the opportunities appropriate for them (Roberts, 1977). According to this view, its primary concern is to meet the needs of the labour market: Brown (1985), for example, writing from a neo-Marxist perspective, sees the Careers Service as part of a state apparatus designed to habituate entrants to the workforce to the requirements of capital.

Other writers use less ideological language to make much the same kind of point. They emphasise that counsellors act as 'gatekeepers' to opportunities (Erickson, 1975; Wrench, 1991). They also note that one of the main functions of guidance is to discourage students from seeking opportunities regarded as 'unrealistic' and to lower their expectations. Guidance is seen as an effective if insidious means of 'cooling out' excessive aspirations (Clark, 1960). It masks inequalities in society by making them seem matters of individual choice, thereby reconciling people to their roles. In doing so, it propagates myths, such as the 'dignity of work' and the concept of 'choice' itself. Thus to suggest to young people 'that there is satisfaction and dignity in that which is their probable economic destiny is not making it possible for them to have "freedom to choose" – it is rather telling them that they should be satisfied with their lot in life' (Sessions, 1975, pp. 315-16; also Grubb and Lazerson, 1975).

---

[31] The use of the term 'liberal' here – as with the subsequent use of the terms 'conservative', 'progressive' and 'radical' – is specific to guidance ideologies and does not imply any necessary association with political Liberalism.

Such comments, it should be noted, refer to the functions of guidance rather than to conscious intentionality. The comments tend to be made by brief visitors to the field, who are concerned with pointing out the gulf between its liberal rhetoric and what they see as being its conservative reality. At the same time, the reality they describe does have some direct congruence with policy-makers who view guidance as being concerned primarily with serving the needs of the labour market, and with guidance writers and practitioners who emphasise 'realism'.

To counter the sociological critique of the liberal position, some guidance writers have adopted a more progressive stance, viewing guidance as a means of individual change. The emphasis shifts to a proactive approach, seeking in particular to raise the aspirations of individuals from deprived backgrounds. This incorporates attention to using active role models so as to increase expectations, to adopting forms of coaching and assertiveness training so as to improve self-confidence, and to engaging in forms of advocacy designed to remove obstacles to the individual's progress. The assumption tends to be that the individual's interests are best met by seeking to achieve the highest level that is possible within the status hierarchy of the opportunity structure. The conflict of identity and loyalty that, for example, young people from working-class backgrounds may experience in moving into middle-class roles (Jackson and Marsden, 1962) are regarded as difficulties to be overcome rather than as legitimate objections to seeking advancement.

The progressive approach is open to the criticism that encouraging some degree of movement of individuals within the status hierarchy merely reinforces the hierarchy itself, with no benefits for those who remain at the lower levels within it. Some have accordingly argued that guidance should seek to adopt a more radical stance, concerned with promoting social change. The basic assumption here is that it is not possible to advance the interests of certain groups of individuals without some change in social structures. This might materialise in guidance practice as a more generalised advocacy role on behalf of groups of individuals (Ranson and Ribbins, 1988), or as a feedback role which seeks to change the opportunity structure in the interests of such groups (Oakeshott, 1990).

More radically still, it might involve seeking to help such individuals to view their situation in group rather than individual terms: enabling them to understand, for example, the unequal and exploitative nature of the employment system. Such an approach has drawn sustenance from the work of Willis (1977) with working-class boys, showing how personal choices are bounded by norms and perceptions linked to shared identity: this has been interpreted by some as implying the need for interventions to engage with the group culture and develop its socio-political consciousness. Thus some careers teachers in London schools were reported as indicating that they were not disposed to co-operate with any 'tinkering' efforts to improve individual prospects but that their concern was rather to 'conscientise' young people (*New Society*, 14 May 1981).

A broadly similar position was elaborated within the Schools Council Careers Education and Guidance Project:

> Society and the range of job and other opportunities were regarded as more incompatible than compatible with the goal of encouraging the development and expression of human potential. This led to an emphasis on stimulating pupils to assess critically society and the occupational roles available and to act as an influence for social change, particularly in the world of work. (Bates, 1990, p. 71)

Bates analyses the political conflicts which surrounded the Schools Council project, and particularly the tensions between the radical and liberal positions. She also describes how teachers tended to ignore the different political nuances evident in the project publications and to regard them in a pragmatic and politically uncritical way as a source of lesson materials which could lift careers education out of its job-information rut. She further notes how even this was modified by pressure from pupils to revert to the traditional job-information approach. This provides a valuable reminder of how even sharply defined ideological stances can become modified by the practical constraints of the context in which they are implemented and by the negotiation with clients which effective guidance arguably requires.

The four approaches we have identified can be arranged on two dimensions, according to whether their core focus is on society or on the individual, and according to whether their concern in each case is with accepting the status quo or changing it in prescribed directions. This is illustrated in figure 26, with the former dimension represented vertically and the latter one horizontally.

Figure 26: Four socio-political approaches to careers education and guidance

	Core focus on society	Core focus on individual
Change	Radical (social change)	Progressive (individual change)
Status quo	Conservative (social control)	Liberal (non-directive)

Source: Adapted from Watts and Herr (1976)

It is worth noting that there is also some lateral correspondence within the table. Thus both the conservative and progressive models tend to assume what Katz (1993) terms a 'single optimisation model' for meeting both societal and individual interests: the notion that opportunities are arranged in a single hierarchy, and that the issue is who 'wins' or 'loses' particular places within this hierarchy. The liberal and radical approaches, by contrast, question in different forms the dominance of the hierarchy: the liberal approach by arguing that differences in values mean that individuals can 'win' in different ways; the radical approach by questioning the 'game' itself. The extent to which it is feasible and/or legitimate for guidance to adopt a fully-fledged social-change approach is open to question. Certainly it is likely to attract political opposition, as when a Minister of State for Employment accused careers officers of being 'social engineers ... incapable or unwilling to help employers by encouraging young people to take up opportunities on offer' (Morrison, 1983). More fundamentally, Halmos (1974) argued that there is an intrinsic incompatibility between the personalist orientation of counselling (in its various forms) and political activism. He contended that any attempt at 'hybridisation' of the roles was a serious mistake. Halmos further argued that the radical critique of counselling was misconceived: 'no social system, least of all the favoured utopias, can come about and subsist without a generously staffed personal service to individuals' (p. 147).

This leaves open, however, the issue of whether some elements of the social-change approach might be necessary to achieve the personal emancipation valued by the liberal approach. We will explore this issue further in the sections that follow.

The challenge of unemployment

Of the four approaches outlined in the previous section, the liberal and progressive approaches tend to be dominant in most careers education and guidance practice at the level of conscious intentionality. This is mainly because they focus on the individual, which – as noted earlier – is the natural focus of attention at the point of guidance intervention. When opportunities are relatively plentiful and/or expanding, this dominance is more likely to be uncontested. When, however, opportunities contract, it tends to come under growing pressure. This is particularly the case when levels of unemployment rise. Unemployment calls into question the concepts of 'opportunities' and 'choice' on which the liberal and progressive approaches are essentially based. Responses to unemployment thus provide a particularly fruitful area in which to explore the impact of different socio-political ideologies on educational provision in general and on guidance practice in particular (Watts, 1978a; 1983a; Fleming and Lavercombe, 1982; Watts and Knasel, 1985).

The most common immediate response of guidance services to rising unemployment is to pay more attention to active ways of helping their clients to secure the opportunities that remain available. In particular, there tends to be increased focus on employability. This includes job-search skills, and skills of self-presentation on paper and in selection interviews. It also includes exploration of possibilities for education and training which may increase employability. Eventually, however, guidance services have to confront the fact that while guidance along these lines may be helpful and effective for some of the individuals concerned, it does little or nothing to increase the number of jobs, and that many clients may remain unemployed. In such cases, guidance programmes limited to employability may only increase the stress and sense of inadequacy that stem from repeated failure, making it seem that this failure is due to personal inadequacy.

Attention may accordingly extend to focus on coping. This may include helping people to claim the benefits to which they are entitled, and to survive on a limited budget. It may also include helping them to explore opportunities for making good use of their increased 'leisure' time – hobbies, voluntary work, skill exchanges, non-vocational educational opportunities and helping them to cope in mental-health terms. Excessive focus on coping is, however, open to attack on the grounds that it is encouraging people to tolerate the intolerable, particularly in a society in which employment remains the chief source of status, of social identity, and of income.

A further extension therefore focuses on opportunity creation. This involves helping people to explore possibilities for becoming self-employed or setting up a small business or co-operative. The rise of unemployment in the early 1980s indeed saw a huge growth of attention to such possibilities, linked to the 'education for enterprise' movement (Watts and Moran, 1984). Again, however, too much focus on encouraging people to be 'enterprising' in this sense could imply that this represents a societal solution to unemployment, and that people who do not take up this option are feckless: this could be aligned to political arguments for reducing or withdrawing their benefits, so again becoming a classic case of 'blaming the victim'.

In each of these cases, therefore, options which appear liberal-progressive in nature are open to attack on the grounds that they are hidden forms of social control. This is reflected clearly in the attitude taken to hidden-economy activity. For many unemployed people, activities within the hidden economy are important forms both of coping and of opportunity creation. Because, however, they are officially proscribed, they tend to be ignored in guidance programmes (see chapter 3).

Some careers teachers, careers officers and other guidance workers find it acutely uncomfortable to accept the social-control nature of their work. They are aware that their efforts to help people with their individual problems fail to address the social context from which these problems largely stem. Moreover, they may begin to feel that they are helping to reinforce the social context by shifting attention away from it: by suggesting that what is needed is not socio-political reform but ways of making good the inadequacies of individuals.

In response to this, they may seek to focus also on the context itself. This may involve helping people to understand the extent to which responsibility for unemployment lies at a societal rather than individual level, and to explore possible forms of social, political and community action in response to it. This may be justified in liberal-progressive terms: if unemployed people understand that unemployment is not due to personal inadequacy, this may make it easier to avoid the destructive effect which unemployment may have on their confidence and self-respect. But it may also be justified in more radical terms, as raising people's consciousness of the social causes of unemployment and helping them to work collectively for social change. This too, however, is open to objections: increased awareness of the size and complexity of the forces that cause unemployment could lead unemployed people to feel a sense of impotence in the face of these forces; this in turn could lead to a fatalism which not only reduces their personal chances of finding a job but also produces a more general sense of alienation and disenchantment; it is likely to attract opposition from the public authorities on whose support most guidance provision depends; and it places the unemployed in the forefront of political pressures for change, which may expose them to risk and may mean that excessive expectations are raised for a group whose power is relatively limited.

In the end, resolving these dilemmas is a question of finding the optimal balance between the different options that is appropriate to the particular guidance context in question. To focus exclusively on any one option poses considerable ethical and professional difficulties. But an appropriate balance between them may make it possible to avoid or at least minimise such difficulties. In this sense, the difficulties tend to be more acute in careers education programmes than in, for example, the counselling interview, where the balance between the various options can be more flexibly negotiated with the individual client. On the other hand, socio-political context issues tend to be difficult to address in one-to-one counselling sessions and may be easier to tackle in group situations. For our present purposes, however, the various guidance options available in response to the challenge of unemployment illustrate very clearly the socio-political dilemmas that lie beneath all guidance provision.

Gender issues

Issues of socio-political ideology also arise in relation to gender. Here they assume a particularly acute form because of the fixed nature of gender allocation: whereas people can move between social classes, they cannot do so (*pace* transsexualism) between genders. Since gender segregation in the labour market is still strong, with many women confined to relatively low-paid and low-status jobs (Martin and Roberts, 1984; Rees, 1992; Killeen, 1996c), guidance is faced with the question of whether it serves to reinforce or challenge such segregation.

Traditionally, guidance clearly tended to reinforce the segregation. Prout (1983) argues that until the mid-1970s guidance not only reflected gender-stereotyped assumptions about male and female roles in society, but overtly encouraged them. The Youth Employment Service (now the Careers Service) had separate sections for boys and girls, with distinct staff, records and job-vacancy lists. Careers literature referred to 'girls' jobs' and 'boys' jobs'. Pictures in such literature tended to show men at work doing positive and demanding tasks, whereas women were shown in supportive roles as secretaries, in caring roles as nurses, or in decorative roles as florists and hairdressers. Child-rearing and home-making were assumed to play central roles in women's careers but not in men's.

These practices and assumptions have been strongly challenged by the feminist movement and changes in social mores. The more overtly segregated practices were abandoned, and explicit stereotyping is now scrutinised much more critically. Nonetheless, there is some evidence that in practice guidance services still tend to perform a conservative, social-control function in relation to gender issues. Several studies have shown, for example, that careers officers and teachers have been perceived as offering little help, and often positive discouragement, to girls who want to choose gender-atypical occupations (Benett and Carter, 1982; Breakwell and Weinberger, 1987; Cockburn, 1987; Devine, 1993).

The stance of careers advisers themselves is often liberal in nature. Most of them claim to be following equal-opportunities policies, at least in a passive sense. But their adherence to a non-directive approach means that they are inclined to take their clients' interests and preferences at face value. They are concerned about whether it is ethically legitimate for them to seek 'to reshape youngsters' aspirations and views of themselves' (Gottfredson, 1981, p. 577). They are also anxious to avoid rejection or ridicule from their clients (Cockburn, 1987). They accordingly may be reluctant to present gender-atypical options to those who do not volunteer an interest in such options. On the other hand, they may feel that with those who do indicate an interest in gender-atypical options, they should ensure that the individuals concerned are aware of the difficulties involved (Breakwell and Weinberger, 1987). This is easily perceived by such individuals as discouragement. In such ways, the liberal stance of careers advisers can serve conservative ends.

There has accordingly been pressure to adopt a more progressive approach, based on more active equal-opportunities policies (Watts and Kant, 1986). This includes active ways of increasing awareness of gender-atypical options. A particularly common approach is the use of positive role models, through talks, group discussions or work-shadowing schemes. Attention may also be given to providing support to those who want to pursue gender-atypical options, helping them to confront discrimination. Sometimes such programmes include work in single-sex groups, where issues specific to the gender in question can be addressed more directly. This runs the risk of reintroducing segregation and reinforcing gender stereotypes.

There is some evidence that progressive programmes of these kinds have only limited success in terms of direct impact on immediate choices (Brooks et al., 1985; HMI, 1982; Sultana, 1990). This demonstrates the strength and persistence of gender stereotypes. Gottfredson's (1981) theory of career development emphasises that gender-role conceptions are fundamental to people's sense of personal identity and that this produces strong resistance to relinquishing gender-type perceptions in choosing an occupation. It seems likely that such resistance will be particularly strong during adolescence, when young people are still developing their sexual identity and beginning their sexual careers. Such concerns seem to pose even greater problems for boys than for girls in choosing gender-atypical options for their occupational careers: such choices are viewed as irrational in selecting lower-status and lower-paid 'feminine' occupations, and tend therefore to be regarded as casting doubts on the individual's sexual identity (Hayes, 1986). Yet, arguably, the movement of males into 'feminine' occupations is critical if females are to be able to move more easily into 'masculine' occupations.

A common progressive response to these difficulties in relation to careers education programmes in schools is to seek to start them much earlier, before gender stereotypes are rigidly formed. Indeed, this forms one of the chief arguments for beginning careers education programmes in primary schools, in advance of puberty. A second response is to argue that such programmes need to be broader in approach, incorporating attention to domestic and child-rearing roles as well as occupational roles (Van Dyke, 1981). This enables the interaction between such roles to be addressed, and the gender distribution of work in the home as well as in employment to be brought into question.

Such responses can be incorporated within a liberal-progressive approach, but some writers have suggested that a more radical stance needs to be taken. It is argued that the concept of equal opportunities is not adequate as a framework for countering gender discrimination and women's disadvantage: that instead an anti-sexist approach is required based on challenging patriarchal power bases (Weiner, 1985). Attempts have been made to develop curriculum units based on anti-sexist principles designed to influence occupational choice by developing a broader critical consciousness of gender divisions and stereotyping (Chisholm and Holland, 1986; Blackman, 1987). Griffin (1985), by contrast, attached importance to such critical consciousness as an end in its own right. She argued that careers advisers and teachers should not try to force young women into non-traditional jobs where they will be detached from the support of other women: instead they should develop the students' understanding of why their choices are so limited.

Beneath these different approaches, two key issues can be identified. The first is whether it is the responsibility of guidance to represent the world of work as it is, or as it might be. The conservative and liberal approaches tend to be concerned with presenting the world as it is, with its existing inequalities and discrimination. Thus the fact that certain occupations are gender-segregated is regarded as valid occupational information. The progressive approach, on the other hand, tends to place more emphasis on the world as it might be from the individual's perspective, attaching particular importance to positive images and role models. Thus significance is attached to representing occupations non-stereotypically or even counter-stereotypically, so that a male-dominated occupation is represented visually by equal numbers of men and women. This makes it easier for girls to see the occupation as accessible to them, even though it misrepresents the current reality (Birk et al., 1979) and pays no attention to the structural changes required to achieve change. The radical approach, by contrast, sees it as important to address the current reality but to expose its structural foundations to radical critique.

The second issue is the balance between the approaches which is most likely to encourage individual autonomy. Such autonomy requires individuals to be able to envisage a range of possible selves in possible futures and to transcend the prescriptions of their situation and their socialised self (Law, 1981a). It is important to recognise that the test of such autonomy must include the possibility of choosing conventional as well as non-conventional options, but choosing them as an act of informed volition rather than as a result of conditioning. The danger with the progressive and radical approaches is that they tend implicitly to devalue traditionally feminine occupations, and the traditionally feminine roles of home-making and child-rearing, and to impose on women a male definition of career achievement (Hashizume and Crozier, 1994). On the other hand, it is arguable that the critical understanding of traditionally feminine roles developed by such approaches, and the awareness of alternatives, are essential if these roles are to be assumed as a matter of genuine choice. In other words, some elements of the progressive and radical approaches are necessary to detach liberal approaches from their conservative tendencies, but in the end the progressive and radical approaches have to be reconciled with the liberal one if individual autonomy is to be affirmed. It may be that the recognition of this point explains why a survey of teacher attitudes found stronger support for the statement 'It is important that careers education should encourage people to look critically at sex roles in society', which is concerned with awareness-raising at the exploration stage, than for the statement 'A careers teacher should make positive efforts to encourage pupils to consider taking up subjects or careers that are not normally done by their sex', which suggests directive intervention closer to the point of decision-making (Pratt et al., 1984, pp. 185-86).

Ethnicity issues

Ethnicity is a particularly socio-political issue for the 'visible ethnic minorities', i.e. people 'likely to be discriminated against on the basis of colour' (Forbes and Mead, 1992, p. 1). By 1989 such people constituted about 4.7 per cent of the total population of Britain. Most are systematically disadvantaged in the labour market, although the nature and degree of such disadvantage varies according to the country of origin (ibid.). As with gender, ethnic identity is in principle immutable; but in contrast to gender disadvantage, ethnic disadvantage applies to whole families and communities. This, along with the fact that some ethnic groups arrived in Britain only relatively recently, means that they may have only limited quantities of relevant 'cultural capital' (Bourdieu and Passeron, 1977) on which to draw. Accordingly, they may need more active support in order to secure access to opportunities.

One of the results is that black youngsters of Afro-Caribbean or Asian descent tend to be much more dependent on formal guidance services than do white youngsters. They are less likely to be able to obtain from their family or friends the informed help they need in order to gain access to opportunities. They are accordingly more likely to have recourse to careers officers or teachers (Brooks and Singh, 1978: Lee and Wrench, 1983; Sillitoe and Meltzer, 1985; Verma and Darby, 1987).

In response to such demands, some careers officers and teachers adopt the liberal 'colour-blind' stance that 'we treat them all the same'. Such a stance tends to deny the existence of systematic discrimination against ethnic minorities within the labour market, and to attribute any lack of success on the part of these minorities to their cultural attributes (Cross et al., 1990). There appears to be little if any evidence of overt ethnic discrimination on the part of guidance services (Roberts et al., 1981). Nonetheless, there is evidence that careers advisers tend to assess the occupational aspirations of ethnic-minority young people less favourably than those of white young people with similar qualifications, and to be more likely to regard such aspirations as unrealistic. Moreover, they are inclined to engage in 'protective channelling', directing ethnic-minority young people away from opportunities where they suspect these youngsters will be rejected (Cross et al., 1990). This means that discrimination on the part of employers is not even tested, let alone challenged. In such ways, careers advisers operating within a liberal framework which rejects racism nonetheless can help to produce racist outcomes. Concepts such as 'realism' act to conceal the underlying racism. Indeed, Brown (1985) argues that such 'racist non-racism' is able to hold the racist model together precisely because it represents itself as an individualistic, meritocratic and informal set of practices based on common sense.

In response to such critiques, one or more of three rather different positions seem to be adopted. The first is a reformed liberal approach based on pluralistic multicultural principles. This seeks to pay more attention to understanding and accepting the cultural background of ethnic-minority groups. It may include acceptance of cultural factors that constrain the range of opportunities. It might also, however, include training for careers advisers in avoiding cultural stereotypes, and strategies for recruiting careers advisers from ethnic-minority groups.

The second is a progressive approach based on active assimilation. This may include providing compensatory teaching for ethnic-minority groups in employability skills and/or knowledge of the labour market. It may also include providing access to positive role models, and extending the range of informal networks to which ethnic-minority individuals have access (Watts and Law, 1985).

The third is a more radical approach based on anti-racist principles. This seeks to develop a stronger critical understanding of the power relations underlying racism. It might include 'racism awareness training' for careers advisers, seeking to help them to confront their own latent racism, though this has sometimes alienated careers staff and been counter-productive in its effects. 'Anti-racist training', aimed more at organisational strategies for combating racism, has been suggested as being more fruitful in practical terms. This might include strategies for combating racist recruitment practices on the part of employers (Cross et al., 1990). At the level of guidance interventions, strategies might include examining within careers education programmes socio-political issues related to the opportunities open to ethnic minorities, and preparing ethnic-minority individuals to confront discrimination and racism (Watts and Law, 1985).

As in the case of gender, the choice of strategies in relation to ethnicity has to wrestle with complex issues related to identity as well as social context. This is particularly the case when there are tensions between attitudes and behaviours valued within the ethnic-minority subculture, and attitudes and behaviours required to achieve success within the white-dominated labour market. Liberal approaches tend to attach more importance to the former, and progressive approaches to the latter; attempts may be made to reconcile these by seeking to help ethnic-minority groups to become effectively bicultural. Radical approaches, by contrast, seek to address the tensions themselves within a broader critical analysis.

Conclusion

During most of this chapter, the four different approaches to careers education and guidance have been presented as alternatives. In these terms, each is vulnerable to attack.

The conservative approach, focused on social control, accepts and seeks to reinforce the social status quo. It thereby conserves existing inequalities which constrain opportunities for many individuals.

The liberal approach is in practice closely aligned with the conservative one. It tends to regret any inequalities, but its non-directive character means that it avoids confronting them.

The progressive approach, focused on individual change, seeks to alter the distribution of opportunities but not the opportunity structure itself. It therefore accepts the social status quo in a more direct way than the liberal approach does. On the other hand, it in some respects places more pressure on the opportunity structure by raising expectations which this structure may be unable to meet. This is a familiar feature of the 'diploma disease' (Dore, 1976): expectations of vocational advancement lead more individuals to apply for higher levels of education; this leads to an expansion of educational opportunities at a rate which exceeds the pace of change in the skill-mix of the economy; the result is frustration of the very vocational aspirations which have set the process in motion. This is likely to increase individual discontent: the objective degree of social inequality needs to be distinguished from the felt inequality, which is experienced only in relation to the reference groups with which those at the lower levels of the hierarchy compare themselves; the effect of raising aspirations is to extend these reference groups, thus increasing the sense of relative deprivation (Runciman, 1966). Moreover, because the progressive approach focuses on the individual without questioning the social context, the individual is left carrying the full weight of the deprivation.

The radical approach addresses the social causes of inequality and seeks to remedy them through social change. In its more extreme forms, it is prepared to increase individuals' sense of relative deprivation and alienation, on the grounds that this is necessary in order to achieve the level of social consciousness which will stimulate change. In this sense, it may be prepared to sacrifice immediate individual satisfaction in the interests of possible future social reform. This can be aligned to a dogmatism which views alternative viewpoints as 'false consciousness'. It also tends to be utopian in nature: if such utopias turn out to be chimerical, the individual sacrifice it has demanded will be in vain.

Such arguments are, however, based on narrow extrapolation to reductio ad absurdum extremes. In reality, no guidance intervention is likely to be sufficiently powerful to achieve the effects envisaged here. Moreover, most guidance interventions are likely to contain some mix of the approaches, particularly if they are to involve some negotiation with clients. Indeed, the earlier argument in relation to gender can be applied more broadly: elements of the progressive and radical approaches can help to rescue liberal approaches from their conservative inclinations, particularly for individuals and groups whose immediate access to genuine choices is limited; but in the end they need to be reconciled with the liberal approach if the autonomy of the individual is to be respected and supported. The appropriate mix is likely, however, to vary in different situations and with different clients. The professional task of the guidance practitioner is to identify what is morally and pragmatically appropriate in particular contexts. The discussion in this chapter may be helpful in thinking through the options and the issues involved.

12. The Implications of School-Leaver Unemployment for Careers Education in Schools[32]

> You know all that careers work we did at school. It's just a big waste of time. They never told us how to be unemployed. (County Durham school-leaver.) (Institute of Careers Officers, 1972).

> I hope we shall never 'educate for unemployment', which is a contradiction in terms and the sort of defeatist realism we can do without. (Headmaster, Newcastle upon Tyne.)

I wish at the outset to state clearly that I harbour no illusions that school-leaver unemployment is an educational problem. In my view it is basically an economic and political problem, and any adequate response to it must be economic and political in nature. Nonetheless, if school-leaver unemployment is not an educational problem, it is a problem for education. It is with the problems it poses for careers education in particular, and with possible ways in which such problems might be confronted, that this report is primarily concerned. It is based on a study supported by a grant from the Inner London Education Authority, whose help is gratefully acknowledged.

The scale of school-leaver unemployment

The basic facts can be presented briefly. In July 1977, over 708,000 young people aged under 25 were registered as being out of work in Britain. Of these, 242,000 were school-leavers, representing over one-third of the summer's leavers. The remaining 466,000 were young people who had either been unemployed for some time, or – having found a job – had quickly become unemployed again (Department of Employment, 1977). Admittedly the median duration of unemployment for young people aged under 18 is lower than that for other age groups, but it is now well over 10 weeks (MSC, 1977a), and significant proportions, of course, remain unemployed for much longer. Moreover, all of these figures relate only to those who are registered as unemployed, and clearly underestimate the full extent of youth unemployment (Phillips, 1973).

To some extent the high level of school-leaver unemployment is just one facet of the high level of general unemployment. This seems to be becoming a cyclical phenomenon, corresponding to the economic cycle. Three crucially important points need, however, to be noted. First, the cyclical character of general unemployment

---

32 Editorial footnote: Reprinted, by permission of the publisher, from *Journal of Curriculum Studies*, Volume 10 No. 3, September 1978. DOI: 10.1080/0022027780100305.

conceals an underlying upward trend: in each recession since 1961, the peak of unemployment has tended to be higher than in previous ones; and each recovery period has tended to have a low point of unemployment higher than in the previous recovery (see Department of Employment, 1977). Second, a significant deterioration is taking place in the relative unemployment rates of young people: whereas in 1966 the unemployment rate for males aged under 20 was lower than for all males, by 1975 it was over twice as high (Metcalf, 1976) (for a good analysis of the reasons for this trend, see British Youth Council, 1977). Third, the number of school-leavers is currently shooting up: present projections indicate that whereas there were 816,000 school-leavers in 1975/76, there will be over 900,000 in 1980/81 (though the figure will decline thereafter) (MSC, 1976). It seems unlikely, therefore, that the problem of school-leaver unemployment will diminish significantly over the next few years, however successful Britain's economic policies may be: a more likely possibility is that it will assume even larger dimensions.

The demoralising effects of prolonged unemployment have been exhaustively documented by a variety of studies (e.g. Marsden (1975); for a useful summary see Harrison (1976)). It is traumatic and destructive enough for adults, who have already achieved a work role identity, and who – because of their life experience and knowledge – may find it possible to see unemployment as a social rather than a personal problem. School-leavers however have no such identity or experience to sustain them, and their resulting sense of rejection and worthlessness may well reinforce negative self-images which have already been established at school. The young people who are most vulnerable to unemployment are those who have already experienced 'failure' against the criteria of schools (National Youth Employment Council, 1974). Such young people often look forward with anticipation to the freedom and independence that work will provide. When this is not forthcoming, their self-confidence takes a further blow: they have 'failed' again (Ashton & Field, 1976). The social implications of such discouragement are considerable. The Manpower Services Commission (1976) has indeed declared its fear that the failure of young people to get a job may permanently alienate them from the world of work and from society. Not only does this bode ill for the future productivity of the country's potential labour force, but it is also likely to cause high levels of crime and social unrest, especially since youth unemployment tends to be disproportionately concentrated among ethnic minorities in the inner cities (British Youth Council, 1976).

To alleviate these problems, and following the work of the Holland Report (MSC, 1977a), the Government has consolidated and considerably enlarged its programmes of temporary alternatives to unemployment: notably, courses to prepare young people for work, and work-experience schemes of various kinds. It had been hoped in some quarters that these programmes would be expanded to the point where they could form a Youth Opportunity Guarantee, ensuring that all young people would be offered a choice between a range of education, training, employment, and community work options (e.g. National Youth Bureau, 1977; Watts, 1977b). In the event, however, the Government has decided that places on the new programmes will normally be available only to those who have been unemployed for at least six weeks since leaving school (MSC, 1977b). Moreover, there is no guarantee that those who have completed particular schemes within the programme will not then return to the dole. It seems clear therefore that for large numbers of school-leavers over the next few years, unemployment is likely to be an experience they will face on leaving school, and probably indeed at several future stages in their lives.

Unemployment and careers education

This being so, the question arises of whether schools have some responsibility to prepare students for the possibility of being unemployed. An emerging area of the school curriculum for which this is a particularly pressing issue is careers education, which – according to the most recently available survey – appears in one form or another on the curriculum of about 70 per cent of secondary schools (DES, 1973), though it is often poorly implemented (see chapter 5). Careers education tends at present to be focused around the concept of occupational decision-making: helping students to become more aware of their own attributes, and of the various occupations open to them, so that they can make an appropriate choice of employment. Accordingly, the existence of high levels of school-leaver unemployment is liable to undermine what commitment there may be to careers education as an activity within the school. Moreover, if in a school situated in an area of substantial school-leaver unemployment the careers education programme ignores the issue, proceeding on the assumption that opportunities suited to each student's capacities and interests will be available, it will have failed to prepare the students for the immediate realities that may well face them – which presumably is one of its prime aims. Such a programme is also likely to lose all credibility in the eyes of students. Their suspicion that it is 'just another lesson' – as divorced as most of the others from the world they experience outside school – will be confirmed.

Despite all this, our experience suggests that few schools have attempted to deal seriously with the issue of unemployment in their careers education programmes. In an inner-city school studied by Law and Watts (1977), for example, the transition from the careers education programme to the harsh realities represented by the careers officer was felt by students to be almost as abrupt, and as bewildering, as the transition from school to 'work'. Again, at a meeting of representatives of four I.L.E.A. schools which had been specially selected by the local Careers Guidance Inspector for the quality of their careers education programmes and their location in areas of relatively high school-leaver unemployment, it was found that none had paid any significant curricular attention to unemployment.

From our discussions and observations, it would seem that this situation might be due to a number of reasons. The first is that teachers feel they do not have the first-hand experience or the competence to tackle it effectively. This feeling is not of course confined to the issue of unemployment, but it is given added weight by the second factor, which is teachers' tacit awareness of the highly political and highly emotional nature of the issue. A third and more directly educational reason is teachers' fear that raising the issue of unemployment may lead to students questioning not only the work ethic in the wider society but also the work ethic within the school. The two ethics are clearly aligned by the implicit (and often explicit) assurance that 'if you work hard, you'll get a job'. To question the validity of this assurance is to call into question the value of examination qualifications and thus to challenge many of the basic assumptions on which the legitimation of the school's activities are based (Law and Watts, 1977).

A fourth and final reason for teachers' reluctance to tackle the issue of unemployment is their instinctive hostility to the concept of 'preparation for unemployment'. They suspect that this implies conditioning a particular group of students to accept unemployment as inevitable, and they are concerned both about the implications of labelling a particular group in this way, and about the danger that it may lead to these students believing themselves to be 'unemployable' (see Chambers & Engel, 1976). They may also point out, cynically, that the students to whom a programme of unemployment might be most relevant are those who are most likely to be absent from school, truanting.

The latter set of arguments are essentially ranged against a particular kind of programme on unemployment, not against the idea of covering unemployment as such. It is highly arguable, for example, that unemployment should not be treated separately from other aspects of careers education, but rather that the latter should be broadened to cover family, community, and leisure roles – including 'unemployed' roles (see Watts and Herr, 1976). Under such a conception, unemployment would be included for all students as an integral part of the programme, recognising that for all of them, unemployment may be an option – or an imposition – at some stage during their lives. In other words the aim would not be preparation for unemployment, but preparation for adult roles in a society in which paid employment might not always be available. The underlying issue of the extent to which the curriculum is concerned with adapting students to the situation they face, or with one of a variety of alternative possible aims, remains an open question – and one to which I shall return shortly.

In my view, a school in the current economic climate which avoids giving unemployment any curricular attention is abdicating one of its most important responsibilities: that of preparing students for their transition to the outside world. This argument is particularly compelling if the school is situated in an area of substantial school-leaver unemployment. Schools tend to be insulated institutions – self-validating, self-perpetuating, and unable to respond readily to the changing nature of society (Rubber and Plastics Processing Industry Training Board, 1976). It may be tempting for them to think that they can best serve the interests of their students by maximising their educational qualifications and, thereby, their chances of getting a job, and to think that recognising the existence of unemployment may vitiate this by sapping students' motivation. Such a policy would, however, be short-sighted. Concentrating solely on the rules of a race, which some must lose, does nothing to serve the interests of the losers: it accentuates their sense of failure, and also their sense of alienation when – even if they have worked hard as their teachers recommended – they still fail to get a job.

At the same time, it is important to recognise that for a school to confront the issue of unemployment without adequate preparation and thought could potentially have a very negative and demoralising effect. Timing is critically important here: the issue should ideally be introduced at a time when it seems real, but not yet too immediate to make it difficult to create a learning situation. Equally important is clarity about aims and objectives. The next section of this paper will accordingly be concerned with examining the aims and objectives which could be pursued.

What schools can do

As a first step, we analysed the main careers education curriculum materials which pay significant attention to the issue of unemployment.[33] On the basis of this analysis, and of our discussions with teachers who have attempted to cover the issue in schools or in colleges of further education, we have identified, in table 1, seven possible curricular objectives related to unemployment. As will be seen, they cover a wide area, and provide the basis for a not insubstantial programme. Many of them are not exclusively related to the issue of unemployment, and – as has already been implied – we are not suggesting that they should be exclusively covered in the light of that issue. All, however, represent direct responses to the possibility that students may face being unemployed on leaving school.

A basic problem underlying the implementation of many of these objectives is how to make their content seem real to the students. It is important that the treatment should be as experience-based and action-oriented as possible: for example, it would be useful to try to incorporate some direct contact, preferably away from the school premises, with school leavers from the previous year who are currently

---

33 This analysis was prepared in conjuction with A. D. Crowley, whose help here and in other parts of the project is gratefully acknowledged.

unemployed. In some cases, the implications of an experience-based approach for the educational process are considerable. For instance a serious attempt to teach students the skills of managing the use of their own time (objective V(d)) might require structuring at least part of the school curriculum so as to give them experience in implementing plans for using their own time in a self-fulfilling way. Many schools design their curriculum in a form which essentially prepares students to submit to the kind of externally-structured environment characteristic of the work-place: in doing so, it deskills them in terms of their ability to use negotiable time effectively (Besug, 1975).

Figure 27: Some possible curricular objectives relating to the issue of unemployment

Objectives	
I	**Employability skills. To equip students with skills which will increase their chances of finding and keeping a job:** a) Employable skills which may not have been developed in the basic curriculum (social skills, etc.). b) Job search skills c) Job acquisition skills (interview techniques, application forms etc.). d) Job retention skills. e) Skills of foreseeing forces which may affect prospects in particular kind of employment.
II	**Adaptability awareness. To extend the range of employment opportunities which students feel are possible for them:** a) Awareness of jobs other than those which are immediately attractive. b) Awareness of possibility of travelling to work or living away from home, and relevant skill training (how to ride cheap mechanised transport etc.).
III	**Survival skills. To equip students with the knowledge and skills they will need to survive if they are unemployed:** a) Knowledge of unemployment benefits and supplementary allowances. b) Knowledge of redundancy rights. c) Knowledge of welfare rights in general. d) Skills of claiming rights. e) Skills of handling a limited budget. f) Awareness of local possibilities for 'fiddling' (e.g. 'illegal' part-time jobs), and of its possible consequences. g) Awareness of psychological effect of being unemployed, and skills for coping with it. h) Awareness of social pressures on the unemployed, and skills for coping with them. i) Knowledge of after-care and support services in the community.

	Objectives
IV	Contextual awareness. To help students to determine the extent to which the responsibility for being unemployed lies with society rather than with the individual: a) Awareness of possible alienating effects of work. b) Awareness of effects of technological change. c) Awareness of possible economic and political solutions to unemployment. d) Awareness of possible alternative patterns of work and leisure.
V	Leisure skills. To equip students with knowledge and skills which will help them to make good use of their increased 'leisure' time while they are unemployed: a) Knowledge of possible leisure activities and local leisure activities. b) Knowledge of local Youth Service activities for unemployed young people. c) Knowledge of local possibilities for voluntary community work. d) Skills of managing use of own time.
VI	Alternative opportunity awareness. To make students aware of official alternatives to employment and unemployment: a) Knowledge of courses in further education, in skillcentres, etc. b) Knowledge of the Government's Work Experience Programme, Community Industry etc.
VII	Opportunity creation skills. To equip students with the knowledge and skills they need to be able to create their own employment: a) Knowledge of job-sharing possibilities and procedures. b) Knowledge of self-employment possibilities (window-cleaning, etc.). and of legal and social security problems involved. c) Awareness of alternative, self-sustaining life-styles (communes, etc.). d) Skills of thinking about work in a proactive rather than a reactive way.

An overarching element common to several of the objectives is self-confidence. For example, it is important that students should not only know about the benefits and rights available to them if they become unemployed (objectives III (a)-(c)), but should also have the confidence to claim them. Again, self-confidence is an important component of job search and job acquisition skills (objectives I (b)-(c)). Furthermore, if students are to be able to make good use of their increased 'leisure' time while they are unemployed (objective V), they need to have a strong enough self-image to resist the corrosive effects of unemployment on energy and motivation. Building up such self-confidence is a difficult enough task: equally important, however, is the task of designing strategies for sustaining it. The understanding that the responsibility for being unemployed does not necessarily lie with the individual (objective IV) is important here.

So too is recognising the importance of forming a reference group of young people in a similar situation, as a source of support. Ashton (1975) has suggested that where the experience of unemployment is shared by a group of young people who have access to a set of beliefs that explains their situation and supports their self-image, the psychological consequences of prolonged unemployment may be less damaging.

There are, however, conflicts here. The notion of societal responsibility for unemployment, and the building-up of alternative group identities, can easily provide the basis for a delinquent subculture in conflict with the dominant norms of society: many teachers would find such a consequence unpalatable. Even the more modest objective of presenting the positive possibilities of being unemployed (objective V) is difficult in a society which seems to have a strong need to believe that life on the dole is characterised by suffering and misery. That it is so characterised has been convincingly documented by, for instance, Marsden (1975), who states clearly that for those interviewed, talk about the 'opportunity' or 'leisure' afforded by unemployment seemed decidedly premature. The strength of the social pressures to sustain this situation are demonstrated by, for example, the way in which unemployed people who are able to present a more positive self-image are persistently presented by the press for public obloquy as 'scroungers'. In view of this, teachers attempting to pursue objective V may be doubly constrained by the feeling that they are presenting possibilities which may not exist, and whose feasibility society is in any case unwilling to acknowledge. Focusing on socially approved and socially useful roles outside employment – e.g. voluntary work – may be the most generally acceptable approach, but clearly the presentation of alternative social identities, based on positive role-models, is highly problematic. The basic issues here are whether the teacher should model or should question society's attitudes to the unemployed, and whether – even if the latter course is desirable – it is also feasible in view of the strength of the pressures against which the teacher is working.

The objectives which are probably most consonant with current social attitudes to the unemployed are objectives I and II: to equip students with skills which will increase their chances of finding and keeping a job, and to extend the range of employment opportunities which students feel are possible for them. Certainly there is a strong argument for the former in particular to be part of a curriculum programme designed to confront the issue of unemployment, because employability skills become more and more important at times when unemployment is high. It is, however, important to recognise that the advantages such skills offer are essentially relative rather than absolute: their effects are not by and large to increase the number of jobs, but rather to influence the way in which the jobs that exist are distributed. Thus, if all schools focus heavily on the development of these skills, the advantages potentially offered by such a programme may, to some extent, be cancelled out. This is not an argument for neglecting objective I: compensatory training in the skills is for example necessary to equalise the employment chances of different groups of young people – without it, certain ethnic and other groups are likely to be even more severely disadvantaged in the job hunt than they would be otherwise; moreover, it may help to increase the employment chances of young people as against adults in competition for the same jobs. But it is important to recognise that it is no panacea. Furthermore, exclusive focus on job-finding and job-keeping can easily sustain the myth that there are satisfying jobs available to anyone who has the skills and persistence to find them. Such a belief conveniently defines unemployment as being due to individual inadequacy, and thus distracts attention from society's responsibilities. It also means that when, despite all his efforts, the young person still fails to find a job, the effects on his morale and self-respect are likely to be much more destructive. As Orwell (1937: 76) commented when he first saw unemployment at close quarters: 'The thing that horrified and amazed me was to find that many of them were ashamed of being unemployed'.

Aims

It seems clear, therefore, that in designing a curriculum programme relating to the issue of unemployment, careful attention needs to be paid to the overall aims of such a programme. Watts and Herr (1976) have suggested that careers education as a whole could have any of four very different socio-political functions.[34] The first is as an agent of social control, adapting individuals to the career opportunities which realistically are open to them. The second is as an agent of social change, making students aware of deficiencies in the employment system and of how they can help to change it. The third is as an agent of individual change, accepting the social system as it is and aiming to maximise the chances of individual students within it. And the fourth is non-directive, making students aware of the full range of opportunities and helping them to be more autonomous in choosing the alternatives suited to their own needs and preferences.

These approaches can be distinguished along two dimensions: one concerned with whether the primary focus is on society or on individuals; the other with whether the approach basically accepts the status quo or is concerned with changing it in prescribed directions. Although in figure 28 each is represented as being divided into two discrete categories, for practical reasons they are perhaps better regarded as continua: the designers of a careers education programme will inevitably find a place somewhere within the two-dimensional space represented by the continua.

The same is true in figure 29, where possible aims related to the issue of

---

34 Editorial footnote. This model was later reworked in "Socio-political ideologies in guidance" (see chapter 11).

unemployment have been elaborated for each of these four approaches. They are not as mutually exclusive as the figure suggests: nonetheless, the tensions between them will become evident when attempts are made to reconcile them. The objectives have simply been assigned to the aim with which they seem to be most directly linked. Some of the assignments are disputable: I have already suggested, for example, that objective I has a clear social-control function, though in my judgement this is subsidiary to its individual-change function of maximising students' chances of finding meaningful 'employment'; the converse could be argued in relation to objective II. The implication of the analysis, however, is that as objectives more directly linked to other aims are added, the overall stance being taken moves closer to the central parts of the figure. It is important that the assumptions and values implied by such decisions be explicitly recognised and accepted.

Figure 28: Four alternative approaches to careers education

	Focusing on society	Focusing on individuals
Change	Social-change approach	Individual-change approach
Status quo	Social-control approach	Non-directive approach

Figure 29: Four alternative curricular aims relating to the issue of unemployment[35]

	Focusing on society	Focusing on individuals
Change	Social-change approach To help students to see unemployment as a social phenomenon which can only be resolved by political and social change (objective IV).	Individual-change approach To maximise students' chances of finding meaningful employment (objectives I, VI and VII).
Status quo	Social-control approach To reinforce students' motivation to seek work, and to make them feel that unemployment is a result of personal inadequacy (objective II).	Non-directive approach To make students aware of the possibility of unemployment, and to help them to determine how they might cope with it and use it positively (objectives III and V).

The choice of aims and objectives will obviously depend a great deal on the personal values of the teacher concerned. Certainly I believe that before teachers launch

[35] The objectives referred to are those listed in figure 27.

into the topic of unemployment, they should be very clear about their own values, about the values on which their programme is to be based, and about how any discrepancies between these two sets of values are to be handled. For example, a teacher who basically believes that the unemployed are layabouts may have difficulty in attempting to follow a 'non-directive' aim. One 'litmus paper' indicator of one's values in this respect might be whether one believes that unemployed people should always accept a job offered to them – whatever that job may be – rather than 'live off the state'. Another might be one's attitude to 'fiddling' (see Marsden, 1975).

The longer term: explanations, responses and strategies

I have suggested that a crucial question to be decided when covering the issue of unemployment is whether the primary focus is to be on societal needs or on individual needs. I suspect that for many teachers the primary concern will be individual needs. While having some sympathy with this view, I accept also that any aim, however focused on individual needs, will imply some set of assumptions about the future role of work in society. My concern is that such assumptions are too often implicit and untested. To stimulate more thought on this issue, I feel it might be useful in the final section of this paper to offer my own analysis. I do so with some timidity: the issues with which it is concerned are large and complex. I hope however that it may provide a fruitful stimulus to debate.

There are basically three explanations of the currently high level of unemployment. The first is that it is 'voluntary' – in other words, that it is due to the erosion of the wish to work. The second is that it is cyclical, corresponding to the economic cycle of recession and recovery. And the third is that it is structural, reflecting a major shift in the relationship between capital and labour, which has resulted from technological innovation and from management practices designed to improve productivity and reduce unit labour costs.

Each of these three explanations suggest different educational responses. If the problem is seen as one of 'voluntary' unemployment, the task of careers education might be seen as being that of reinforcing the work ethic, or alternatively it might be seen as strengthening and articulating this questioning process, on the grounds that it reflects a valid questioning of work that is not fit for people to do. If unemployment is seen as a purely cyclical phenomenon, reinforcing the work ethic is again important, ensuring that the work force is there to maximise expansion during the upward swing of the economy: attention is also however needed to help people to cope with what may be recurrent phases of unemployment throughout their lives. Finally, if unemployment is seen as a more long-term structural problem – and pending any political and economic solutions to it – attention shifts to equipping at least some people to cope with the long-term effects of being unemployed: in this respect, reinforcing the work ethic for all school-leavers could be positively dysfunctional since it may raise expectations that are not capable of being fulfilled.

Of the three explanations, it seems clear that the voluntary unemployment thesis has little substance. Of all the myths of the Welfare State, stories of the work-shy and scroungers have been the most persistent, yet the least well-founded on evidence (Marsden, 1975). In a study of the available data, Mukherjee (1974) firmly dismisses it as being in any sense a substantial explanation for the high rate of joblessness. He also rejects the cyclical theory as an adequate explanation of what is happening, in the light of the underlying upward trend in unemployment rates described earlier. It would seem therefore that the problem is, at least in part, a structural one.

At a political and economic level, the responses to this problem seem so far to have been locked into three kinds of approach. The first is that of hoping it will be solved at a macroeconomic level by stimulating the economy, so increasing the demand for 'real' jobs. Seeing training as a solution is, in effect, based on this approach, since it assumes that there will be jobs at the end: if there are not, such training could easily prove socially counter-productive, increasing disillusionment. The approach is based in essence on a cyclical interpretation of unemployment trends, and seems certainly to have been the dominant theme of government policies to date. The major objective of the Government's measures following the Holland Report, for example, is to help unemployed young people to gain permanent employment as soon as possible (MSC, 1977a). Yet the Holland Report, itself, quoted the view of the National Institute for Economic and Social Research that to return to full employment would require an annual growth rate over five years of nearly five per cent, and also pointed out a number of other factors that might prevent such an outcome even in the unlikely event of such a growth rate being achieved: for example, the existing spare capacity in the economy, and the effects of basic changes in the occupational structure. Moreover, in the medium and long term there must be serious misgivings about both the feasibility and the desirability of continued economic growth, particularly bearing in mind the awesome multiplicative power of compound interest (see, for example, Mishan, 1977; Hirsch, 1977).

A second approach has been that of job maintenance, as reflected in such measures as the Temporary Employment Subsidy (see British Youth Council, 1977) and the investment of public money in Chrysler UK (see Young and Hood, 1977). Such an approach respects the social relationships and social ties which may have been formed around workplaces, but in a broader perspective clearly may make neither social nor economic sense. The Chrysler saga, for example, arguably involved maintaining classically alienating production-line jobs to produce environment-polluting cars for which there was inadequate market demand. Similarly, Chanan (1976/1977) recounts the successful efforts of a group of shop stewards in the aerospace industry to defend themselves against threats of redundancy, and points out how they were disturbed by the realisation that their struggle to stay in work had entailed a struggle for society to continue making products which, in their own wider judgement, were anti-social. A policy of job maintenance clearly has to pay some attention to defining the social and economic ends which are being sought.

A third approach, which is subject to the same caveats, is that of job creation. Such measures have so far been tentative, because of the fears of creating inflationary pressures and distorting market forces, and also because of the high public expenditure costs which are seemingly involved. But the latter need to be set against the savings in unemployment benefits, and the social security contributions and taxes that are generated, when a person ceases to be jobless and becomes employed: Mukherjee (1976) has calculated if the government paid a rate up to 90 per cent of the average earnings of industrial workers in order to enable people to work rather than be unemployed, this would lead not to an increase but to a reduction of the budget deficit. And this takes no account of the benefits of their output, or of likely savings in public expenditure for dealing with the pathological effects of unemployment – crime, delinquency, mental illness etc. (for an interesting American analysis of these indirect costs, see Brenner, 1977). Moreover, the view that high wage rates and inflation are a direct function of the overall level of unemployment is being called increasingly into question (Lutz et al., 1976). The ironical feature of the Government's job creation policies to date is that they have proceeded side-by-side with severe cuts in spending on public services, based on the arguments of economists like Bacon and Eltis (1976) that one of the causes of Britain's economic problems has been that too many workers have been leaving 'productive' jobs and moving into 'non-productive' jobs. The implication that economic growth has been held back by labour shortages seems highly questionable, to say the least.

Mukherjee's (1974) proposals for dealing with unemployment are based on an adaptation of dual-labour market theory. This theory distinguishes between a primary labour market characterised by training, promotion opportunities, security, and protection from competition, and a secondary labour market where recruitment, training etc. are controlled directly by relatively unconstrained economic forces (see Doeringer & Piore, 1971; Bosanquet & Doeringer, 1973). Mukherjee suggests that the two sectors can be defined in age terms, and that what is needed is training for the unemployed in the primary or 'inner' labour market (i.e. males aged 24-55), and job creation for those in the secondary or 'outer' labour market (i.e. males aged 16-24 or 55-64).

Mukherjee, however, virtually totally ignored women. This is critically important, because women have increasingly been exerting pressure to enter the labour force and to have the same pay and opportunities as men. This derives largely from the recognition that work is the main source of status and identity in our society, as well as a major determinant of income. Such recognition has also been advanced as an important cause of the problems experienced by other groups excluded from the labour force: it has, for instance, been argued that a significant cause of student unrest over the last ten years has been the student's lack of an accepted social role (e.g. Hatch, 1972; Silver, 1965), and the same kind of explanation has been given for the distress and anomie experienced by many old people once they retire (e.g. Burgess, 1960).

All of these groups depend for their income on benefits made available to them by the state (or, in the case of women, by husbands) and feel that they lack a respected role. The prevailing ideology of social equality means that they are no longer as content to accept low-status and dependent positions. Yet these pressures on the labour force are occurring at a time when, as we have seen, there are strong forces tending to reduce its size. Labour tends still to be regarded narrowly as a cost, and in these terms is becoming steadily less cost-effective as compared with automated methods. In order to sustain a competitive position in international markets, the current ethos is accordingly concerned with using fewer people to do the same, rather than using more people to improve standards of service and performance. In this situation, the future validity of a narrowly based work ethic becomes highly questionable. Such an ethic may be healthy and necessary in a society which 'needs' as many of its members as possible to be engaged in economic production. But in a society where this is not the case, it will raise expectations which society is not able to meet, and thus produce individual distress and social unrest.

The implication seems clear. If society is to maintain an ideology of social equality, it has to choose between two courses. One possibility is to recognise labour not just as a cost but as intrinsically valuable (or potentially so) for the people who perform it (see e.g. Schumacher, 1973). The implication of this is that the right to work would be recognised, and jobs would have to be created to implement it. Such provision might be made easier by work-sharing schemes or banning overtime[36] (see e.g. British Youth Council, 1977), but in principle the opportunities for service work are virtually unlimited, and a positive effort might also be made to stimulate labour-intensive industries (British Youth Council, 1977). This approach, however, has considerable implications not only for job creation but also for job design. It suggests that in creating employment, attention should be paid not only to the product of the work but also to the needs of the worker: in other words, the extent to which the work allows people to use and develop their individual interests, skills and values. It may also mean giving employment status to functions which are not given such status at present – for example, child-rearing and homemaking (O'Toole et al., 1973). The definition of work might become 'an activity that produces something of value for

---

[36] Cox and Golden (1977) have argued that so much overtime is worked in industry that to ban it would almost eliminate unemployment (within the labour market as currently defined).

other people' (O'Toole et al., 1973: 3): this would allow society to circumscribe the content of at least part of the lives of its members, though within these boundaries considerable freedom of choice could be offered.

The second, alternative approach is to define work as being a necessary evil concerned with the performance of tasks necessary to meet the basic needs of society. Since structural changes in industry mean that the efforts of a decreasing proportion of the adult population are required for this purpose, ways would need to be found of enabling some people to achieve social status and self esteem without being dependent on paid employment. This could be done by allowing people the option of choosing whether to work or whether to have total control over what to do with their time. To avoid labelling particular groups as dependent and inferior, it would be important that this be their choice, rather than imposed on them as a result of (for example) their age: to this extent, proposals for raising the age of entry into the worker role, or for reducing the age of retirement, would seem to be dangerously rigid and retrogressive. It would also be important to devise means of distributing resources which would not stigmatise those outside paid employment. Theobald (1963), for instance, suggested the principle of Basic Economic Security, which would establish an 'economic floor' under each member of society without any connotation of personal inadequacy or any implication that an undeserved income was being received from an over-generous government.

The choice between these two alternatives basically revolves around the importance that is attached to work as 'the major point of connection between the individual's creative energies and the purposes and policies of the whole society' (Chanan, 1976/1977). The first course regards this as important; the second does not. As a compromise, Galbraith has suggested that the way should be open for the individual who wishes to satisfy his needs for food, clothing and simple houseroom with 10 to 20 hours of labour a week to do so. An alternative compromise suggested by Rehn (1974) would allow individuals much greater freedom to diversify and vary the balance of their working lives, and would use this as the means of undertaking adjustments in the labour market, rather than using the most vulnerable and least adaptable for this purpose.

Of course, Britain is not an economic island, and under all these approaches incentives would still be needed to attract people to work in the wealth-generating parts of the economy and to perform the tasks without which society cannot function. Such jobs would increasingly command higher salaries than those jobs which were less necessary to society and more self-actualising to their occupants (the changing relative income position of miners over the last 20 years is a sign that this may already be happening). But society already has considerable discretion over the types of job it can make available without affecting its productivity (Levitan & Johnston, 1973). It now needs to release itself from the behaviour determining hold of concepts of work which it no longer requires and indeed can no longer fulfil. As Bertrand Russell (1935: 19) argued many years ago: 'Only a foolish asceticism, usually vicarious, makes us continue to insist on work in excessive quantities now that the need no longer exists'.

Educational implications

If society has the courage to move towards either of the scenarios sketched above, the implications for education in general – and for careers education in particular – are profound. In relation to the second scenario, for example, Theobald (1963) recognises that 'the right to a due-income would allow the individual to make his own decisions and the income would be adequate to allow him to pursue his own interests': accordingly, he argues that 'the discovery of the proper uses of freedom is a fundamental task of the remainder of the twentieth century'. Even if society takes the alternative step and moves towards extending the concepts of employment to provide more work for more people, it should allow people more autonomy over what they do: not only can it afford to do so, but it arguably needs to do so if the self-actualising potential of work is to be realised.

Both of these approaches suggest that a prime task of education will be to equip students with the skills, concepts and information they need to be able to define who they are, who they want to be, and what community needs they can help to meet. This will need to be a recurrent activity: in other words, people will return to educational institutions periodically through their lives to reorientate themselves as well as to acquire additional skills which they need in order to perform new roles. Careers education will become a central activity in a system of recurrent education, and will now be able legitimately to be based on the concept of vocational choice as a means of self-actualisation (an approach which at present is frequently attacked as being unrealistic for a large sector of the population – see, for example, Roberts, 1977). Rather than being concerned with slotting people into the pre-created jobs that exist (or do not exist) for them, it will be able to encourage and equip people, if necessary, to create their own work.

Such ideas, of course, require major social and political changes before they are converted into realities. In the meantime, the extent to which designers of careers education programmes can afford to take cognisance of them is open to question. On the one hand, schools clearly have a responsibility to prepare students for the realities of the world into which they are going to move once they leave. On the other hand, students leaving school at the minimum leaving age in 1978 will still be under 40 by the year 2000, when some of the changes we have described may have happened. Moreover, if the concept of democracy means anything, schools arguably have at least some responsibility to help students develop the ideas of the kind of society they would like to create. Furthermore, there is a danger in off-loading responsibility and waiting for government action: if the problem is structural, then structural change must come – at least in part – from the grass roots.

This suggests that careers education programmes might pay more attention than they often do at present to the concept of self-actualisation, recognising that it may often be attainable not in work roles, but in family, leisure or community roles, with work providing the instrumental means to implementing the individual's non-work aspirations. In other words, careers education could be focused around the concept of what Dubin (1956) has called 'central life-interests'. Loughary and Ripley (1974) for example have drawn a distinction between 'job' (what one does to survive), 'vocation' (one's most important activities) and 'leisure' (what one does for fun and relaxation), recognising that 'vocation' may spill over into either 'job' or 'leisure', or in both. Perhaps the central concern of careers education should be not 'job' but 'vocation'?

In addition, there would seem to be a strong argument for the government measures being developed for school-leavers to incorporate some experimental proactive approaches which would encourage young people to develop their own projects, as was done with the Local Initiatives Programme in Canada (see Mukherjee, 1974): for example, funding young artists and sportsmen, or providing phasing-out grants and advisory and training support for self-enterprise co-operatives, or supporting job creation projects focused on community needs but devised by groups of young people themselves. If this was done, it might be possible for experimental projects of this kind to be integrated with careers education programmes during the final year of school, the programmes being designed to help the students formulate the projects for which they would seek support. Objective VII in table 1 was designed to encourage such an approach. If taken seriously, it could provide an exciting response to the immediate problems of unemployment, which might help to pave the way for the society of the future.

13. The Impact of the 'New Right': Policy Challenges Confronting Careers Guidance in England and Wales[37]

Careers guidance services in England and Wales have hitherto been conceived largely as part of public social-welfare provision. Most are funded by government, whether central or local, and whether directly or through an educational institution. They are, therefore, potentially or actually, instruments of public policy. Yet most view their primary clients as being the individuals with whom they are working. Professional associations and a professional literature have been developed to affirm this as their key operating principle.

The last few years have seen some tensions between the public-policy and the professional roles of guidance services. These have been linked to the growing influence of 'New Right' ideology, particularly under the Prime Ministership of Margaret Thatcher between 1979 and 1990. The 'New Right' is suspicious of the welfare state and is concerned to establish market principles for public activities. It is also suspicious of the 'new class' which staffs the welfare state, and of professional self-interest in general. It thus potentially poses major challenges (and threats) to existing guidance services and practices.

In this paper I will attempt to analyse these issues in more depth. I will first briefly outline the historical evolution and structure of careers guidance services in England and Wales. Next I will explore the relationship between guidance and public policy. I will then identify some of the main strands of 'New Right' thinking and will examine some of the ways in which they have had an impact on guidance policy. Finally, I will discuss the extent to which 'New Right' ideology is congruent with guidance philosophy and practice.

Origins and structure of guidance services

The origins of careers services in Britain stem from the twentieth century, when several public and private labour-market bureaux were in intermittent operation, run by Local Authorities and charitable organisations. These early services were characterised in part by concern for individual welfare, and in part by the growing recognition of classical economists that government intervention was necessary

---

37 Editorial footnote: Reprinted, by permission of the publisher, from *British Journal of Guidance and Counselling*, Volume 19 No. 3, September 1991. DOI: 10.1080/03069889108260388.

to help the labour market work more effectively (Heginbotham, 1951; Bradley, 1990). They were gradually formalised into a Juvenile Employment Service, which in 1948 became the Youth Employment Service and in 1973 the Careers Service. Although the structure of the service has gone through a number of changes, it has traditionally rested on a 'system of checks and balances' (Roberts, 1971). Since 1973 this has involved authority being distributed between the Local Education Authorities (which have administered the service) and the Department of Employment (which has provided guidance of a general nature and has inspected the service); this has represented a balance between both education and employment interests, and between local and national interests.

The traditional main concern of the Careers Service has been young school-leavers. In addition, many schools have appointed careers teachers within the school to provide guidance to their pupils. Daws (1972) locates the origins of this role between 1926 and 1932, and identifies its original basis as being to help people to find suitable employment. The role has developed considerably with the emergence of careers education programmes within schools. Such programmes often involve other teachers too, including tutors and subject teachers. The nature of these roles and their guidance responsibilities have been largely defined by individual schools.

Other educational institutions, too, have developed careers services of their own. The universities, for example, set up appointments boards – 'generally organised with an eye to the employment of graduates in business, though other occupations were not entirely neglected' (UGC, 1964, p.3). The first such board was set up at Oxford in 1892; the other universities gradually followed over the next 60 years or so. In the 1960s and 1970s these boards were converted, in function and then in title, into careers advisory services concerned not only with placement but with a wider range of guidance functions. Many polytechnics and colleges of higher education also established services of this kind.

A further development in the late 1960s and 1970s was the emergence of guidance services for adults. In 1966 the Government established an Occupational Guidance Service, which by 1978 was based in 49 centres and saw around 54,000 clients a year (MSC, 1978). In addition, a number of educational guidance services for adults were set up. Originating with the setting up of a service in Belfast in 1967, these services grew despite the fact that they were usually funded from a variety of sources, often on a short-term, and therefore vulnerable, basis. Such services have been concerned to improve the match between the learning needs and wishes of adults and the learning opportunities available to them, both through guidance to individuals and through feedback on their learning needs to providers (ACACE, 1979).

Finally, some careers guidance services have grown up in the private sector. The MSC (1978) estimated that fee-charging agencies saw about 10,000 clients a year, three-quarters of these being seen by two particular agencies.

In general, however, the vast majority of guidance services have been funded by public authorities and have been free to clients. They have clearly therefore been viewed in social welfare terms. At the same time, guidance practitioners formed themselves into professional associations, which by the late 1970s included the Institute of Careers Officers, the National Association of Careers and Guidance Teachers, and the Association of Graduate Careers Advisory Services (a later addition has been the National Association of Educational Guidance Services, subsequently retitled the National Association for Educational Guidance for Adults). Their functions have included promoting the status and interests of the nascent guidance profession, facilitating communication and co-operation between their members, and supporting professional development.

Although, as we have seen, the origins of careers guidance services in Britain go back to the turn of the century, many of the ideas and theories which underpin recent guidance practice emerged in the 1960s and early 1970s. It was then, for example, that the developmental theories of Super and Ginzberg, and the client-centred approaches of Carl Rogers, made their way across the Atlantic and began to have an impact in Britain (Daws, 1976). It was an age of increasing interest in individual expression within a political climate dominated by Keynesian economic thinking and a broad social-democratic political consensus. The new approaches to guidance, contrasted with the talent-matching ideas that had dominated previous practice, fitted well into this climate. The emphasis on individual autonomy and on plurality of values suited the prevailing liberalism in the social sphere. At the same time, this was modified by a concern to compensate for, rather than to reinforce, inequalities in access to opportunities: this reflected, and fitted, the social-democratic spirit of the times (for a contemporary theoretical analysis of these perspectives on career development, see Watts, Super and Kidd, 1981).

Many of the structures and concepts outlined in this section have survived through the very different political climate of the 1980s and into the 1990s. They have however come under pressure, as will be outlined shortly. First, though, we need to examine more closely the relationship between guidance and public policy.

Guidance and public policy

In policy terms, it is important to recognise that guidance services serve a number of different constituencies. In addition to individuals, they are important to education and training providers, in increasing the effectiveness of their provision by helping learners to be linked to programmes which meet their needs; to employers, in helping them to find employees whose talents and motivations are matched to the employer's requirements; and to governments, in making maximum use of the society's human resources and relating this to chosen social and political ends. In particular, guidance services can play a significant role in fostering efficiency in the allocation and use of human resources, and in fostering social equity in access to educational and vocational opportunities (Watts, Dartois and Plant, 1988).

It is primarily for these reasons that guidance services are supported from the public purse. At the same time, those involved in the provision of such services have tended consistently to argue that their primary client must be the individual. There are good practical as well as ethical reasons for this, not the least of which is the point that guidance services can only serve the interests of their secondary clients if they retain the confidence and trust of the individuals with whom they are working – whose interests must accordingly be given primacy. This requires a kind of self-denying ordinance on the part of public authorities: they may justify guidance services on the grounds that they serve public purposes, but they have to abnegate this as the operating principle on which the practice of the services should be based. It means that careers guidance needs to be viewed not as a direct instrument of public policy, but more as a lubricant of such policies and of the operations of the labour market (Watts, 1980). Under this view, guidance services have a responsibility to ensure that individual choices are well-informed in terms of the opportunity structure, but they have no responsibility for selecting, recruiting or directing individuals to meet the requirements of institutions, employers or others. In the end, the main concern of guidance is seen as being to enable individuals to take responsibility for their choices in terms of what is in their own best interests.

In general, this view of the role of guidance services has been affirmed and protected by their professional associations, and respected by their funding authorities. At times, however, services have come under pressure from these authorities to serve interests which may or may not be congruent with the individual's interests. As an example, school-based guidance services have at times been placed under pressure to encourage pupils to stay on at school into the sixth form, since school resources and staff salaries are significantly affected by the proportion who do so. Other instances of this kind have grown in recent years, partly as a result of increasing political pressures on guidance services. These have been linked to some extent to the influence of the 'New Right' on the political climate and on public policy, and it is to this that I now turn.

The 'New Right'

The 'New Right' has represented a wide range of groups and ideas, with many internal divisions and conflicts. But its essence is, as political analysts like King (1987) and Gamble (1988) have pointed out, a curious yet powerful amalgam of liberalism in the economic sphere and conservatism in the social sphere. The dominant strand has been liberalism, with its concern for individualism, limited government intervention and free market forces. What is distinctive about the 'New Right', however, has been the way in which such liberal principles have been combined with conservative concerns for societal order based on tradition, authority and national identity. There are clearly tensions between these two strands: liberalism is at root permissive and individualist; conservatism is authoritarian and statist. They share, however, a hostility to the ideas, practices and institutions of social democracy. Their internal tensions have been resolved – in political if not philosophical terms – by seeing a key role of the state as being to restore market principles to social areas where (in the eyes of 'New Right' protagonists) they have been subverted, and thenceforth to protect the market from vested interests and restrictive practices.

One of the main aims of the 'New Right' has thus been to restrict and where possible to dismantle the welfare state. Goodin (1982) identified six respects in which the welfare state is alleged to reduce freedom: by infringing the freedom of taxpayers to dispose of their property as they please; by limiting the range of services; by paternalistically directing citizens towards defined choices; by imposing bureaucratic and/or legal restrictions on individuals; by producing dependency among welfare recipients; and by creating its own supporting interest groups among bureaucrats and beneficiaries, who then oppose alternative social and political arrangements. The latter point has been developed by public choice theorists like Niskanen (1971), who argue that the welfare state induces its bureaucrats to be self-interested budget maximisers, and that this – allied with the absence of profit criteria and with pressure on politicians to promise goods and services to voters in order to get elected – encourages the public sector to expand in a reckless manner. Among the 'new class' anathematised by the 'New Right' as sharing a self-interest in the preservation and expansion of the welfare state are doctors, social workers and teachers. It is worth noting that the way had been paved for this 'backlash against professional society' (Perkin, 1989) by critiques from the left from writers like Illich (1973; 1977).

The 'New Right' is concerned to restore or introduce market principles to social and economic activities wherever it can. The assumption is that the market-based production of goods and services ensures greater responsiveness to consumer choice and greater efficiency in production because of the profit incentive (see King, 1987). For writers like Hayek (1944) individualism is allied with market relations because the latter maximise liberty as voluntary choice and reduce coercion to a minimum. Such writers invoke Adam Smith's (1776) famous dictum that individualists in pursuit of their self-interest are led by an 'invisible hand' to promote an end which was no part of their intention – the public interest – and do so more effectually than when they intend to promote it.

At the same time, the 'New Right' is prepared to concede some exceptions to their veneration of market forces. The social-conservative wing is very concerned about protection of family values, and has protested strongly against the way in which, as women have increasingly participated in the labour force, various forms of work previously done in the home have been shifted to the market (Eisenstein, 1982). Some economic liberals have been attracted to this argument too because they see the reassertion of the traditional family as being a way of reducing the pressure for social-welfare provision.

Beyond this, most branches of the 'New Right' see a residual role for state intervention, particularly in view of the social-conservative wing's concern for law and order. There are some exceptions: American libertarians like Rothbard (1977) have argued that all taxation represents a violation of individual rights and that even such state functions as the police, the courts, the bureaucracy and the military should be privatised. But most accept the legitimacy of what Adam Smith referred to as 'the duty of erecting and maintaining certain public works and certain public institutions, which it can never be for the interest of an individual, or small number of individuals, to erect and maintain; because the profit could never repay the expense to any individual, or small number of individuals, though it may frequently do much more than repay it to a great society' (Smith, 1776, Book 4, ch.9).

Many, too, recognise that some residual state programmes are required for the less fortunate, but they wish to restrict these to a minimum, and wherever possible to adopt market-based measures such as cash vouchers which recipients can then use as they wish within the competitive market system: such vouchers are redistributive interventions in the free flow of the market, but at least – in the view of their advocates – their effects are contained by market disciplines and stimulate market activity. In addition, some writers see an active role for the state in offsetting market failures through such measures as improved information flows.

These, then, are some of the main currents of 'New Right' thinking. In a British context they have become closely identified with 'Thatcherism' (Gamble, 1988) and closely associated with the Conservative administrations headed by Margaret Thatcher. The crucial break with Keynesian demand-management policies had, however, occurred several years earlier under a Labour Government. It is also important to recognise that 'New Right' ideology had a limited impact on government policy even under Thatcher: the growth of public spending was contained, but such spending was not in general reduced, and indeed the Thatcher Government was concerned at times to emphasise how it had increased its expenditure on education and on health in particular. Nonetheless, the 'New Right' increasingly set the terms of political debate during this period, and its hegemony can be seen in most areas of public policy – including, as we shall now see, public policy related to careers guidance.

Conflicting currents

Guidance services have been affected in contrasting ways by the political currents of the last decade or so. They have certainly been affected by the restrictions which the 'New Right' has encouraged on government spending. On the other hand, they have been viewed by economic liberals and by government as important mechanisms for making students and their institutions responsive to the needs of the labour market. Accordingly, they have benefited from a variety of government programmes which have incorporated guidance elements. Some of these programmes, however, have carried with them political pressures – stemming in part from the social-conservative wing of the New Right – which have challenged the professional independence of guidance services. There have also been attempts to make guidance services themselves more responsive to market forces.

These countervailing forces are evident in relation to, for example, guidance services for adults. An early casualty of public-expenditure cuts was the Occupational Guidance Service, which was dismantled in 1980/81. On the other hand, some LEA Careers Services during the 1980s extended their services to adults. The number of educational guidance services for adults also continued to grow: by 1988, 43% of LEAS contained at least one such service which was a member of the National Association of Educational Guidance Services (NEGI, 1990). At the same time, the Employment Training scheme involved the appointment of Training Agents whose task was to help unemployed adults to define the training needs they sought to address through the scheme. The Careers Service accounted for around only 20% of the National Training Agents network (DE, 1990a); the majority of the remainder were private-sector organisations. The issue of whether and how to develop a more comprehensive guidance service for adults remains a key unresolved policy issue.

A more specific example of the conflicting impact of political currents relates to the effects on careers education and guidance in schools of the Technical and Vocational Education Initiative (TVEI)[38] and the National Curriculum. TVEI has included mandatory provision for careers education and guidance and also for such closely related elements as work experience and records of achievement. Indeed, the Focus Statement issued by the Training Agency in April 1989 for TVEI Extension, which is to extend the scheme to all schools and colleges by 1992, included as one of its core principles 'making sure that young people have access to initial guidance and counselling, and then continued education and training, and opportunities for progression throughout their lives'.

---

38 Editorial footnote: The Technical and Vocational Education Initiative (TVEI) was a curriculum initiative for 14-18 year olds that ran from 1983 to 1997.

The place of TVEI in relation to 'New Right' thinking is a complex one. It clearly is grounded in the concern of the economic liberals to develop the kinds of attitudes and skills which are likely to foster market activity. But it is based on the notion that, if such concerns are to be met, the content of the curriculum cannot be left to the autonomy of the individual school. Instead, forms of state intervention are needed to achieve educational change. Such intervention is less familiar and acceptable to the economic liberals than to the social conservatives. Yet the changes sought by TVEI are in many ways direct attacks on the academic curriculum which the social conservatives prize. Indeed, with their emphasis on cross-curricular projects and on active, experiential learning, they incorporate many elements of the progressive education which the social conservatives have condemned as being responsible for the ills of the education system (see Jamieson et al., 1988). Accordingly, Jones (1989) finds it necessary to identify such programmes as being principally developed by a third group, which he terms the 'Conservative modernisers'.

The reaction of the social conservatives to such ideas is evident in the National Curriculum introduced by the Education Reform Act 1988. This is largely based on conventional conceptions of learning embodied in traditional school subjects. Significantly, careers education and guidance is accorded a much less significant place in such a curriculum. It was not even mentioned in the original consultative document (DES, 1987) – despite statements in a Government document issued only a couple of months previously that careers education and guidance 'are essential to the vision of education as a vital force for a vital economy' (DES/DE, 1987, p.9). It has since been included as one of a number of 'cross-curricular themes' (NCC, 1990) which are to be delivered largely through the mainstream subjects.

There are, however, no mechanisms within the National Curriculum for ensuring that these themes are implemented, and the pressures imposed by the statutory parts of the curriculum could make them vulnerable. The main current assurance for careers work in schools is offered by the contractual nature of TVEI, but this is a short-term programme and there is anxiety about what will happen when it comes to an end.

Strands of influence

In general, it seems that the main impact of 'New Right' thinking on guidance policy can be analysed in relation to three concepts. The first is the notion of guidance as social control: this has been particularly evident in relation to responses to unemployment. The second is the notion of guidance as market-maker: this has been developed particularly in relation to training credits for young people. The third is the notion of a market in guidance: this is reflected in recent proposals regarding the funding of guidance services. Each of these concepts and illustrations will now be examined in more detail.

Guidance as social control

From a guidance perspective, the early years of the Thatcher administration were dominated by the impact of the massive rise in unemployment in general and youth unemployment in particular. A succession of programmes were set up in response to the social problems this posed, notably the Youth Opportunities Programme and the Youth Training Scheme. Some young people resisted entering such schemes, regarding them as poorly-paid forms of exploitation that were unlikely to lead to worthwhile jobs: they accordingly preferred to remain on the dole. In September 1983 Peter Morrison, Minister of State at the Department of Employment, made a speech to the Institute of Careers Officers Annual Conference in which he accused careers officers of being 'social engineers' – 'incapable or unwilling to help employers by encouraging young people to take up opportunities on offer'. He continued:

> Employers want the Careers Service to encourage young people to display a positive attitude to the world of work, to accept necessary work disciplines, and to be prepared to take up opportunities on offer at realistic rates of pay. (Morrison, 1983)

The issue was subsequently exacerbated when the Government instructed the Careers Service to report young people who turned down YTS placements, so that benefit sanctions could be applied: at least one LEA service refused to co-operate with this demand, and others quietly ignored it (see Lee et al., 1990). Along with the pressures to act as a recruitment agency for YOP/YTS, it was seen by some careers officers as being in conflict with the unequivocal statement in the Government's guidelines to LEAs that 'in advising unemployed young people about the programme, and in matching them to suitable opportunities, the main consideration will be the best interests of the young person concerned' (DE, 1980, p.18). The issue remained: who was to define what those best interests should be?

Similar issues arose in a more acute way in relation to the Government's own direct guidance provision for the adult unemployed. In 1986 it introduced its Restart programme, under which all of those who had been out of work for a year were 'invited' to their Job Centre for a guidance interview, with the promise that they would be offered one of a range of ways towards finding work; the latter included a one-week Restart course to help them assess what they were good at and to develop their job-seeking skills. The 'invitation', however, included warnings that eligibility for continued receipt of benefit would be affected by failure to attend. Many of them saw the content of the interviews as being concerned with harassment rather than with counselling, and as placing pressure on them to accept low-paid work (Gray, 1987). A lot of the people who attended the courses thought that they were compulsory: when they found that they were voluntary, some left (MSC, 1988; Sharp, 1988). In 1990 it was announced that Restart courses would become compulsory for claimants who 'have been unemployed for two years or more and who, at their next Restart interview, reject all offers of help'.

The Restart programme, it should be noted, has been firmly controlled by central government. The interview programme has been conducted by its own staff; the Restart courses have been sub-contracted to a variety of private- and public-sector organisations, particularly colleges of further education, but within very firmly-set contractual parameters. There has therefore been limited space for assertion of the professional principle outlined earlier in this paper: that the primary client must be the individual.

Unemployment has indeed opened up in a major way the tensions between government policy and professional practice in relation to careers guidance. These tensions are much easier to reconcile where there are no evident conflicts between government interests and individual interests. At a time of high unemployment, however, the government's interest are best met by encouraging individuals to invest all their energies in competing for the jobs that remain. Yet arguably some individuals might rationally decide that their interests will be better met, for example, by inertia (thus avoiding the depression of continued rejection), by collective action to attack the roots of unemployment, or by working through the informal rather than the formal economy. Governments are unlikely to be willing to support services which encourage individuals to examine all these options in a rational and unbiased way (Watts, 1980c). The Thatcher Government showed its active hostility to the collective-action option by its attacks on 'political activities' within government schemes (Watts, 1983a, p.72; 1983b). The only alternative option which it was prepared to support was the notion of self-employment: thus substantial sums of public money were invested in supporting schemes designed to encourage individuals to consider the possibility of creating their own employment and to develop the skills it requires (Watts and Moran, 1984; Rees, 1988). Such activities were clearly attractive to a government concerned to encourage enterprise attitudes and values. At the same time, however, it in general resisted any overt links to stimulating informal-economy activity – which a wholly libertarian ideology would have been prepared to encourage. Here again, then, the 'New Right's' economic liberalism was evident, but so was the brake applied by its social conservatism.

Guidance as market-maker

Towards the end of the 1980s, greater attention began to be given to developing a rationale for guidance services which would be more closely in line with 'New Right' thinking. It was based on the notion that guidance could be viewed as a tool for making markets work, ensuring that the supply-side had access to market information and was able to read market signals. This was very close to the 'lubricant' argument presented earlier. It provided a rationale for publicly-funded but client-centred guidance services which could invoke Adam Smith (1776) himself in claiming that in enabling individuals to pursue their best interests, guidance services could – via the 'invisible hand' – promote the interests of society too. It thus transformed guidance into what in 'New Right' terms could be viewed as 'that most politically acceptable of professions: the market makers' (McNair, 1990).

The most significant development of this argument was constructed, somewhat unexpectedly, by the Confederation of British Industry (1989a; 1989b). Concerned about Britain's need to improve skill levels in order to compete with world markets, it suggested that one of the main criticisms of the current system was that it had always given the needs of providers higher priority than the needs of individuals. It accordingly argued that the way forward was to 'put individuals first' and to encourage them to develop their skills and knowledge throughout their working lives. For an organisation representing corporate interests to initiate such an argument was remarkable. The CBI saw the notion of 'careership' as a concept which should be applicable to all individuals, and to give it practical form it recommended a system of credits which would give all young people post-16 a publicly funded right to education and training and control over the form it should take. It viewed effective careers guidance as the essential means of ensuring that such individual decisions were well-informed, and proposed that careers guidance required a 'new rationale, reinvigoration and extra investment' (CBI, 1989b, p.23).

The Government clearly found these proposals ideologically attractive. Accordingly it announced that by April 1991 it intended to set up ten training-credit pilot schemes covering up to 10% of the national total of 16- and 17-year-olds leaving full-time education. Each scheme was to include 'quality careers advice, working through the Careers Service and careers teachers, so that young people make the best choices about use of their credits' (DE, 1990b, p.4). Bids from Training and Enterprise Councils were accordingly to include indications of 'how the TEC will work with schools and the Careers Service to improve and enhance careers advice for young people' (ibid, p.9).

The notion of guidance as market-maker thus offers the prospect of significant extensions of guidance provision. At the same time, however, it views guidance principally in informational terms as a source of market intelligence. How far its proponents are prepared to attend to the complexities of helping individuals to process such information, and to relate it to their own personal needs and values, remains to be seen.

A market in guidance

A further effect of the CBI report was to bring into question the funding and structuring of careers guidance services. The issue had already arisen in a different context in higher education, where the pressure of cuts in government funding to institutions had encouraged the proposal that careers services should become 'self-funding' through a levy on employers recruiting their graduates. While certain institutions took significant steps to generate some income from employers (e.g. Steptoe, 1990), the Association of Graduate Careers Advisory Services stated unequivocally that to ask employers 'to bear the entire cost of providing the Service would be entirely inappropriate, because they are not the main clients of the Service' (unpublished briefing paper, July 1989).

Within the context of the LEA Careers Service, the CBI had initially indicated that it was 'not convinced that careers education and the Careers Service as currently organised and resourced can deliver what is needed'. It also stated that 'experience with Training Agents in Employment Training does not suggest that building in a new independent guidance system based on training providers is more likely to be successful'. It went on to suggest that transferring the responsibility from the LEAs to the (employer dominated) Training and Enterprise Councils was 'probably the most appropriate way of ensuring that a local service is developed to meet local needs' (CBI, 1989a, p.24). This proposal was subsequently dropped and replaced with the proposal that 'a major review be undertaken to clarify the role, responsibilities and relationships of the major guidance agencies'. It suggested that this review should 'examine how the interests of the various client groups could best be served and how the funding should be arranged to ensure that those interests are met'. It further suggested that 'this might involve the separation of responsibility for professional direction from that for service delivery'. This might include 'services to schools and colleges negotiated and paid for individually', a 'basic service to employers specified and funded in a contract with, for example, the Training and Enterprise Council', and 'other services negotiated on a normal contractual basis'.

In 1990 the Government announced that it was launching an internal review of organisational arrangements for careers guidance 'with the aim of recommending the most relevant system for delivering careers information, advice and guidance for young people in the 1990s' (DE Press Notice, 10 May 1990). In the meantime, it was reported that the government, 'under heavy pressure from employers to take the service out of the hands of local authority education departments', was encouraging three LEAs to hive off their careers services into newly-formed companies which would employ the careers staff and contract with its local-authority and other users to provide services. Options ranged from council-owned 'arms-length' agencies to private enterprises formed by selling careers departments to their own managers (Times Educational Supplement, 28 September 1990; see e.g. Coopers & Lybrand

Deloitte, 1990).

Pursuit of such options has been encouraged by the White Paper published in May 1991 in the wake of the government review (DES/DE, 1991). The White Paper left open a variety of possible organisational models for the Careers Service, with permission for local diversity. This included enabling LEAs to contract the Careers Service out to the private sector through competitive tender if they so wished. The Government also declared that it proposed to take reserve powers to require LEAs to put the service out to tender if experience showed this to be a good way of managing it.

Further, the White Paper announced that the government would extend the training credits scheme so that by 1996 it would cover all 16/17-year-olds leaving full-time education. This could have a significant effect on the form the funding for careers guidance takes. Entitlement to guidance services could be built into the credits themselves. An alternative being considered by some TECs, however, is that the credits could incorporate the option of 'buying' guidance services, and individuals could then decide whether to spend part of their credit in this way or not. This latter proposal would do what the current funding structures fail to do: ensure that the chief beneficiary of guidance is also its purchaser. It would also place pressure on guidance services to ensure that they are genuinely serving the self-perceived interests of the individuals with whom they work. On the other hand, the notion that opting for guidance will reduce the training entitlement could discourage young people from seeking the guidance which – in the eyes of the CBI and the Government – is the means of ensuring that their choices are informed by market forces.

The interest in training credits is not confined to young people. Proposals have been developed for immediately applying the same notions to the long-term adult unemployed, and eventually to much wider groups of adults. Such discussions have given considerable attention to the notion of counselling vouchers, including the idea of encouraging competition between counselling providers (see e.g. Full Employment UK, 1991).

Conclusion

It is evident that there are tensions between the three strands of influence we have identified. The notion of guidance as market-maker implies universal access to guidance, but the notion of a market in guidance may impose restrictions on such access. Again, the notion of guidance as market-maker implies that guidance services must be independent and view individuals as their primary clients, yet the notion of guidance as social control is concerned to influence the content of the guidance that is offered and to ensure that it meets the immediate needs of government and/or employers.

How far are the values and practices of guidance services identified earlier in this article sustainable in a political climate in which such influences are predominant? Certainly the notion of careers guidance services being delivered free of charge by a strong and coherent public sector is under sustained attack. Their role as 'market makers' may place them in a stronger position to survive such attacks than other social services. But the pressures are likely to continue, and public-sector institutions like local education authorities – themselves under continuous pressure – may not be the most comfortable or supportive environment in which to pursue their professional purposes.

There are aspects of 'New Right' ideology which are in principle congruent with guidance philosophy and practice. The CBI report, in particular, embodied some of these ideas in forms which potentially offer an attractive opportunity to guidance services. They give guidance an unprecedented prominence in public-policy debates. They offer the prospect of a significant increase in guidance provision. They also attach considerable importance to the principle that such services should be 'independent'.

Whether their organisational proposals offer the best way of assuring such independence is open to question, but they re-contour the debate about how this can best be achieved. Moreover, they recognise that guidance (and training) must be available to all, not only to those who are able to pay. Their voucher proposals are thus in principle egalitarian in nature. As Le Grand (1989) points out in a more general context, the fact that the idea of vouchers has in recent years been colonised almost exclusively by the Right does not mean there is anything inherently right-wing in what is perhaps their principal merit: that they empower the welfare client.

The full implementation of the CBI's proposals could also at last lead to a more comprehensive careers guidance service for adults. The notion of 'careership' was viewed by the CBI as a process of continuous personal development. It noted that 'with the accelerating pace of change in the labour market, there will be many opportunities for important careers choices throughout a working life' (CBI, 1989a, p.19). One of its main criticisms of current provision was that 'it is very much a youth and education centred system and this does not bode well for a greater emphasis on lifetime learning' (ibid, p.24). This was played down somewhat in the CBI's final report (CBI, 1989b), and the subsequent close association of the CBI proposals with the training-credits pilot schemes for young people has meant that it has not yet received close attention. But one of the tests that needs to be applied to the new organisational arrangements which emerge from the 1991 White Paper is the extent to which they foster improved provision for adult guidance.

The effects of 'New Right' thinking on the professional independence of careers guidance are ambivalent. The economic-liberal wing of the 'New Right' is very concerned to support the free choices of individuals. On the other hand, its social-conservative wing is, as we have seen, concerned to limit this freedom to the economic arena, and is suspicious of choices which are motivated by social and political values of which it disapproves. While public provision for guidance remains, periodic pressures from the latter faction on professional guidance values seem likely to continue.

In this context there are dangers that guidance services will be evaluated by the behavioural outcomes of the decisions taken by their clients – i.e. by their destinations. This is clearly at variance with the principle that it is the client who is responsible for the decision and for determining whether the decision meets his or her needs. The implications of the latter view is that guidance services should be evaluated not in terms of the outcomes of their clients' decisions but in terms of the process through which the clients make their decisions: whether they have been adequately informed about the opportunities available and have thought them through adequately in relation to their own values and other attributes. In this respect, it may be significant that an internal review of guidance provision conducted by the Training Agency in 1989 concluded that the focus of evaluation should be not destinations but learning outcomes – a more professionally acceptable outcome measure.

The hegemony established by the 'New Right' in the 1980s may not survive through the 1990s. Thatcher's fall from power in late 1990 reduced its political hold, and its intellectual hold had already begun to look more vulnerable – particularly in the light of the growing concern with environmental issues, which are classic examples of problems that cannot be resolved by unbounded market forces. Nonetheless, any new political trend will have to start from the ideas the 'New Right' has promoted and the ways in which these ideas became institutionalised under the Thatcher Government. Moreover, the collapse of communism in Eastern Europe makes it clear that market principles are likely to be incorporated in any counter-revolution from the Left – as the current interest in 'market socialism' (Le Grand and Estrin, 1989) affirms. Clarifying the relationship of careers guidance to 'New Right' thinking is therefore not just of historical, analytical interest: it is also likely to be important for shaping the direction of professional development for guidance services in the future.

14. Career Guidance and Social Exclusion: A Cautionary Tale[39]

Introduction

Since the advent of the 'New Labour' Government under Tony Blair in spring 1997, public policy in the United Kingdom related to career guidance for young people has been dominated by the issue of social exclusion. In 1998, the Department for Education and Employment introduced a policy of focusing the attention of the Careers Service more strongly on those who had already dropped out of the education, training and employment system, or were at risk of doing so (DfEE, 1998a). Then in 1999 the government announced, in a report from the Social Exclusion Unit within the Cabinet Office, the details of a new youth support service incorporating the Careers Service, parts of the youth service and a range of other specialist agencies designed to address the needs of young people, 'especially those from disadvantaged backgrounds or experiencing particular difficulties' (SEU, 1999, p. 78). Ministers subsequently indicated that the Careers Service was to disappear as a visible national entity: the statutory duty to provide careers services under the Employment and Training Act 1973 would remain, but would henceforth be delivered through the new youth support service, to be termed the Connexions Service (Baroness Blackstone, House of Lords Hansard, 17 February 2000).

It is important to note the extent of the policy shift denoted by these measures. Under the previous Conservative Government, the Careers Service had been 'marketised' by contracting it out on a competitive tendering basis (Watts, 1995), but the service had been clearly defined as a universal one, addressing the needs of all young people. Indeed, steps had been taken to extend the universal entitlement to cover the earlier years of compulsory schooling as well as the period of transition from school or college (Morris, 1996). Guidance-related programmes designed to address the distinctive needs of young people who had dropped out of the education, training and employment system (see e.g. Ford, n.d.) were mounted largely on the initiative of individual careers services, supported by European funding, and remained marginal to the main officially-endorsed Careers Service provision. Now, under the 'New Labour' Government, the marginal programmes have become mainstream, and the service itself is being subsumed within the wider entity which such mainstreaming is seen to require.

These changes pose major challenges for the future of career guidance provision

---

39 Editorial footnote: Reprinted, by permission of the author and publisher, from *British Journal of Guidance and Counselling*, Volume 29 No. 2, May 2001. DOI: 10.1080/03069880020047111.

for young people in England (rather different approaches are being adopted in the rest of the United Kingdom). The notion of career guidance as an entitlement for all young people, and the extent of the service provided to them, are at risk of being subordinated to the government's social exclusion agenda. It is accordingly important to analyse the nature and origin of this agenda, the impact it has had so far on career guidance policy and practice, and the issues which it poses for the future.

The concept of social exclusion

'Social exclusion' is a new term in British political debates, subsuming and in some eyes replacing the traditional left-wing preoccupations with poverty, inequality and disadvantage. It is defined by Room (1995) as 'the process of becoming detached from the organisations and communities of which the society is composed and from the rights and obligations that they embody' (p. 243). Its intellectual roots lie in Durkheim's concern with the ways in which social integration, solidarity and social cohesion can be effected in advanced industrial societies (see Levitas, 1998, Chapter 9). *L'exclusion sociale*, and the complementary notion of *l'insertion sociale*, have been a focus of political debate in France since the 1960s (Silver, 1994). The concept of social exclusion has also exercised a growing influence on social and economic policy within the European Union (see e.g. European Commission, 1994).

The concept is a contested one. Levitas (1998) has pointed out that it is embedded in three different discourses. The first is a redistributionist discourse, primarily focused on poverty, which draws on traditional left-wing concerns with reducing inequality. The second is a moral underclass discourse, centring on the moral and behavioural delinquency of the 'excluded' themselves, which draws on American right-wing analyses of the growth of an 'underclass' fostered by welfare dependency and moral irresponsibility (see Murray, 1990). The third is a social integrationist discourse, which focuses on participation in paid work as the key to social inclusion.

In a careful and detailed analysis of how these discourses have been interwoven in recent UK political debates, Levitas notes that the dominant influence on New Labour Government policy has been the social integrationist discourse, with some moral underclass overtones. Concerns for distributional equality have been marginalised. Instead, social inclusion is defined primarily in terms of participation in paid employment. This is viewed as the key to other social and economic goals, including reduction of crime and of welfare costs. Achieving such participation is seen as the moral responsibility of the individual: the right to work is replaced by the individual's duty to secure employment or, as a means to this end, to enhance his or her employability through, in particular, participation in education and training. The role of the state is to ensure that all have opportunities for participation in education, training or employment, and to encourage individuals to take advantage of such opportunities through a mixture of 'carrots' and 'sticks' . The New Deal and 'Welfare to Work' programmes are central parts of the government's strategy for carrying out this role.

Within this broad policy frame, particular attention has been addressed to young people who have dropped out of the education, training and employment system. The substantial rise in youth unemployment in the late 1970s and 1980s led to a range of youth training schemes, and to a 'youth training guarantee' of access to such schemes; the existence of this guarantee was used as a rationale for withdrawing unemployment benefits for 16/17-year-olds. The result was that many young people who were unwilling to take up such a place disappeared from official statistics, and their existence was officially ignored and even, on occasion, denied (Williamson, 2000). A study in South Glamorgan (Rees, Williamson & Istance, 1996) estimated that the local monthly totals of young people in this 'status zero' group varied between 16% and 23% of the age cohort. National figures, based on more limited data-sets, have tended to produce figures of around 7-8% (Robinson, 1999).

The 'NEET' group (Not in Education, Employment or Training) is volatile. Many young people change tracks frequently, moving in and out of school, college, training schemes, jobs, and being unemployed (see e.g. Hodkinson, Sparkes & Hodkinson, 1996). Youth Cohort Study data indicated that in their first 2 years after the end of compulsory schooling, 6% of young people were NEET for more than 6 months in total, and that 4% had more than one NEET spell. Only 1% of the cohort were NEET throughout the 2 years (Payne, 2000).

The policy concern for social exclusion is not confined to 16/17-year-olds. In terms of younger age groups, substantial numbers of young people drop out of school before the age of 16. The number of young people permanently excluded from schools in England rose from 2,910 in 1990/91 to 13,581 in 1995/96, dropping slightly to 13,041 in 1997/98 (Parsons, 1999). In addition, nearly 10% of pupils have been recorded as truanting at least once a week or more, and 1.6% as doing so every day, during the final year of compulsory schooling; these figures are likely to be underestimates (O'Keeffe, 1994). Such data represent the visible part of the iceberg: beneath the surface lie a larger number of pupils who attend school but are disaffected from formal learning and therefore can be regarded as being at risk of dropping out from formal systems. These include, according to Barber (1994), a disruptive minority of 10-15% who express their disaffection through their behaviour and seriously undermine the quality of schooling for as many as half of all secondary-school pupils.

Williamson (2000) suggests that young people who have become disengaged from education, training and employment can be divided into three main groups: the 'essentially confused', the 'temporarily sidetracked' and the 'deeply alienated'. Many suffer from multiple personal and social problems, including dysfunctional family backgrounds, personality and behavioural difficulties, and experience of traumatic events (Stone, Cotton & Thomas, 2000). They are more likely than their peers to be involved in drugs and in crime (SEU, 1999). The policy attention devoted to them stems partly from concern for their welfare and partly from the social threat they are perceived to represent.

The design of appropriate policy responses to social exclusion in general and NEET young people in particular depends on the view adopted of the relationship between the sociological concepts of agency and structure. This relationship is the pivotal concern of recent social theory, and arguably has always been the central sociological dilemma (Archer, 1995). The relationship is a complex one: as Giddens (1993) argues, 'social structure is both constituted by human agency and yet is at the same time the very medium of this constitution' (pp. 128-129). The stance adopted on the balance and interaction between the two in policy debates is however of considerable practical significance. The widespread use of the term 'disaffection', for example, tends to view the young person as the author or agent responsible for their own life situation, suggesting that remedies need to be found in sanctions or incentives aimed at changing their attitudes and behaviours. On the other hand, the use of the term 'socially excluded' can permit the young person to be viewed as the victim of structural factors which have to be removed or improved if their situation is to be ameliorated (Hodgson, 1999; Merton & Parrott, 1999; Pearce & Hillman, 1998). The risk of an analysis based on a narrowly structural position (e.g. Byrne, 1999) is that it leads to a sense of impotence in the absence of major political change. The danger of an analysis based on a narrowly agency-based position is that it can lead to naïve solutions which are doomed to failure.

In practice, as Merton and Parrott (1999) point out, all programmes and projects focusing on direct work with young people are based on the idea of young people as agents. So if – as they and other commentators affirm – it is likely that the situation of disengaged young people occurs as a result of a complex interaction between agency and structure, this has consequences for the design of such programmes. First, some degree of modesty is needed in setting expectations for the programmes' results. Second, care needs to be taken, in planning the programmes, to start from the assumption that young people's disengagement may not be pathological but be based on a rational response to their structural situation (Piper & Piper, 1998/99).

The role of career guidance

These issues are particularly pertinent to the role of career guidance in relation to social exclusion. This role is mainly twofold: preventive, helping young people to avoid such exclusion; and reintegrative, supporting those currently excluded to gain access to education/training and the labour market. In its preventive role, it can, for example, clarify the links between education and the achievement of vocational goals, and prevent 'false moves' which lead to failure and undermine future participation. In its reintegrative role, it can operate directly to support educational participation and to incorporate individuals into the labour market, as well as operating collaboratively with other agencies in contributing to holistic multi-agency approaches to addressing multiple disadvantage (Killeen, Watts & Kidd, 1999). In addition, Morgan and Hughes (1999) identify a recovery role, aimed at bringing young people back into learning provision specifically designed to meet their needs (this is perhaps best seen as a 'stepping stone' within the reintegration role of helping them into mainstream provision). Certainly guidance has an important role to play in innovative education and training programmes designed to attend to the needs of 'at risk' young people (Watts, 2000b).

But those involved in offering career guidance to young people who have dropped out of the formal education, training and employment system, or are at risk of doing so, are unlikely to be effective unless they address the reality of the current lifestyles of such young people and are able to do so within the young people's own phenomenological perspective. Many such young people are engaged in work, not within the formal economy, but within one or more of the three informal economies: the household economy, covering production for internal consumption within the home of goods or services for which substitutes might otherwise be purchased for money; the communal economy, involving the production of goods or services that are consumed by people other than the producers, but not sold on a monetary basis; and the hidden economy, involving work conducted wholly or partly for money which is concealed from the taxation and regulatory authorities (Gershuny & Pahl, 1979/80, 1980; Watts, 1983a).

Johnston, MacDonald, Mason, Ridley and Webster (2000), in a study of a deprived housing estate in Teesside, identified six career routes which young people might take in such a neighbourhood, three of which were located in the informal economies. They used the term 'career' as a tool for theorising the complexity and diversity of transitions and pathways the young people appeared to follow. The first was domestic and home-centred careers, concentrated largely on childcare and domestic labour. The second was careers involving extensive or repeated engagement in informal economic activity, such as volunteering, self-employment and cash-in-hand 'fiddly work' . Much of this work was found through word-of-mouth via local contacts. In many cases it was legitimate, in the sense that it did not infringe tax or benefit regulations, but sometimes it was linked to criminal enterprises like the selling on of stolen or counterfeit goods. The third was more specifically criminal careers, often linked to the sale of drugs.

Most of the young people in Johnston et al.'s study did not remain within any one of these career routes, but moved between several of these and the other more formal routes during their post-school years. From their own perspective, however, they were engaged in work even when they were operating in the informal economies. Moreover, within the context of their neighbourhood, many of them did not feel 'socially excluded'. Indeed, their access to local knowledge and their capacity to navigate local networks – in other words, their sense of social inclusion within their own community – was the key to their survival.

Of the three alternative routes outlined by Johnston et al., the criminal route was the most distinct. A recurrent theme amongst those who regarded themselves as criminals was their perception of crime as an alternative form of work, offering many of its psychological benefits: enforced activity, social contacts, social identity, and goals and purposes within a time structure. Coles (1995) indicates how criminal careers can develop in a series of staged career progressions through which some young people move from minor acts of hooliganism, through more persistent offending, to accepting a life of instrumental crime punctuated by periods of imprisonment. Within particular communities, gaining access to informal forms of work can provide access to a social network which can offer 'opportunity structures' including apprenticeship in the techniques of entrepreneurial crime. Craine (1997) argues that such career routes have been systematically under-reported in ethnographic youth research.

From the individual's point-of-view, entering such a career route may be perceived to be economically rational, at least within a short-term time perspective. It may also offer more social status within the local peer culture: 'rather than tolerating regular hours for low pay, there can be more status in proving one's ability to get by without surrendering to the system' (Roberts, Noble & Duggan, 1982, p. 174). Entering low-paid training schemes and jobs may be viewed with derision: 'slaving your bollocks off for £30 – I can nick that in 10 minutes' (quoted in Rees et al., 1996, p. 228).

Guidance services paid for by the government are likely to have to view such issues differently, condemning activities which are regarded as being illegal or anti-social. Many informal-economy activities, however, do not fall clearly into these categories, and here judgements are much more open to question. For example, Craine (1997) found that for unemployed young women in his study, the 'mothering option' provided a socially acceptable alternative to the limited opportunities available for employment (see also Wallace, 1987). Are such young women feckless and morally irresponsible drains on the welfare state, as social-underclass theories (e.g. Murray, 1990) contend? Or misguided individuals cutting themselves off from the mainstream opportunity structure? Or responsible young adults committing themselves to the demands and responsibilities of parenthood? Public policy under the New Labour Government has tended to adopt the second of these positions, with some undertones of the first (see Levitas, 1998). A credible social case can however be made for the third. At the very least, it raises the issue of how far governments should seek to take firm prescriptive positions on the personal and moral issues involved in such decisions, or leave them for individuals to resolve. Even if they use financial and other incentives to favour particular options, should they thereafter adopt a 'self-denying ordinance' and permit guidance services to be client-centred in weighing up these and other pros and cons (Watts, 1996b)?

There are important political and ethical issues here, but there are also practical issues. If Careers Advisers are to be able to intervene effectively with young people who have dropped out of the formal system or are at risk of doing so, they need to understand and to be prepared to work to some extent within the subjective frame of reference of the young people with whom they are working. As Coles (1988) puts it, they need to be not only experts in local labour market intelligence but also 'ethnographers of local "youth culture" ' (p. 83).

Traditionally, however, formal career guidance services have paid little if any attention to the informal economies. Indeed, even within the formal economy they have tended to be drawn to its more bureaucratic parts, such as the professions and large organisations, where educational credentials tend to be more important; somewhat less attention has in general been given to the more entrepreneurial parts, including small firms and self-employment. This is not surprising, since formal guidance services tend to be located within or closely connected to the formal education system, which is significantly legitimated through the structure of credentialism that such services support. In secondary schools, in particular, the chief basis for organisational control is the promise that: 'If you work hard and pass your exams, you'll get a (good) job'. The premise underlying this promise is much more valid in the bureaucratic sectors of the labour market than in its entrepreneurial sectors. When guidance programmes emphasise the bureaucratic sectors, therefore, they are serving the interests of the school itself (see chapter 3).

The tendency for formal career guidance services to relate narrowly to the formal education, training and employment system explains why strategies addressed to social exclusion have tended to focus on building close working links between career guidance services and youth/community services. The latter are more likely to have contact with, and credibility with, the young people concerned, because they know more about the informal systems within which the young people live, and are more prepared and better equipped to work within their frame of reference. On the other hand, if the policy aim is to encourage the young people to move back into the system, the career guidance services can provide the information and support they need in order to do so. The 'street knowledge' of the youth/community services is thus in principle complemented by the 'formal knowledge' of the careers services; the process-oriented methods of the former mesh with the more formal methods of the latter (see e.g. Morgan & Hughes, 1999).

Such partnerships can adopt a number of different strategies. In a six-country European project on 'non-formal guidance' for young people at risk, the non-formal guidance agents were defined to include not only youth/community workers but also significant adults or peers who had ongoing relationships with the target-group of young people or might be able to form such relationships on an informal basis. Three strategies were developed for linking the formal and non-formal guidance providers (Watts & McCarthy, 1996). The first was for the non-formal guidance agents to act as referral points for accessing the target-group to the formal guidance system. The second was concerned with outreach: for the formal guidance services to develop new methods for working with the non-formal guidance agents and with the target-group itself. The third focused on capacity building: helping the non-formal guidance agents to be initial deliverers of guidance to the target-group. The latter was carried out through training programmes designed to develop the guidance skills of the non-formal guidance agents (Watts & McCarthy, 1998).

The inclusion of unpaid volunteers within the project raised a number of complex issues (Watts & McCarthy, 1998). How far should the project be concerned to formalise the non-formal, or to respect and value its non-formality? For example, should the volunteers be paid, particularly where they were unemployed themselves; should, indeed, they be given opportunities for using the training courses as the first step towards a professional qualification in youth and community work or related fields? Or, especially in the case of the 'deeply alienated' young people identified by Williamson (2000), would unpaid non-professionals find it easier to secure young people's trust than adults paid by the state? Beneath these issues lay the definition of 'social exclusion' being adopted by the project. If it was defined as being outside the formal education, training and employment system, then the unemployed volunteers were socially excluded too. Should the project seek to 'include' them (as they were seeking to 'include' the young people) by offering them training and a paid post with the public expenditure this would require? Or should it, in effect, reinforce and utilise their 'exclusion'?

The partnership design of such projects can be seen as an attempt to manage the tensions and the ethical and practical dilemmas involved in designing guidance strategies to achieve the voluntaristic participation of young people in formal systems which they have rejected. These tensions and dilemmas are also evident when defining the outcome criteria by which the success of the projects will be measured. If these are defined too rigidly as reintegration into the formal system, this assumes that such an outcome is the only desirable one, and thus fails to respect the autonomy of the young person: their right to determine the course of their own lives. As well as being ethically questionable, this may be pragmatically counterproductive: attempts to drive too directly towards such an outcome may be resisted and therefore reduce the chances of achieving the outcome itself. Accordingly, it is argued that the outcome criteria should be framed in terms of 'graded steps' which are valuable in relation to achieving viable and socially legitimate lifestyles outside the formal system, as well as enabling young people to move towards the formal system as and when they wish to do so (Watts & McCarthy, 1998).

Many of the same issues emerged from the major career guidance initiative addressed to the needs of 'at risk' young people under the Conservative Government that held power in the mid-1990s: the Mentoring Action Project. This represented an example of an 'outreach' strategy: developing the 'mentoring' skills of careers service staff so that they were equipped to work in more informal ways with disengaged young people. The project was initiated not by the government but by careers services themselves, through the Institute of Careers Guidance, with funding from the European Commission's Youthstart programme. It stemmed from the recognition by careers services that: 'The increasing emphasis placed nationally on the main core of pupils and students in full-time mainstream education meant that young people who had left school and were encountering difficulties – for a variety of reasons – in adjusting to the formal system and progressing into education, training and work, were at risk of losing the ready access to in-depth career guidance services which they required if they were to establish a clear sense of personal direction' (Ford, n.d., pp. 16-17). By the end of the project in December 1997, there had been a change of government, and the focus of concern was being precisely reversed.

'Foregrounding' social inclusion

Prior to the General Election of 1997, the Labour Party had been working on a policy statement entitled *A Successful Career: the Careers Service in the 21st Century*. The document stated that: 'The Skills Revolution will demand the creation of a Careers Service integrally and inextricably linked to a learning-led culture and economy'. It made a number of proposals for extending services to adults, including the introduction of personal learning advisers: 'Our aim is that everyone should have an entitlement to meet with a personal learning adviser at least every two years.' The Careers Service was seen as being 'at the centre of a network of providers, be they schools, further and higher education, the Employment Service (ES), TECs or individual companies and LEAs' (Labour Party, 1997, p. 2). The move was towards a universal all-age careers service. The only reference to young people who had fallen out of the system was a statement that new ways of targeting such young people needed to be explored (p. 6).

This document, colloquially known as the 'Byers/Gee document', was nearing publication when the General Election was called. In a speech to the Careers Services National Association in June 1997, shortly after the Election, David Blunkett (Secretary of State for Education and Employment) referred to 'the emerging paper that we didn't quite manage to get out in time for the General Election' and declared that: 'We will manage to get it out in the weeks and months ahead as fully fledged Government paper.' But it was never published.

Instead, the first major government statement came in a speech by Dr Kim Howells, a junior Minister, at a Careers Service Conference held at Heathrow in November 1997. He included a passage in which he emphasised the priority attached by the government to social inclusion:

> We want *all* young people to have the help they need… But we also want to concentrate some of our resources, and activity, in schools on those who are *most at risk*, or who have 'dropped out'… And we want schools and colleges to take more responsibility for preparing pupils to take careers decisions. This will free up services to concentrate more on the areas where they are most needed to focus their professional skills more on those who need it most, and supporting lifelong learning… For young people over the age of 16, we want services to concentrate on those who are *not in education, training or employment.*

This 'focusing agenda', as it came to be called, meant that careers services ceased to carry out careers interviews with all young people in schools (a practice that was already beginning to be modified in some areas by the growth of small-group work). The agenda had, in principle, two facets: allowing greater flexibility of response, so that more attention could be given to young people of all kinds who were 'ill-informed or undecided' ; and targeting attention on young people who had already dropped out of the formal system or were deemed to be at risk of doing so (DfEE, 1998a). In practice, the targeting agenda predominated. In a growing number of schools, young people who were performing well but were uncertain about what they wanted to do found it difficult or impossible to secure a careers interview.

Then, in June 1999, the government moved the issue of social exclusion centre-stage. It issued a White Paper in which it indicated its intention to create 'a comprehensive structure for advice and support for all young people beyond 13, improving the coherence of what is currently provided through organisations such as the Careers Service, parts of the Youth Service and a range of other specialist agencies' (DfEE, 1999a, p. 51). Significantly, the details of this new service were published soon afterwards in a report from the Social Exclusion Unit within the Cabinet Office, entitled *Bridging the Gap: New Opportunities for 16-18 Year Olds Not in Education, Employment or Training* (SEU, 1999). The report indicated that the service would take the form of a single national agency, which would contract with a single lead body locally to be accountable for providing the service in its area.

Subsequently, a policy statement on this new Connexions Service, as it was to be called, indicated that it would operate through a 'new profession' of Personal Advisers, who would 'end the current fragmentation of services' and 'take responsibility for ensuring all the needs of a young person are met in an integrated and coherent manner'. These Personal Advisers would 'be drawn from a range of backgrounds including the Careers Service, Youth Service, Social Services, teachers and Youth Offending Teams, as well as from the voluntary and community sectors'. They would operate at three levels of priority: 'intensive sustained support for those with multiple problems' ; 'in-depth guidance for those at risk of disengaging' ; and, for the rest, 'information and advice on career/learning/employment choices with minimum levels of intervention' . Alongside these Personal Advisers, the service would also 'encourage and provide training to members of the community to act as mentors' (DfEE, 2000a, pp. 35, 39, 41, 45).

While there was some consultation following the White Paper, it was on points of detail rather than on the key design features of the proposals. It is accordingly important to note that the proposals themselves did not emerge from any in-depth analysis involving research and open consultations with professionals in the field. They were significantly influenced by Demos, a policy think-tank. Geoff Mulgan, the former Director of Demos, had been appointed as adviser to the No. 10 Policy Unit and was the *eminence grise* behind the Social Exclusion Unit (Levitas, 1998). Demos had published an analysis of the problems of marginalised youth (Bentley & Gurumurthy, 1999), supported by a report on the views of young people who had experienced various aspects of social exclusion (Bentley & Oakley, 1999). The former report recommended, in particular, that the government should create 'a new profession: the youth broker, responsible for supporting young people in creating pathways to independence'. This 'national service… could be created through the long-term merger of the youth, careers and education welfare services'. It should include 'the offer of a mentor to any at-risk young person who wants one' (Bentley & Gurumurthy, 1999, pp. 105-106). All of these ideas were clearly evident in the design of Connexions. Although the title 'youth broker' specifically referred to in *Bridging the Gap* (SEU, 1999, p. 83) as an idea that was being examined was not subsequently adopted, the concept was, in the proposals for the 'new profession' of Personal Adviser.

Thus the key design features of Connexions stemmed essentially from an analysis related to the needs of young people at risk of social exclusion. The core of the analysis was the belief that a key cause of the ineffectiveness of current provision was the proliferation of specialist agencies, each dealing with a disconnected part of the young person's life. Bentley and Gurumurthy (1999) quoted and endorsed the view of an American commentator who saw the basic problem as being the inclination of agencies to protect their own turf: 'Every agency has a speciality, a catchment area, a *raison d'être*. Every profession has its own area of expertise... They are suspicious of, if not downright unfriendly to, others who may approach the problem from a different angle' (Ianni, 1989). This was reinforced by Merton's (1998) comment that 'young people often feel as if they are being passed from pillar to post and each time they meet an official from yet another agency they have to tell their story again' (p. 21). Accordingly, there was a widely-held view that the agencies needed to be brought more closely together, and that as part of this process there was a strong case for each young person to be linked to a key worker who could form a relationship of trust with them, see their problems as a whole, and 'broker' the support of the relevant specialist agencies.

In transferring this analysis into the design of Connexions, however, there were two fundamental design flaws. The first was linked to the fact that Connexions was designed not just for young people at risk of social exclusion but for all young people: it was both a targeted and a universal service. The conventional and logical way to reconcile these dual aims is first to design the universal service and then extend it to ensure that the distinctive needs of the targeted group are satisfactorily addressed. But Connexions was designed on the reverse basis. Significantly, a key rationale given by Ministers in the Parliamentary debates on the Learning and Skills Bill was the principle that 'if "poor people's services" are just for poor people, they tend to be poor services': accordingly, 'it will be a universal service for all people, because that is the most civilised and dignified way of giving support to the most disadvantaged' (Malcolm Wicks, House of Commons *Hansard*, 27 June 2000). In other words, universality was a second-order consideration. As a result, efforts were made to extrapolate to all young people measures designed to address the needs of the primary target-group. If the needs of young people at risk were perceived to require the merging of services, then the services must be merged as a totality. If young people at risk were to have a Personal Adviser, then all young people must have one.

The second design flaw was that the original Demos aim of merging the youth, careers and educational welfare services was only part-implemented. The only service totally subsumed within Connexions was the Careers Service; the other services remained as entities, but expected to participate in and pass some of their resources to the Connexions Service. The main reason for this distinction was administrative convenience: the Careers Service was the only budget that the Department for Education and Employment (DfEE) as the main government department responsible for the planning of Connexions was able to control; without it, the funding base for the new service looked fragile. But the decision to commit the whole of the Careers Service budget to Connexions, alongside the failure to secure similar commitments from other budget-holders, immediately produced an imbalance in the structure of Connexions partnerships. It also meant that careers services' existing mainstream work was placed under threat.

Problems

A number of problems stemmed from one or both of these two design flaws. The first related to case-loads. It was felt that ways had to be found of securing Personal Advisers for all young people. But, on cost and staffing grounds, the case-load outside the 'at risk' group would have to be much higher. Unpublished working papers produced within DfEE suggested that Personal Advisers might work with '10-20 young people with multiple problems, 250 young people in need of in-depth guidance or more than 800 young people who only [sic] need a guidance interview' . While such specific figures did not appear in official public statements, the principle of three levels implying very different case-loads was regularly mentioned (e.g. DfEE, 2000c, p. 35). With large case-loads, however, the rationale for the role of a Personal Adviser able to form a relationship, view the young person in holistic terms, broker specialist services was clearly neither credible nor sustainable.

The second problem related to staffing. DfEE calculated, presumably on the basis of its initial ratios, that between 15,000 and 20,000 Personal Advisers would need to be recruited (Baroness Blackstone, House of Lords *Hansard*, 17 February 2000, col. 1380). The notion was that these would initially come mainly from the Careers Service and the Youth Service. But there were only just over 7,000 Careers Advisers working in the Careers Service in the whole of England, Scotland and Wales (ICG, n.d., p. 10). In order to meet the target, as many of these as possible might need to be recruited as Personal Advisers. DfEE accordingly became reluctant to commit itself to the inclusion of Careers Advisers among the specialist services to which Personal Advisers would broker access (e.g. DfEE, 2000a, p. 41; SEU, 1999, p. 81). The notion grew that in the case of career guidance, Personal Advisers might be expected to deliver what was required. But, of course, not all Personal Advisers would have been trained to provide career guidance. It was suggested that a small element of training in a short generic course might fill this gap (DfEE, 2000d). This raised the danger of serious erosion of professional standards in service delivery.

When, later, a clearer distinction was established between generic Personal Advisers and specialist support in vocational guidance, the issue was still blurred by using the term 'specialist personal advisers' for the latter – these being distinguished from those who wished to become 'fully qualified Connexions personal advisers' (DfEE, 2000e, para. H7). Locating Careers Advisers as specialists within a new profession of Personal Advisers, in which they were not regarded as being fully qualified, seemed paradoxical, confusing and indeed demeaning.

The third problem concerned the role of pastoral-care structures in schools and colleges. In the initial design of Connexions, such structures were virtually ignored. *Bridging the Gap* included an analysis of the range of functions which might be performed by the Connexions Service, identifying by whom they were currently performed: on the function of 'providing a network of Personal Advisers to provide a single point of contact for each young person and ensure that someone has an overview of each person's ambitions and needs', the only pre-16 reference was to 'learning mentors being introduced into schools in some inner city areas as part of Excellence in Cities' (SEU, 1999, p. 81). Yet for pupils in schools and colleges, tutors clearly fitted this job description – much more credibly so, indeed, than Personal Advisers with case-loads of between 1:250 and over 1:800. When, belatedly, a Ministerial speech acknowledged that 'tutors are usually closest to pupils, and may be important in identifying initial needs', it added that they 'can give advice on courses themselves, and refer young people to Personal Advisers for further help or guidance' (Malcolm Wicks' speech to Annual Conference of the National Association of Careers and Guidance Teachers, 6 July 2000). Since Ministers had already by this stage indicated that, where appropriate, Personal Advisers would refer young people to specialist careers advice, this seemed to suggest a cumbersome three-stage model, in which the intermediate stage had no evident rationale. By late 2000, policy statements were suggesting that Personal Advisers might only be needed for those requiring intensive support (DfEE, 2000e, para.H3).

The fourth problem related to impartiality. Because the role of Personal Advisers pre-16 was focused largely on combating disaffection from learning, there appeared to be a strong case for basing them in schools. Following lobbying from headteachers' associations, a circular was issued stating that: 'Personal advisers working in schools and in Pupil Referral Units will be appointed and managed by the Head Teacher or teacher in charge but will also operate as part of the integrated Connexions Service' (DfEE, 2000b, p. 3). This immediately raised concerns about the long-standing issue of the impartiality of advice offered on post-16 options in 11-18 schools which had a financial interest in persuading their pupils to stay on rather than move elsewhere (e.g. Ofsted, 1998, p. 16). The main assurance of impartiality of advice was access to Careers Advisers based outside the school: this was the rationale for mandating such access in the Education Act 1997 (DfEE, 1997). But if many Careers Advisers were to be replaced by Personal Advisers appointed and managed by headteachers, the extent of this access seemed likely to be severely reduced; and insofar as career guidance was in future to be offered by these Personal Advisers, the likelihood of overt or subtle pressures being placed on their impartiality was significantly enhanced. The DfEE's *Planning Guidance* nonetheless reiterated the principle that 'all young people [should] have access to impartial careers information, advice and guidance' , and stated that: 'The Connexions Service should have the final say on how this is to be achieved' (DfEE, 2000e, para. I8). The potential for conflict or collusion here seemed considerable. Confidence was not enhanced by a Ministerial statement that the proposed Connexions Direct website and helpline could be 'one route for giving them access to impartial guidance on post-16 choices, or for gaining a second opinion if they are not convinced by what they hear in school' (Malcolm Wicks at NACGT Annual Conference, op. cit.). A key issue here was whether 'reactive impartiality' , requiring student initiative, was sufficient, or whether agreement should be based on 'positive impartiality', requiring positive steps to be taken to make students aware of the full range of choices (Watts & Young, 1997).

The fifth problem was more generally concerned with standards of career education and guidance provision in schools and colleges. As noted earlier, the 1997 statement by Kim Howells indicated that the government wanted schools and colleges 'to take more responsibility for preparing pupils to take careers decisions', in order to 'free up [careers] services to concentrate on the areas where they are most needed'. But an official survey of careers work in schools stated that 'the wide variation in content, organisation, and time allocated for careers work is unacceptable' (Ofsted, 1998, p. 17). Had significant steps been taken to address this situation, then a serious and credible strategy to move towards a more school/college-based model of provision would have been discernible. But no such moves were made.

All of these problems related to the services provided for mainstream young people. But even in relation to the primary target-group of 'at risk' young people, further confusions were evident. Roles were ill-defined. It was unclear how far the Personal Adviser was expected to be a first-in-line adviser, a nominated specialist with an additional generic role, a new additional generalist, or a merging of existing specialists into a multi-skilled generalist. All had very different implications for the competencies required of Personal Advisers (Watts, 1999b). Young people at risk were to have access not only to a Personal Adviser but also to a volunteer mentor: the relationship between the two roles was not clear. Further confusion was added by initially using the term 'Learning Mentors' – adopted from the Excellence in Cities programme (DfEE, 1999b) – to describe Personal Advisers based in schools. To compound the confusion still further, initial statements indicated that 'The Personal Adviser for most 13-16 year old children will be a Learning Mentor based in their school' (DfEE, 2000a, p. 53); whereas later it was stated that, in Excellence in Cities areas, Connexions advisers were to 'work alongside EiC Learning Mentors' (DfEE, 2000b, p. 3) – with no indication of how their roles were to be differentiated.

Moreover, there was little sensitivity in the policy statements on Connexions to the complexities of working with disengaged young people. *Bridging the Gap* made no effort to conceptualise or even acknowledge the informal economies: when referring to lone parents, for example, it stated that there was no reason to believe that they 'could not participate in learning or work given the opportunity and help in doing do' (SEU, 1999, p. 22) – so denying the status of child-rearing as legitimate work.

Again, the initial policy statement on Connexions appeared to see no contradiction or tension between on the one hand a young-person-centred service able to command the trust of young people and understand their needs, and on the other a service that would be required to carry out the control function of ensuring school attendance pre-16 and whose performance would be measured by prescribed outcomes related not to subjective measures of satisfaction and appropriateness but to objective measures of participation in the formal education and training system (DfEE, 2000a, pp. 34, 35, 56). In this context, the liberal intentions of co-ordinated support for young people could easily be turned into its obverse: co-ordinated surveillance (Kelly, 2000) 'weaving an all-pervasive web of "social control"' (Rose & Miller, 1992, p. 175).

It is difficult not to conclude that all of these problems stemmed, in one way or another, from the decision to seek a structural solution to the problems of 'at risk' young people rather than building on the programmes and partnerships that were already in place. Other studies of linkages between guidance services have classified them at five different levels: communication, co-operation, co-ordination, cross-fertilisation and integration (e.g. Miller, Taylor & Watts, 1983; Watts, Dartois & Plant, 1988). Initiatives like the Mentoring Action Project (Ford, n.d.), the Stepping Stones project (Ford, 2000a), New Start (Morgan & Hughes, 1999) and the Learning Gateway (GHK Economics & Management, 2000) were already successfully developing linkages between careers services, youth services and others based on the more modest levels, including cross-fertilisation (where efforts are made to encourage services to share and exchange skills, and in effect to work across professional boundaries in ways that are likely to re-draw the boundaries themselves). These developments appeared to be achieving effects: official Labour Force Survey figures for young people aged 16-18 who were not in education, training or employment fell from 185,000 in 1998 to 157,000 in 1999 (Malcolm Wicks at NACGT Annual Conference, op. cit.) (though, of course, causality cannot be assumed). The decision to move to integration, however, meant that instead of these developments progressing organically, the focus of attention shifted to organisational restructuring, which had major unforeseen side-effects on mainstream provision. The problems and confusions analysed in this paper demonstrate the efforts of policy-makers to struggle with these side-effects.

It is significant in this respect to note that Scotland and Wales decided not to follow the Connexions route. In Scotland, the Beattie Committee (1999) recommended that careers service companies should have adequate resources to work with 'at risk' young people, including identifying those who would benefit from the support of a 'key worker' and/or mentor in collaboration with schools and guidance staff, but it proposed building stronger links between the Careers Service and other agencies rather than seeking to restructure them. In Wales, a report from the National

Assembly for Wales Policy Unit (2000) explicitly stated that it had examined and rejected the option of restructuring all sources of funding for youth support into a new single funding stream for allocation at local level across providers. Its reasons were telling: that 'the disruption caused by restructuring would be unlikely to be justified by gains in delivery'; that 'restructuring would be a distraction from service improvement'; and that 'there is a good case for maintaining the Careers company input as a centrally funded stream to preserve the independence of vocational advice to young people' (p. 72).

Indeed, instead of moving towards horizontal integration of support services for young people, Wales and Scotland have decided to move towards vertical integration of all-age career guidance services.[40] Following a report from the Education and Training Action Group for Wales (1999), steps are being taken to establish Careers Wales as a national all-age information, advice and guidance service. Based on the current role of the eight careers service companies in Wales, it is drawing together provision from the Careers Service, the Adult Guidance Initiative and Learndirect. A broadly similar model is being adopted in Scotland, where the Duffner Committee (2000) has recommended that the Careers Service be responsible for ensuring the provision of an all-age careers guidance service, and be given a new collective identity as Careers Scotland. The all-age model is that proposed for England too by the 'Byers/Gee document', noted earlier. But it contrasts sharply with what has subsequently occurred in England, where the government's adult guidance strategy based on local Information, Advice and Guidance for Adults (IAGA) partnerships (DfEE, 1998b) is at risk of being undermined by the fact that careers service companies which in most areas have been the lead partner in these partnerships are in some cases to be totally subsumed with the local Connexions partnership.

In other areas of England, careers service companies may continue, carrying out work for Connexions on a sub-contractual basis. As a final irony, the *Planning Guidance* states that 'where a Partnership subcontracts for services an open and transparent competitive tender exercise should be undertaken' (DfEE, 2000e, para. L29). It seems, therefore, that in those areas where careers service companies wish to remain in being, they will have to return to the competitive tendering introduced by the previous Conservative Government. Yet the 'Byers/Gee document' was critical of these arrangements, proposing to replace them with licenses and franchises as later recommended by the National Audit Office (1997). It noted: 'the costs of contracting out have been substantial . . . This money could be put to better use' (Labour Party, 1997, p. 4).

---

40 Editorial footnote: For a later review of these and other all-age services, see: Watts, A.G. (2010). National all-age career guidance services: evidence and issues. *British Journal of Guidance and Counselling*, 38(1), 31-44.

Conclusion

The analysis of the development of Connexions in this paper has taken the story up to the end of 2000, and has focused on design faults and the problems that have ensued from them. Other commentators have been more optimistic. Law (2000), for example, has suggested that Connexions offers opportunities for reframing support for career on a broader and deeper basis. Roberts (2000) has pointed out that: 'Many careers officers have long aspired to broaden out into life counselling. They will now have that chance' (p. 27). There are possibilities for innovation in using information and communication technologies (Offer & Watts, 2000) and in taking steps to ensure that the integration of services working with schools is mirrored by schools taking a similarly holistic view of their work supporting pupils (Andrews, 2000). Ford (2000b) has identified a number of common elements between Connexions and IAGA partnerships which could provide the basis for all-age strategies.

But it is clear that many problems remain to be solved if these potential benefits are to be realised, and to outweigh the risks. Unless the fundamental flaws are acknowledged and addressed, workable solutions are unlikely to be found. Current policy seems to favour solutions being found at local level, and over a longer time-frame than originally envisaged (Weinstock, 2000). These represent classic responses of policy-makers when faced with intractable difficulties in original policy design.

Many of these difficulties could have been avoided. The way in which the design of Connexions emerged, from think-tank exercises supported by some limited scanning of the views of young people, represents a clear case of what le Fanu (2000) terms 'the culture of ignorance', demonstrating that this culture, 'nourished during the Thatcher years, flourishes still'. Its distinctive feature is that 'its adherents mistrust those with specific skills or expertise, suspecting that they are interested only in feathering their own nests' (p. 23). The failure to conduct any open consultation of professionals in the field meant that the implications of the measures recommended were not thought through. To add insult to injury, Ministers subsequently appeared to take the view that they were battling against a recalcitrant profession rigidly attached to the bureaucratic target-driven regime established by the previous government. The fact that, with little official support, careers services had carried out innovative work addressed precisely to the problems which the new government was concerned to prioritise, was given little if any attention, and the opportunity to learn from this experience was missed. It will not be surprising if, when a new government in due course gains power, Connexions Services are similarly excoriated for neglecting the needs of mainstream young people and the labour market.[41]

---

41 Editorial footnote: Indeed this did prove to be the case in the Milburn report (2009) which echoed many of the criticisms of Connexions that are made in this chapter.

This demonstrates the dangers of guidance services being directly subject to the ebbs and flows of political processes. In such situations, they are vulnerable to destabilising swings of priority, as well as being used as scapegoats for the perceived deficiencies of the preceding government. Much depends on key civil servants understanding the distinctive nature of guidance services and being able and willing to inform Ministers of likely implications before the government commits itself to particular courses of action. In the case of Connexions, this role seems to have been inadequately performed.

The emergence of the Connexions Service provides a salutary demonstration of the dangers of giving excessive prominence to the issue of social exclusion in framing policy on career guidance services. Certainly such services have a potentially important role to play in strategies designed to address social exclusion. But in the end, the social benefits of guidance are not limited to participation: they are concerned with individual progression and development, and with linking societal needs to individual needs on a voluntaristic basis (Watts, 1996b). In short, the primary role of guidance services lies in lubricating the societal structures to which inclusion is being sought.

15. The New Career and Public Policy[42]

Careerquake

The concept of career has been a significant feature of advanced industrial societies in the twentieth century. For individuals, it has provided the structure for a coherent and continuous working life which has helped to shape and sustain social identity, linked to a faith in the future and a sense of the future self. For organisations, it has provided a means of motivating employees, and a structure through which their development can be linked to organisational goals. It has also bound individuals to the wider society, and so helped to stabilise it (Wilensky, 1961).

But career structures in many countries are now being fractured. Work organisations are less prepared to make long-term commitments to individuals. Many have been reducing their size, and seeking to operate in more flexible ways through a small core of key workers and a growing contractual periphery.

This process has gone further in some countries than in others. It is strongly evident in English-speaking countries, and particularly in the USA, which has been concerned to restrict labour-market regulation and to trust the free flow of market forces. Although deregulation has created jobs, many have been low-skill in nature. Combined with low levels of social-welfare expenditure, this has resulted in marked social disparities, linked to high levels of crime, drugs, and violence.

In other countries, the process has been constrained by cultural and political factors (Albert, 1993; Hutton, 1995). In Japan, for example, the 'lifetime employment system' has been eroded somewhat but remains influential; economic relationships are based on trust and continuity, supported by an interventionist state providing the infrastructure for economic development. Continental European countries like Germany, France, and the Scandinavian countries, too, have sought to regulate markets, underpinned by corporate partnerships between the state, employers, and unions, in order to encourage employment security and social protection. It seems, however, that relative stability in these countries is being bought at the price of higher levels of unemployment.

The UK could be in a position to offer a 'third way'. It has traditionally had a stronger welfare ethos than the USA. But its tentative flirtations with corporatism have been largely abandoned, and in recent years it has engaged in extensive US-style deregulation aimed at securing greater labour-market flexibility. Its task now is to

---

[42] **Editorial footnote:** Reprinted, by permission of the publisher, from Collin, A. & Young, R.A. (eds.): *The Future of Career*. Cambridge: Cambridge University Press, 2000. DOI: 10.1017/CBO9780511520853.017.

see whether it can re-cast its welfare ethos in forms which can be reconciled with such flexibility.

Labour-market flexibility is not necessarily unwelcome to those affected by it. But for many, it is seen as offering a threat rather than an opportunity (National Association of Citizens Advice Bureaux, 1997). This is particularly the case for the low-skilled, who can be exploited on low wages, without benefits or security, and then thrown back on to the labour market when no longer needed. Flexibility here becomes a euphemism for the naked exercise of employers' labour-market power.

This raises the critical issue of how flexibility can be reconciled with the need to secure the high skill levels required for economic competitiveness. As Reich (1991) points out, well-trained workers and modern infrastructure attract global webs of enterprise, which invest and give workers relatively good jobs; these jobs, in turn, generate additional on-the-job training and experience, thus creating a powerful lure to other global webs (see also Porter, 1990). High levels of skill make it possible to generate products which compare on the basis of quality rather than purely on the basis of price: this alone can yield the high returns that sustain high wages. But in flexible labour markets, employers tend to restrict their training commitment to their limited core workers. While some peripheral workers may be prepared to plan and finance their own training to maintain employability, those with lower skills and lower pay are unlikely to do so; even less so are those caught in poverty traps and cultures of unemployment which limit their hold on the labour market.

This in turn poses threats to social cohesion. Hutton (1995) has described the emergence of the 40: 30: 30 society: the growing divisions between the 40% who are relatively privileged, in reasonably secure employment or self-employment; the 30% who are marginalised and insecure, in jobs that are poorly protected and carry few benefits; and the 30% who are disadvantaged, being either unemployed or economically inactive. Such divisions threaten a decline into an ever more selfish, splintered, violent society. In the USA, Reich (1991, p. 303) has pointed to the risk that what he calls the 'symbolic analysts' – the new work aristocracy, with the high-level skills that can make flexibility work to their advantage – are losing their sense of belonging to a wider community, and becoming resentful of any support for the well-being of others. He notes that their sense of enclosure is illusory: that 'the peace of mind potentially offered by platoons of security guards, state-of-the-art alarm systems, and a multitude of prisons is limited'.

The key policy question, therefore, is whether it is possible to reconcile social equity and upgrading of skills with a flexible labour market. One response is to view low-skill jobs in life-cycle terms (Esping-Andersen, 1994). Instead of being a life sentence for certain groups, such jobs could be seen as a temporary phase, giving individuals an initial experience of work disciplines, filling in gaps, or helping to fund further education, after which they can move on to more demanding roles. The Confederation of British Industry (1989) has advanced the concept of 'careers for all' – linked to continuous learning throughout life – as the means of achieving the 'skills revolution' needed to achieve competitive advantage in the global economy.

This suggests that what is needed is a much broader concept of career, supported by appropriate social institutions and incentives. In the industrial era, the dominant concept of career has been progression up an ordered hierarchy within an organisation or profession. Instead, career should now be viewed as the individual's lifelong progression in learning and in work. 'Learning' embraces not only formal education and training, but also informal forms of learning, in the workplace and elsewhere. 'Work' includes not only paid employment and self-employment, but also the many other forms of socially valuable work, in households and in the community (including child-rearing and elder care). 'Progression' covers not only vertical but also lateral movement: it is concerned with experience as well as positions; with broadening as well as advancing. 'Progression' does however retain the sense of development: career is more than mere biography.

Such a concept recognises not only skill development but also fluctuations in the life-cycle due to changing family commitments and changing values. It provides a framework for encouraging everyone to continue to learn and develop throughout life, linked to a sense of having a stake in society. It thus makes it possible to reconcile flexibility with a just society, in Rawls's (1972) challenging definition of the term: one we would choose to live in if we did not know what position within it we ourselves would occupy.

If future careers in this broader sense are to be accessible to all, new social ligatures are needed: new bonds between individuals and social structures. These are the issues for public policy which this chapter discusses. Much of it is drawn from a pamphlet written for the policy think-tank Demos (Watts, 1996d); many of its themes have also more recently been addressed by Bayliss (1998). Whilst written mainly from a UK perspective, most of the issues are of broader international relevance.

More flexible financial-support structures

The most fundamental ligature is to reform the welfare state to provide support to more flexible and individually driven careers, linked to a wider concept of work. The welfare state that emerged after the Second World War was based on a series of assumptions about the family, work, and the life-cycle (Esping-Andersen, 1994). The family was assumed to combine a full-time stably employed male wage-earner, with a wife primarily devoted to her work within the home. It was further assumed that their life-cycles were orderly, standardised, and predictable, that male employment was assured, and that the welfare state could therefore concentrate on childhood (schooling) and old age (pensions), being largely passive during the active middle part of the life-cycle except in supporting men affected by frictional or cyclical unemployment.

All of these assumptions are now in question. Women are now spending much longer periods in the labour force, with shorter gaps for childrearing. Young people are entering the labour force later, and taking longer to secure an independent foothold within it. Dislocation and significant changes in mid-career are more common. Some older workers are adopting a more gradual process of disengagement from full-time employment. In short, the life-cycle is becoming more flexible and diverse (e.g. Gaullier, 1992).

These changes place an ever-greater burden on the welfare system as currently constructed, with longer periods of dependency during the lifespan and shorter periods of contribution. This is producing a fiscal crisis in which the basic tenets of welfare as a basis for social equity and citizenship are being increasingly challenged, and levels of support eroded.

The most radical proposal for supporting a more flexible concept of career is to collapse the present tax and social-benefits systems into a basic citizen's income, received as a right by every individual – man, woman, and child. This would enable people to make flexible choices about the extent of paid employment in which they engage. The concept of unemployment – an industrial-era notion (Garraty, 1978) – would be redundant. With it would go poverty traps and the alternative lure of the black economy. More flexible patterns of work would be positively encouraged rather than – as at present – discouraged. The concept has appeal both to the political left, because it provides an egalitarian base, and to the right, because it liberates the market.

There are, however, objections to the citizen's income. The first is fiscal: the costs of the level needed to provide the basis for a satisfactory quality of life. After exhaustive costings of alternative models, Parker (1989) concluded that while it is not politically realistic to move immediately to a full citizen's income, it could be phased in. The second objection is political: a basic income would not of itself solve the problems of social exclusion, but might erode the political will to do anything further to address them. Certainly there would be a need for further measures to transform, for example, the infrastructure of poor neighbourhoods in terms of resources, housing, education, and economic opportunities. The third objection is ethical: by providing income without duties, the basic income undermines the concept of reciprocal obligation, traditionally the basis of active citizenship (Gray, 1996). It would however recognise that social contribution can take a variety of forms other than paid employment; and would be preferable to the present benefit system, which provides income only so long as people can demonstrate that they are doing little or nothing of social value.

To those who regard the ethical objection as decisive, the debate moves to some form of 'work test'. Taken to its logical conclusion, it leads to the notion of replacing current benefit systems with a 'workfare' scheme, in which unemployment benefits are paid only to those who engage in work constructed through public-policy interventions. The administrative costs of such schemes are, however, considerable, and there are difficulties in ensuring that they do not undermine the operations of the market. They also, if too narrowly drawn, tend to have a stigmatising effect, associated with 'make-work' rather than 'real work'. If, however, the boundaries of what is regarded as acceptable social contribution are broadened to include voluntary work, childcare, and education and training – as suggested by the concept of a 'participation income' (Commission on Social Justice, 1994) – this danger is more easily avoided. It then becomes a matter of balancing the costs of policing such a system – and the invasion of individual dignity which such policing systems can involve – against the benefits of maintaining an assurance of social obligation.

In the meantime, steps need to be taken to devise ways of coping with the effects of more flexible and discontinuous career patterns on mortgages, pensions, and private health-care insurance, all of which have hitherto been based on assumptions of continuous employment. Thus the great majority of those whose homes are repossessed because of mortgage default are people who have lost their job, whose earnings have fallen, or whose businesses have failed (Ford, Kempson, & Wilson, 1995). Wider use of payment 'holidays' and similar devices is needed to help mortgage payers to schedule their payments in line with their fluctuating career commitments, including helping them through temporary loss of work or the birth of children.

Stronger incentives to learning

Learning is the key to progression in work. If workers are to be able to move from contract to contract with some sense of development rather than mere survival, they need to find ways of enhancing their skills and knowledge on a continuing basis. Some of this will happen informally; some will happen formally alongside their work; some will require breaks from work.

Within a flexible labour market, employers need to be encouraged to replace a narrow approach to training with a broader approach to career development. This would include development in the workplace as well as on training courses, and focus on future employability as well as the skills required for immediate use. Some organisations are already doing this, as part of a new 'psychological contract' in which they seek to assure employees' security not by offering a 'job for life' but by providing training and development which will extend their marketable skills and sustain their 'career resilience' (Herriot & Pemberton, 1995; Waterman, Waterman & Collard, 1994).

In general, however, the rhetoric here is running well ahead of the reality (Hirsh & Jackson, 1996). Employers readily acknowledge the need to encourage people to participate in learning throughout their working lives. Most, however, are unwilling to provide any training that is not strictly related to immediate job needs (Metcalf, Walling & Fogarty, 1994), and their performance management systems pressure individuals to perform rather than to learn. In a market environment, the rational self-interest of employers requires access to skills, but offers little incentive to invest in their development, because they cannot be privately appropriated (Streeck, 1989, 1992). Employers investing in skill development are adding to a common pool which is accessible to other employers, including direct competitors, in their industry or locality. The result is that most firms have a chronic tendency to invest less in training and development than their own longer-term interest demands. Flexible labour markets greatly accentuate this tendency.

On the other hand, training is not an area where state provision is able readily to respond to market failure (Streeck, 1989). The record of government training schemes is not impressive. The notion that places of work and places of learning should be kept neatly apart, to serve their separate interests, is now widely questioned. Workplaces – particularly those using state-of-the-art technology – are engines of learning as well as of production.

A key policy question therefore is what measures need to be taken to encourage employers to invest in training and development in their collective interest, and whether these measures should be voluntary or include an element of compulsion. An idea of particular interest in this respect is individual learning accounts, to which government, employers, and individuals would all contribute, thus providing a mechanism for recognising mutuality of interest by sharing the costs (Commission on Social Justice, 1994). For the unemployed or self-employed, the lack of an employer contribution could be compensated through enhanced state contributions.

A more flexible and responsive learning system

Stronger incentives to learning require a learning system able to respond to learners' more flexible needs. In the industrial era, learning structures have tended to reflect work structures. Both work and learning have been concentrated in large bureaucratic organisations. Young people have been concentrated in schools and colleges, where they have acquired the attitudes and behaviours, plus the base of skills and knowledge, required for their likely future in the workplace (Bowles & Gintis, 1976). An important role of these institutions has been to sort out those destined for different levels of careers and of jobs – largely on the basis of examination performance (Dore, 1976).

Within this model, formal education has largely preceded employment. As the demands of the workplace have grown, the minimum school-leaving age has been progressively raised, further and higher education expanded, and the age of entry to the workplace deferred. But education has continued to be heavily 'front-loaded'. The relatively stable nature of work organisations has meant that any subsequent work-related learning has been largely provided within the organisation, with little need for further recourse to formal learning systems.

Now, however, new models of career are calling these traditional models of learning into question. The pace of technological change means that the 'shelf-life' of work skills and knowledge is getting ever shorter. 'Just-in-time' work systems require 'just-in-time' learning. More frequent movement between jobs requires regular acquisition of new competencies. More and more jobs require 'multi-skilling': a broader and more flexible range of skills, demanding a wider base of understanding. Learning no longer precedes work: it is interwoven with work, on a lifelong basis.

Lifelong learning does not necessarily mean lifelong education. It embraces training, as well as more informal learning in the workplace and outside it. The education system has, however, an important role to play in supporting such varied forms of learning, as well as providing formal learning opportunities detached from the immediate concerns of the workplace. It accordingly needs to be much more flexible than in the past. It needs to establish much stronger links with the world of work: to view employers as its partners in learning, not as receivers of its products. In addition, course structures need to be adapted to enable individuals to move easily in and out of the formal learning system, and to design their own learning pathways, drawing from provision in different kinds of institution where appropriate. In other words, education institutions need to be integrated into a flexible and co-ordinated learning system, providing resources for individuals to use as and when they have particular learning needs.

Technology is likely to play a powerful change-agent role in this respect. It liberates knowledge, and the learning process, from institutions (Hague, 1991). The traditional emphasis on class attendance is outdated. Learning packages can now be used in the home, the workplace, community centres, and elsewhere. Learners can start when they like, work at their own pace, and complete when ready to do so. The value added by more direct forms of learner support needs to be more personal and more interactive: in one-to-one or small-group situations, and focused not on transmitting information but on deepening understanding.

More flexible learning systems imply new roles for teachers, with implications for their staff development and career structures. The first role is as a learning designer – with 'products' ranging from books and video lectures to programmed-learning packages, multi-media learning kits, and various forms of experiential learning. The second is as a learning co-ordinator, linking human and material resources to objectives and methods so that they meet the needs and readiness of the learner. The third is as a learning consultant or mentor, helping the learner to overcome learning blockages and to engage at a deeper level with the meaning of what they are learning. The fourth is as a learning assessor, evaluating and accrediting the individual's learning regardless of where and how it has been obtained.

Such a concept of lifelong learning transforms the role of schools. Hitherto their models of learning have been dominated by public examinations, linked to their 'sorting' function. This has tended to encourage a narrowly instrumental approach to learning, focused on the 'exchange value' of examination certificates rather than the 'use value' of the learning itself (Saunders, 1993). Now, however, the key role of the school is to foster young people's motivation and confidence, and to develop their skills for learning how to learn. This requires very different curriculum models, with weaker emphasis on the boundaries between traditional school subjects, more stress on the interaction between theory and practice, and more use of community resources. Kolb's (1984) four-stage learning cycle – concrete experience, reflective observation, abstract conceptualisation, and active experimentation – needs to be built more strongly into school curricula.

This implies that relationships between learning and work need to be established more strongly at an earlier stage. Perhaps because of education's early-industrial-era role of protecting young people from child labour, its boundaries with the world of work have been sharply marked, and tightly patrolled. This has begun to change, and needs to change further. Experience-based learning in workplaces and other forms of education-business partnership enrich the learning process, and help young people to engage at an earlier age in the interaction between learning and work which is the essence of lifelong learning (Miller, Watts & Jamieson, 1991): such activities need to be extended, with stronger employer commitment. This could be linked to other changes in schools, mirroring those in the world of work: more 'portfolio' teachers combining teaching with other work roles, more 'contracting out' of parts of the curriculum to business and industry, more use of information technology for independent learning, more opportunities for problem-solving projects involving students working in supervised teams in varied settings, and more flexi-time arrangements that give teachers and students a stronger sense of control and reduce the sense of oppressive routine and predictability (Hargreaves, 1994).

Lifelong learning can be viewed as comprising three overlapping stages: foundation (up to the age of 16), instilling the habit of learning; formation (ages 14-21), developing workplace readiness; and continuation (age 18+), based on independent learning (Ball, 1991). A more flexible learning system constructed along these lines would mirror the new more flexible work system, and enable individuals to construct career paths intertwining the two.

A national qualifications framework

Within this new model of learning, the role of accreditation is critical. If individuals are to move more regularly between different work organisations, their learning must be accredited in ways which make it portable. This means accreditation not only of formal learning, but also of informal learning, including learning in the workplace. Individuals who are responsible for their own career development need to be assured that the learning they have acquired in the course of any work contract is accredited, to enable its value to be recognised by other possible employers. This could be the basis of a new mutually beneficial 'psychological contract' focused around employability rather than secure employment.

In the UK, the structure of National, and Scottish, Vocational Qualifications (NVQs/SVQs) represents an important move in this direction. It is competence-based, but does not prescribe the process by which the individual should achieve this competence. The framework is designed to cover all work-related learning, and to facilitate movement between as well as within particular occupations (Jessup, 1991). The framework has been extended to cover competences acquired through unpaid work in the home and the community. Its approach is, however, widely criticised for being narrowly behaviourist in nature and not paying sufficient attention to underpinning knowledge and theory (e.g. Hodkinson & Issitt, 1995). This could be a particularly significant limitation at higher occupational levels, where progress is still at an early stage.

As the same time, the post-compulsory education system is increasingly developing credit accumulation and transfer systems (CATS) to enable students to move more easily between different courses and institutions. The pace of such development is still uneven, with different credit 'tariff' systems being used by different institutions, with a continuing divide between the systems used within further and higher education respectively, and with some institutions being concerned with intra- rather than inter-institutional mobility (Robertson, 1994).

In principle, the roles of these two systems are complementary. The criticisms of NVQs/SVQs for neglecting knowledge and theory are mirrored by criticisms of educational courses accredited in CATS schemes for neglecting skills (in particular, transferable core skills). Effective learning experiences are likely to need to encompass attention to knowledge/theory and skills, though in varying balance –

both need to be accredited. Whether this is based on a system of dual accreditation of single learning experiences, or on an integrated accreditation system, is open to debate. But whichever approach is adopted, the new model of career requires an integrated qualifications framework. Such a framework will provide a clear, comprehensible, and widely recognised climbing frame for career development for all. Schools should then be seen as providing young people not with life-sentences based on terminal assessments, but with their initial foothold within the frame.

Action is also needed to make the resulting framework the basis for a 'licence to practise' in work roles. At present, such requirements exist in Britain only within occupations dominated by strong professional associations (e.g. medicine, the law, architecture, accountancy) and within some skilled trades (e.g. welding, electrical work). Such professional licencing could be applied to other occupational groups, as in Germany, both by legislation and by other forms of pressure and encouragement. It could be extended by requiring evidence of continuing professional development to maintain one's licence. The result would be greater protection of the consumer through product and service quality, plus a stronger incentive for individual career development.

Lifelong access to career guidance

Within the industrial era, the role of career guidance has been limited. The destiny of individuals within both the education system and the employment system has been determined largely by selection processes. Career guidance has been a limited switch-mechanism to fine-tune the passage from one system to the other. Hence career guidance services have been concentrated around the transition from full-time education to employment. In practice, the two systems have usually been so well synchronised that it has not had too much to do. It has been a marginal and low-status activity.

Now, however, its role is moving centre-stage. If individuals are to take responsibility for their career development, career guidance is critical, in three respects: helping individuals to clarify and articulate their aims and aspirations; ensuring that their decisions are informed in relation to the needs of the labour market; and empowering them in their negotiations with employers and other purchasers of their services. Careers are now based not on single decision points, but on a long series of iterative decisions made throughout life. Guidance needs to be available at all these decision points.

This means that a national strategy is required for lifelong access to guidance in support of lifelong career development for all (Watts, 1994a; Watts, Law, Killeen, Kidd & Hawthorn, 1996). No single agency can deliver what is needed. A three-pronged strategy is required, with each prong supported by strong and clear quality standards (Hawthorn, 1995).

First, career guidance should be an integral part of education. In particular, compulsory schooling should lay the foundations for lifelong career development. This emphasises the importance of career education within the curriculum, designed to develop competence in career self-management: the skills, knowledge, and attitudes which will enable young people to make and implement career decisions both immediately and in the future. Career education has traditionally been marginal to a curriculum dominated by academic subjects. It now needs to be the core of a new curriculum, preparing students for lifelong learning.

In addition, within but also beyond compulsory schooling, all educational provision should provide regular opportunities for students to relate what they are learning to their future career development. This has implications for the whole curriculum. It also requires tutorial support, and specialist guidance services within the institution. The importance attached to such services is likely to grow as course structures become more flexible, with the development of modular courses and systems of credit accumulation and transfer.

A particularly significant development both in schools and in further and higher education is the growing practice of encouraging students to engage in regular recording of achievement (reviewing their learning experiences, inside and outside the formal curriculum, and defining the skills and competencies acquired) and action planning (reviewing their long-term goals, their short-term learning objectives, and ways of achieving these objectives). These processes are of value in their own right; they also help to develop and support the skills of reviewing and of planning which are crucial to career self-management.

Second, guidance should be an integral part of work organisations. Here, too, individuals are increasingly being given opportunities to review their progress and their future plans – either within appraisal systems, or through parallel systems of development reviews. In addition, a growing number of organisations are introducing other activities to support career self-management, such as career planning workshops, assessment centres, career resource centres, and mentoring programmes (Kidd, 1996). Such practices tend, however, to be more common in larger organisations.

A potential advantage of embedding career guidance within educational and employing organisations is that they have more continuous contacts with individuals based within them, and so are able to deliver more substantial and sustained support than any external service can do. In particular, through their processes of regular development reviews, they are able to deliver the career equivalent of the dental check-up (Goodman, 1992). Furthermore, they are in a stronger position to influence the opportunities they offer in response to individuals' needs and demands, as revealed through the guidance process (see, e.g., Oakeshott, 1990).

Guidance can thus not only help individuals to choose between the opportunities already available, but also encourage organisations to develop new opportunities to meet individuals' preferences and requirements. But career guidance within education and employment will not cover everyone: many people spend significant parts of their lives outside such organisations – because they are unemployed, for example, or engaged in child-rearing. Moreover, guidance provision within organisations does not always have a sufficiently broad view of opportunities outside that organisation. Again, the organisation can have a vested interest in the outcomes of the individual's decision, which can make it difficult to provide guidance that is genuinely impartial. In the UK, for instance, schools with sixth-forms are rewarded financially if their students stay on beyond the age of sixteen: some are tempted to bias their guidance in favour of their own offerings at the expense of the opportunities available elsewhere. Employers, too, may be reluctant to encourage valued employees to explore opportunities in other organisations.

For these reasons, individuals also need access to guidance with a broader and more impartial perspective. Some will be able to gain sufficient help and support from friends and relatives. Many, however, will need access to a neutral service with professional counselling skills and access to high-quality information. This could have two levels (Watts, 1994b). Its foundation provision would be available free of charge to all. It could comprise a national telephone helpline (now available in the UK), plus open-access information centres in every sizeable town and city, with 'satellites' in rural areas. These centres would offer high-quality information, supported by brief 'diagnostic guidance' interventions designed to identify guidance needs for which further provision might be needed. This enhanced provision – counselling interviews, psychometric testing, etc. – would be available from a range of accredited providers, and would be costed: those able to pay would be expected to do so, perhaps from their individual learning accounts; public funding would be targeted at groups where the ability to pay was low and/or the public interest in take-up was high (notably the unemployed, women returners, and the low-waged).

To bring together these various strands of guidance provision within a coherent strategic framework, strong co-ordinating structures are needed. At national level, the National Advisory Council for Careers and Educational Guidance in the UK now brings together the major stakeholder organisations and guidance professional organisations, with observers from the relevant government departments. Strategic frameworks for lifelong access to guidance are also needed at local level (Watts, Hawthorn, Hoffbrand, Jackson & Spurling, 1997).

The changing concept of career has considerable implications not only for the structure of guidance delivery, but also for its processes. Full use needs to be made, for example, of the opportunities for global access to information and contacts offered by the Internet. It also seems likely that there will be a need for stronger links between career guidance and financial guidance (Collin & Watts, 1996).

Stronger intermediary organisations between individuals and employers

Independent guidance services are intermediaries between individuals and employers. Other intermediary organisations need to be strengthened too, to provide additional supports on which individuals can draw, and where appropriate to act as brokers in their relationships with employers.

The main social institutions which exist to provide such support to individuals at present are professional associations and trade unions. Unions have hitherto tended to be pre-occupied with collective wage bargaining, but this role has been in decline in the UK. Both they and professional associations now need to pay more attention to supporting individual career development within a flexible labour market. This requires greater attention to services to individual members, including professional development and career guidance, and possibly acting as agents and advocates for individuals in their negotiations with employers. Use of commercial agents is already common in fields like sports and the arts where the practice of short-term contracting is well established: professional associations and unions could take on similar roles as such contracts are introduced elsewhere. Their concern should be more with maintaining their members' employability than with seeking to protect their existing jobs; their role should be heightened rather than weakened when their members experience unemployment. Where the collective bargaining role of unions survives, it should cover employers' career management practices, and pay more attention to the procedural equity of the individual contracting process than to the pursuit of common outcomes (Herriot & Pemberton, 1996). It may be that the roles of professional associations and unions in these various respects will increasingly blur into one another.

There is also a growing role for 'deployers' – firms with a long-term relationship with individuals whose labour they deploy to others. Other intermediary organisations with increasingly significant roles include commercial agents, voluntary organisations representing particular client groups (e.g. one-parent families), self-help groups, and networks. Social networks represent personal communities (Wellman, Carrington & Hall, 1988): they are important in providing colleagueship and support, in exchanging ideas and information, and in supplying links to potential customers and employers. The Internet is likely to provide a powerful impetus to networks of all kinds.

The social importance of these various intermediary organisations needs to be publicly recognised, and where appropriate supported by facilitative legislation and in other ways. In recent years, legislation in the UK and elsewhere has been used to restrict the power of (particularly) trade unions, based on their traditional functions. In other countries, however, it is recognised that – effectively channelled – they form part of a structure of civil society which can greatly aid economic performance (Streeck, 1992). The task now is to strengthen the new social forms that will perform this function in a post-industrial society characterised by a flexible labour market.

Conclusion

Flexible labour markets could make it possible for more individuals to achieve more of their potential than has been the case in the past. But they will only do so if they are linked to a new concept of career, made available to all, and buttressed by appropriate support structures. Some of these structures should continue to be provided by employers: appropriate forms of regulation and encouragement are needed to ensure that employers carry out their responsibility in offering such support, in their own longer-term self-interest. But increasingly, within a flexible labour market, more support structures need to be available directly to individuals.

Assuring the availability of such support is an important issue for social policy. Attending to the implications of the new career is one of the most pressing tasks for public policy as we enter the new millennium.

Section Four:
International Career Development

Section Introduction

A full understanding of career development requires that we examine it over time, across space, and throughout the lifespan. Over time addresses the stage of economic development of countries from primitive societies through to the increasing complexity of post-industrial, globalised labour market conditions. Across space reflects the variety – and inequalities – between countries and continents. The lifespan is a concept related to the individual, but profoundly related to the time and space which individuals move through in the course of their – increasingly lengthening, increasingly mobile – lives.

In this section Tony Watts offers broad overviews allied with detailed studies of complexity. In The Role of Career Guidance in Societies in Transition, he traces the reasons for the emergence of career development services and their form, or absence, under varying political regimes. Developing the theme of 'career' as the means through which individuals engage with their socio-political and economic setting, he reverses the question to consider how political systems frame the individual, and what are the resultant implications for guidance theory and career development practice. In International Perspectives, Watts expands consideration to other aspects of society and culture, including – across space – the interaction within societies of individualism, of collective familial and communal traditions, and of class or caste systems.

Evident throughout Tony Watts' career was a commitment not only to understand and elucidate, but to act. National and international policies both permit and limit the help that is accessible to the individual citizen. For much of the last two decades of his working life, Watts developed conceptual frameworks and action agendas addressed to policy-makers, aiming to stimulate and guide the actions of those holding the power to realise career guidance as both a public and a private good.

The role of policy-makers in enabling individuals to access information, help and support is explored in an elaboration of the policy challenges facing countries. The context for these challenges includes the need for lifelong development for ageing populations as well as labour market entrants, and the movement to active labour market polices to meet global challenges. The policy challenges are discussed in Policy Challenges for Career Guidance which forms the first chapter of the OECD report that Tony Watts co-authored with Richard Sweet in 2004. The questions raised in this chapter are discussed in Career Guidance Policies in 37 Countries (co-authored with Ronald Sultana). Embedded in the service-delivery questions are searching challenges to career development practitioners to explore changing work methods in order to achieve cost-effective models of service delivery in response to policy imperatives .

These chapters demonstrate Tony Watts' engagement with international policy and practice in career development. This interest in policy is driven by a commitment to developing systems which reflect local cultures and within which individuals can thrive and pursue their careers.

16. The Role of Career Guidance in Societies in Transition[43]

This title seems particularly appropriate for an international conference being held in Romania[44]. The issue of what role career guidance has to play in societies in transition is especially acute in the countries of central and eastern Europe, which have been experiencing such a major political, economic and social transformation since the revolutions of 1989. But in fact, of course, all our societies are in transition. All advanced industrial societies are experiencing the discomforts and confusions of the transition to a post-industrial era. And Third World countries are experiencing the fallout from these massive changes, sometimes in the form of new opportunities, but sometimes in the forms of new threats reinforcing old bondages.

I will divide my paper into four parts. First, I will discuss the economic and political conditions which favour attention to career guidance and give it significance as a social phenomenon: I will draw here on a paper I gave to an earlier IAEVG conference (Watts, 1996c). Second, I want to make some comments on the role of career guidance in certain countries in marked transition, drawing on recent experience in central and eastern Europe, and also in South Africa. Third, I want to explore the role of career guidance in relation to social change in more general terms. Finally, I want briefly to outline some possible implications for guidance theory.

Conditions Favouring the Growth of Career Guidance

In broad terms, the growth of careers guidance is closely related closely to economic development. In relatively primitive societies, based on a subsistence economy, there is little division of labour. As agrarian-based societies become more wealthy and sophisticated, with more trade, there is greater diversity of roles, but allocation of such roles is determined largely by the family, caste or class into which one is born. It is with the growth of industrialisation that the division of labour eventually extends to a point where these traditional mechanisms of role allocation start to break down, and formal guidance services may be developed to supplement them. This explains why it was at the turn of the century that the first vocational guidance

---

43 Editorial footnote: Reprinted, by permission of the author and the International Association for Educational and Vocational Guidance, from *Educational and Vocational Guidance Bulletin*, No. 61, 1998.

44 A plenary address to an International Association for Educational and Vocational Guidance conference on "Career: Chance or Planning?" held in Brasov, Romania, on 22-24 September 1997.

services began to appear both in the USA and in Europe (Brewer, 1942; Keller and Viteles, 1937), It also explains why in Third World countries formal guidance services are a much more recent development, and are still very limited in nature (Drapela, 1979).

At least as important as economic factors, however, is the impact of political systems. Unless individuals have some significant degree of free choice, guidance services have no role to play. In Maoist China at the time of the Cultural Revolution, for example, all guidance services were disbanded (Weiyuan, 1994). All school-leavers were sent to the countryside, without any choice, to spend a period working in agriculture. Those who went to university were assigned to courses with no consideration for what they were interested in – "that would be individualism, a capitalist vice" (Chang, 1993 edn., p. 605). Neighbourhood councils decided what training and occupations a member of the community should embark upon. To quit one's job was to incur severe social disapproval (Brammer, 1985). Individuals, in short, had little or no say in the direction of their working lives.

This is an extreme example, but countries with planned economies and totalitarian political systems, whether right-wing or left-wing, tend to have no space for guidance or to view it as a directive process designed to meet labour-utilisation needs. In the USSR under communist rule, for example, there was an obligation on all citizens to work, and on the authorities to find work for them. Jobs were commonly assigned by placement commissions: advancement was dependent significantly on membership of the Communist Party. Because society was viewed as composed of classes rather that individuals, individualistic activity was regarded with suspicion, and "careerism" in terms of personal quest for career success was disparaged (Skorikov and Vondracek, 1993). The concept of vocational guidance was blurred with vocational selection (Nowikova, 1991; Zajda, 1979); the task of vocational guidance was to adjust the individual's subjective view to reality to make it consistent with the objective needs of society (Machula, 1989). Teachers in schools were made responsible for vocational guidance, but their programmes tended to be no more that general orientation on current manpower needs along with appeals to fill the labour quotas (Drapela, 1979).

In general, it is in countries with market economies and democratic political regimes that guidance systems are likely to be viewed as significant social institutions, in three respects. The first is economic efficiency: a means of making the labour market operate more effectively. Guidance can, for example, ensure that the individual decisions through which the labour market operates are well-informed; it can reduce some of its market failures – for instance, drop-outs from education and training, or mismatches between supply and demand; and it can support institutional reforms designed to improve the normal functioning of the labour market (Killeen et al., 1992). The second is social equity in access to educational and vocational opportunities: guidance can perform a valuable role in raising the aspirations of disadvantaged groups of individuals, making them aware of opportunities, and supporting them in securing entry to such opportunities. The third is individual liberty: the emphasis on the "active individual", affirming the value attached in democratic societies to people's rights to make free choices about their own lives. This latter is the most distinctive rationale for guidance, suggesting as it does that to tackle economic efficiency and social equity through structural reforms alone is not enough. In a sense, guidance can be viewed as a kind of brokerage between individual needs and societal needs. It addresses both individual rights and individual responsibilities within a societal context. It is a means of encouraging individuals to participate in determining their role within, and their contribution to, the society of which they are part. In this sense it is a vital tool of civil society.

Central and Eastern Europe

The relevance of all this to the countries of central and eastern Europe is evident. Since the revolutions of 1989, the economic systems of these countries have been in transition in a number of respects: from the stability of price controls to the uncertainty of markets; from very high ratios of state-sector employment to growing ratios of private-sector employment, including self-employment and small businesses (Sorrentino, 1992). Their political systems have also been in transition, from totalitarian regimes to democratic structures. These transitions have been easier to manage in countries like the Czech Republic, which the reforms have in effect reconnected with their pre-Second World War history, than in countries like the former Soviet republics which have no past experience of democracy or of being a modern market economy (Barr and Harbison, 1994). They have also been easier to manage politically in countries where the old system was associated with oppression by a foreign Soviet regime, and people have been prepared to pay a price for freedom; the situation is different in countries like Russia and Romania where the repression of democratic culture was severe and imposed by their own government (Crawford and Thompson, 1994; Gallagher, 1995).

In all of the countries, however, the short-term result of the transition has been considerable disruption of life-styles and living standards, and high levels of unemployment. The extent and pace of the change should not be underestimated. In December 1989, the main unemployment office in Warsaw paid benefits to five people; a year later, more than a million Poles were unemployed, and by mid-1993 the figure was 3 million (Barr and Harbison, 1994). Alongside unemployment have come massive growth in poverty levels, in crime rates and suicide rates; and political instabilities which can be fanned and exploited by demagogic politics and xenophobic nationalism.

The hope is that this pain will be transient, and that the reforms will in due course lead to higher living standards. The limitations of the command economy have been exposed: it is incapable of galvanising human energies in a sufficiently flexible way to respond to change. The free market appears ultimately to be more effective, partly because it taps more deeply the motivational power of individual commitment, and partly because it is a self-adjusting system: the state can never have as much information, nor the capacity to respond to it as quickly or effectively, as the market (Barr, 1994). Hence Adam Smith's famous dictum that individuals encouraged to pursue their own interests are led by an "invisible hand" to promote an end which is no part of their intention – the public interest – and to do so more effectually that when they intend to promote it (Smith, 1776).

This paradox may explain Vaclav Havel's statement that the material aim of the reforms is subordinate to their "true aim", which is "to empower individual citizens" (Havel, 1994). Havel may have meant that it is subordinate morally, but it is also subordinate temporally, in the sense that it is from the sense of empowerment that the material benefits will eventually stem. Such empowerment involves giving people "knowledge and the freedom to use it". It requires "transferable job skills and well-functioning labour markets which allow people some power over their work" (ibid). An important form of such power is the power to choose their work, in a well-informed and well-thought-through way.

There are however problems here. In many areas, the conditions necessary for private markets to be efficient are absent. This is particularly the case in the labour market, where the initial effect of the reforms has largely been to destroy economically inefficient jobs, without generating the means to replace them. This is why there is a need for active labour-market policies, linked to economic development. Governments have to intervene in order to make the markets work. But this requires different kinds of intervention than the old command-economy model: interventions designed to support markets rather than replace them. In particular, it requires measures to be taken to build markets, to regulate markets, and – where necessary – to compensate for market failure.

Career guidance, as I have suggested, is a classic intervention of this kind. It is a means of helping individuals to maximise their choices within the situations with which they are confronted. It cannot of itself, beyond narrow limits, act as an instrument of economic regeneration. But linked to a range of structural measures, it can provide a means of lubricating these measures and reconciling them with the individual empowerment which ultimately is the engine that will determine their effectiveness. The subtlety of its modus operandi means that its importance can easily be overlooked by impatient policy-makers, and belies its potential power and significance.

Certainly there are signs of regeneration of career guidance services in central and eastern Europe. The aid programmes provided by the World Bank and other international organisations, as well as by private foundations like the Soros Foundation, have played an important role in supporting such developments. Many of them have, understandably, been linked to the imperative to respond to high unemployment levels. This has dangers attached to it, particularly if the guidance is largely placement-oriented and based on a narrow matching model. In this situation, the paucity of vacancies can easily cast guidance into disrepute. Some initiatives have however included more active approaches to job-seeking, utilising job clubs and the like (see e.g. Pauly, 1994). Some have also paid attention to encouraging entrepreneurship, helping individuals to explore possibilities for setting up businesses of their own. The boundary between entrepreneurship and black-economy activity is though a thin one, and the extent of the black economy in central and eastern Europe and the threat its growth poses to civil society – together with the tensions between the bureaucratic and entrepreneurial mind-sets – make this a difficult issue for official and officially-sponsored agencies to address.

The same is true of two further functions of guidance in relation to unemployment, identified in the European Commission's Eurocounsel programme. The first is activation: assistance in finding ways of being active which do not involve a full-time permanent job in the primary labour market. The second is coping: supporting those who have little realistic chance of re-entering the labour market, perhaps through ill health or for other reasons, in finding ways of maintaining a fulfilling life and an active role in society (EFILWC, 1996). Arguably, too, there is an argument for some attention to context: helping individuals to understand the economic and political causes of unemployment, partly as a source of psychological survival (Watts and Knasel, 1985). Official employment services are unlikely to be able to manage broad approaches encompassing this range of functions. This argues for a multi-agency approach making use of private-sector and third-sector as well as public-sector organisations.

Within the countries of central and eastern Europe, such broad approaches may be difficult to develop. It is however important that they develop quickly, if career guidance is to be able to respond credibly to the challenge of unemployment. A further challenge is to move as quickly as possible away from reactive, crisis-oriented responses to unemployment, towards more proactive approaches to career development. Strong guidance programmes within schools and other educational institutions are critical here: one of their key roles is to help students develop the skills, knowledge and attitudes which will enable them to take responsibility for managing their own careers. This is not easy in school systems which under the communist regime encouraged dogmatic teaching and strictly restricted individual choice and diversity. One of the major structural obstacles to effective career guidance provision is that governmental responsibility for it tends to fall between ministries of education and of employment, and accordingly to be marginalised within both. This is true in central and eastern Europe (e.g. Ritook, 1993) as it is elsewhere. Effective structures which connect or cross-cut these ministries are critical to the quality and effectiveness of guidance programmes.

A final observation about the career guidance initiatives in these countries in the post-communist era is the attention which is being given to information systems and the use of information technology in such systems. Career information is essential, if not sufficient, for effective career guidance. Under the communist regime, career information systems designed for individual usage were ill-developed; the reforms mean that they now have a much more complex and volatile reality to relate to. High-quality systems need to be developed for describing the structure of educational and vocational opportunities and for ensuring that such descriptions are accurate, objective, comprehensive and up-to-date. Information technology is a powerful instrument for collecting, managing and disseminating such data. In addition, sophisticated computer-aided guidance systems can be developed which enable IT to be used not just for information but for delivering guidance itself. The Internet potentially greatly increases the range and accessibility of possible applications. The effective use of such technologies could provide a powerful means of accelerating the pace of change for guidance services within societies in transition.

South Africa

I have so far focused on central and eastern Europe. Before making some more general points, it might be instructive to look at another and more different example of a society in transition – South Africa – where I can draw more directly from personal experience. I did some work in South Africa on two occasions: in 1979, at the height of the apartheid regime; and in 1994, soon after the election of the new African National Congress government under Nelson Mandela.

Under the apartheid regime, severe restrictions were placed on the choice of work for blacks within the white areas – which was where most employment opportunities were located. Accordingly, a sophisticated career guidance system for the white community – strongly influenced by Christian Nationalist ideology – co-existed with a limited or non-existent service for the black community (Watts, 1980b). The contradictions of apartheid, however, led to the emergence of a small number of community agencies, funded by overseas governments and foundations and by large international companies, which attempted on a thin resource base to develop career guidance services for black people. They were part of a range of non-governmental organisations in a variety of fields, which played an important role both in developing services and in contesting apartheid (Harding, 1994). The career centres were concerned to make information on opportunities and on the obstacles to opportunities available, partly to help black people to make career decisions, but partly also to encourage them to agitate for political change (Walters, 1989). They led a vulnerable existence, with regular friction with government as they tested the boundaries of official tolerance.

With the political transformations of the early 1990s, the role of the career centres moved centre-stage. They had an experience of working with black people, and a credibility with black communities, which contrasted with the rigidity of the formal guidance system and its association with the discredited nationalist regime. The key issue was whether the professional resources of the formal guidance services could somehow be harnessed with the experience and innovative capacity of the centres. The issue was an urgent one, because with the end of apartheid and the advent of a new constitution, the funding for non-governmental organisations – which previously had come from sources opposed to the nationalist government – was in decline or being channelled through the new government. An important related question was whether the role of the centres was to be a transitional one, in due course becoming integrated into the formal structures: or whether they were to be enduring institutions, supplementing and complementing the official services.

The South African case accordingly raises with greater clarity the issue of the relationship between public-sector guidance service and third-sector services in societies in transition. Government has a responsibility, and alone has the means, to develop a strong guidance infrastructure. But the political imprint on its activities can undermine the credibility of its provision and pervert the purpose of such provision. Such strains become particularly evident at times of market transition. Third-sector services, for all their structural weaknesses, have a fluidity and a grass-roots groundedness which enables them to facilitate change and respond more effectively to change.

Career Guidance and Social Change

I have so far focused on some recent examples of societies in which the pace of transformation has been particularly rapid. As I mentioned at the beginning, however, all societies are in transition. In particular, all advanced industrial societies are currently experiencing the transition to a post-industrial era, in which the structures of work and of career are being massively reshaped. The pace of change stems from two linked forces: the impact of new technology, and the globalisation of the economy. The result is that all work organisations have to be prepared to change much more regularly and rapidly than ever before. Accordingly, they are less prepared to make long-term commitments to individuals. The psychological contract between the individual and the employer is being restructured: the old long-term relational contract, based on security and reciprocal loyalty, is in many cases being replaced by a short-term transactional contract based on a narrower and more purely economic exchange; where the relational contract survives, it commonly involves exchanging job security for task flexibility; either way, therefore, it needs to be constantly renegotiated (Herriot and Pemberton, 1995; Rousseau, 1996). Individuals now have to take more responsibility for their own career development, including learning new skills and knowledge. Security increasingly lies not in employment, but in employability, accumulating skills and reputation that can be invested in new opportunities as they arise (Kanter, 1989). These changes represent a "careerquake" (Watts, 1996b). The old concept of career was based on orderly progression up a hierarchy within an organisation or profession. The foundations of this concept are being shaken and in many cases destroyed. In its place, a new concept of career needs to be built, redefined as the individual's lifelong progression in learning and in work. This new concept is in principle accessible to all, not just to the few. But it requires policy supports. One of these supports is life-long access to career guidance.

This raises the question, however, of how such guidance is to be provided and funded. Hitherto guidance services have in the main been concentrated around the transition point from full-time education into the labour market. The resource base required has been reasonably modest. But if guidance is to be available on demand throughout people's lives, a major scaling-up of resources is needed. What is the role of government in relation to such scaling-up?

One model is for government to organise and administer the guidance provision. This however raises the difficulties already discussed about the bureaucratic and political constraints this imposes on the nature of the provision. At the other extreme, some have argued that guidance should be viewed as a market good, like any other: if individuals want it, they will pay for it. But this ignores the public interest in guidance as a public good, in the terms outlined earlier: as a means of making the labour market work more effectively, and reconciling economic efficiency with social equity and individual liberty. It also ignores the fact that many of the people who most need guidance are in the least position to pay for it.

This suggests that in reviewing appropriate structures for career guidance, we need to look at mixed models in which there may be roles both for the public and private sectors, and for the third sector too. In such models, government may reduce or withdraw from its role as provider, but maintain roles as funder and/or as regulator and/or as facilitator. The different models adopted in Germany, France and the UK (Watts, Guichard, Plant and Rodriguez, 1994; Rees et al., 1996) are of interest in this respect.

In Germany, vocational guidance has for some time been a formal monopoly of the Bundesanstalt für Arbeit, which is a self-governing legal body financed by contributions from employers and employees to the social pensions insurance scheme. This body is controlled by the three social partners – employers and unions as well as government – which in effect ensure that their respective vested interests are balanced and that the individual's interests are given primacy. Other institutions – including schools and universities – have been prohibited from offering vocational guidance; private agencies have not been permitted. The rationale has been to help individuals to realise their basic right, enshrined in the German constitution, of free vocational choice. The monopoly has now been successfully challenged by a plethora of private-sector organisations in the executive outplacement market, and of third-sector organisations focusing on the needs of disadvantaged groups, the latter often combining guidance with other activities. The core services, however, remain highly centralised and strongly regulated.

In France, most services remain publicly-funded and free to the individual, but are more pluralistic, and increasingly based in the third sector. Services for school pupils are centralised and provided by civil servants employed by the Ministry of Education. Many of the organisations providing guidance to adults, however, are non-profit associations or public-sector agencies. Funding is provided on a contract basis or through capitation payment for the clients they attract. These involve quasi-market elements, through competition for the state contracts or, in the case of the capitation payments, for clients.

In the UK, the quasi-market elements have been taken further. In the case of young people, the statutory Careers Service has been contracted out on a competitive basis. Although in most cases the contracts have been won by the existing providers, these have been reconstituted as private companies – most of them non-profit companies limited by guarantee. There have also been some "new entrants", including a private-sector commercial company; and some "expansionism", with existing providers winning contracts for areas other than their own. In adult guidance, on the other hand, the government policy has recently been based on a two-level model: a foundation level, comprising free access to information plus some limited guidance support (this is to include a national telephone helpline and local information centres); and a second level, consisting of a range of services (e.g. individual counselling, group session, psychometric testing) supplied by a variety of providers in the public, private and third sectors, for which users are expected, where possible, to pay. The extent to which the new Labour government will maintain this policy is as yet unclear, but it seems unlikely that it will radically transform it.

These models provide a range of different responses to the need to reshape the role of government in relation to services in societies in transition. The German model is based largely on a centralised operation, at one remove from government, with some diversification at the fringe. The French model is based on centralised, public-sector provision for young people, but on greater decentralisation and quasi-market elements for adults. The UK model is based on decentralisation and quasi-market elements for young people, and on an adult guidance strategy incorporating elements of public provision but also elements of a real market in guidance.

Implications for Guidance Theory

Finally, I would like to make a few comments about the implications of social change not only for the way in which guidance services are structured organisationally, but also for the way in which their work is conceived theoretically. Trait-and-factor approaches based on matching individuals to opportunities have a role to play in most guidance services. On their own, however, they are static conceptions, taking no account of change either in the individual or in the opportunity structure. Their inadequacies become particularly exposed at times of rapid change.

The developmental approaches promoted by Super (1957) are an attempt to respond to these limitations. They recognise the changing nature of the individual, and seek to support such change on a continuing basis. They are however predominantly psychological in nature, and only weakly framed to take account of social change.

Perhaps we now need models of guidance which pay more attention to the social context, to its changing nature to the individual's dynamic relationship with that changing context. Plant (1997) has advocated the concept of "green guidance", in which individuals are encouraged to consider the environmental implications of their career choices. A criticism of this approach is that it imposes one particular value frame on the guidance process. Giddens (1991), however, has pointed out that one of the distinctive features of the late modern age is that the self now has to be constructed as a reflexive process of connecting personal and social change. Personal decisions are also political decisions. This is particularly true of decisions relating to work, which is a key transaction through which individuals act on the world and influence it. Perhaps guidance should pay more attention to helping individuals explore the political nature of their personal choices, and to addressing the way in which they can be agents of – rather than victims of – social change.

17. Career Guidance: An International Perspective[45]

Introduction

There are at least three reasons for studying guidance systems in other countries than one's own. The first is that it demonstrates the cultural relativity of one's own practices. By showing that things are done differently elsewhere, it causes one to question practices which otherwise tend to be taken for granted. The second is that it permits policy borrowing. While direct transplanting of practice from one country to another is problematic, new possibilities can be indicated which can be adapted to one's own situation. The third is that it facilitates international co-operation. Within an increasingly global economy, the growing mobility of students, trainees and workers between countries means that guidance services need to work more closely together: understanding the similarities and differences between guidance systems can help to facilitate such co-operation and make it more effective.

Studying guidance systems can be a revealing lens through which to seek to understand another country. It brings into focus the education and training system and the economic system, and the relationship between the two. It also illuminates the social and political structure, and cultural factors concerning the relationship between the individual, the family, and the wider society.

Despite all this, the comparative literature on guidance systems is remarkably limited. There are a number of 'travel reports', based on studies conducted by brief visitors. Because these tend to be limited to single countries, however, they usually lack a strong comparative framework. The same is true of collections of country-studies such as Drapela (1979). Some studies have attempted to develop a comparative framework from separate country-studies provided by other authors (e.g. Watts and Ferreira-Marques, 1979; Plant, 1990; Watts, 1992). In other cases, the methodology has included first-hand visits by the main author(s), so strengthening the comparative frame (e.g. Keller and Viteles, 1937; Reubens, 1977; Watts et al., 1988; 1994). Further reports and commentaries have drawn more impressionistically from conferences, visits made over a period of time, and the like (e.g. Reuchlin, 1964; Super, 1974).

The paucity of comparative guidance studies contrasts with the now very extensive and theoretically sophisticated literature on comparative education (for a useful overview, see Halls, 1990). Comparative guidance studies can draw on this literature,

[45] Reprinted, by permission of the author and publisher, from Watts, A.G., Law, B., Killeen, J., Kidd, J.M. & Hawthorn, R.: *Rethinking Careers Education and Guidance: Theory, Policy and Practice.* London: Routledge 1996.

of course, but they need a broader frame of reference.

The present chapter attempts to develop a framework for looking at guidance systems in an international perspective. It draws from the existing studies, and particularly from various studies in which I have been personally involved over the last twenty-five years. It pays particular attention to the key differences between guidance systems in different countries, and the reasons for these differences. It looks in turn at the extent to which such differences relate to stage of economic development, to the political system, to social and cultural factors, to the education and training system, and to professional and organisational structures. Finally, it explores the pressures towards convergence and divergence between guidance systems. Many of the points made in the chapter are effectively hypotheses based on selective illustrative evidence rather than conclusions based on exhaustive enquiry. It is hoped, however, that they will encourage more rigorous comparative studies in the future.

Impact of stage of economic development

Formal guidance services are, in part at least, a product of economic development. In relatively primitive societies, based on a subsistence economy, there is little division of labour. As agrarian-based societies become more wealthy and sophisticated, with more trade, there is a greater diversity of roles, but allocation of such roles is determined largely by the family, caste or class into which one is born. It is with the growth of industrialisation that the division of labour eventually extends to a point where such traditional mechanisms of role allocation start to break down, and formal guidance services may be developed to supplement them.

It was accordingly at the end of the nineteenth century and in the early years of the twentieth century that the first vocational guidance services began to appear both in the USA and in Europe (Brewer, 1942; Keller and Viteles, 1937; Heginbotham, 1951). In Third World countries, formal guidance services are a much more recent development, and are still very limited in nature (Drapela, 1979).

Stage of economic development can influence not only the extent of guidance services but also their orientation. For countries still in the early stages of economic development, guidance services tend to be dominated by labour-utilisation considerations, channelling individuals into fields of education, training and work that are deemed necessary for the national economy. A common policy role for formal guidance in developing countries, for example, is to encourage young people to move into technical and vocational education rather than aspiring to higher education (Watts and Ferreira Marques, 1979; UNESCO, 1980). It is only in conditions of relative affluence that greater attention may begin to be given to individual human development (Super, 1954; 1985).

More speculatively, it seems possible that as societies move into a post-industrial stage, with more emphasis on knowledge occupations (Drucker, 1969) and more flexible educational and occupational structures (Handy, 1989), the role of guidance may become more salient and more pervasive than it has been in the past. In industrial societies, labour has tended to be concentrated in large organisations, individuals have tended to stay in such organisations for long periods of time, and any career progression they may have experienced has tended to be managed by the organisation; much the same has been true of the system of education, which has preceded employment rather than being interwoven with it; guidance has tended to be concentrated at the interface between the two systems, supporting individuals in their passage between them. In post-industrial societies, all these generalisations are likely to be less valid. The case for lifelong access to guidance in support of continuous career development, in mediating the 'psychological contract' between individuals and organisations (Argyris, 1960; Herriot, 1992) on an iterative basis, and in supporting the construction of self as a 'reflexive project' (Giddens, 1991), accordingly becomes stronger and more pressing (Watts, 1994a; 1996f; Collin and Watts, 1996).

Impact of political systems

If the development of formal guidance services is linked to industrialisation, it also seems to be linked to democratisation. Unless there is some degree of free choice for citizens, guidance services have no role to play. In Maoist China at the time of the Cultural Revolution, for example, all guidance services were disbanded (Weiyuan, 1994). All school-leavers were sent to the countryside, without any choice, to spend a period working in agriculture. Those who went to university were assigned to courses with no consideration of what they were interested in – 'that would be individualism, a capitalist vice' (Chang, 1993, p. 605). Neighbourhood councils decided what training and occupations a member of the community should embark upon. To quit one's job was to incur severe social disapproval (Brammer, 1985). Individuals, in short, had little or no say in the direction of their working lives.

This is an extreme example, but countries with planned economies and totalitarian political systems, whether right-wing or left-wing, tend to have no space for guidance or to view it as a conservative, social-control process, using directive methods to meet labour-utilisation needs. In the USSR under Communist rule, for instance, there was an obligation on all citizens to work, and on the authorities to find work for them. Jobs were commonly assigned by placement commissions. Advancement was dependent significantly on membership of the Communist Party, and 'careerism' in terms of personal quest for career success was disparaged (Skorikov and Vondracek,

1993). The concept of vocational guidance was blurred with vocational selection (Nowikowa, 1991; Zajda, 1979); the task of vocational guidance was to adjust the individual's subjective view of reality to make it consistent with the objective needs of society (Machula, 1989). Teachers in schools were made responsible for vocational guidance, but their programmes tended to be no more than general orientation on current manpower needs along with appeals to fill the labour quotas (Drapela, 1979).

In Germany in the 1930s, the guidance system was strongly influenced by the overtly racist (and ultimately genocidal) policy of the National Socialist regime. The concern was not just for social but for biological selection. Even before the concentration camps, Jews and other non-Aryans were forced into the least desirable jobs. Keller and Viteles (1937) reported – in terms that in retrospect seem chillingly portentous – that in testing programmes, great stress was laid upon heredity: 'Entire family trees are reconstructed. The characteristics of all the relatives are given, and on the basis of the general pattern the boy is advised as to the kind of work in which he is mostly likely to succeed' (p. 135). They also recorded that counsellors were selected with great care and 'must have the quality of leadership, as expressed in the tenets of the National Socialist Party' (p.137).

In South Africa under apartheid, a sophisticated guidance system for the white community – strongly influenced by Christian Nationalist ideology – co-existed with a limited or non-existent service for the black community. Severe restrictions were placed on the choice of work for blacks within the white areas – which was where most employment opportunities were located. Migrant workers were classified by labour bureau officers into particular categories of employment, in which they were likely to have to stay for the rest of their working lives. In 1975 there were 30 trained counsellors to provide all psychological services for nearly 3.75 million black school children. Much of their time was spent administering tests, the results of which were used largely for statistical research rather than guidance purposes. A section on 'vocational guidance' was included in the social studies curriculum: it included a heavy emphasis on 'cultivating realistic attitudes, ideals and expectations' and on 'the importance of manual labour' (Watts, 1980b; Dovey, 1980; Dovey and Mason, 1984). The emphasis was thus on bringing students to accept politically-constructed reality: any attempt to encourage a critical approach to this reality was taboo (much the same has been true of counselling in Arab schools in Israel – see Mar'i, 1982).

All of these are clear examples of the constraints placed on guidance services by totalitarian regimes. South Africa under apartheid was, however, different from the earlier examples because it aspired to liberal-democratic principles even though it confined the application of these principles to the white community. This led it to permit the establishment of a small number of community agencies, funded mainly by overseas governments and foundations and by large international companies, which developed careers guidance services for black people. These were part of a wide range of non-governmental organisations in a variety of fields, which played an important role both in developing services and in contesting apartheid (Harding, 1994). The careers centres were concerned to make information on opportunities and on the obstacles to opportunities available, partly to help black people to make career decisions but partly also to encourage them to agitate for political change (Walters, 1989). Therefore, they provided an example of community-based guidance agencies pursuing a radical social-change agenda in reaction to an official guidance system operating a conservative social-control strategy (see chapter 11). With the end of apartheid and the advent of a new black-dominated government in South Africa, the experience of the community-based careers centres may be crucial in developing an official guidance system capable of addressing the needs of the black communities. The South African case thus provides an example both of contrasting socio-political models within the same country, and of how such models become recontoured when the political system changes.

In general, countries with market economies and democratic political regimes are inclined to attach more importance to guidance. They are also more likely to view it in liberal-progressive terms, seeing it as a non-directive process or as a process designed to maximise individual achievement. In these terms, guidance can be seen both as a way of making the labour market work more effectively and as a means of affirming the value attached in democratic societies to the rights of individuals to make free choices about their own lives.

In practice, tensions between societal needs and individual needs mean that even within liberal-democratic societies, guidance sometimes comes under pressure to revert to a conservative social-control model. Some countries, however, may attain a sufficient level of democratic sophistication to view these tensions in a different way, and to recognise the validity of guidance as a more radical process of ongoing social change. The most notable case is Sweden, where an official policy statement on guidance issued in 1971 (quoted in Watts, 1981a) included radical as well as liberal-progressive aims. It suggested, for example, that guidance should develop a critical awareness of sources of information and influences on choice:

> Among other things, a critical attitude implies the querying by pupils of the facts selected in the information they are given and the theoretical foundations of that information. For instance, it is important for them to be made aware of the unreliability of forecasts and tests and critical of categorical statements concerning labour market developments.

It placed individual decision-making within a pluralistic social context in which issues of conflict and inequality were not to be avoided:

> Pupils should ask questions and obtain facts concerning social relations and work-places, the values of different groups, problems such as the goal of activities, pay differentials, occupational status, relations between superiors and subordinates, sex roles, etc., and then discuss these matters and relate them to their own problems of vocational decision.

It did not regard obstacles to freedom of choice as given, but instead specifically charged the counsellors to work against them wherever possible:

> SYO [educational and vocational guidance] should counteract restrictions of vocational choice due, e.g., to social background, sex, lack of motivation for the analysis of one's own situation etc., even if this involves questioning decisions taken by the pupil and even if, by increasing the number of alternatives apparent to the pupil, it has the effect of making it more difficult for him [sic] to choose.

It recognised that individual choices could themselves act as agents of change in society, and positively supported such effects:

> One of the tasks of SYO is to supply the individual with true and detailed information, and this may also result conceivably in an increased labour shortage in certain sectors coupled with a labour surplus in others, e.g., due to greater light being shed on the differences between different occupations in terms of remuneration and prospects of job satisfaction. This in turn may lead to long-term changes in the labour market.

Finally, it recognised that some of the social changes necessary to meet the career interests of individuals could not be achieved through individuals working alone, and asserted the links between guidance and the development of political consciousness:

> SYO should among other things be related to instruction and debate concerning trade union and political organisations, and the ability of the individual to influence developments.

In all of these respects, it recognised officially the positive role that guidance could play in promoting constructive social change on a continuous basis. The reality of guidance practice, however, tended to be more prosaic and limited than these radical aims would suggest (Watts, 1981a).

A further recent example of the impact of political systems is the attempt in some countries influenced by the 'New Right' to explore the application of market principles to the organisation of guidance delivery (see chapter 13). This has included encouraging the growth of guidance services within the private sector, and moving public guidance services into quasi-market situations where they have been exposed to the forces of competition. Such developments have been particularly evident in the United Kingdom (Watts, 1996f), but they have also been visible in Australia (Pryor, 1991), in New Zealand (Hesketh and Kennedy, 1991) and to a lesser extent in some other European countries, notably the Netherlands (Watts, Guichard, Plant and Rodriguez, 1994).

Impact of social and cultural factors

In addition to economic and political factors, the significance attached to guidance and its nature are also strongly influenced by social and cultural factors. In social-structural terms, for example, countries with strong social stratification are likely to have relatively limited needs for formal guidance services: individuals tend to make choices within socially circumscribed limits, and are able to get much of the help they need from their family and from informal networks. In societies with relatively high levels of social mobility, on the other hand, formal guidance assumes greater importance: individuals have a wider field of choice available to them, and their family and informal networks are less likely to provide informed help in relation to the full range of opportunities; accordingly, there is likely to be more recourse to formal guidance services to provide the help that is required.

In countries with traditionally strong class systems, the contestation of such systems seems to lead to more attention being paid to sociological dimensions in guidance. This is certainly the case in Britain and Scandinavia, where sociologists have made influential contributions to the theoretical guidance literature (Killeen, 1996). In the USA, on the other hand, the guidance field has been almost entirely dominated by psychologists. This seems linked to cultural and historical factors. Even though social mobility rates in the USA are not substantially different from those recorded in other economically advanced societies (Blau and Duncan, 1967), the USA has from the beginning of its independent existence been committed to the proposition that 'all men [sic] are created equal' and that any American, however humble his or her origin, can become President. Moreover, the existence of a frontier moving gradually westwards long sustained the possibility of escaping economic and social oppression and becoming wealthy and self-respecting through effort and native wit alone (Turner, 1921). The psychological dominance of guidance thus seems closely linked to the individualism on which American culture is based (Watts, 1981b). Counsellors in the USA appear to have more difficulty than those in Britain in recognising the relevance of socio-political issues to their work.

Individualism is not, however, confined to the USA. In most western industrialised countries, it is an important element of national culture (Hofstede, 1984). In many eastern and Third World cultures, on the other hand, the role of the individual is subordinated to the collectivity, whether to the nuclear family, the extended family, or the tribe. This is linked to Tönnies' (1957 edn) classic distinction between *Gemeinschaft* (a community based on strong common ties in which the individual is not sharply differentiated) and *Gesellschaft* (a society based on individuals forming associations for different purposes). Where *Gemeinschaft* survives, guidance in its individualist form is unlikely to find a place. Esen (1972), for example, pointed out that in Nigeria the central concept of guidance – that of the self-determining individual – was inappropriate, since individual identity was considered subordinate to group – and especially tribal – identity:

> Since the group embodies reality and is the framework within which the people can hope for a degree of self-actualisation that would be difficult to attain otherwise, the views of the group's accredited spokesmen tend to become the conscience of the people. Authority, rather than reason or free choice, becomes the guiding principle of the individual's life. (Esen, 1972, p. 795)

Again, Moracco (1979) noted that in Arab families, individuals were subordinated to the group and in decision-making were influenced strongly by the values and needs of the family. If these conflicted with their own, individuals were expected to conform to family values, expressed in most cases by the father. Similar points have been made in relation to Latin America (Espin, 1979) and to Chinese communities (Scaff and Ting, 1972; Saner-Yui and Saner-Yui, 1985).

In some cases, the concept of individual choice may be further limited by religious fatalism. Amongst the Yoruba in Nigeria, for example, it is believed that all individuals have a predestined occupation as part of their *ori* – a detailed 'blueprint' of the life they will lead and the role they will play within the tribe. To discover this blueprint, it is necessary at each decision point to consult the *bataiawo*, an Ifa priest (Ipaye, 1989).

All of these traditions can influence what happens when, as part of the process of industrialisation, formal guidance services grow up in eastern or Third World countries. Thus in countries with a strong emphasis on respect for authority, such guidance is likely to be directive in nature. In Latin America, for instance, students tend to expect the counsellors to tell them exactly what to do, and may judge the counsellor to be incompetent if this does not happen. Extensive emphasis on psychometric testing fits well into this tradition (Espin, 1979). The extent to which guidance services are inevitably in conflict with traditional structures, or could and should seek to accommodate themselves to such structures, is an important issue to which we shall return later in this chapter.

Impact of education, training and employment systems

Within these broad economic, political and social structures, and cultural mores, the organisational structure of education, training and employment systems also have an impact on careers guidance provision. Turner (1960) distinguished between educational systems based on 'contest mobility', with weak and late tracking, and those based on 'sponsored mobility', with strong and early tracking. The former are likely to attach much more importance to guidance than the latter. Thus schools in America, Turner's exemplar of a contest-mobility model, historically developed much more sophisticated guidance and counselling systems than did schools in England, his exemplar of a sponsored-mobility model. It was the introduction of comprehensive schools in Britain, with their greater flexibility and less rigid tracking, which gave rise to a significant increase in the importance of guidance systems (Daws, 1968).

The curriculum theory adopted by a particular educational system is also likely to influence the place of formal guidance within it. Nicholas (1983) distinguished three models: European classicism, in which objective knowledge is pursued for its own sake, and the search for wisdom, truth and beauty is regarded as the highest form of human activity, which should not be sullied or tainted by the practical world; Marxist-Leninism, in which the political purpose of schooling is to act as an agent in the production of the new Communist society, inculcating the skills, knowledge, attitudes and behaviour which will be needed; and liberal-pragmatism, in which schools are seen as servicing the needs of the individual, in his or her pursuit of freedom and social mobility. Formal guidance would seem likely to have very little place in relation to European classicism, a limited and highly directive place in relation to the Marxist-Leninist model (as already noted above), and a much more central, though less directive, role in relation to liberal-pragmatism. This helps to explain why careers education has been able to establish a place within the curriculum more readily in some countries (e.g. the USA, Denmark, Netherlands, and *Realschulen* in Germany) than in others (e.g. France, and *Gymnasien* in Germany).

The nature of the vocational education and training system is relevant too. Systems which are largely based on apprenticeship within the workplace are likely to locate their main guidance services within labour-market institutions, whereas those which are largely education-based tend to locate them within education. Thus in Germany, with its strong apprenticeship system, vocational guidance is a formal monopoly of the Bundesanstalt für Arbeit, a labour-market organisation. In France, with its structure of vocational education, on the other hand, the main guidance services are part of the education system (Watts, Guichard, Plant and Rodriguez, 1994).

The issue of whether formal guidance services are located in educational or labour-market institutions is important, because it tends to influence their orientation.

Services based within education tend to focus on educational-choice processes, to be somewhat detached from the world of work, and to emphasise personal-development aspects of guidance. Services based within labour-market institutions, by contrast, tend to focus on occupational choice and job placement, and to emphasise labour-market realities. The choice of location may not only influence such considerations but also be influenced by them: countries with strong labour-utilisation rather than individual-development concerns are more likely to base guidance services within employment services and other labour-market institutions rather than within education. Many countries, of course, have guidance services in both sectors, and/or in 'agency' structures located between them.

The nature of the employment system also has an effect on the structure and nature of guidance services. In Japan, for example, the 'lifetime employment system' means that men in particular tend to make their primary commitment to an organisation rather than to an occupation, and to stay in the same organisation throughout their career (Watts, 1985). Indeed, their corporate membership tends to occupy a major part of their self-identity (Ishiyama and Kitayama, 1994). The result is that guidance and placement services for facilitating movement between organisations are not well developed, whereas there has been a growth of services designed to facilitate career development within organisations. In addition, in guidance services for young people there is a much heavier emphasis than in most other countries on choice of organisation. Much of the careers information made available in guidance services for young people entering the labour market is accordingly classified by organisation rather than by occupation (Watts, 1985).

Impact of professional and organisational structures

A final set of international differences in guidance provision is related to the professional and organisational structures within which guidance is located. The professional identity and training of those occupying formal guidance roles varies considerably. In many cases their primary professional identity is as psychologists, as teachers, or as labour-market administrators. In such cases, their guidance training is regarded as being incorporated into, or supplementary to, the training for their primary professional role. This explains why their guidance training is sometimes limited in scale and even optional in nature. It is only in a residual number of cases that the primary professional identity of guidance professionals is as counsellors or guidance workers, with their own specialist training (Watts, Dartois and Plant, 1988; Watts, 1992).

To some extent, of course, professional identity is linked to sectoral location: services based in educational institutions will tend to be staffed by teachers; services in labour-market organisations by labour-market administrators; services in separate agencies by psychologists or specialist counsellors. This is not, however, invariably the case. In Sweden, for example, the SYO counsellors are based in schools but are not trained as teachers (Watts, 1981a). Again, psychologists are to be found in schools and in labour-market organisations as well as in separate agencies. Reuchlin (1964) points out that the delivery of services by psychologists tends to be related to an emphasis on psychometric testing.

The definition of the focus of the counsellor's role also varies between countries. A common conceptual distinction is between educational guidance (e.g. on educational options, or on learning problems), vocational guidance (e.g. on choice of occupations and work roles), and personal and social guidance (e.g. on behaviour problems, or emotional issues). In some cases – Germany, for example – there is clear-cut distinction between these forms of guidance, which are allocated to wholly separate agencies. In other cases, all three forms of guidance are brought together: in Belgium, through different roles based in one agency (the Psycho-Medico-Social Centre); in schools in such countries as Ireland, through a single role (the school counsellor or guidance counsellor) (Watts, Guichard, Plant and Rodriguez, 1994).

The combined effect of professional identity, sectoral location and role focus leads to very varied models of provision across countries in relation to schools in particular. Broadly, there are three main ways in which careers guidance provision is organised within schools (Watts, 1988a).

First, it can be based on specialists outside the school. These specialists may be based in education authorities (e.g. France) or in labour-market authorities (e.g. Germany). They may cover all three forms of guidance (e.g. Belgium) or they may focus mainly on educational or vocational guidance (e.g. France and Germany respectively). They commonly go into schools to offer interviews, give talks, and so on, but they do so from an external base.

Second, careers guidance can be provided by specialists inside the school. In some cases these are non-teachers (e.g. Sweden). In others, they are initially trained as teachers but have had substantial in-service training in counselling and now spend most of their time on guidance and counselling activities: in effect, their guidance role has taken on the attributes of a sub-profession within the teaching profession. In such cases, their roles usually cover educational and personal/social as well as vocational guidance: this is true of school counsellors in such countries as Canada, Ireland, the Philippines and the USA. Where the role is confined to educational and vocational guidance, the level of specialist training in guidance and of time allocated to guidance roles tends to be much more limited: this is the case, for example, with careers teachers in Greece and the Netherlands.

Third, careers guidance can be more fully integrated into the school, by encouraging most or all teachers to be involved in it. This may be attempted by seeking to integrate it into academic-subject teaching, which has been tried in such countries as Germany (Busshoff, quoted in Watts and Ferreira-Marques, 1979) and the USA (Watts and Herr, 1976), though it has proved difficult to implement successfully. Alternatively, careers guidance can be integrated into the 'pastoral' structure of the school: this is the case, for instance, in Japan, where it is regarded as part of the responsibility of the 'home-room' teacher (Watts, 1985); in Venezuela, where all teachers are expected to take on the role of guidance counsellor in addition to that of specialist teacher of a specific subject (Kim, 1987); and in Singapore, where careers education is delivered through a curriculum in pastoral care implemented by form tutors (Watts, 1988b).

These organisational models are not mutually exclusive, and many countries have elements of more than one model. In England and Wales, for example, there are elements of all three: careers education and guidance is offered by careers officers based outside the school, by careers teachers based inside the school, and by tutors who form the basis of the school's pastoral-care structure.

The same kinds of distinctions can be drawn in relation to guidance services available to young people and adults after leaving school. These services are in many countries less well-developed than services for young people in schools. But a study of guidance systems within the European Community found significant between-country differences in guidance services in tertiary education, in guidance services for young people based outside full-time education (in apprenticeship structures, in transition programmes, and in youth and community services), and in guidance services for adults (within public employment services, in adult education, in the voluntary and private sectors, and in the workplace) (Watts, Guichard, Plant and Rodriguez, 1994).

Convergence or divergence?

Much of this chapter has focused on variations between formal guidance systems in different countries. Some of these variations have been essentially organisational in nature; others have been more conceptual and ideological. They have been linked to economic, political, socio-cultural, educational and professional factors. Across societies, these factors are interwoven in complex ways: the implications of these textures needs more detailed exploration than has been possible here.

The focus on variations requires, however, to be balanced by a recognition that there are some tendencies to professional convergence which may transcend such differences. Thus a four-stage model of the development of conceptions of careers guidance in schools (from a focus on information, through a focus on interviewing and then the addition of careers education to the curriculum, to the integration of careers education across the curriculum) which was originally developed in relation to the UK (Law and Watts, 1977), appears to have a wider validity as a way of explaining such development in other countries too (Watts, 1988a).

Again, it seems that across the guidance systems within the European Community, three common trends can be identified. The first is towards guidance as a continuous process, which should start in schools and be accessible throughout adult and working life. The second is towards a more open professional model, in which the concept of an expert guidance specialist working with individual clients in a psychological vacuum is replaced or supplemented by a more diffuse approach in which a more varied range of interventions is used and more attention is given to working with and through networks of other individuals and agencies. The third is a greater emphasis on the individual as an active agent, rather than a passive recipient, within the guidance process (Watts, Guichard, Plant and Rodriguez, 1994). These trends are evident in advanced industrialised countries in other parts of the world too.

Such convergence is supported by international links as mediated through such organisations as the International Association for Educational and Vocational Guidance (IAEVG) and the International Round Table for the Advancement of Counselling (IRTAC). It is also fostered by aid programmes and international use of consultants. Many countries with less developed guidance systems have looked to countries with more developed systems for models and support. International borrowing of this kind can lead to difficulties. In countries such as Ghana and Malaysia, for example, individualistic client-centred models of guidance were imported from the USA and Britain which seemed inappropriate to the culture and meant that insufficient attention was paid to basic priorities such as the provision of occupational information (Bolger, 1978; Watts, 1978b; see also Kim, 1987). Underlying the issue of convergence or divergence is the extent to which guidance is a technique or a philosophy. Morris (1955) suggests 'that guidance is purely a technique, that it is only a means, and that the ends which it serves will be determined both by the cultural tradition within which it operates and by the detailed way in which it interprets that tradition in its modes of operation' (p. 124). Patterson (1978), on the other hand, takes the view that counselling 'is neither time-bound nor culture-bound; it transcends time and culture, since it is based upon the universal unity of human nature' (p. 231). According to Patterson, counselling is concerned essentially with self-actualisation, which 'is an ultimate, universal value, not one that is man-made or culture-bound'. He is careful to note that self-actualisation is not necessarily identified with western culture and with its 'extreme individualism, selfish aggrandisement, and competitive dog-eat-dog ethics, with the devil taking the hindmost'. But he argues that the values and forms of every culture 'must be judged or evaluated in terms of their contribution to the self-actualisation of the individual' (pp. 237-38). In this sense, the goals of counselling are universal, not culture-specific. These arguments are developed in relation to counselling in general, but could equally be applied to careers education and guidance in particular.

The arguments and evidence we have presented in this chapter offer some support for both these views. Guidance is able to take many different forms. Certainly its organisational features vary considerably, as do its techniques and approaches. But at the heart of the concept of guidance is a set of values which call into question whether guidance services in, for example, Nazi Germany represented guidance in a 'true' or 'complete' sense.

Formal guidance services, as we have seen, are linked to industrialisation, to democratisation, to social mobility, and to cultural individualism. In societies where these processes are less evident, the values which are central to guidance philosophy – of respect for the individual, and of concern for individual growth and development – may still be present, if within a very different cultural context. As the pace of change encourages the growth of guidance services in such countries, it is important that such services respect and work with elements of the culture which are congruent with their own.

18. Policy Challenges for Career Guidance[46]

Introduction

This chapter describes the expectations, many of which are long-standing, that policy-makers in OECD countries have for career guidance services. It then sets out the special challenges that lifelong learning and active labour market policies pose for career guidance, and concludes by describing what these policy challenges imply for how career guidance services are organised and provided.

The chapter's key policy conclusions are that:

- While policy-makers in some OECD countries expect career guidance to be centred upon individual goals, in all countries they also expect it to contribute to public policy objectives: making education systems more efficient; contributing to the improved efficiency of the labour market; and helping to improve social equity.

- Many of these expectations are long-standing. The progressive adoption of lifelong learning strategies in OECD countries, and an emphasis upon active employability in labour market policies, pose new challenges for career guidance. It needs to shift from being largely available to selected groups, at particular points in life, to being much more widely available throughout the lifespan. And services need to shift from an approach largely focused upon helping people to make immediate decisions though face-to-face interviews, to a broader approach that also encompasses the development of career self-management skills such as the ability to make and implement effective career decisions.

- OECD countries need, then, to work towards the development of lifelong guidance systems.

---

[46] Co-authored with Richard Sweet; published under the authorship of OECD. Republished, by permission of the OECD, from *Career Guidance and Public Policy: Bridging the Gap*. Paris: OECD, 2004. OECD Publishing. http://dx.doi.org/10.1787/9789264105669-en

What do policy-makers expect of career guidance[47]?

Public policy has not in the past been of great interest to most career guidance practitioners, whose primary motivation quite properly is a desire to help people. Similarly, the details of how career guidance is provided have often been of limited interest to public policy-makers. Nevertheless public policies set the frameworks for career guidance and provide the funds for much of it. Career guidance becomes increasingly important for public policy as education and employment policies seek to widen individual choices and to create systems that can respond to very different needs throughout life. This report is about how the gap between career guidance and public policy can be bridged.

Support by public policy-makers for career guidance has traditionally rested upon a belief that it can improve the efficiency and effectiveness of labour markets and educational systems, as well as contribute to social equity. Indeed formal career guidance has its origins in a concern in the early parts of the 20th century to use systematic methods to help underprivileged young people to choose an occupation when they were leaving school and about to look for a job (Parsons, 1909). Some of the policy challenges that career guidance must respond to in OECD countries are long-standing: to improve the knowledge and skills base of the population; to keep unemployment low and ensure that labour supply and demand are in harmony; and to ensure that education and employment opportunities are distributed equitably. Others, as we shall see below, are more recent, and pose new challenges for career guidance.

Countries participating in the OECD review of career guidance policies were asked to indicate the key goals and objectives of their career guidance services. They were also asked to indicate the major educational, labour market and social influences that are shaping their career guidance policies. Some countries – Denmark and Norway are examples – made it clear that they expected the goals of career guidance to be centred on the individual: for instance by increasing personal satisfaction, improving career decision-making, or increasing personal development. All countries made it clear that they also expected career guidance to serve a number of important public objectives. And all indicated that their career guidance services are being strongly influenced by current issues and developments in public policy. These public policy goals, issues and developments fall into three broad categories: learning goals; labour market goals; and social equity goals.

---

[47] In some countries terms such as "vocational guidance", "vocational counselling", "career counselling", "information, advice and guidance" and "career development" are used to refer to the range of activities that is included here within the term career guidance. In this report career guidance encompasses all of these, and no attempt is made to distinguish between them. Figure 30 expands on the meaning of the term career guidance.

Figure 30: What is career guidance?

> Career guidance refers to services intended to assist people, of any age and at any point throughout their lives to make educational, training and occupational choices and to manage their careers. Career guidance helps people to reflect on their ambitions, interests, qualifications and abilities. It helps them to understand the labour market and education systems, and to relate this to what they know about themselves. Comprehensive career guidance tries to teach people to plan and make decisions about work and learning. Career guidance makes information about the labour market and about educational opportunities more accessible by organising it, systematising it, and making it available when and where people need it.
>
> In its contemporary forms, career guidance draws upon a number of disciplines: psychology; education; sociology; and labour economics. Historically, psychology is the major discipline that has under-pinned its theories and methodologies. In particular differential psychology and developmental psychology have had an important influence (Super, 1957; Kuder, 1977; Holland, 1997). One-to-one interviews and psychological testing for many years were seen as its central tools. There are many countries where psychology remains the major entry route.
>
> However in most countries career guidance is now provided by people with a very wide range of training and qualifications. Some are specialists; some are not. Some have had extensive, and expensive, training; others have had very little. Training programmes are still heavily based upon developing skills in providing help in one-to-one interviews. On the other hand, psychological testing now receives a reduced emphasis in many countries as counselling theories have moved from an emphasis upon the practitioner as expert to seeing practitioners as facilitators of individual choice and development.
>
> While personal interviews are still the dominant tool, career guidance includes a wide range of other services: group discussions; printed and electronic information; school lessons; structured experience; telephone advice; on-line help. Career guidance is provided to people in a very wide range of settings: schools and tertiary institutions; public employment services; private guidance providers; enterprises; and community settings.

Learning goals

In some cases, countries expressed the significance of career guidance for education, training and skills development in quite broad terms. For example, Australia, Austria, Canada, Finland, Germany, Ireland, the Netherlands and the

United Kingdom made it clear that career guidance is an important part of their approach to lifelong learning. Canada and Korea saw it as one way in which public policy can support the development of human resources.

Some countries were more specific about the learning goals that career guidance supports. Austria saw it as one of the ways in which the permeability and effectiveness of educational pathways can be improved. Finland, the Netherlands and Norway saw its importance rising with the growing individualisation and diversification of school programmes. The Netherlands argued that career guidance is needed to support the more active approaches to learning that are important in developing lifelong learners. The United Kingdom saw career guidance as an important tool in its efforts to improve levels of basic skills, again an important part of its lifelong learning strategies.

More broadly, it is very common for countries to see career guidance as a tool that can help to improve the efficiency of their education systems. Denmark, Finland, Germany and the Netherlands believed that it can support the attainment of high rates of educational qualification by youth and adults. Austria, Denmark, Finland, Ireland, the Netherlands, Norway and Spain argued that it can help to reduce dropout rates and improve graduation rates.

Countries also saw career guidance as a way to improve the interface between education and the labour market. Austria and Norway explicitly said that it is a way to improve the match between the two. Australia, Korea and the United Kingdom saw it as important in improving the school-to-work transition. The Netherlands regarded career guidance as one way to support qualifications upgrading in response to labour market change.

Finally, three European countries – Austria, Finland and Germany – saw career guidance as growing in importance as education becomes increasingly internationalised: for example by helping to provide information and advice on international study opportunities. A similar motivation under-pinned the creation in 2003 by the European Commission of a website portal to provide information on learning opportunities throughout Europe (www.ploteus.net).

Labour market goals

As with learning goals, countries often expressed the importance of career guidance for labour market policies in quite general terms. For example, Australia, Canada, Denmark, Germany and the United Kingdom argued that it is important in helping to improve labour market outcomes or labour market efficiency. Denmark argued that it can help to reduce the effects of labour market destabilisation. Austria, Denmark, Finland, Germany, Korea and Spain indicated that it can help to prevent or reduce unemployment.

There are a number of specific labour market objectives that countries saw career guidance as helping to achieve. For example, Austria and Spain both argued that it can improve labour mobility. Austria, Canada and Luxembourg argued that it can help to improve the match between supply and demand. In a similar vein, Austria, Finland, Germany, Ireland and the Netherlands believed that it can help to improve labour supply and is a way of addressing skill shortages. Canada, Germany, the Netherlands and Spain argued that career guidance can assist active labour market policies by helping to reduce individual dependency upon income support.

Some countries also argued that career guidance is an important part of policies that support adjustments to the broad changes that are occurring in labour markets. Denmark, Finland, Germany and the Netherlands saw it as important in helping to deal with the effects of an ageing society, or in reducing early retirement. Korea and the United Kingdom saw career guidance as important in helping to support the notion of a lifelong career, as opposed to a lifelong job. Austria, Finland, Germany and Norway argued that it can support the growing internationalisation of the labour market. Canada believed that career guidance can help address the impact of migration on the labour market.

Social equity goals

Somewhat less frequently, countries argued that career guidance can help to achieve a number of social equity goals: both within education and the labour market, and more broadly. Australia and the United Kingdom argued that it can help to promote greater social inclusion. Denmark and Spain argued that it can address the needs of marginalised groups and of the disadvantaged. Finland, Germany and Norway believed that career guidance is important in supporting the social integration of migrants and ethnic minorities.

Some countries indicated a more specific focus to their social equity goals. Germany and Ireland argued that career guidance can support the integration of the disadvantaged and the poorly qualified in education, and, together with Spain, in employment. Canada argued that it can address growing polarisation in the labour market.

Some countries focused specifically on gender issues. The Netherlands and Spain believed that career guidance can support rising female labour force participation. Austria, Germany and Norway argued that it can help to address gender segmentation in the labour market.

The special challenges of lifelong learning and active employment policies

The steps that many OECD countries are taking to implement lifelong approaches to learning pose particular challenges for career guidance policies and programmes. In broad terms, a commitment to lifelong learning sees learning taking place throughout the lifespan. Just as importantly, it promotes substantial individual control over what is learned, and over the timing, location and mode of learning. It places a strong emphasis not only upon achieving formal skills and qualifications, but also upon developing the motivation to learn and the skills to manage one's own learning (OECD, 2001a).

In specific terms, these approaches involve a higher proportion of the population attaining initial educational qualifications at upper secondary and tertiary level. They need more flexible pathways to be created through initial education and training. This requires people to have the knowledge and skills to navigate their way through these pathways and to manage their own learning. And the creation of more learner-driven education systems increases the scope for individual choice in learning. Commitments to broad lifelong learning goals require countries increasingly to make it possible for adults to return to learning, with appropriate assessment and recognition of the knowledge and skills acquired through work and experience.

It is difficult to see how learning systems such as these can operate in the absence of highly developed systems of information and advice, any more than it is possible to see how financial markets could operate in the absence of appropriate information and sources of advice to guide financial investment decisions. Such systems of information and advice are needed both within initial education and within further education and training, and at the interface between both of these and the labour market. Within initial education highly developed information and advice systems are needed to support the development of learning management skills, to support flexible pathways, and to ensure that the benefits of investing in extended education are not lost through making inappropriate choices. Within further education and training they are needed to make sure that adults have the right information and advice to return to study after periods of absence. In particular, well developed information and advice systems are needed to help support people who have low qualifications and low skills. These are the least likely to be able to navigate their way into and through complex education systems, and they are likely, without advice and information, to make poor choices or to drop out of formal learning (OECD, 2003a).

Closely related to these challenges are ones that emerge from new views of labour market policy. Three developments in approaches to labour market policy, in particular, pose challenges for career guidance: the introduction, in a number of OECD countries, of active, mutual obligation approaches to the payment of unemployment benefits and to welfare dependency; growing interest in the notion of employability as a tool of labour market policy; and the employment implications of ageing societies.

Active, mutual obligation approaches to welfare dependency

With the rise in unemployment levels in OECD countries in the mid-1970s, attention focused upon shifting policy away from the payment of passive unemployment benefits towards more "active" approaches based upon labour market programmes that involve education, training or subsidised employment. Subsequently, approaches towards active labour market policies shifted, and the term came also to connote approaches that involve a mutual obligation. Such mutual obligations involve the unemployed person being required to actively search for work or to undertake training to continue to qualify for unemployment benefits. An emphasis upon earlier intervention to help the unemployed is part of such approaches. A similar approach is part of approaches to the payment of welfare benefits in many OECD countries.

The European Employment Strategy, which was formulated in 1997, is an example of such approaches. It requires member countries to intervene to offer unemployed young people assistance before the end of six months of unemployment. It requires unemployed adults to be offered a similar "fresh start" before reaching twelve months of unemployment: either by being offered training, work practice or another employability measure, or by accompanying individual career guidance (European Commission, 1998).

A key element in many such approaches is the development of an individual action plan, worked out between the benefit recipient and an adviser. A similar approach can be seen in the early intervention programmes that have been introduced, with apparent success, in a number of Nordic countries to deal with early school leavers (OECD, 2000a). If such approaches to unemployment policy and welfare dependency are to be successful, public employment offices and welfare administration centres need greatly improved access to information on education and training opportunities. Their staff need an increased capacity to act in an advisory or guidance role, in addition to a benefit administration, vacancy administration and job placement role.

Employability as a tool of labour market policy

A closely related approach focuses upon the concept of employability. The notion of employability has a number of interpretations (Gazier, 1999). One of these is the more active approach to dealing with unemployment outlined above. A broader view sees employability as a collection of individual attributes such as the ability to find and keep a job, and the capacity to adapt to a changing labour market and new job requirements. Translating such thinking into practical policies and programmes has not gone very far in most OECD countries. However it is hard to see how such thinking about employment policy could be translated into practical programmes without a strong career guidance component.

The employment implications of ageing societies

Another challenge that career guidance needs to face is the employment implications of ageing societies. To date much of the policy debate that surrounds ageing societies has focused upon reform to the retirement age and reformed income support arrangements (OECD, 1998a). Debate is emerging on the importance of financial and legislative reforms being accompanied by more flexible working arrangements in the latter periods of life. More flexible working arrangements might allow a sudden shift from full-time work to retirement to be replaced by a more gradual and more flexible transition. Over a longer period this could include options such as part-time work, self employment and voluntary work. Debate is also emerging on the importance of public policies supporting more active ageing, so that additional free time is not used passively, partly to utilise the social contribution of older people, and partly to reduce health expenditure. And it is becoming clear that whether people use their increased leisure actively in their retirement is very much determined by how they use their time when employed (OECD, 2000b).

Alongside the important role that financial planning plays in helping people to prepare for and enjoy their retirement, career guidance has a clear role to play in supporting increased flexibility in time use in the transition from full-time employment to full-time retirement, as well as in helping people better to prepare for the transition (Department for Education and Skills, 2003).

What do these policy challenges imply for career guidance?

The theoretical basis of career guidance has long emphasised the developmental nature of career decision-making. Yet this has less often been reflected in the ways that services are organised and delivered. In most OECD countries, career guidance has traditionally been provided in two main settings. The first of these has been schools, where career guidance has largely focused upon helping young people at the point of leaving school with key decisions such as which occupation or which course of tertiary study to choose. The second main setting for career guidance has been the public employment service, where career guidance has largely focused upon helping the unemployed with immediate job decisions. In both settings face-to-face interviews have been the career guidance method, supplemented by career information, usually in printed form. In both settings information provision and immediate decisions have predominated over the development of career-management skills.

Inevitably, this emphasis results in gaps in provision. In particular, there is relatively little provision, in most OECD countries, for tertiary students, for employed adults, and for adults not in the labour market.

There are many variations on these two principal models, and in many countries career guidance is increasingly being provided in a wider range of settings and in more varied ways. Nevertheless, the traditional model of career guidance does not appear well suited to the full range of contemporary policy challenges that it is expected to meet. The wide range of challenges that policy-makers in OECD countries believe career guidance should be able to address, and in particular the challenge of helping to implement lifelong approaches to learning and active approaches to labour market policy, imply radically different ways of organising and providing career guidance services.

The policy challenges for career guidance set out above imply that, at the least, career guidance services need to broaden from largely providing assistance with decisions at limited and selected points in people's lives to an approach which also encompasses the development of career-management skills. In addition, countries need to greatly expand access to career guidance so that it is available to people throughout their lives, and so that it can be available not just to selected groups such as school students or the unemployed, but to all. If this changed emphasis and expanded access were to be achieved solely through the traditional way in which career guidance is provided – face-to-face interviews – there would inevitably be a substantial increase in costs. Both to minimise cost increases, and to meet the needs of a greatly expanded and more diverse range of clients, career guidance needs to be made available much more flexibly in time and space, and to adopt a wider range of delivery methods. [48]

---

48 Editorial note: The OECD report concludes with a list of ten features of lifelong guidance systems which policy-makers should use in examining the adequacy of the current systems. The final chapter of the OECD report lists six issues (later expanded to seven) which policy-makers should address. As both lists are included in the following chapter, they are not reproduced here.

19. Career Guidance Policies in 37 Countries: Contrasts and Common Themes[49]

Introduction

Internationally, career guidance is higher on the public policy agenda than ever before. This paper outlines the key findings from three overlapping reviews of career guidance policies, which together have covered 37 countries. The first was a review conducted by the Organisation for Economic Co-operation and Development (2004) which covered 14 countries: Australia, Austria, Canada, Czech Republic, Denmark, Finland, Germany, Ireland, Korea, Luxembourg, Netherlands, Norway, Spain and the United Kingdom. An adapted version of the OECD questionnaire was then used for a World Bank review of career guidance policies in seven middle-income countries: Chile, Poland, Romania, the Philippines, Russia, South Africa and Turkey (Watts & Fretwell, 2004). Finally, at the request of the European Commission, the OECD questionnaire was completed by all European Union member-states and acceding countries that had not taken part in the OECD review, and synthesis reports were produced covering first the acceding countries (Sultana, 2003) and then (Sultana, 2004) the full range of 29 European countries: Austria, Belgium, Bulgaria, Cyprus, Czech Republic, Denmark, Estonia, Finland, France, Germany, Greece, Hungary, Iceland, Ireland, Italy, Latvia, Lithuania, Luxembourg, Malta, Netherlands, Norway, Poland, Portugal, Romania, Slovakia, Slovenia, Spain, Sweden and the United Kingdom. Of these, 13 had also taken part in the OECD or World Bank reviews, which included review visits by external experts; the other European countries completed questionnaires but did not have such visits. A significant stimulus for the co-ordination of the three reviews was provided by two international symposia on career development and public policy, held in Canada in 1999 and 2001 (Bezanson & O'Reilly, 2002; Hiebert & Bezanson, 2000).

The definitions of career guidance adopted for the three reviews were virtually identical. The term was defined as referring to services intended to assist individuals, of any age and at any point throughout their lives, to make educational, training and occupational choices and to manage their careers. These may include services in schools, in universities and colleges, in training institutions, in public employment services, in companies, in the voluntary/community sector and in the private sector. The services may be on an individual or group basis, and may be face-to-

---

[49] Co-authored with Ronald Sultana. Reprinted, by permission of the publisher, from *International Journal for Educational and Vocational Guidance*, Volume 4 No.2-3, 2004. IJEVG is the journal of the International Association for Educational and Vocational Guidance. DOI: 10.1007/s10775-005-1025-y. With permission of Springer Science+Business Media.

face or at a distance (including helplines and web-based services). They include career information (in print, ICT-based and other forms), assessment and self-assessment tools, counselling interviews, career education and career management programmes, taster programmes, work search programmes, and transition services.

The present paper aims to identify the key common issues which have emerged from the three reviews, and the conclusions which can be drawn from them. First, though, some contrasts across the countries will be examined. Finally, a few closing reflections will be added.

Some contrasts

There are difficulties and dangers in carrying out and synthesising a comparative analysis on this scale. The main danger is downplaying the extent to which each country has its own traditions and history of provision, with the same terms and concepts sometimes concealing quite different shades of meaning. The dynamics of globalisation have led to a great deal of inter-country convergence in the practice of career guidance: all countries face a similar set of broad challenges for education, labour market and social policies related to career guidance systems. Nevertheless, it needs to be constantly kept in mind that all guidance services reflect the economic, political, social, cultural, educational and labour market contexts – as well as the professional and organisational structures – in which they operate (Watts, 1996e).

Some of these contrasts emerge less strongly in these reviews than one might have anticipated. Thus the OECD report on Korea, one of the few non-Western countries covered, notes the influence of Korean values (stemming largely from Confucian tradition) of respect for elders, deference, and obedience to authority; and also of endurance (learning to bear one's problems), maintaining social face and avoiding embarrassment; these mores are not reflected explicitly, however, in the subsequent analysis of services. Similarly, the EC and World Bank reports note the importance in middle-income countries of the informal economy, much of it unregulated, in which individuals gain a living in semi-legitimate, entrepreneurial ways; but the reports find few guidance practices that attend to this economy and its importance in the work-lives of many individuals.

In part the lack of such contrasts may be a commentary on guidance systems themselves, which are inclined to be formal in nature and to be heavily influenced by European and North American models. The downplaying of differences may also be exacerbated by the OECD questionnaire used for all of the reviews, which tended – for understandable reasons – to emphasise formal structures at the expense of informal ones, and systems and structures at the expense of contents and processes.

Despite this, there are some specific differences between countries which emerge clearly from the reviews. These include, for example, differences between educational systems with strong early streaming and tracking mechanisms and those with more flexible pathways: guidance services tend to play a more important role in the latter than in the former. They also include differences between countries in which most public services – including career guidance services – are delivered by the state or state agencies, and countries in which there has been a strong policy to deliver services through the private and voluntary sectors wherever possible: the latter tends to lead to greater diversity of service provision.

Two contrasts seem particularly worthy of note. One is the importance of level of economic development. While no low-income countries were included in the reviews, it would seem unlikely that formal career guidance services would have a significant role to play in such economies (though informal community-based services might). It is only as economic activity becomes more formalised and diversified, and resources are available to attend to the problems this poses, that formal guidance services start to grow. The World Bank review shows that middle-income countries tend in general to have less well-developed career guidance systems than high-income countries, and in particular more limited career information to support such systems. This may be partly because of low levels of public resources, partly because the range of choices for many individuals is more restricted, and partly because more people are preoccupied with economic survival rather than with development and growth.

The second is the relationship of career guidance services to the development of market economies and democratic political institutions. This is particularly relevant to the countries of central and eastern Europe which have been moving from command to market economies; and to South Africa which has been in transition from the apartheid regime to a more integrated and open society. In centrally planned economies under the Communist regime, for example, there was little perceived need for career guidance services: unemployment did not officially exist, and people were largely allocated to their roles by selective processes; career was linked with individualism, and regarded as a social vice. Career guidance services distinctively affirm the value attached in market-based democratic societies to the rights of individuals to make free decisions about their own working lives, linking personal goals to the socio-economic needs of the society in which they live.

Particularly in middle-income and transition countries, but also elsewhere, there is much evidence of "policy borrowing", in terms of strategies, tools, resources and training. In some respects, the United States is the "absent centre" from the reviews, since it is not directly included and yet its influence on career guidance practice is evident in most if not all of the participating countries. In recent years, Canada has been particularly successful in exporting its practices, The Real Game

– a career development programme involving role-play and simulation – being a prominent but not unique example. There are also examples of other links, often influenced by historic, linguistic, economic or cultural ties. Thus German models have been influential in several central and east European countries; French models tend to be visible in Francophone countries. In some countries, collaborative and support programmes financed by the European Commission and World Bank have had considerable impact. To some extent such programmes tend to promote a process of convergence, but they seem to be most successful when they include a process through which they are customised to the distinctive needs of countries and respond to country conditions.

Key common issues

With these caveats, we will now identify the key common issues which emerged from the three reviews. We will do so under five broad headings: rationale, evidence, delivery, resourcing, and leadership.

Rationale

The reviews indicate that in all countries policy-makers clearly regard career guidance as a public good as well as a private good. The public-policy goals which they expect career guidance services to address fall into three main categories. The first are learning goals, including improving the efficiency of the education and training system and managing its interface with the labour market. The second are labour market goals, including improving the match between supply and demand and managing adjustments to change. The third are social equity goals, including supporting equal opportunities and promoting social inclusion. The balance between and within these categories varies across countries. A challenge for all countries is to maintain an appropriate balance between them in the provision of services.

These goals are currently being reframed in the light of policies relating to lifelong learning, linked to active labour market policies and the concept of sustained employability. The result is that countries increasingly recognise the need to expand access to career guidance so that it is available not just to selected groups like school-leavers and the unemployed, but to everyone throughout their lives.

This is arguably the key point in the reports, with huge implications. It requires not just expansion but transformation. If the expanded access that is required were to be achieved solely through public services and such traditional methods as face-to-face interviews linked to psychometric testing, there would inevitably be a massive increase in costs. For these and other reasons, efforts are being made to diversify the methods and sources of provision and to seek innovative and more streamlined forms of service delivery. As part of this, there is a move towards self-help approaches, including approaches designed to help individuals to develop the skills of managing their own careers. These trends are supported by recent trends in career development theory, which emphasise that career guidance should be available throughout life, should be viewed as a learning experience, and should foster the individual's autonomy.

Recent OECD work on human capital (OECD, 2002) suggests that the career management skills which are now a growing focus of career guidance policies and practices may play an important role in economic growth. It points out that less than half of earnings variation in OECD countries can be accounted for by educational qualifications and readily measurable skills. It argues that a significant part of the remainder may be explained by people's ability to build, and to manage, their skills. Included in this are career-planning, job-search and other career-management skills. There is a close harmony between this wider view of human capital and concepts of employability. Seen in this perspective, it seems that career guidance has the potential to contribute significantly to national policies for the development of human capital.

Evidence

In this context, the available empirical evidence on outcomes from career guidance is of great interest to policy-makers. Of course, policy-making is not a wholly rational process: power processes matter too, and anecdotal evidence can often be persuasive. It is important to acknowledge that many social activities are supported by public funds without such evidence: the teaching of history or literature, for example. But sound empirical evidence is helpful if sceptics are to be convinced.

The OECD report reviews the existing evidence at three stages: immediate learning outcomes from career guidance, including attitudinal changes and increased knowledge; intermediate behavioural changes, including entry into a particular career path, course or job; and longer-term outcomes, such as success and satisfaction with these paths or placements.

In these terms, there is substantial evidence of the learning outcomes which individuals derive from career guidance interventions. This is important, because in general career guidance interventions are concerned not with telling people what to do but with helping them acquire knowledge, skills and attitudes that will help them make better career choices and transitions. It is also congruent with the growing attention to the development of career management skills.

In the aggregate, there is also growing evidence of positive behavioural outcomes in terms of impact upon participation in learning and in work: more such studies are needed. On long-term benefits in relation to success or satisfaction – to which some policy outcomes in relation to economic and social benefits are linked – adequate studies have not yet been conducted. There is a case for a major international initiative, possibly linked to continuing OECD work on human capital, to determine what is feasible in this respect: the methodological difficulties and cost implications of long-term longitudinal studies are formidable. Meanwhile, it can be concluded that the available evidence on the benefits of career guidance is not comprehensive, but that what exists is largely positive.

Delivery

The reports go on to examine the current delivery of career guidance services in relation to the changing rationale outlined above. They demonstrate that no country has yet developed an adequate lifelong guidance system. But all countries have examples of good practice, and across the range of countries these indicate what such a system might look like – recognising that in terms of its detail it will take different forms in different countries. Twelve general points relating to delivery are particularly worth noting here.

The first is the growing recognition of the importance of career education and guidance in schools, not only in helping young people to make the immediate choices that confront them but also in laying the foundations for lifelong learning and lifelong career development. This is evident, for example, in the inclusion in many countries of career education in the curriculum, incorporating career awareness, career exploration, and the development of career management skills. This can be a separate subject, or subsumed into a broader subject, or infused across the curriculum (though the latter approach is difficult to implement successfully); alternatively, it may be provided in the form of seminars and workshops. Such programmes are greatly enriched where they include active involvement of employers, parents and other stakeholders, and opportunities for pupils to engage in experiential learning: course tasters; and active experiences of the world of work through visits, simulation, shadowing or actual work experience. The longer-term perspective is also evident in the introduction of profiling and portfolio systems designed to encourage students to engage in regular review and planning and to manage their own learning. As with career education, such approaches can start in primary school. They have implications for the whole school, evident for example in the concept of *l'école orientante* (the guidance-oriented school) in Quebec.

Second, there is a risk of career education and guidance in schools being marginalised within a broad concept of guidance. Many countries have guidance counsellors with a holistic role covering personal and social as well as educational and vocational guidance. In such schools, there is consistent evidence that career guidance tends to be marginalised, in two respects: the pressing nature of the personal and behavioural problems of a minority of pupils mean that guidance counsellors spend much of their time on these problems, at the expense of the help needed by all pupils in relation to their educational and vocational choices; and guidance on such choices tends to focuses mainly on educational decisions viewed as ends in themselves, rather than on their vocational implications and on longer-term career planning. In Norway, accordingly, the career guidance role is being split off, partly to protect its resourcing, and partly to address its distinctive competence requirements, including knowledge of the labour market. In Poland, too, separate career counsellors are now being introduced into schools.

Third, it is clear that alongside career education and guidance within the school itself, there is merit in making career guidance available in a specialist form from the employment service or some other agency based outside the school – as is the case, for example, in Germany and the UK. Such an agency can offer closer links with the labour market, and stronger assurance of impartiality in the guidance they provide. In several countries there has been some erosion of such agencies in recent years, with damaging consequences. On the other hand, other countries are exploring the possibility of setting up new agencies of this kind. In such cases there is a need for clear partnership models with schools, to avoid confusion and unnecessary overlap.

Fourth, there has in many countries been a growing policy concern for at risk young people who have dropped out of formal education and training with few or no qualifications, and who are drifting in and out of unemployment, labour-market inactivity and marginal unskilled work. In Denmark, for example, municipalities are obliged to make contact with, and offer guidance to, such young people. Successful strategies for this work involve a highly individualised approach which attends to their personal and social as well as their educational and vocational guidance needs: in contrast with our earlier comments on schools, this is a case where holistic approaches are highly desirable. Such strategies can be managed through close partnership working between career guidance workers and youth workers, using outreach approaches. An alternative model is to have a single generic first-in-line role, supported by a range of specialists (including career guidance specialists) who can be brought in when their distinctive help is needed.

Fifth, it is evident that in several countries career guidance services in tertiary education are inadequate or non-existent. Ironically, guidance roles within education tend to be least strongly professionalised in higher education, which is the sector responsible for much of the professional training in the field as a whole. In some countries such guidance as is available is confined largely to choice of studies: the assumption seems to be that students can manage their own transitions into the labour market without any support. This may have been sustainable when their student body covered a small academic elite, who normally entered a narrow field of work related to their studies. It is much more questionable when the number of students is much larger and more diverse, and when the links between their studies and the fields open to them are much more complex. There is accordingly increasing recognition of the need to strengthen career guidance services in tertiary education. These include not only central careers services, but also developments in the curriculum including career management courses, opportunities for work experience, and profiling and portfolio systems, extending and enhancing earlier such provision in schools.

Sixth, there is a widespread need to integrate public employment services more closely into lifelong learning strategies in general and strategies for lifelong access to guidance in particular. Huge public resources are concentrated in these services. They tend at present to be targeted narrowly at particular groups (notably the unemployed) and short-term goals (immediate employment and removal from the benefit system). But they could be transformed into well-publicised career development services for all, helping people to sustain their employability and respond flexibly to change. This could also enable their work with the targeted groups to be preventive rather than purely remedial and to avoid the stigma which can undermine the effectiveness of such work. A strong model could, for example, be developed by bringing together the respective strengths of the career information centres (BIZ) in Germany with the innovative capacity of the public employment service (Aetat) in Norway, including the design quality of the latter's walk-in services, the user-friendliness of its website, its inventive range of web-based tools, and its plans to set up a call centre for information on learning and work.

Seventh, there is a need for enhanced career guidance services to be provided in the workplace by employers for their employees. These can include career planning workshops and regular review and planning processes, paralleling those within education. They tend to be stronger in large organisations than in small- and medium-sized enterprises. While employer interests may impose constraints on the impartiality of such services, they are an important part of lifelong guidance provision. They can be supported by public policy through voluntary quality-mark schemes, and by including career guidance provision within expenditure allowable against training levies. There is also interest in a number of countries, including Austria, the Netherlands and the UK, in the role of trade unions in providing career guidance services for their members.

Eighth, career guidance can have a particularly dynamic role to play in adult education. Some access provision for people returning to learning or to work includes strong guidance elements. Again, procedures for the accreditation and recognition of prior learning can develop into a guidance dialogue, in which individuals are helped not only to identify the knowledge and competencies they have acquired informally, but also to explore new opportunities to which they might be transferable. Career guidance services can also be used to improve the responsiveness of educational institutions to consumer needs through advocacy on their behalf and through feedback to providers on their unmet needs. In an experiment in Sweden, learners were not permitted to start an education or training programme without first seeing a guidance counsellor and drawing up a learning plan.

Ninth, a life-stage where current provision is particularly inadequate is the third age. Many countries are expressing growing concerns about their ageing populations and difficulties in funding adequate pension provision, and the consequent need to encourage people to stay longer in the labour force. There is also growing interest in encouraging those who have left the labour market to continue their involvement in learning and in voluntary work in the community, so reducing health bills and harnessing their social contribution. But no country has yet systematically addressed the potential role of guidance services in these various respects, and more generally in helping individuals to manage more gradual and more flexible approaches to retirement.

Tenth, good-quality career information is essential for good-quality career guidance and good-quality career decision-making. Governments have an important role to play in funding the collection, publication and distribution of career information. Even where information is produced by others, they should also seek to assure its quality. Too often career information is driven by producer needs rather than consumer needs. There is a need for strong cross-pathing between educational and occupational information – showing, for example, the occupational implications of educational decisions, and the educational pathways that lead to particular occupational destinations. This requires close collaboration between education and labour authorities. ICT-based systems make integration of this kind easier to deliver, and also make it possible to add a diagnostic front-end to enable individuals to input their characteristics and preferences and be guided to appropriate opportunities. The National Career Information System in Australia is a good example of what can be produced.

Eleventh, while information is necessary, it is not sufficient. If individuals are to be able to find the information they need, to understand this information and relate it to their personal needs, and then to convert it into personal action, many will need some form of personal support. Some such help, however, can be provided at a distance. There is much scope for using helplines and web-based services to extend access to guidance, and for integrating such services more creatively with face-to-face services. In the UK, the Learndirect helpline was launched in February 1998; in five years since then it has responded to over five million calls. In principle, flexible but integrated use of helplines, websites and e-mail, linked closely with face-to-face facilities, opens up new strategic opportunities for the delivery of career guidance. It means that individuals can initially access help in the form which is convenient and comfortable for them, and then where appropriate be moved on to other media to maintain the dialogue.

Finally, there is scope to redesign the physical facilities of all career guidance services on a self-help basis. Some services, particularly in some middle-income countries, are designed solely for one-to-one consultations, with information resources kept in counsellors' offices rather than on open display. Elsewhere, though, it is increasingly common for a variety of ICT-based and other resources to be on open access, with clear signposting, and with specialist career counsellors being available for brief support as well as for longer counselling interviews. Diagnostic help can then be provided on reception to help clients decide whether they can operate on a self-help basis, need brief staff assistance, or require intensive professional help.

Resourcing

Under the heading of resourcing, there are two key issues which have implications for the nature and quality of career guidance services. The first is how such services are staffed. The second is how they are funded.

On staffing, there is a need for stronger occupational structures in the career guidance field. In many countries, the current structures are weak in comparison with those in related professions. Many services are provided by people who do it for only part of their time (the rest being devoted to teaching, job placement, or guidance on personal or study problems) and little appropriate training. Often, qualifications from apparently related fields – such as teaching and psychology – seem to be regarded as proxies for guidance qualifications, without any verification of whether they assure the requisite competencies or not. Guidance strategies can include delivery through others – teachers and mentors of various kinds, for example; there is also a need for wider use of trained support staff. But clarity is needed about the role of guidance professionals within such diversified delivery systems. Their training should include consultancy and management roles, and embrace the types of cost-effective and flexible delivery methods that can widen access to guidance.

Supporting such diversified training provision, there is also a need for competence frameworks which can embrace but also differentiate a variety of guidance roles – and provide a career development structure for guidance staff themselves. The Standards and Guidelines for Career Development Practitioners, developed in Canada through a long process of consultation between all the professional groups involved, is of particular interest in this respect. The international standards recently developed by the International Association for Educational and Vocational Guidance provide a useful reference point for such processes.

On funding, policy options include devolving funding either to regions and localities as part of decentralisation, or to individual educational institutions. This can result in stronger local ownership and customisation of services, but can also produce wide variation in their level and quality. Steps that can be taken by central governments to avoid this include staffing formulas, performance contracts and legislative-based entitlements.

Some governments have contracted out a range of employment services, including career guidance services. This can result in cheaper services and, particularly in the case of the voluntary, community-based sector, in services that are more closely attuned to the needs of particular groups. It can also, however, result in services that are fragmented. In Canada, it is estimated that there are over 10,000 community-based organisations delivering career development services. Alternatively, a few countries have trialed voucher schemes in which funding is channelled through the clients, who can use their voucher to "buy" the service from a provider of their choice.

Contracts and vouchers can also be linked to pump-priming private markets for career guidance service delivery. There are strong markets in a number of countries in career publishing, in placement agencies, and in outplacement services. But in general markets for career guidance per se are supported largely by contracted-out public employment services and by employers. Only in a few countries, notably Australia, Canada, Germany, the Netherlands and the United Kingdom, is there much evidence of a market in career guidance supported by fees paid by individuals themselves, and even here this market is still limited. It is as yet unclear whether this is a transitional problem, linked to users being accustomed to such services being free of charge, or a systemic problem, based on difficulties in treating career guidance as a commodity in the ways a market would require.

In all countries, more information is needed on the extent and potential of these markets. Since guidance is widely viewed as a public as well as a private good, the roles of government in relation to a mixed-economy model of provision would seem to be threefold: to stimulate the market (through contracts and incentives) in order to build its capacity; to ensure that it is quality-assured, both to protect the public interest and to build consumer confidence; and to compensate for market failure by addressing needs which the market cannot meet, where this is viewed as being in the public interest.

Leadership

Governments have an important role in providing strategic leadership. But they need to do so in association with other stakeholders: education and training providers, employers, trade unions, community agencies, students, parents, other consumers, and career guidance practitioners.

Evidence and data are important tools for policy-making. Stronger infrastructures are required to build up the evidence base for both policy and practice, and to do this cumulatively so that experience is not wasted and mistakes repeated. This should include evidence on users, on client needs, on which services are delivered to whom, on the costs of services (on which remarkably little information is available at present), and on the immediate and longer-term outcomes of guidance interventions. The limited extent of such data at present is due to the absence of an accountability culture among professional guidance staff and to the lack of pressure from policy-makers to collect the data. Some of the information should be collected on a routine basis; some requires sophisticated studies. To date, few countries have established specialist career guidance research centres or research programmes to develop the knowledge base in a systemic way. There is also a need for university chairs to provide status and intellectual leadership for the field: few countries have such chairs at present.

Legislation can be another instrument for steering career guidance services. It plays an important role in this respect in some countries, but none at all in others. Where legislation exists, it tends to be general in nature. Much of it is sector-specific: Denmark is a rare example of a country which has a specific career guidance Act covering all sectors. The value of legislation as a policy steering tool would be increased if it was used to define client entitlements.

A need is evident in many countries for stronger co-ordination and leadership mechanisms in order to articulate a vision and develop a strategy for delivering lifelong access to guidance. Such mechanisms are required within government, where responsibility for guidance services is often fragmented across a number of ministries and branches. Strong co-operation between education and employment portfolios is particularly important: for example, to ensure that educational and occupational information are integrated; and that a strong labour market perspective is included in schools' career guidance programmes.

Co-ordinating mechanisms are also needed more broadly at national level, to bring together the relevant stakeholder groups and the various guidance professional bodies (which in some countries are very fragmented). Parallel mechanisms are then required at regional and/or local levels, closer to the point of delivery.

The UK has a strong model in these various respects, with its National IAG[50] Board to bring the relevant government departments together, its Guidance Council to bring the stakeholders together, its Federation of Professional Associations in Guidance to bring the professional groups together, and its information, advice and guidance (IAG) partnerships of local adult guidance providers. Another promising exemplar is the National Forum for Vocational Guidance in Poland. In some other countries, by contrast, seminars set up for the OECD and World Bank reviews seemed to provide an unusual opportunity for the relevant groups to come together, and led to proposals to develop a more sustainable infrastructure for joint action.

An important focus for such collaborative action is identifying gaps in services and developing action plans for filling them. Another is the development of strategic instruments which can be operationally useful across the whole range of the career guidance field and hold it together. Competence frameworks for career guidance practitioners of the kind developed in Canada are one. Another is organisational quality standards of the kind developed in the UK, covering how individuals are helped and how services are managed: these can be voluntary in nature, but can also be made mandatory for organisations in receipt of public funding. A third type of instrument, developed in Canada drawing from earlier work in the USA, is the Blueprint for Life-Work Design, a list of the competencies which career education and guidance programmes aim to develop among clients at different stages of their lives, with accompanying performance indicators. The systematic publication of data linked to such indicators could provide a way of introducing more coherent accountability across a co-ordinated career guidance system. Together, these three instruments could harmonise the system, particularly if they could be linked to common branding and marketing of services.

Conclusions

The conclusions in the three synthesis reports are framed in rather different ways. In the European report, they are framed in terms of trends in the nature of guidance, and to whom, when, where, by whom and how it is offered. In the World Bank report, they comprise four general conclusions, one of which identifies five priorities for middle-income countries. The OECD report defines 10 features of lifelong guidance systems and six issues for policy-makers to address. Since the features and issues identified by OECD embrace most of the European trends and the World Bank conclusions, they can – with a few small additions and modifications – serve as conclusions for the three studies.

---

50 Editorial footnote: Information, Advice and Guidance (IAG) was a term commonly used to describe career development work in the UK from the 1990s, but is now falling into disuse.

The 10 features of lifelong guidance systems can be framed as criteria which policy-makers can use to examine the adequacy of their current guidance systems in lifelong terms, and to determine priorities for action. The ten features are:

- Transparency and ease of access over the lifespan, including a capacity to meet the needs of a diverse range of clients.

- Attention to key transition points over the lifespan.

- Flexibility and innovation in service delivery to reflect the differing needs and circumstances of diverse client groups.

- Processes to stimulate individuals to engage in regular review and planning.

- Access to individual guidance by appropriately qualified practitioners for those who need such help, at times when they need it.

- Programmes for all young people to develop their career-management skills.

- Opportunities to investigate and experience learning and work options before choosing them.

- Access to service delivery that is independent of the interests of particular institutions or enterprises.

- Access to comprehensive and integrated educational, occupational and labour market information.

- Active involvement of relevant stakeholders.

The (now) seven issues which the creation and management of such lifelong guidance systems require policy-makers to address are:

- Ensuring that resource allocation decisions give the first priority to systems that develop career self-management skills and career information, and that delivery systems match levels of personal help, from brief to extensive, to personal needs and circumstances, rather than assuming that everybody needs intensive personal career guidance.

- Ensuring greater diversity in the types of services that are available and in the ways that they are delivered, including greater diversity in staffing structures, wider use of self-help techniques, and a more integrated approach to the use of ICT (including helplines as well as the Internet).

- Exploring the scope for facilitating measures, including appropriate incentives, designed to encourage the development of career guidance services within the private and voluntary sectors.

- Working more closely with professional associations and training bodies to improve education and training for career guidance practitioners, preferably on a cross-sectoral basis, producing professionals who can manage guidance resources as well as be engaged in direct service delivery.

- Improving the information base for public policy making, including gathering improved data on the financial and human resources devoted to career guidance, on client need and demand, on the characteristics of clients, on client satisfaction, and on the outcomes and cost-effectiveness of career guidance.

- Developing better quality assurance mechanisms and linking these to the funding of services.

- Developing stronger structures for strategic leadership.

Postscript

Finally, there are three general points which may be helpful in reflecting on these findings.

The first point is the importance of viewing career guidance services within each country as a coherent system. In reality, of course, they are not a single system. Rather, they are a collection of disparate sub-systems, including services in schools, in tertiary education, in public employment services, and in the private and voluntary sectors. Each of these is a minor part of some wider system, with its own rationale and driving forces. But in the reviews these different parts have been brought together, and viewed as parts of a whole. From the lifelong perspective of the individual, it is important that they should be as seamless as possible. If career guidance systems are to play their role in national strategies for lifelong learning linked to sustained employability, it is essential that the holistic vision adopted in the reviews be sustained and collectively owned by a council or other structure with the breadth and strength of membership to implement the vision. This is why stronger strategic leadership structures are so necessary.

Second, within lifelong learning strategies there is a strong case for viewing career guidance in more proactive terms than has been the case hitherto. Until recently, such services have been viewed largely as a reactive device, designed to help young people to manage the necessary transition from education to the labour market, and unemployed people to return to work as quickly as possible. This means that services need to be made available only when they have a problem which services can help them to solve. Within the context of lifelong learning, however, it can be argued that such services need to be available at times and in forms which will encourage all individuals to continue to develop their skills and competencies throughout their lives, linked to changing needs in the labour market. Such services accordingly need to be viewed as an active tool, and individuals positively encouraged to use them. This requires rationing mind-sets to be replaced by active marketing strategies linked to cost-effective models of service delivery.

Third, career guidance is essentially a soft rather than a hard policy intervention. At its heart is the notion of the "active individual": that individuals should be encouraged to determine their role in, and their contribution to, the society of which they are part. The primacy of the individual's interests is commonly a core principle in codes of practice for career guidance services. There are practical as well as ethical reasons for this, not least that such services can only serve the public good if they retain the confidence and trust of the individuals they serve. For policy-makers, this raises the issue of whether they expect practitioners to pursue the outcomes defined by policy objectives in their dealings with an individual client; or whether they are willing to support practitioners in addressing the individual's interests, in the confidence that, when aggregated, this will meet the public objectives too. Several countries in the reviews made a point of centring their definitions of career guidance around the needs of the individual. In principle, career guidance could be viewed (not only by economic liberals) as a classic case of Adam Smith's famous dictum that individuals encouraged to pursue their own interests are led by an "invisible hand" to promote an end that is no part of their intention – the public interest – and to do so more effectually than when they intend to promote it (Smith, 1776). In this sense, career guidance services could represent Smith's invisible hand made flesh. Their role is to not to determine what individuals should do, but to ensure that their decisions are well-informed (in terms of, among other things, the needs of the labour market) and well-thought-through. If there could be a clear understanding between policy-makers and practitioners on this issue, it would greatly enhance collaboration between the two.

Career guidance services have often in the past been viewed as marginal services in terms of public policy. Reviews by three influential international bodies have affirmed that this view is no longer adequate. Such services need now to be brought into the mainstream of policy formation.

Section Five:
Looking Forward

Section Introduction

This book demonstrates Tony Watts' visionary thinking about career development. He has variously wrestled with the disciplinary base of the field, created models for policy and practice, and described, analysed and influenced career development at home and overseas. His work has been defined by his ability to understand how the field is situated, conceive of where it might go, and map out the route between one and the other. In this final section he addresses both the future of work and the future of the career development field.

Unemployment and the Future of Work was originally delivered in Dublin in 1984 to the International Association of Educational and Vocational Guidance. In it Watts discusses how the visions of the leisure society that were so popular in mid-twentieth century science fiction have dissolved into a society which is concerned not with leisure, but unemployment. The chapter argues that those who are interested in career development must attend to the place of work in society and consider how this might, and should, change as society itself changes. He sets out four scenarios: unemployment; leisure; employment; and work. In the final scenario he returns to themes that have been covered already in this book about the importance of the informal economy and of non-alienated labour. It is here, he suggests, that the best future lies.

In Career Development: Looking Back; Moving Forward Tony Watts reflects on his own career and discusses how it has intertwined with policy and the development of the field within which he has worked. Ever insightful he skewers recent policy in the career development field, showing how the politicians and civil servants have failed to learn from many of the mistakes of history and are consequently doomed to repeat them. However, ever optimistic he identifies both progress and cause for hope both internationally and in the currently beleaguered climate of career development in England.

Career Development: Looking Back; Moving Forward is Watts' last public word on career development. His voice has rung clearly for 50 years, defining the field and acting as one of his strongest advocates. He has left behind a field changed by his engagement in it; he has also left behind numerous institutions, models and practices. However, most vitally, he has left behind a huge contribution to research, scholarship, practice and policy in his writings. It is this contribution that this book has sought to represent and celebrate in order to inspire future generations in the career development field.

20. Unemployment and the Future of Work[51]

The title of this seminar – "The Future of Work and Leisure" – is redolent of the 1960s or early 1970s. At that time we were growing rapidly more aware of the opportunities which automation held for reducing the hold of work on people's lives and for increasing the role of leisure. In careers guidance, we more and more began to talk about the importance of "life-styles": about enabling young people to choose "a life rather than simply a living" (Daws, 1972, p. 5).

In the more troubled and pessimistic 1980s, the title seems more problematic. It is "unemployment" rather than "leisure" which now preoccupies us. The statement of the seminar theme refers to the fact that "almost all countries" are now "experiencing severe economic recession and accompanying high levels of unemployment". It is in this new context that we are being invited to consider "the changing relationship between work and leisure and the implications this has for educational policy and the quality of life".

This in my view makes it essential that we do not evade the problematic economic, political and social realities which surround us. We must guard against the temptation to slip back in a facile way into sixties optimism. At the same time, it is equally important that we do not allow our vision and our imagination to be confined by the pessimistic assumptions of the eighties. It may be that the opportunities we perceived in the sixties are still there. But we need to be more aware of the political and social changes that will be needed to bring them to fruition.

The concept of unemployment

It is important at the outset to recognise how historically bounded our concepts of employment and unemployment are. In a subsistence economy, people work for their own survival. In an economy based on slave labour, slaves are obliged to labour for life, and cannot "lose their jobs", much as they might wish to do so. In a feudal society, serfs are bound to their lords by a range of obligations, rights and protections which are inviolable and extend far beyond work.

---

[51] Paper delivered to an international seminar on 'The Future of Work and Leisure', held at Dublin on 10-13 September 1984, under the auspices of the International Association of Educational and Vocational Guidance. Reprinted, by permission of the author and the IAEVG, from *Educational and Vocational Guidance Bulletin*, No. 43, 1985.

It is only with industrialisation, and with the development of capitalist productive relations, that our present concepts of employment and unemployment have evolved. Unemployment was barely written about by economists until the 19th century (Garraty, 1978). Even now, within advanced centrally-planned socialist economies, unemployment is officially unthinkable, since the whole of the available labour force is in principle assigned to production units. It is only when workers are free to offer or withdraw their labour, but (in Marxist terms) are separated from the means of production, that unemployment becomes meaningful.

In short, the problems we are addressing here are likely to be essentially those of western industrial societies. In socialist countries, or in Third World countries, these problems assume a very different form. Their problematic nature for us stems from the way in which our societies have been built around economic and social structures that may have operated well enough during our industrial age, but may not work as well in the post-industrial era into which many of our countries now seem to be moving.

The difficulties have of course been exacerbated by the prolonged recession. There appear now to be serious doubts about the feasibility of continued economic growth of the levels we became accustomed to in the 1950s and 1960s. But even if sustained growth is resumed, it may well not solve the unemployment problem. Within the manufacturing sector, industries are likely to invest not in labour-intensive methods but in capital-intensive methods, using the potential of automation and robotics to achieve the productivity increases that will enable them to compete in world markets. Such labour-intensive industries as remain are likely to continue to migrate to the "less developed countries", where labour costs are cheaper. Moreover, the assumption that the services sector will expand to encompass those released from manufacturing now seems questionable too. Many services are based within the public sector, and the advent of the "tax revolt" and of monetarism have led in most countries to pressure for reductions rather than further increases in public expenditure. Moreover, many services within the market economy have tended to price themselves out of the market: this is because wages and salaries tend to rise alongside those in manufacturing, but with less opportunity for compensating productivity rises.

The result of all this has been not only heavy unemployment but also a growing sense that we are unlikely, within present assumptions and structures, to return to anything approaching full employment for the foreseeable future. This is a huge change in social attitudes. In Britain it was not many years ago that newspaper leader writers confidently asserted that there was no way in which any government could survive unemployment rising over one million. Yet last year we voted back into power, with a massive majority, a government which had presided over an increase in unemployment to over three million – a figure unprecedented since the worst days of the depression in the thirties.

One possible scenario for the future, therefore, is that high unemployment as currently conceived will continue. There are however other possible scenarios. A second is that those outside employment, instead of being stigmatised, could form the basis of a new leisure class. A third is that ways could be found of distributing employment, and the income and status associated with it, more evenly. A fourth is that the concept of work could be broadened beyond that of employment, and greater value attached to self-employment and to forms of work outside the formal economy. The implications of these four scenarios are that the groups who are at present unemployed (1) remain unemployed, (2) are regarded as being "at leisure", (3) are offered employment, or (4) are seen as "working", if outside formal employment structures. I have explored the four scenarios in more detail elsewhere (Watts, 1983a). What I want to do in the main part of this paper is to present their main features and to identify some of the key underlying issues they raise.

The unemployment scenario

The unemployment scenario is based on a profound contradiction. It is a scenario in which employment continues to be regarded as the main source of status, identity and income, but is then denied to large numbers of the adult population. The results are enormously costly for the individuals concerned. The research evidence in Britain and elsewhere shows clearly that for the vast majority of unemployed people, it is a profoundly dispiriting, demoralising and impoverishing experience (for a review of this evidence, see e.g. Hayes and Nutman, 1981). There are strong grounds for supposing that it is closely associated with mental and physical ill-health, with suicide, and with crime and delinquency (see Watts, 1983a). These effects are also costly for the public purse, as are the costs of unemployment benefits and allowances, and of tax revenues foregone. The danger therefore is that an advanced society with high unemployment experiences a downward spiral effect, in which there is increased pressure for benefits and public services, but reduced capacity to pay for them. The gap between the employed and the unemployed tends to grow, as does the gulf between areas of the country where unemployment is high and those where employment is more buoyant

Unemployment also tends to hit some groups more than others. In particular, it usually has particularly severe effects on the weaker groups in the labour market: the young, the old, the women, the handicapped, the unskilled, the ethnic minorities. The first three of these groups have access to alternative socially-acceptable roles: the young as students or trainees, the old as pensioners, the women (some of them, anyway) as housewives. But in recent years, many people who have assumed these alternative roles have expressed dissatisfaction with the dependent status attached to them, and have pressed for access to the labour market. Women, in particular, have been asserting strongly that if employment continues to be the main source of status, identity and income, they want to have access to it on the same terms as men.

Finally, it is worth noting that unemployment has ripple effects right through the labour market in terms of the "under-employment" it causes, At a time of high unemployment, many more people are forced to accept jobs which do not make use of their talents, skills and qualifications; and many people who are dissatisfied in their existing jobs are unable to move to something better. The unemployment scenario is thus one in which the sense of confidence and fulfilment of many people is gradually eroded, and in which the social fabric is placed under increasing pressure.

The leisure scenario

A potentially more positive scenario of the future is the concept of the "leisure society". Its basic underlying notions are two-fold. The first is that, because of technological advances, work in the dimensions we have known is no longer necessary: Stonier (1983), for instance, has estimated that by early in the 21st century, a labour force no more than 10% of its present size will be required to provide us with all our material needs. The second is that since most work is no longer necessary, it is also no longer desirable: as Bertrand Russell (1935) put it, "only a foolish asceticism, usually vicarious, makes us continue to insist on work in excessive quantities now that the need no longer exists" (p. 19).

The notion of the ultimate preferability of a "leisure ethic" has deep roots in Western culture. The Book of Genesis can be seen as viewing work as punishment for sin, and idleness as the natural condition of the blameless soul. The yearning for the return to the Garden of Eden is a basic thrust in Christian tradition. The Greeks saw leisure in more elevated terms as a disciplined quest for higher values, but they too saw it as superior to work undertaken for gain – which, as Aristotle put it, "absorbs and impoverishes the mind" (1959 ed., p.222). Significantly, the Greek word for work – ascholia – defined it in negative terms as "lack of leisure": a salutary contrast with the precisely opposite way in which the word "unemployment" is now used in our own society. Of course, the Greeks had their slaves. But we have new technology. And Peter Walker, a Minister in the current British Government, has talked of new technology as enabling us to "create Athens without the slaves" (1978, p. 10).

What seems to be envisaged here is, in Gabor's words, a "technological paradise in which the work of a small minority is sufficient to keep the majority in idle luxury" (1964, p. 10). There would, of course, be a need for some to work. There would therefore be a division between a new working class and a new leisure class. The power would be in the hands of the working class: the leisure class would not have any significant control of capital, or the power to withdraw their labour. There would have to be incentives for the working class to create the wealth on which the livelihood of the leisure class would be depend. Yet it would be essential for the conditions of this latter livelihood to be sufficiently attractive to prevent the leisure class being tempted to challenge the power of the working class. It would also be important that joining the leisure class should be a matter of choice rather than an imposition due to, for example, one's age or sex. Finally, it would be important for income to be distributed to the leisure class not as allowances but as a guaranteed minimum income received as of right (for an excellent discussion of guaranteed-minimum-income schemes, see Roberts, 1982).

It is important to recognise the scale of the changes that would be needed for these conditions to be satisfied. At present, unemployment benefits and allowances are widely seen not as a right but as a grudging gift from a munificent state, and are passed over with clear signals of stigma and guilt. The notion that people can properly choose to be unemployed and live on social security is widely regarded as reprehensible and as threatening not only the economic but also the ethical base of society. Frith (1981), for example, has argued that some young people in response to unemployment have begun to construct their own leisure identities, but are being inhibited by "officials, the police, teachers, every adult concerned to stop the young carving out their own space". He continues:

> The state's fear is that the more successfully the young do survive nonwork, the less they'll ever be willing to do 'real' work. Hence the ideological and physical crackdown (which black people have long experienced) on any suggestions that the young unemployed are enjoying themselves ... If the young learned to enjoy 'unearned' leisure then the concept of earned leisure itself is thrown into question. Youth's most disruptive demand is not the right to work, but the right not to work (p. 5).

Frith's argument emphasises how leisure in our society has conventionally been seen not as an alternative to work but as essentially complementary to it. Most definitions of leisure define it in relation to work: Parker (1976), for instance, defines leisure as "time free from work and other obligations" (p. 12). So close is the link between the two that it is questionable whether unemployed people have "leisure" at all: they have plenty of spare time, but they do not have the resources to use it fruitfully, nor the sense of having earned their right to do so. Significantly, studies of those who become unemployed suggest that the extension of their free time results not in an increase but in a diminution both of the range of their leisure activities and of the enjoyment they derive from them (see e.g. Jahoda et al., 1972 ed; Economist Intelligence Unit, 1982).

The employment scenario

If it is the case that leisure is dependent upon work, then a case can be built for a third scenario in which steps are taken to sharing or redefining employment so as to make it available to all. This case becomes stronger if work is seen as having important intrinsic virtues of its own. Just as there is a tradition in Western culture espousing the superior virtues of leisure, so there is a contrary tradition espousing the superior virtues of work. In contrast with the notion of work as a product of the Fall, it can be seen as an opportunity to share in the divine activity of creation and recreation of the universe. Through work, one discovers and grows in one's understanding of God: as the hymn puts it,

> "Raise the stone, and thou shalt find me, cleave the wood and I am there."

The Protestant work ethic taught men the need to apply their talents with sobriety and thrift to their work so that they could avoid sin and prove – not least to themselves – that they were among the elect. Support for the importance of work also comes from very different religious and philosophical traditions. Schumacher (1973), for example, has pointed out that "the Buddhist point of view takes the function of work to be at least three-fold: to give a man a chance to utilise and develop his faculties; to enable him to overcome his egocentredness by joining with other people in a common task; and to bring forth the goods and services needed for a becoming existence" (p. 49).

In these respects, of course, "work" is not necessarily equated with "employment" – a point to which I will return shortly. Nonetheless, in modern industrial societies, the two concepts have become so closely equated that we readily slip from one word to the other as though they were synonyms. Moreover, employment has increasingly assumed a key social and political role as "the major point of connection between the individual's creative energies and the purposes and policies of the whole society" (Chanan, 1976/77, p.43). Indeed, one can fruitfully view employment as a key modern form of the "social contract" between the individual and the wider society, whereby individuals agree to devote some of their time, energies and skills to wider social purposes, in return for which they receive a social status and identity, plus income which they are free to use in their own time in whatever way they choose. If this is the case, then surely there is a "right to work". Such a right is indeed clearly affirmed in the Universal Declaration of Human Rights issued by the United Nations in 1948:

> Everyone has the right to work, to free choice of employment ... and to protection against unemployment. (article 23)

The problem, of course, is how to deliver this right. Two broad approaches can be conceived. The first is based on the notion that there is a finite amount of work, that it seems to be contracting, and that ways accordingly need to be found of sharing it out more evenly. Methods include encouraging more part-time jobs, job-splitting, reducing the length of the working week, introducing longer holidays and sabbaticals, and banning overtime. The difficulty is that such measures, if they are to be effective in work-sharing terms, also imply income-sharing, which means reduced living standards on the part of those whose work is cut. Trade unions resist this, in which case the measures do not create more jobs. Recent studies in Britain of reductions in the working week in particular industries have shown that they have had little or no effect in generating employment (White, 1980: Incomes Data Service, 1982).

The alternative approach to achieving full employment without massive economic growth takes a more radical stance. Instead of seeking to share out the existing employment more equally, it seeks to create new forms of employment. After all, there is no shortage of work: only a shortage of employment. If the existing economic, social and political mechanisms are not making employment available to all, these mechanisms could in principle be changed. People could be paid for forms of work which are not paid for at present.

One way of implementing this approach is to attempt to return to pure market forces. If the labour market were permitted to operate strictly according to market principles, then – in accordance with classical economic theory – the price of labour would fall to the point at which it would become purchasable. Arguably, however, the nature of advanced economies is so complex that even if this is regarded as an ideal, it is unattainable. Meanwhile, frustrated attempts to move in this direction may only exacerbate the unemployment problem.

An alternative approach is to accept the structural constraints on market forces, but to extend them in a way which creates more jobs. After all, many jobs are based not in the market economy but in the public sector – schools, hospitals, the armed forces, the police, government bureaucracies. Even within the market economy, there is a lot of over-manning. This can be regarded as wasteful. But it stimulates domestic demand. Moreover, in Japan, it has been estimated that up to 2.5 million workers in employment are surplus to requirement, but the security of employment offered to many workers through the "lifetime employment system" (Watts, 1984) has helped to make workers acquiescent to the technological changes in which the prosperity of the Japanese economy has been substantially based (Sleigh and Boatwright, 1979).

These arguments suggest that a strong economic as well as social case can be mounted for artificial job maintenance and job creation. This however poses other questions. What are the kinds of work which should be sustained in this way? Is any kind of work acceptable? Or should some criteria be laid down in terms of the social value of the services or products it produces, and/or the quality of the work and the satisfactions it offers to the worker? How can such forms of work be prevented from undermining market mechanisms? And does the right to work imply an obligation to work in return for state benefits, or does this imply an intolerable intrusion into individual liberties?

The work scenario

The final scenario is based upon a clearer and more sustained distinction between "work" and "employment", and upon greater valuing of the considerable amount of work that takes place outside employment. William Morris (1888), for example, distinguished "useful work" from "useless toil": to him, the craftsman and the artist were the epitome of "useful work", partly because of the worker's independence and identity with the product of his work. Marx, too, pointed out how being employed by another alienates the worker from his work, so that "in work he does not belong to himself but to another person" (1963 ed., p. 178). Marx was particularly concerned with such effects within capitalism, but arguably they are equally present within socialism. Gorz (1982) accordingly argued that "post-industrial socialism" should not seek to artificially sustain the "relations of subordination, competition and discipline" that characterise the employment system, but rather to appropriate areas of autonomy outside the system (pp. 72-73).

Even within the formal economy, many people already work not for others but for themselves – whether as self-employed, as owners of small businesses employing others, or as members of co-operatives. There is currently greater interest in Britain in these areas. Often it is linked to the notion of the "electronic cottage" (Toffler, 1980): the idea that new telecommunications systems are going to make it much easier for more work to be done from home, possible on a fee rather than on a wage/salary basis. Certainly there is evidence that the self-employed have higher levels of job satisfaction than those who work for other people (Consumers Association, 1977). The proportion of self-employed people in the labour force in Britain is still well under 10%, but is rising (Department of Employment, 1983).

Beyond this, there is also a massive amount of work outside the formal economy, within three informal economies. First, there is the black economy, which consists of work conducted wholly or partly for money concealed from the tax authorities. This ranges from undeclared criminal and immoral earnings (prostitution, drug trafficking), through office pilfering and perks, to undeclared income earned by the self-employed, by moonlighters and by the unemployed. Estimates of its extent in Britain range between 3% and 15% of the Gross National Product, and suggest that it may be increasing (Macafee, 1980; Feige, 1981); in Italy, estimates of its extent vary between 10% and 40%, and it is clearly to some extent tolerated by the state (Hansen, 1979; de Grazia, 1980). Attitudes to its social morality depend largely on whether its victims are seen to be the clients of the welfare state or its bureaucrats. Again, however, there is evidence that black-economy work, even where it is not greatly lucrative, can offer considerable job satisfaction: not only control over one's work, but also the pleasure of "beating the system" (Henry, 1978; Outer Policy Research Circle, 1979).

Second, there is the communal economy, covering the production of goods or services consumed by people other than the producers, but not sold on a monetary basis. This ranges from baby-sitting circles or car pools which operate on the basis of a formal exchange of tokens or credits, through exchanges of skills or equipment between friends and neighbours, to voluntary and gift activities for which no reciprocity is expected. Many communities, including those hard-hit by unemployment, contain rich networks of reciprocal support which mean that less recourse has to be made to the formal economy.

Third, there is the household economy, consisting of all the work within the home involving production for internal consumption of goods or services for which approximate substitutes might otherwise be purchased for money. This includes cooking, decorating, laundry, childcare, home repairs, garden produce, etc. In the USA, it has been estimated that if all the work done within the household was converted into monetary form, the total would be equal to the entire amount paid out in wages and salaries by every corporation in the country (Burns, 1975).

It seems possible that although the amount of work within the formal economy is contracting, the amount of work within the informal economies is increasing. The irony at present, as illustrated in recent research in Britain by Pahl (1984), is that the employed are much more likely than the unemployed to engage in many of these forms of work. This is largely because of Britain's present social-security arrangements, which means that the unemployed are constrained and discouraged from engaging in other forms of work, and in any case have little money for the tools and other resources they need to do so. This again reiterates how tightly our existing social arrangements are bound to the institution of employment, from which so many people are excluded.

Ways could be sought of bringing more informal-economies work into the formal economy – through "wages for housework", for example. This however raises wider issues. In particular, it raises the question of how far we want work to be built around a cash-nexus or around other kinds of relationships. In modern times, the market – which in earlier societies was subordinated to social and religio-cultural goals – has come to set the goals of industrial societies. Economic growth has become the prime aim of governments; increasingly, forms of service have been based around the cash-nexus. Yet we all recognise the devaluation that occurs when human activities are turned over to the market-place: when, as it were, making love becomes prostitution.

The establishment of the welfare state, in which services like education and health care are made freely available to the public, is one response to this. It does however raise its own difficulties. Those offering such services – nurses, social workers, teachers – have shown increasing concern with financial rewards, and a growing willingness to subordinate their clients' interest to strikes. In a society which judges worth in monetary terms, this is hardly surprising or reprehensible. But it limits the extent of the service which is offered, and can erode the sense of altruism and commitment which is so crucial to the quality of such work both for the worker and for the client.

In the end, every society is held together by activities for which payment is neither given nor expected – by activities motivated not by acquisitiveness but by love, caring, creativity, curiosity, energy. Yet the capacity to devote all one's time to working without monetary rewards implies access to money without effort, which in turn – unless it takes the form of inherited wealth – implies a form of dependency. Traditionally, it is women who have been chief sources of "gift" work in households and communities. Dependent on the incomes of their husbands, they have performed many of the unpaid caring and expressive roles – looking after young children and elderly parents, carrying out voluntary services for friends and neighbours, simply giving people time and attention – which are so crucial to the social cohesion of communities and to the quality of life within them. From the viewpoint of social status, and of access to power and wealth, these roles are demeaning and entrapping; from the viewpoint of social value and moral quality, they are arguably superior to much if not all paid employment.

Hitherto, the rigid division of sex-roles has tended to confine such roles to women, and to give women little choice in accepting them. My sexist use of the male pronoun in discussing the philosophical roots of the employment and work scenarios demonstrates how clearly men's work has been distinguished from women's work. Women understandably are now challenging this. But the result may be to place gift work under greater threat. Feminism until recently has more readily taken the form of claims to male prerogatives and privileges, than of affirmations of the superiority of traditionally female roles and values. Men, meanwhile, have shown little inclination to give up their power, status and wealth in the quest for social and moral virtue. So what happens to the re-evaluation of sex-roles, and to the relationship between gift work, the welfare state and the market economy, are in my view likely to be crucial to the future of work

Final comments

I have attempted to sketch out, briefly and crudely, four possible scenarios of the future. In reality, of course, the future is likely to contain elements of all four scenarios, as indeed the present already does. The scenarios, however, pose choices for society in terms of dominant social attitudes regarding the relationship between work, employment and leisure. Their merit, I believe, is that they address our attention to the separable issues of which scenarios we regard as the most probable for the future, and which as the most preferable, The key questions underlying these issues are five-fold:

1. How far do we value work as against leisure?

2. How far do we value paid work as against unpaid work?

3. What are the forms of work we are prepared to pay for?

4. How are these forms of work to be distributed?

5. How is this distribution to be related to the generation and distribution of wealth?

These are profound and complex questions. Arguably, the answers to which we have become accustomed since the Industrial Revolution are not going to work any more. They lead into the social and economic whirlpool of the unemployment scenario. If, however, we could summon the courage and energy to find new answers and so to move in a substantial way towards one or more of the other scenarios, this might produce a society that would offer the chance of a more fruitful and fulfilling life to more of its members than has been possible during the industrial phase of our history.

Guidance services have an important role to play in the quest for such alternatives. Certainly we need to re-examine our current practices in relation to them. In particular, we need to recognise the extent to which careers guidance has traditionally been tied to the bureaucratised concepts of employment structures that have characterised our industrial society (Watts, 1981). The traditional "matching" approach has required that broad categories of jobs be described in ways which have made it possible to match individual attributes to them. It accordingly has been drawn towards the bureaucratised sector of the labour market, where jobs are formalised in groups, with formal entry channels defined in terms of educational qualifications. In doing so, it has performed an important task both in oiling the operations of the employment bureaucracies, and in relating to them operations of our correspondingly bureaucratic educational structures.

Many of these assumptions have tended to survive the move towards more developmental guidance theories and methods, which in principle could provide a much wider and more flexible approach. Although we talk in terms of broad concepts of developing life-styles, and although Donald Super's (1981) concept of the "career rainbow" provides a useful framework for this, the concepts which underlie our resources and practices still tend in the end to be narrowly employment-focused. Moreover, the effect of growing unemployment has in many cases been to lock guidance services even more rigidly into job-seeking and job-placing activities. I would argue that to confront the realities that now face our clients, we need to break down our concepts both of "means" and of "ends", so that we focus on how (a) employment and/or (b) other paid work and/or (c) unpaid work and/or (d) leisure can contribute towards (i) their personal identity and fulfilment, (ii) their contribution to society, and (iii) their economic survival (see figure 31).

Figure 31: A post-industrial model for careers guidance

	"Means"			
	(a) Employment	(b) Other Paid Work	(c) Unpaid Work	(d) Leisure
"Ends"				
(i) Personal identity and Fulfilment				
(ii) Contribution to Society				
(iii) Economic Survival				

Finally, I would like to suggest three procedural maxims for subsequent discussions of "The Future of Work and Leisure". The first is that we should distinguish carefully and consistently between the term "leisure" and the term "unemployment", recognising that for the unemployed to experience leisure would, in many of our countries, require major changes in our social attitudes and mores. The second is that we should distinguish carefully and consistently between the term "employment" and the term "work", recognising that much work takes place outside employment. The third is that while recognising that guidance practitioners are concerned essentially with helping individuals, and tend to be caring optimists, we should not underestimate the deeply philosophical and deeply political nature of the questions we are addressing here.

21. Career Development: Looking Back; Moving Forward[52]

Introduction

It was a great honour to give the first Annual Lecture in this series, back in 1999 (see chapter 2). It is an even bigger honour to be invited to give this second one, as my final lecture on career development. I decided around 18 months ago to retire around now from all professional activities. I have spent the intervening time trying to complete the various programmes of work in which I have been involved, to do some summative writing, and to hand over as much as possible to others. I now hope to give more time to my other interests. I am running a class next term for the University of the Third Age on Handel operas and oratorios, and am available to anyone who wants a lecture on those wonderful works. But on career development, this is the last.

What I plan to do is to look back over my 50 years in this field, and to try to pull out some of the key lessons I would draw from the work I have done. I will include some sharp comments on the damaging developments of the last few years. I intend to follow Dylan Thomas's advice, not to go gentle into that good night. But I will end on a very positive note, because I believe there are good grounds for optimism.

Beginnings – and why it matters

I came into this field in January 1964 when Adrian Bridgewater and I set up the Careers Research and Advisory Centre – CRAC (an innocent acronym in those days). I was 21, and had started work at Cornmarket Press, which published books in the careers field. Adrian and I talked. We felt – partly on the basis of our own inadequate experiences – that this was a field in which much needed to be done, and that it would be much more possible to do it within a non-profit organisation than within a publishing company. Adrian had some business experience; I had some ideas on what we might do. So we started what would now be known as a social enterprise, registered as an educational charity.

Our aims were two-fold: to improve the quality of careers work, in schools and beyond; and to develop closer links between the worlds of education and of work. These have continued to be the core mission of my own career, as for many

---

[52] **Editorial footnote:** Originally given as the 17th iCeGS Annual Lecture. Published with permission of the author and the University of Derby, from an International Centre for Guidance Studies paper. Derby: International Centre for Guidance Studies, University of Derby, 2014.

other people attending this lecture: to improve other people's careers. I believe passionately in the importance of this work.

There are, periodically, siren voices which urge dropping the word 'career' and finding a better one to describe our field. This is a futile quest. There is no other word that brings together learning and work, grounds them in the individual, and is about progression. Certainly we need to move away from the old definition: progression up an ordered hierarchy within a profession or organisation. This was a middle-class, elitist concept: some people had careers; most had jobs, or no jobs. But, like many English words, it has always been richly ambiguous: we also refer to 'careering about', with very different connotations. The growing definition now, which we must assiduously foster and promote, is lifelong progression in learning and work. 'Learning' because it is about education, but also about training, and informal learning. 'Work' because it is about paid employment, but also about self-employment, and unpaid work within households and communities. But it is also, of its essence, about progression and development – lateral as well as vertical. In principle, this concept of career is inclusive, accessible to everyone. The core task of the careers profession is to help to make it so.

This matters, deeply. Our careers significantly define how we spend a lot of our lives, the people we become, and the contributions we make to the societies of which we are part. Our paid work represents a kind of social contract, through which we agree to devote a substantial part of our time to wider social purposes, in return for which we receive income, which we can then spend in whatever ways we choose. If we engage in forms of learning and work which utilise our distinctive abilities, interests and values, we are likely to lead more fulfilling lives. We are also likely to be more motivated and therefore more effective, with benefits for the wider society and economy.

The philosophical roots of this perspective are deep and inspiring. As Ronald Sultana has recently reminded us in a brilliant essay (Sultana, 2014), for Socrates every person has an 'arete' or excellence, and it is by being the best that one can be, through putting one's talent at the service of the community, that one attains virtue. This was echoed by Karl Marx, who stated that 'the chief guide which must direct us in the choice of a profession is the welfare of mankind and our own perfection'.

Of course, none of this can ever be perfect. Many people still experience enormous constraints on their lives, related to inequalities of many kinds. But almost all can do more than they think they can do, and one of the tasks of career development support is to help them to realise this and to do so. Career development work can thereby support social mobility, social equity and social justice.

It is such important work. Where it is done well, it can transform people's lives.

Yet it is too often derided, usually by people who have made no effort to discover what it is or what it comprises. The roots of this derision are complex: they may have had poor career guidance themselves; or they may want to take the full credit for their own successful careers – which good career guidance would, of course, have encouraged them to do. But the arguments for serious attention to career development are, in my view, incontrovertible. And while useful career conversations can be had with many people, the contributions of careers professionals are distinctive. Their role is not only to deliver services, but also to build the capacity of others. Without them, I am convinced, no serious improvement in career development support is possible.

Progress

Over the past 50 years, we have made much progress. When I entered this field, careers services were very limited. Some schools had careers teachers, with a few periods a week, mainly to manage a small careers library; some schools did not even do that. The Youth Employment Service visited schools, largely to match early leavers to jobs using a simple diagnostic device called the Seven Point Plan. Universities had appointments boards, focusing mainly on job placement. And that was largely it.

But in the 1960s and 1970s, this began to be transformed. The twin concepts of careers education and counselling began to evolve, based on a much more complex understanding of what was needed. The previous model had been a quasi-medical model: diagnosis and prescription, possibly using psychometric tests or other devices, with the careers adviser doing the work. Now the model shifted to learning, with the active individual at the centre. Moreover, the focus began to shift from choosing a career at a particular point in time (usually around the transition from full-time education to the world of work) to constructing a career, through the series of decisions we make throughout our lives.

This was a massive shift. Careers education programmes began to grow, in schools and colleges but also in higher education. The Youth Employment Service became the Careers Service. Services for adults began to develop: initially with the Occupational Guidance Units; later through a rich community-based tradition of educational guidance services for adults; alongside career development services within some large companies and other employers. A serious research tradition was initiated to support all this work, with attention to theory as well as empirical studies. We identified examples of good practice and sought to learn from them, as a basis for spreading good ideas and encouraging innovation and development.

We had to confront major challenges, not least the massive growth of unemployment in the late 1970s and 1980s, which challenged many of our assumptions and practices. But we did this well, and it brought the field into a position of greater prominence and respect.

We also had to address the challenges posed by the neoliberal policies pursued by the Thatcher and Major Governments, which included the marketisation of careers services in the form of contracting-out and experiments with guidance vouchers. I was critical of these developments, partly on the theoretical grounds that the key role of career guidance within such an ideological perspective was as a market-maker – a way of making the learning and labour markets work – and that it made little sense to marketise the market-maker (Watts, 1995). But the contracting-out of the Careers Service was well-managed by some very competent civil servants – I know, because I was invited by a senior civil servant of the time, Valerie Bayliss, to observe the contracting process from the inside – and it was largely successful, resulting in some fruitful energising and innovation.

Ministers have recently stated that there has been no Golden Age in the provision of careers work in this country. But I agree with Paul Chubb, who has argued in a recent blog (Chubb, 2014) that we came pretty close to it in the mid-1990s. We had an Education Act which mandated careers education in schools and the partnership between schools and the Careers Service. We had the CBI advancing the concept of 'careers for all' as the means of achieving a 'skills revolution' (CBI, 1989a). We had the decision to establish a learning helpline for adults, which subsequently became Learndirect – a world leader (Watts & Dent, 2002). We had the Guidance Council, jointly sponsored by the CBI and the RSA, which brought together the key stakeholders and was supported by the Government to develop quality standards for the field (Alloway, 2008).

We also had a Labour Party paper, on which I worked with Steve Byers and Ruth Gee, which argued the case for the Careers Service to become an all-age service. So when the Labour Party came to power with a massive majority in 1998, all seemed set fair.

And then it started to fall apart, in England at least. John Major had called the General Election early, and the Byers-Gee paper had not been published. Early in the life of the new Government, David Blunkett, the Secretary of State for Education, promised to publish and act upon it. But he never did. Instead, careers services for young people were overtaken by the issue of social exclusion (Watts, 2001b). The Government wanted to bring together all the services concerned with young people at risk; but the only budget it controlled was that of the Careers Service; so it used this to create a new Connexions Service. This had two aims: to provide a careers service for all young people, and a holistic service for young people at risk. But all the performance measures were addressed to the latter group. Moreover, the responsibility for running the service was given to Anne Weinstock, from a Youth Service background, who shamefully banned the use of the word 'careers'. Careers Advisers were to be rebadged as Personal Advisers; their labour market knowledge was neglected. This resulted in serious professional erosion. Moreover, whereas almost all young people had been seen at least once by a professional adviser, the proportion now fell massively.

Towards the end of its time in power, the Labour Government realised the error of its ways. A report of a group chaired by Alan Milburn (Panel on Fair Access to the Professions, 2009) pointed out that in its concern for social exclusion, the Government had neglected social mobility. There were plenty of young people who were not at risk of dropping out, but were under-performing and under-aspiring. Among its acts of repentance, the Government established a Task Force to strengthen the careers profession. Brilliantly chaired by Ruth Silver, its excellent report (Careers Profession Task Force, 2010) was accepted not only by the Labour Government but also by the Coalition Government when it came to power in 2010.

The Conservative Party had included in its Election Manifesto a commitment to establish an all-age careers service. John Hayes, the new Skills Minister, gave an inspiring speech in Belfast in which he promised to establish the all-age service, building upon the best of Connexions and Next Step (the service for adults), to safeguard the partnership between schools and the careers service, and to revitalise the professional status of career guidance. This was the second false dawn (Watts, 2013). Because each of these promises has been, in turn, betrayed.

The initial core of the problem was, as with the Labour Government, conflict with a major policy drive: in this case, school autonomy. The duty to provide careers guidance was moved to schools, to buy in services from outside: so the partnership model was replaced by a contractor-supplier relationship. But not with the new National Careers Service, which would provide a helpline for young people but not face-to-face services – a half-baked all-age service at best. We assumed that the Connexions careers funding (around £197 million) would be transferred to schools, perhaps with some pruning in the light of austerity; but it was not. No announcement was made, but gradually we discovered that it had simply been removed. Schools were to buy in or provide services from their existing budgets. Also removed were the funding for Education-Business Partnerships and AimHigher, and the statutory duties to provide careers education and work-related learning.

We then awaited the Statutory Guidance, which schools needed to inform their budgets. Drafts were circulated for consultation, in confidence: they gradually got stronger. But, unbelievably, the version published was weaker than the first published draft: so vacuous as not to merit publication. In effect, it was clear, schools could now do what they liked: if they did little or nothing, there was no basis on which a legal challenge could be mounted. The Liberal Democrats and others made a fuss, and a supplementary Practical Guide was promised. But after endless delays, a purely advisory document was published, in the last week of the summer term just prior to the long summer break. All this demonstrated a noxious mix of incompetence and malign indifference – very different from the Conservative Government of the 1990s.

The cross-party Select Committee on Education, chaired by a Conservative MP (Graham Stuart), was deeply concerned about what was happening. It launched an inquiry, and produced an excellent, well-evidenced and well-argued report (House of Commons Education Committee, 2013). It noted the merits of the partnership model, but recognised the political difficulties of reinstating it. It made, however, a series of strong recommendations, to strengthen the Statutory Guidance and to give the National Careers Service a capacity-building role in relation to schools. Almost all its recommendations were rejected or ignored by the Government.

Shamefully, they were also ignored by the National Careers Council, a body set up by John Hayes before he left his post to advise the Government on careers matters. I was a member of this body, and I and another member, Heather Jackson, resigned prior to its first report. We did so because of the way in which the processes of the Council were manipulated in the final stages to produce a report for Ministers that failed to address the key issues identified by the Select Committee, and that colluded with what we viewed as unacceptable Government policies.[53] I regret that we had to do what we did, but I have never doubted that it was the right thing to do.

As was reinforced by what happened next. The published NCC report (NCC, 2013) was loosely written and bland. It included an appeal for a 'culture change', without defining with any precision what this should involve. The new Minister, Matthew Hancock, issued what he called an Inspiration Vision Statement (HM Government, 2013), which contained no reference whatsoever to the roles of careers professionals or careers programmes. Instead, it seemed, all that was needed was for young people to have contact with employers and people in jobs. In effect, careers professionals were now written out of the policy script: a direct betrayal of the last of the Government's earlier promises. Hancock claimed that this represented a 'big culture change', directly invoking the Council's terminology. One might have expected the Council at least to point out that the Minister's interpretation was not its own. But at no stage has it done so: indeed, its Chair welcomed the Government's statement, without reservation. The Council very belatedly, in its second and final report published this September, affirmed the role of careers professionals, but did not juxtapose this with the Government's position,

---

[53] For the record, the correspondence from Heather Jackson and myself leading up to our resignation has been deposited on the iCeGS website: http://www.derby.ac.uk/research/icegs/news/2014/icegs-policy-and-research-e-briefing-october-2014.html

which it has never publicly challenged in any way. Instead, its main interest seems to have been self-promotion. It is accordingly culpable of having colluded not only with the massive erosion of careers provision for young people but also with the mindless marginalisation of the careers profession.

Its position has contrasted remarkably with the position of the Select Committee, and its Conservative MP Chair, who have continued to challenge the Government on this issue with clarity, integrity and tenacity. This included an interview last December with Michael Gove, the Secretary of State for Education. We knew that the political narrative underlying the Government's careers policies was that John Hayes's good intentions required support not only from the Department for Business, Innovation and Skills (which has largely fulfilled his promises in relation to provision for adults) but also from the Department for Education, where he had been blocked by Michael Gove. But Gove had resisted meetings with the careers sector, and had never spoken publicly on the topic. Now he did. It was an extraordinary interchange.

He commented that more should be done to engage employers with schools, but also stated, explicitly and unequivocally: 'What I emphatically do not believe is that we need a cadre of careers advisers to operate in between these two'. He set up an idealised view of the role of careers advisers, with perfect knowledge of the labour market and of the psychology and motivations of individuals, and then inferred that because they could not be such 'supermen and superwomen', they should not be made available at all. This was a remarkable non sequitur: on this basis, we would not engage in any human endeavours at all. Then, to add insult to injury, he challenged the 'intellectual rigour' and the 'self-interest' of those who had 'populated the debate' on this topic; when asked to name who he meant, he refused. Intellectual rigour is based on evidence and reasoned argument: both were conspicuously absent from his own statements. In using this term, he sought to rubbish all the work we have carefully built up over the years – of which he had patently read barely a word. All this from a Secretary of State for Education. It was a disgraceful performance, arrogant and ignorant, which demeaned his office. More important, it indicated the poverty of the intellectual foundations on which the Government's careers policies for young people had been based.

The policies pursued by this Government have been among the most damaging I have seen in any country; they have also been pursued with an extraordinary mixture not only of betrayal, mendacity and incompetence but also of casuistry. In the Parliamentary debates on the statutory duty in the Education Act, it was assumed by all that the duty was referring to access to independent and impartial individual guidance from a careers professional. But in the latest revised Statutory Guidance, it now seems that this is not the case. There must be elements external to the school, but the requirement to be impartial can be met, apparently, though access to a range of partial sources – in other words, employers and learning providers. This is pure casuistry. What on earth is the point of a statutory duty based on such definitions?

Employers do have important contributions to make. But they are essentially complementary to, and indeed dependent for their effectiveness upon, the roles of careers professionals and careers programmes. The Careers Sector Stakeholders Alliance (2014) produced a careful and measured document arguing this, which has been endorsed by many employers and employer organisations – though, disappointingly, not by the CBI or the National Careers Council. No response has been evident from the Government.

We now have a new Secretary of State, Nicky Morgan. We await whether there will be some change of direction and act of repentance, comparable to that under the Labour Government. If there is, I hope that it will be substantive and well-informed, not cosmetic.

So what can we conclude from all this? The story of the two false dawns can be interpreted in two main ways. Both were examples of the career development agenda being overtaken by larger government agendas – social exclusion and school autonomy respectively. But in both cases the damage caused was greatly exacerbated by two powerful individuals – Anne Weinstock and Michael Gove – who displayed extraordinary ignorance and unwillingness to listen and learn. As so often in history, what happened was a mix of structural forces and of people.

On the more recent events, the Government's casuistry has been aided by the semantic confusion within the field. In particular, we use the term 'career guidance' both generically, to cover all interventions, and specifically, to cover one-to-one interviews with a careers professional. I admit some culpability here, because it was the adoption of the generic usage in the OECD (2004) report, for which I was jointly responsible with Richard Sweet, that enabled the Government in its Statutory Guidance to apply this usage and thereby exclude the contributions of careers professionals. We urgently need to address this. My proposal is that we embargo the usage of 'career guidance', and adopt 'career development' as the generic term, and 'career counselling' for the one-to-one professional interventions. This is an issue that the CDI[54] needs to address.

The other key conclusion I draw from the saga is that the field must stand up for itself more strongly. There has been far too much collusion, and not enough concerted affirmation. We must hold to our values, and never be afraid to speak truth to power.

---

54 Editorial footnote: The Career Development Institute (CDI) is the major professional body for career development workers in the UK.

Reflections

Enough of this. In my more pessimistic moments, it feels that all that we built up over so many years has been wantonly destroyed. Certainly, the poverty of the thinking underpinning the constant references to 'inspirational talks' from employers as some kind of panacea takes me back to when we started in the 1960s, ignoring so much of what we have learned since.

But, of course, it has not been destroyed. Much of what we have built up is still there, to provide a basis on which to build further. So, looking back on 50 years in this field, what have we achieved? Speaking personally, I would identify five significant changes in which I have been involved, along with many other people.

The first I have already mentioned: the move to a focus on learning as the core concept in career development. This includes addressing individuals' conceptual development, in their understanding both of themselves and of the opportunities available to them, and helping them to develop their competences for constructing their career – which include where and when to look for help. It should incorporate active experiences, programmatic learning, and supported reflection on such learning to convert it into actions that are well-informed and well-thought-through.

Second, we have developed a research culture and a research tradition, based on a multi-disciplinary approach. Psychology will always be a core discipline, because at its heart career development is about individuals; but because it is always about individuals in social contexts, it needs in addition to draw from labour market economics and sociology – including socio-political perspectives. It can also draw fruitfully from other disciplines like philosophy, history and literature. In my view, the tradition we have built up in the UK is broader in these respects than in the USA and most other countries: we should value this.

Third, we have developed a strong tradition of innovation, linked significantly though not exclusively to technology. Having reviewed the first efforts in the USA to apply computers to career development in the 1970s, and been involved in some of the first major projects to do so in the UK, it has been amazing to see the transformations that have taken place as technology has advanced. Managing technology as an agent of change, and its interactive relationship to human interventions, will remain a core challenge.

Fourth, we have established a tradition of policy discourses and policy studies, linked to a vision of lifelong career development. The core argument is that career development is a public good as well as a private good: a key lubricant of learning systems, of labour markets and of social equity. It accordingly requires public policies to deliver it and make it available to all, lifelong. The attention given in recent years to lifelong career development policies, strategies and systems by organisations like OECD, the European Commission, UNESCO, ILO and the World Bank is remarkable, and a major advance.

This is closely linked to a fifth significant change, which is the internationalisation of this field, with many more opportunities for countries to learn from each other. An important role here is played by international studies, based on strong analytical frameworks which enable the similarities and differences between countries to be identified (see Watts, 2014b). It is through such studies that countries can recognise the contingent nature of practices they take for granted, and explore possibilities for innovation and change.

I have written quite a lot on all these matters. My main reason for writing is simple: I do not know what I think until I have written it. In conversation one can get away with loose, exploratory thinking, but in writing it down one has to weigh up the arguments and the evidence, and decide what it all means and where one stands. It is hard work, but important; and if published, it adds to the body of knowledge on which others can draw. I commend it to you as a professional practice.

A lot of my writing has been in collaboration with others. The test of collaboration is whether, when the work is completed, you think that you could have written something better, more easily, on your own. There have been one or two occasions when this thought has crossed my mind! But in most cases, I have been immensely fortunate in my collaborators: Bill Law and other NICEC colleagues, Jim Sampson, Ronald Sultana, Ian Jamieson, Andy Miller, Richard Sweet, Tristram Hooley and others. I have learned so much from them, and am clear that what we produced together was much better than what I could have produced alone.

The other activity which has taken up a lot of my time, again with many other people, is building infrastructures within the career development field which can harness energies and support communities of practice. CRAC, NICEC, the Guidance Council, iCeGS, the International Centre for Career Development and Public Policy, the European Lifelong Guidance Policy Network, the Careers Sector Stakeholders Alliance: all have played important roles. Histories have now been written of several of these organisations (Alloway, 2008; Smith, 2010; Hyde, 2014; Watts, 2014a; Watts, Bezanson & McCarthy, 2014). I have always been interested in the relationship between formal organisational structures and networks: most of these initiatives have been hybrids in this respect, enabling creative balances between sustainability and flexibility. All have been dependent upon small groups of people, often initially two or three, coming together to make something happen. I have been enormously fortunate to work together with so many dedicated and creative people in these and many other projects.

As I leave this field after 50 years, I feel very optimistic about the future. We have very strong foundations on which to continue to build. Internationally, we have IAEVG, along with ICCDPP and the tradition of international policy symposia. In Europe – I am a passionate European – we have three networks: ELGPN for policy, Euroguidance for practice, and NICE for training and research. All these will need to continue to evolve and change, but the base is there.

In the UK, we now have the basis of a world-class quality-assurance system with a service standard (Matrix), organisational standards (nationally validated through the Quality in Careers Standard), and professional standards developed by the new Career Development Institute representing the profession as a whole. The previous professional splintering of the field was a significant source of weakness. I do urge all of you to join the CDI and make it a success. In particular, I hope that those who are members of AGCAS, the one organisation which has stayed outside the fold, will resolve its relationship with CDI. I have heard all its arguments, and have been unimpressed by them. Either AGCAS is a professional association, in which case it should join CDI; or it is not, in which case it should actively encourage its members to do so. If there was ever a time for the profession to come together and to affirm its professionalism, this is it. For a relatively privileged group like those in universities to stand outside this process is, in my view, indefensible.

A related development which has particularly delighted me is the evolution of NICEC from a research and development organisation into a learned society – unique in the world, so far as I am aware – and the partnership it has forged with the CDI through which the excellent NICEC journal is distributed to all CDI members. This is an important development, providing a bridge between research and practice which affirms and strengthens the enhanced professionalism of the field.

I am also thrilled by the way in which iCeGS has developed over the last few years. Deirdre Hughes did a fine job in building up the centre, but when she left there was a hiatus, and the university could easily have dismantled it. To its great credit it did not do so, and under Tristram Hooley the centre has moved to a new level both intellectually and in the range of its work. I have worked recently with an international consultancy company which has reviewed career development service providers globally, and it described iCeGS as, in the wondrous jargon of such companies, a 'best-in-class' research centre, in world terms. The university's motivation for setting up the centre was that, as a teaching-led university, it should concentrate its research activities in niches linked to its values – which included extending access to opportunities. It should be very proud of its support for the centre, and what the centre has achieved.

I have been very privileged to work in a field populated by so many good people, dedicated to helping others through their work. Despite my astringent comments in parts of this lecture, I have immensely enjoyed my career in careers, have derived rich satisfactions from it, and have made many great friends through it. As that wonderful actor John Le Mesurier said in his last words: 'It's all been rather lovely.'

Abbreviated Bibliography

The following list sets out an abbreviated bibliography of the writing of Tony Watts. It sets out all of his books, book chapters and peer reviewed articles. It also provides a summary of his other publications including reports, other articles, briefings, policy commentaries, careers books and curriciulum materials, interviews and unattributed publications.[55]

Books

Diversity and Choice in Higher Education. London: Routledge & Kegan Paul, 1972.

Schools, Careers and Community (co-authored with Law, B.). London: Church Information Office, 1977.

Counselling at Work (edited book). Standing Conference for the Advancement of Counselling. London: Bedford Square Press, 1977.

Career Development in Britain (edited with Super, D.E. & Kidd, J. M.). Cambridge: CRAC/Hobsons, 1981.

Education, Unemployment and the Future of Work. Milton Keynes: Open University Press, 1983.

Work Experience and Schools (edited book). London: Heinemann, 1983.

Educational and Vocational Guidance Services for the 14-25 Age-Group in the European Community (co-authored with Dartois, C. & Plant, P.). Maastricht, Belgium: Les Presses Interuniversitaires Européennes, 1988. (Also translated into French).

Mirrors of Work: Work Simulations in Schools (co-authored with Jamieson, I. & Miller, A.). Lewes, Sussex: Falmer, 1988.

Rethinking Work Experience (co-authored with Miller, A. & Jamieson, I.). London: Falmer, 1991.

The Economic Value of Careers Guidance (co-authored with Killeen, J. & White, M.). London: Policy Studies Institute, 1992.

Guidance and Counselling in Britain: a 20-Year Perspective (edited with Dryden, W.). Cambridge: CRAC/Hobsons, 1993.

Rethinking Careers Education and Guidance: Theory, Policy and Practice (co-authored with Law, B., Killeen, J., Kidd, J.M. & Hawthorn, R.). London: Routledge, 1996. (Parts also translated into Danish).

News Skills for New Futures: Higher Education Guidance and Counselling Services in the European Union (co-authored with Van Esbroeck, R.). Brussels: VUB University Press, 1998. (Also translated into French).

Adult Guidance Services and the Learning Society: Emerging Policies in the European Union (co-authored with Bartlett, W. & Rees, T.). Bristol: Policy Press, 2000.

Handbook of Career Development: International Perspectives (edited with Arulmani, G., Bakshi, A.J. & Leong, F.T.L.). New York: Springer, 2014.

---

[55] A complete list of Tony Watts' publications (running to 39 pages) is available from http://www.derby.ac.uk/media/derbyacuk/contentassets/documents/ehs/icegs/PUBLICATIONS-1964-2014.pdf.

Book chapters

"A Structure for Careers Education". In R. Jackson (ed.): *Careers Guidance: Practice and Problems*. London: Arnold, 1973.

"Some Thoughts on the Relationship between Higher Education and Employment". In Williams, G. (ed.): *Graduate Employment Problems*. London: Society for Research into Higher Education, 1973.

"La Fonction d'Orientation des Contenus de l'Education" (co-authored with Super, D.E., Busshoff, L. & Pellerano, J.). In D'Hainaut, L. (ed.): *Programmes d'Etudes et Education Permanente*. Paris: UNESCO, 1979.

"Malaysia". In Drapela, V.J. (ed.): *Guidance and Counseling Around the World*. Washington, DC: University Press of America, 1979.

"Pastoral Care and Careers Education" (co-authored with Fawcett, B.). In Best, R.E., Jarvis, C.B. & Ribbins, P.M. (eds.): *Perspectives in Pastoral Care*. London: Heinemann, 1980.

"Karriärubbilning och Läroplan". In Franke-Wikberg, S. & Lundgren, U.P. (eds.): *Karriär och Levnadsbana*. Stockholm: Wahlström & Walström, 1980.

"Counselling in Work Settings – Areas and Issues". In Bolger, A.W. (ed.): *Counselling in Britain: a Reader*. London: Batsford, 1982.

"Research Needs in Pastoral Care: the Vocational Aspect" (co-authored with Law, B.). In Lang, P. & Marland, M. (eds.): *New Directions in Pastoral Care*. London: Blackwell, 1985.

"Education and Employment: the Traditional Bonds". In Dale, R. (ed.): *Education, Training and Employment: Towards a New Vocationalism?* Oxford: Pergamon, 1985.

"Arbejdsloshed og Fremtidens Arbejde". In Plant, P. (ed.): *Fremtider: Om Arbejde og Uddannelse*. Fredensborg, Denmark: Forlaget Studie og Erhverv a/s, 1987.

"Education, Unemployment and the Future of Work – Implications for Guidance and Counselling". In de Weerdt, P., Stern, E. & Deen, N. (eds.): *The Social Relevance of Counselling*. Utrecht: Rijksuniversiteit Utrecht, 1988.

"Connecting Curriculum to Work: Past Patterns, Current Initiatives and Future Issues". In Wellington, J.J. (ed.): *The Work Related Curriculum*. London: Kogan Page, 1993.

"The Changing Guidance Role of University Careers Services". In Dunsmore, R. (ed.): *Graduate Recruitment: a 25-Year Retrospective*. Cambridge: CRAC/Hobsons, 1993.

"Handlingsplaegning: Grundlaget for Livslang Karriereudvikling?" In Plant, P. (ed). *Handling og Forvandling*. Fredensborg: Studie og Erhverv, 1995.

"Careers Guidance Systems in the European Community". In Bush, L. & Green, A. (eds.): *World Yearbook of Education 1995: Youth, Education and Work*. London: Kogan Page, 1995.

"Guidance and the Transition from School to Work: a European Union Perspective". In *Från Skola till Arbete*. TemaNord 595. Copenhagen: Nordisk Ministerråd, 1995.

"The Policy Context". In Barnes, A. & Andrews, D. (eds.): *Developing Careers Education and Guidance in the Curriculum*. London: Fulton, 1995.

"Careers Education and Guidance in Schools: Policy and Practice". In Frost, D., Edwards, A. & Reynolds, H. (eds.): *Careers Education and Guidance*. London: Kogan Page, 1995.

"Towards a Strategy for Lifelong Guidance to Support Lifelong Learning and Work" (co-authored with McNair, S.). In Bradshaw, D.C.A. (ed.): *Bringing Learning to Life: the Learning Revolution, the Economy and the Individual*. London: Falmer, 1995.

"The Changing Concept of Career: Implications for Career Counseling". In Feller, R. & Walz, G. (eds.): *Career Transitions in Turbulent Times: Exploring Work, Learning and Careers.* Greensboro, NC: ERIC/CASS Publications, University of North Carolina at Greensboro, 1996.

"Mentoring". In Palmer, S., Dainow, S. & Milner, P. (eds.): *Counselling: the BAC Counselling Reader.* London: Sage, 1996.

"Computers in Guidance". In Sultana, R.G. & Sammut, J.M. (eds.): *Careers Education and Guidance in Malta: Issues and Challenges.* Malta: Publishers Enterprises Group, 1997.

"International Perspectives". In Sultana, R.G. & Sammut, J.M. (eds.): *Careers Education and Guidance in Malta: Issues and Challenges.* Malta: Publishers Enterprises Group, 1997.

"Svetovanje za Kariero v Luci Socialno-Politicnih Ideologij". In Niklanovic, S. (ed.): *Prispevki o Poklicnem Svetovanju.* Ljubljana: Izida, 1997.

"Models of Student Guidance in a Changing 14-19 Education and Training System" (co-authored with Young, M.). In Hodgson, A. & Spours, K. (eds.): *Dearing and Beyond: 14-19 Qualifications, Frameworks and Systems.* London: Kogan Page, 1997. (Reprinted in Edwards, R. Harrison, R. & Tait, A. (eds.): *Telling Tales: Perspectives on Guidance and Counselling in Learning.* London: Routledge/Open University, 1998.)

"Applying Market Principles to Delivery of Careers Guidance Services: a Critical Review". In Bartlett, W., Roberts, J.A. & Le Grand, J. (eds.): *A Revolution in Social Policy: Quasi-Market Reforms in the 1990s.* Bristol: Policy Press, 1998.

"Det Samfundsmaessige Udbytte af Uddannelses- og Erhvervsvejledningen". In *Vejlednings-Perspektiver i det 21 Arhundrede.* Copenhagen: RUE, 1999.

"Synthesis". In Hiebert, B. & Bezanson, L. (eds.): *Making Waves: Career Development and Public Policy.* Ottawa: Canadian Career Development Foundation, 2000.

"The New Career and Public Policy". In Collin, A. & Young, R.A. (eds.): *The Future of Career.* Cambridge: Cambridge University Press, 2000.

"The Role of Guidance within Innovative Training Structures". In *Career Guidance: Constructing the Future.* Stourbridge: Institute of Career Guidance/Trotman, 2000.

"Theory and Practice of Career Development". In Sallay, M. (ed.): *Careers Guidance and Counselling: Theory and Practice for the 21st Century.* Budapest: National Institute of Vocational Education, 2000.

"Connexions: Genesis, Diagnosis, Prognosis". In *Career Guidance: Constructing the Future.* Stourbridge: Institute of Career Guidance, 2002.

"Virtual Guidance – Visions and Values". In *Quality and Ethics in Web-Based Guidance.* Stockholm: International Programme Office for Education and Training, 2002.

"Introduction". In Bezanson, L. & O'Reilly, E. (eds.): *Making Waves: Volume 2, Connecting Career Development with Public Policy.* Ottawa: Canadian Career Development Foundation, 2002.

"OECD'n Koordinoiman Ohjauksen Toimintapolitiikan Arviontihankkeen Valirapotti". In Vuorinen, R. & Kasurinen, H. (eds.): *Ohjaus Suomessa 2002.* Jyvaskyla, Finland: Koulutuksen Tutkimuslaitos, 2002.

"Verso un Master Europeo ed il Counselling nell'Istruione Superiore" (co-authored with Van Esbroeck, R.). In Adamo, S., Giusti, P. & Valerio, P. (eds.): *Servizio di Consultazione Psicologica e di Orientamento per Studenti Universitari: Ambiti di Intervento e Percorsi Formativi Specifiche e Percorsi Formativi – Atti del Convegno.* Naples: Istituto Italiano per gli Studi Filisofica, 2003.

"Disconnecting Connexions". In Reid, H. & Bimrose, J. (eds.): *Constructing the Future: Transforming Career Guidance.* Stourbridge: Institute of Career Guidance, 2006.

"Current Trends in Higher Education Policies and Career Guidance Provision" (co-authored with Sweet, R.). In Vuorinen, R. & Saukkonen, S. (eds.): *Guidance Services in Higher Education: Strategies, Design and Implementation.* Jyvaskyla, Finland: Institute for Educational Research, University of Jyvaskyla, 2006.

"Career Guidance within Public Employment Services: a Review of Services in Finland within a European Perspective" (co-authored with Sultana, R.G.). In *Ammatillisen Ohjauksen Vuosikirja: Arsbok för Yrkesinriktad Vägledning*. Helsinki: Edita Prima Oy, 2006.

"Concetto e Pratica dell'Orientamento alla Carriera nella Società della Conoscenza". In *La Scelta Universitaria: Istruire la Pratica*. Turin: Fondazione Giovanni Agnelli, 2007.

"The Use of Telephone Help Lines in Career Information and Guidance" (co-authored with Dent, G.). In Malone, J.F., Miller, R.M. & Walz, G.R. (eds.): *Distance Counseling: Expanding the Counselor's Reach and Impact*. Ann Arbor, MI: Counseling Outfitters, LLC, 2007.

"Higher Education Careers Services: Transformation and Diversification". In Butler, T. & Dane, M. (eds.): *Reflections on Change 1967-2007*. Sheffield: Association of Graduate Careers Advisory Services, 2007.

"Towards a 'Guidance and Counselling in HE Charter': Reflections on the Implications of Recent International Policy Reviews". In Katzensteiner, M., Ferrer-Sama, P. & Rott, G. (eds.): *Guidance and Counselling in European Union Member States*. Aarhus, Denmark: Counselling and Support Centre, University of Aarhus, 2008.

"Career Guidance in England: Where Are We and Where Might We Be Going?" In Reid, H. (ed.): *Constructing a Way Forward: Innovation in Theory and Practice for Career Guidance*. Southborough, Kent: Centre for Career and Personal Development, Canterbury Christ Church University, 2008.

"Career Guidance and Public Policy". In Athanasou, J.A. & Van Esbroeck, R. (eds.): *International Handbook of Career Guidance*. Dordrecht, Netherlands: Springer, 2008.

"Origins and Reflections". In Alloway, J. (ed.): *The Story of the Guidance Council*. Leicester: National Institute of Adult Continuing Education, 2008.

"Personal Development Planning and Employability" (co-authored with Ward, R.). In *Personal Development Planning and Employability* (revised edition). Learning and Employability Series. York: Higher Education Academy, 2009.

"The Conceptual Framework: New Map and New Tools" (co-authored with Barnes, A.). In *ICT Skills 2: ICT Tools and Training for E-Guidance Practitioners*. Bologna: ASTER, 2009.

"Synergies and Exploitation" (co-authored with Cogoi, C. & Barnes, A.). In *ICT Skills 2: ICT Tools and Training for E-Guidance Practitioners*. Bologna: ASTER, 2009.

"Career Information, Advice and Guidance in the UK: the State of the Nation" In Reid, H. (ed.): *The Re-emergence of Career: Challenges and Opportunities*. Southborough, Kent: Centre for Career and Personal Development, Canterbury Christ Church University, 2010.

"Career Guidance Policy Development under the Coalition Government: a Critical Analysis". In Reid, H. (ed.): *Vocation, Vocation, Vocation: Placing Meaning in the Foreground of Career Decision-Making*. Southborough, Kent: Centre for Career and Personal Development, Canterbury Christ Church University, 2011.

"Quality in Career Guidance – an International Perspective". In *Perspectiven guter Beratung: Weiterentwicklung der Qualität und Professionalität in der Bildungs- und Berufsberatung*. Berlin: nfb, 2012.

"Careering through the Web" (co-authored with Hooley, T. & Hutchinson, J.). In Iacob, M. (ed.): *Good Practices in the Use of ICT in Providing Guidance and Counselling*. Bucharest: Jobtribu, 2012.

"Career Guidance in the European Union: Promoting Policy Collaboration and Development". In Schober, K. (ed.): *Shaping Career Guidance: Four Decades of Leadership for Guidance Services*. Bielefeld, Germany: W. Bertelsman Verlag, 2013.

"Career Guidance and Orientation". In *Revisiting Global Trends in TVET: Reflections on Theory and Practice*. Bonn, Germany: UNESCO-UNEVOC Centre for Technical and Vocational Education and Training, 2013.

"Career Helplines: a Resource for Career Development" (co-authored with Flederman, P.). In Arulmani, G., Bakshi, A.J., Leong, F.T.L. & Watts, A.G (eds.): *Handbook of Career Development: International Perspectives*. New York: Springer, 2014.

Articles in refereed journals

"Counselling and the Organisation of Careers Work in Schools". *Aspects of Education*, No. 5, March 1967.

"Counselling and Careers Education in the United States: Some Current Trends". *British Journal of Guidance and Counselling*, 1 (1), January 1973.

"Counselling and Career Education in the United States: a Visitor's View". *Vocational Guidance Quarterly*, 21 (4), 1973.

"Higher Education and Employment". *Universities Quarterly*, 29 (1), Winter 1974.

"Career(s) Education in Britain and the USA: Contrasts and Common Problems" (co-authored with Herr, E.L.). *British Journal of Guidance and Counselling*, 4 (2), July 1976.

"A Rationale for Guidance on Higher Education Choices". *British Journal of Guidance and Counselling*, 5 (1), January 1977.

"Careers Education in Higher Education: Principles and Practice". *British Journal of Guidance and Counselling*, 5 (2), July 1977.

"Using Computers in Careers Guidance in Schools". *Journal of Occupational Psychology*, 51 (1), 1978.

"Careers Guidance in a Developing Country: Malaysia". *International Journal for the Advancement of Counselling*, 1 (2), May 1978.

"The Research and Development Programme of the National Institute for Careers Education and Counselling (United Kingdom)" (co-authored with Kidd, J.M.). *International Review of Applied Psychology*, 26 (2), October 1977.

"British and American Models of Career Education: an Overview" (co-authored with Herr, E.L.). *Vocational Guidance Quarterly*, 27 (2), December 1978.

"The Implications of School-Leaver Unemployment for Careers Education in Schools". *Journal of Curriculum Studies*, 10 (3), September 1978.

"Evaluating the Effectiveness of Careers Guidance: a Review of the British Research" (co-authored with Kidd, J.M.). *Journal of Occupational Psychology*, 51 (3), September 1978.

"Educational and Careers Guidance Services for Adults: I. A Rationale and Conceptual Framework". *British Journal of Guidance and Counselling*, 8 (1), January 1980.

"Careers Guidance Under Apartheid". *International Journal for the Advancement of Counselling*, 3 (1), 1980.

"Educational and Careers Guidance Service for Adults: II. A Review of Current Provision". *British Journal of Guidance and Counselling*, 8 (2), July 1980.

"The Implications of Youth Unemployment for Career Education and for Counselling" (co-authored with Herr, E.L.). *Journal of Career Education*, 7 (3), March 1981.

"Careers Education and the Informal Economies". *British Journal of Guidance and Counselling*, 9 (1), January 1981.

"Careers Guidance in Sweden: a British Perspective". *International Journal for the Advancement of Counselling*, 4 (3), 1981.

"Schools, Youth and Work". Editor of special issue of *Educational Analysis*, 3 (2), 1981.

"Careers Guidance and Counselling in England" (co-authored with Avent, C., Sisterson, D., Fawcett, B. & Newsome A.) *Personnel and Guidance Journal*, Volume 61 No. 8, April 1983.

"Guidance and Support in Work-Experience Programmes for Unemployed Young People in the United Kingdom". *International Journal for the Advancement of Counselling*, 7 (1), 1984.

"Computers in Careers Guidance: the British Experience" (co-authored with Ballantine, M.). *The Counseling*

Psychologist, 11 (4), 1983.

"Changing Structures and Conceptions of Careers Guidance in British Schools". *Research in Counselling* (Japan), 8, 1983.

"The BJGC and Guidance and Counselling in Britain 1973-85" (co-authored with Sugarman, L.). *British Journal of Guidance and Counselling*, 13 (1), January 1985.

"The Japanese 'Lifetime Employment System' and its Implications for Careers Guidance". *International Journal for the Advancement of Counselling*, 8 (2), 1985.

"Issues for Careers Education in the Multi-Ethnic Classroom" (co-authored with Law, B.). *Pastoral Care in Education*, 3 (2), June 1985

"The Careers Service and Schools: a Changing Relationship". *British Journal of Guidance and Counselling*, 14 (2), May 1986.

"The Role of the Computer in Careers Guidance". *International Journal for the Advancement of Counselling*, 9, 1986.

"Beyond Unemployment?: Schools and the Future of Work". *British Journal of Educational Studies*, 35 (1), February 1987.

"School Work Tasks as Simulated Work Experience" (co-authored with Jamieson, I. & Miller, A.). *British Journal of Education and Work*, 1 (1), 1987.

"Timing of Employment Selection within the Youth Training Scheme" (co-authored with Knasel, E.G.). *British Journal of Education and Work*, 1 (2), 1987.

"Careers Guidance Services within the European Community: Contrasts and Common Trends" (co-authored with Dartois, C. & Plant, P.). *International Journal for the Advancement of Counselling*, 10 (3), 1987.

"Work Shadowing and Work-Related Learning" (co-authored with Herr, E.L.). *Career Development Quarterly*, 37 (1), September 1988.

"Orientacão Vocacional: Evolucões na Teoria e na Prática". *Journal de Psicologia* (Portugal), 7 (2), May/June 1988.

"Changing Conceptions of Careers Guidance and a Proposed Model for Singapore Schools". *Singapore Journal of Education*, 9 (1), 1988.

"Les Services d'Orientation Scolaire et Professionnelle pour les Jeunes au Royaume-Uni: I. Les Structures et le Personnel". *L'Orientation Scolaire et Professionnelle*, 17 (3), September 1988.

"Les Services d'Orientation Scolaire et Professionnelle pour les Jeunes au Royaume-Uni: II. Les Relations Entre les Services". *L'Orientation Scolaire et Professionnelle*, 17 (4), December 1988.

"Les Services d'Orientation dans la Communauté Européenne: Différences et Tendances Communes" (co-authored with Dartois, C. & Plant, P.). *L'Orientation Scolaire et Professionnelle*, 17 (3), September 1988.

"The Changing Place of Careers Guidance in Schools". *Prospects* (UNESCO), Vol XVIII (4), 1988.

"Reports from the XIIIth International Conference for the Advancement of Counselling, held at the University of Calgary, Canada, on 14-18 August 1988: Counselling with Respect to Educational, Career and Employment Concerns". *International Journal for the Advancement of Counselling*, 12 (1), January 1989.

"School-Based Work Experience: Some International Comparisons" (co-authored with Jamieson, I. & Miller, A.). *British Journal of Education and Work*, 3 (1), 1989.

"Strategic Planning and Performance Measurement: Implications for Careers Services in Higher Education" (co-authored with Sampson, J.P.). *British Journal of Guidance and Counselling*, 17 (1), January 1989.

"The Single European Market and its Implications for Educational and Vocational Guidance Services" (co-authored with Banks, J.A.G. & Raban, A.J.). *International Journal for the Advancement of Counselling*, 13 (4), October 1990.

"The Impact of the 'New Right': Policy Challenges Confronting Careers Guidance in England and Wales". *British Journal of Guidance and Counselling*, 19 (3), September 1991.

"PROSPECT (HE): an Evaluation of User Responses" (co-authored with Kidd, J.M. & Knasel, E.). *British Journal of Guidance and Counselling*, 19 (1), January 1991.

"Los Servicios de Orientacion en la Comunidad Europen: Diferencias y Tendencias Comunes" (co-authored with Dartois, C. & Plant, P.). *Revista de Orientacion Educativa y Vocacional* (Spain), 1 (1), 1991.

"Computer-Assisted Careers Guidance Systems and Organisational Change" (co-authored with Sampson, J.P.). *British Journal of Guidance and Counselling*, 20 (3), September 1992.

"Individual Action Planning: Issues and Strategies". *British Journal of Education and Work*, 5 (1), 1992.

"Careers Guidance Services in a Changing Europe". *International Journal for the Advancement of Counselling*, 15 (4), December 1992.

"The Politics and Economics of Computer-Aided Careers Guidance Systems". *British Journal of Guidance and Counselling*, 21 (2), May 1993.

"The Changing Role of Careers Services in Higher Education in the United Kingdom". *Higher Education in Europe*, 19 (3), 1994.

"Developing Individual Action-Planning Skills". *British Journal of Education and Work*, 7 (2), 1994.

"Occupational Profiles of Vocational Counselors in Europe". *Journal of Counseling and Development*, 73 (1), September/October 1994.

"Applying Market Principles to the Delivery of Careers Guidance Services: a Critical Review". *British Journal of Guidance and Counselling*, 23 (1), 1995.

"The Death and Transfiguration of Career – and of Career Guidance?" (co-authored with Collin, A.). *British Journal of Guidance and Counselling*, 24 (3), October 1996.

"Toward a Policy for Lifelong Career Development: a Transatlantic Perspective". *Career Development Quarterly*, 45 (1), September 1996.

"Careerquake". *Australian Journal of Career Development*, 6 (2), Winter 1997.

"The Role of the Market in Career Counselling Delivery". *Australian Journal of Career Development*, 6 (3), Spring 1997.

"Developing Local Lifelong Guidance Strategies" (co-authored with Hawthorn, R., Hoffbrand, J., Jackson, H. & Spurling, A.). *British Journal of Guidance and Counselling*, Volume 25 No. 2, May 1997.

"The Marketisation of Guidance Services In Germany, France and Britain" (co-authored with Rees, T. & Bartlett, W.). *Journal of Education and Work*, 12 (1), 1999.

"The Relationship between Career Guidance and Financial Guidance" (co-authored with Stevens, B.). *Widening Participation and Lifelong Learning*, 1 (3), 1999; also in *Revista Española de Orientación y Psicopedagogía*, 10 (18), 2nd Semester 1999.

"International Collaboration in Translating Career Theory to Practice" (co-authored with Sampson, J.P., Palmer, M. & Hughes, D.). *Journal of Employment Counseling*, 37 (2), June 2000; also in *Career Development Quarterly*, 40 (4), June 2000.

"Career Development and Public Policy". *Journal of Employment Counseling*, 37 (2), June 2000; also in *Career Development Quarterly*, 48 (4), June 2000; in *Educational and Vocational Guidance Bulletin,* No. 64, 2000; and in *Orientacion y Sociedad* (Argentina), No.2, 2000.

"Networking a Computer-Aided Guidance System within Higher Education Institutions: Practice and Potential" (co-authored with Jackson, C.). *British Journal of Guidance and Counselling*, 28 (1), February 2000.

"Guidance in the United Kingdom: Past, Present and Future" (co-authored with Kidd, J.M.). *British Journal of Guidance and Counselling*, 28 (4), November 2000.

"New Skills for New Futures: a Comparative Review of Higher Education Guidance and Counselling Services in the European Union" (co-authored with Van Esbroeck, R.). *International Journal for the Advancement of Counselling*, 22 (3), September 2000.

"Donald Super's Influence in the United Kingdom". *International Journal for Educational and Vocational Guidance*, 1 (1-2), 2001.

"Working Relationships between Careers Services Within and Outside Higher Education" (co-authored with Hughes, D. & Haslam, D.). *Journal of Education and Work*, 14 (1), February 2001.

"Career Guidance and Social Exclusion: a Cautionary Tale". *British Journal of Guidance and Counselling*, 29 (2), May 2001.

"L'Education en Orientation pour les Jeunes: les Principes et l'Offre au Royaume-Uni et dans les Autres Pays Européens". *L'Orientation Scolaire et Professionnelle*, 30, July 2001.

"Career Education for Young People: Rationale and Provision in the UK and Other European Countries". *International Journal for Educational and Vocational Guidance*, 1 (3), 2001.

"Connexions: The Role of the Personal Adviser in Schools". *Pastoral Care in Education*, 19 (4), December 2001.

"'Let Your Fingers do the Walking': the Use of Telephone Helplines in Career Information and Guidance" (co-authored with Dent, G.). *British Journal of Guidance and Counselling*, 30 (1), February 2002.

"The Role of Information and Communication Technologies in Integrated Career Information and Guidance Systems: a Policy Perspective". *International Journal for Educational and Vocational Guidance*, 2 (3), 2002.

"Career Guidance Policies in 37 Countries: Contrasts and Common Themes" (co-authored with Sultana, R.G.). *International Journal for Educational and Vocational Guidance*, 4 (2-3), 2004.

"Guidance Workers as Learning Brokers" (co-authored with Hawthorn, R.). *Widening Participation and Lifelong Learning*, 6 (3), December 2004.

"Career Guidance Policy: an International Review". *Career Development Quarterly*, 54 (1), September 2005.

"Building Career Guidance Capacity in the Voluntary and Community Sector" (co-authored with Barker, V., Sharpe, T. & Edwards, A.). *British Journal of Guidance and Counselling*, 33 (4), November 2005.

"Devolution and Diversification: Career Guidance in the Home Countries". *British Journal of Guidance and Counselling*, 34 (1), February 2006.

"The 'P' Word: Productivity in the Delivery of Career Guidance Services" (co-authored with Dent, G.). *British Journal of Guidance and Counselling*, 34 (2), May 2006.

"Constructing Futures: an International Policy Perspective". *Australian Journal of Career Development*, 15 (2), Winter 2006.

"Career Guidance in the Middle East and North Africa" (co-authored with Sultana, R.G.). *International Journal for Educational and Vocational Guidance*, 8 (1), March 2008.

"The Evolution of a National Distance Guidance Service: Trends and Challenges" (co-authored with Dent, G.). *British Journal of Guidance and Counselling*, 36 (4), November 2008.

"Navigating the National Qualifications Framework (NQF): the Role of Career Guidance" (co-authored with Walters, S. & Flederman, P.). *South African Journal of Higher Education*, 23 (3), 2009.

"National All-Age Career Guidance Services: Evidence and Issues". *British Journal of Guidance and Counselling*, 38 (1), February 2010.

"Social Exclusion and Career Development: a United Kingdom Perspective". *Australian Journal of Career Development*, 19 (1), Autumn 2010.

"The Involvement of the European Union in Career Guidance Policy: a Brief History" (co-authored with Sultana, R.G. & McCarthy, J.). *International Journal for Educational and Vocational Guidance*, 10 (2), July 2010.

"The Development of a Lifelong Guidance System in Hungary" (co-authored with Borbély-Pecze, T.). *International Journal for Educational and Vocational Guidance*, 11 (1), March 2011.

"The 'Blueprint' Framework for Career Management Skills: a Critical Exploration" (co-authored with Hooley, T., Sultana, R.G. & Neary, S.). *British Journal of Guidance and Counselling*, 41 (2), April 2013.

"False Dawns, Bleak Sunset: the Coalition Government's Policies on Career Guidance". *British Journal of Guidance and Counselling*, 41 (4), August 2013.

"Forty Years of the BJGC: a Personal Review". *British Journal of Guidance and Counselling*, 42 (1), February 2014.

"The International Symposia on Career Development and Public Policy: Retrospect and Prospect" (co-authored with Bezanson, L. & McCarthy, J.). *Australian Journal of Career Development*, 23 (3), 2014.

Other publications

Reports (85) arising from projects, evaluations, collaborations and other commissioned work.

Other articles (274) contributed to non-refereed journals, professional publications, and newspapers.

Briefings (24) which summarise in accessible form the findings of research projects and other investigations.

Policy commentaries and policy bulletins produced for the Guidance Council (22 in 2000-01) and for Careers England (28 from 2005 to 2014) mainly analysing and responding to government and related policy statements.

Careers books and curriculum materials (7 in total, 1965-80) for use by school staff and students.

Interviews (5), including 4 published in the final months before retirement.

Unattributed publications, including 10 items produced under contract with OECD and for which OECD holds authorship. Several are country working papers, but a smaller number are important research reports; these including the widely cited *Career Guidance and Public Policy: Bridging the Gap* (2004, co-authored with Sweet, R.).

Four other co-authored documents are noteworthy within the list of unattributed publications:

Centre for Educational Research and Innovation: *Mapping the Future: Young People and Career Guidance*. Paris: Organisation for Economic Co-operation and Development, 1996. (Written by St John-Brooks, C. & Watts, A.G.)

Organisation for Economic Co-operation and Development & European Commission: *Career Guidance: a Handbook for Policy Makers*. Paris: OECD, 2004. (Written by Sultana, R.G. & Watts, A.G.)

Careers England: *An All-Age Strategy for Career Guidance Services in England*. London: Careers England, 2007. (Written by Watts, A.G., with support from Chubb, P.)

Cedefop: *Establishing and Developing National Lifelong Guidance Policy Forums*. Thessaloniki: Cedefop, 2008. (Written by Kristensen, S., McCarthy, J. & Watts, A.G.)

References

Abt, C.C. (1968). Games for learning. In Boocock, S.S. & Schild, E.O. (eds.) *Simulation Games in Learning.* Beverly Hills, California: Sage.

Advisory Council for Adult and Continuing Education (1979). *Links to Learning.* Leicester: ACACE.

Albert, M. (1993). *Capitalism Against Capitalism.* London: Whurr.

Alloway, J. (ed.) (2008). *The Story of the Guidance Council.* Leicester: National Institute of Adult Continuing Education.

Andrews, D. (2000). *Implications of Connexions for Careers Education and Guidance in Schools* (CRAC/NICEC Conference Briefing). Cambridge: Careers Research and Advisory Centre.

Andrews, D., Law, B., McGowan, B. & Munro, M. (1998). *Managing Careers Work in Schools* (NICEC Project Report). Cambridge: Careers Research and Advisory Centre.

Archer, M. (1995). *Realist Social Theory: the Morphogenetic Approach.* Cambridge: Cambridge University Press.

Argyris, C. (1960). *Understanding Organizational Behavior.* Homewood, IL: Dorsey.

Aristotle (1959 edn). *Politics.* Written 4th century BC; edited and translated by John Warrington. London: Dent.

Arthur, M.B. & Rousseau, D.M. (1996). *The Boundaryless Career.* New York: Oxford University Press.

Ashton, D.N. (1975). From school to work: some problems of adjustment experienced by young male workers. In Brannen, P. (ed.) *Entering the World of Work: Some Sociological Perspectives.* London: HMSO.

Ashton, D.N. & Field, D. (1976). *Young Workers.* London: Hutchinson.

Ashton, D.N. & Maguire, M.J. (1980a). The functions of academic and non-academic criteria in employers' selection strategies. *British Journal of Guidance and Counselling*, 8(2), 146-157.

Ashton, D.N. & Maguire, M.J. (1980b). The careers service and the local labour market. *Careers Bulletin*, Summer, 15-18.

Assistant Masters and Mistresses Association (1988). *Making the Most of Work Experience.* London: AMMA.

Association of Graduate Careers Advisory Services (2005). *Careers Education Benchmark Statement.* Report by Careers Education Task Group. Sheffield: AGCAS.

Audit Commission & Her Majesty's Inspectorate (1993). *Unfinished Business: Full-Time Educational Courses for 16-19 Year Olds.* London: HMSO.

Azrin, N.H., Philip, R.A., Thienes-Hontos, P. & Besalel, V.A. (1980). Comparative evaluation of the Job Club program with welfare recipients. *Journal of Vocational Behavior*, 16, 133-145.

Azrin, N.H., Philip, R.A., Thienes-Hontos, P. & Besalel, V.A. (1981). Follow-up on welfare benefits received by Job Club clients. *Journal of Vocational Behavior*, 18, 253-254.

Bacon, R. & Eltis, W. (1976). *Britain's Economic Problem: Too Few Producers.* London: Macmillan.

Ball, B. & Butcher, V. (1994). *Developing Students' Career Planning Skills: the Impact of the Enterprise in Higher Education Initiative.* Sheffield: Employment Department.

Ball, C. (1991). *Learning Pays.* London: Royal Society of Arts.

Banks, O. (1976). *The Sociology of Education* (3rd edn.). London: Batsford.

Barber, M. (1994). *Young People and their Attitudes to School*. Keele: Centre for Successful Schools, Keele University.

Barnes, D., Johnson, G., Jordan, S., Layton, D., Medway, P. & Yeomans, D. (1987). *The TVEI Curriculum 14-16*. Leeds: School of Education, University of Leeds.

Barr, N. (1994). The role of government in a market economy. In Barr, N. (ed.) *Labor Markets and Social Policy in Central and Eastern Europe: the Transition and Beyond*. Oxford: Oxford University Press.

Barr, N. & Harbison, R.W. (1994). Overview: hopes, tears, and transformation. In Barr, N. (ed.) *Labor Markets and Social Policy in Central and Eastern Europe: the Transition and Beyond*. Oxford: Oxford University Press.

Bartlett, W., Rees, T. & Watts, A.G. (2000). *Adult Guidance Services and the Learning Society: Emerging Policies in the European Union*. Bristol: Policy Press.

Bateson, M.C. (1994). *Peripheral Visions: Learning Along the Way*. New York: HarperCollins.

Bates, 1. (1990). The politics of careers education and guidance: A case for scrutiny. *British Journal of Guidance and Counselling*, 18(1), 66-83.

Baxter, A. (1988). "'Their fault or ours?": The contraction of work and the 'radicalization' of young people. *British Journal of Education and Work*, 2(1).

Bayliss, V. (1998). *Redefining Schooling*. London: Royal Society of Arts.

Bayliss, V. (1998). *Redefining Work*. London: Royal Society of Arts.

Bazalgette, J. (1978). *School Life and Work Life*. London: Hutchinson.

Beattie Committee (1999). *Implementing Inclusiveness: Realising Potential*. Edinburgh: Scottish Executive.

Beck, J. (1981). Education, industry and the needs of the economy. *Cambridge Journal of Education*, 2(2), 87-106.

Benett, Y. & Carter, D. (1982). *Sidetracked?: A Look at the Careers Advice Given to Fifth Form Girls*. Manchester: Equal Opportunities Commission.

Bennett, J. (1983). Work visits. In Watts, A.G. (ed.) *Work Experience and Schools*. London: Heinemann.

Bennett, N., Dunne, E. & Carré, C. (2000). *Skills Development in Higher Education and Employment*. Buckingham: Society for Research into Higher Education and Open University Press.

Bentley, T. (1998). *Learning Beyond the Classroom*. London: Routledge/Demos.

Bentley, T. & Gurumurthy, R. (1999). *Destination Unknown: Engaging with the Problems of Marginalised Youth*. London: Demos.

Bentley, T. & Oakley, K. (1999). *The Real Deal*. London: Demos.

Berg, I. (1970). *Education and Jobs: the Great Training Robbery*. Harmondsworth: Penguin.

Besug, F. (1975). Work-leisure and the school. *Counseling and Values*, 20(1), 25-28.

Bezanson, L. & O'Reilly, E. (eds.) (2002). *Making Waves: Volume 2, Connecting Career Development with Public Policy*. Ottawa: Canadian Career Development Foundation.

Birch, D.L. (1979). *The Job Generation Process*. Cambridge, Massachusetts: MIT Program on Neighborhood and Regional Change.

Birk, J. M., Tanney, M. F. & Cooper, J. F. (1979). A case of blurred vision: Stereotyping in career information illustrations. *Journal of Vocational Behavior,* 15(2), 247-57.

Blackman, S. J. (1987). The labour market in school: New vocationalism and issues of socially ascribed discrimination. In Brown, P. & Ashton, D. M. (eds.) *Education, Unemployment and Labour Markets.* Lewes: Falmer.

Blair, T. (1998). *The Third Way.* London: Fabian Society.

Blau, P. M. & Duncan, O. D. (1967). *The American Occupational Structure.* New York: Wiley.

Bloomer, J. (1973). What have simulation and gaming got to do with programme learning and educational technology? *Programmed Learning and Educational Technology,* 10(4), 224-234.

Bolger, A. W. (1978). Guidance and counseling in a developing country. *International Journal for the Advancement of Counselling* 1(3), 225-29.

Bolton Committee (1971). *Small Firms.* London: HMSO.

Bosanquet, N. & Doeringer, P.B. (1973). Is there a dual labour market in Britain? *Economic Journal,* 83, 421-435.

Bourdieu, P. & Passeron, J.C. (1977). *Reproduction in Education, Society and Culture.* London: Sage.

Bowles, S. & Gintis, H. (1976). *Schooling in Capitalist America.* London: Routledge & Kegan Paul.

Bradley, S. (1990). The careers service past, present and future. *British Journal of Guidance and Counselling,* 18(2), 137-155.

Brammer, L.M. (1985). Counselling services in the People's Republic of China. *International Journal for the Advancement of Counselling,* 8(2), 125-136.

Breakwell, G. M. & Weinberger, B. (1987). *Young Women in 'Gender-Atypical' Jobs: The Case of Trainee Technicians in the Engineering Industry* (Research Paper No. 49). London: Department of Employment.

Brenner, M. H. (1977). Personal stability and economic security. *Social Policy,* 8 (1), 2-4.

Brewer, J.M. (1942). *History of Vocational Guidance.* New York: Harper.

Bridges, D. (1981). Teachers and "the world of work". In Elliott, L., Bridges, D., Ebbutt, D., Gibson, R. & Nias, J. (eds.) *School Accountability.* London: Grant McIntyre.

Bridges, D. (1993). Transferable skills: a philosophical perspective. *Studies in Higher Education,* 18(1), 43-51.

Bridges, W. (1995). *Jobshift.* London: Brealey.

British Youth Council (1977). *Youth Unemployment: Causes and Cures* (Report of a Working Party). London, British Youth Council.

Bromley, R. & Gerry, C. (eds.) (1979). *Casual Work and Poverty in Third World Cities.* Chichester: Wiley.

Bronfenbrenner, U. (1979). *The Ecology of Human Development.* Cambridge, MA: Harvard University Press.

Brooks, D. & Singh, K. (1978). *Aspirations Versus Opportunities: Asian and White School Leavers in the Midlands.* London: Commission for Racial Equality.

Brooks, L., Holahan, W. & Galligan, M. (1985). The effects of a nontraditional role-modeling intervention on sex typing of occupational preferences and career salience in adolescent females. *Journal of Vocational Behavior,* 26, 264-76.

Brown, K. M. (1985). Turning a blind eye: Racial oppression and the unintended consequences of white "non-racism". *Sociological Review,* 33(4): 670-90.

Burgess, E. (1960). *Aging in Western Societies*. Chicago: University of Chicago Press.

Burns, S. (1975). *The Household Economy*. Boston: Beacon.

Butcher, D. & Harvey, P. (1998). Meta-ability development: a new concept for career management. *Career Development International*, 3(2), 75-78.

Byrne, D. (1999). *Social Exclusion*. Buckingham: Open University Press.

Canadian Labour Force Development Board (1998). *Standards for electronic labour market information*. Retrieved 1 September 2001, from www.workinfonet.ca/cwn/english/ clfdbs_e.cfm

Careers Profession Task Force (2010). *Towards a Strong Careers Profession*. London: Department for Education.

Careers Research and Advisory Centre (1986). *Inside Insight Courses*. Cambridge: CRAC.

Careers Sector Stakeholders Alliance (2014). *The Roles of Employers and Career Professionals in Providing Career Support to Young People in Schools and Colleges.* Briefing Note 13.

Carney, M. & Turner, D. (1987). *Education for Enterprise*. Mirfield, West Yorkshire: Osmosis.

Chambers, R. & Engel, J. (1976). *Unemployment and the School Leaver* (Working Paper 21). Ormskirk, Lancashire: National Association of Careers and Guidance Teachers.

Chanan, G. (1976/1977). To sustain life – schools' concepts of adult work. *New Universities Quarterly*, 31(1), 37-46.

Chang, J. (1993 edn). *Wild Swans* (first pub. 1991). London: Flamingo.

Cherry, N. (1980). Ability, education and occupational functioning. In Watts, A.G., Super, D.E., & Kidd, J.M. (eds.) *Career Development in Britain*. Cambridge: CRAC/Hobsons.

Chisholm, L. A. & Holland, J. (1986). Girls and occupational choice: Anti-sexism in action in a curriculum development project. *British Journal of Sociology of Education*, 7(4), 353-65.

Chubb, P. (2014). *Was there ever a golden age for career education and guidance?* Available from http://adventuresincareerdevelopment.wordpress.com/2014/09/24/was-there-ever-a-golden-age-for-careers-education-and-guidance (Accessed 16 April 2015).

Clark, B. (1960). *The Open Door College*. New York: McGraw-Hill.

Clarke, E. (1985). *The Renfrew Experience Based Learning Project 1983-1985: Pupils at Work in the Community*. Glasgow: Vocational Initiatives Unit, University of Glasgow (mimeo).

Clements, S. (1985). Role-play. *NACGT Skill-Share*, 1(2), Autumn.

Cochran, L. (1990). Narrative as a paradigm for career research. In R. A. Young & W. A. Borgen (eds.) *Methodological Approaches to the Study of Career* (pp. 71-86). New York: Praeger.

Cockburn, C. (1987). *Two-Track Training: Sex Inequalities and the Youth Training Scheme*. Basingstoke: Macmillan.

Coles, B. (1988). Post-16 'progression' in a rural shire county. In Coles, B. (ed.) *Young Careers: The Search for Jobs and the New Vocationalism*. Milton Keynes: Open University Press.

Coles, B. (1995). *Youth and Social Policy: Youth Citizenship and Young Careers.* London: UCL Press.

Collin, A. & Watts, A.G. (1996). The death and transfiguration of career – and of career guidance? *British Journal of Guidance and Counselling*, 24(3), 385-398.

Collins, R. (1974). Where are educational requirements for employment highest? *Sociology of Education*, 47(4), 419-442.

Collins, R. (1979). *The Credential Society*. New York: Academic Press.

Commission on Social Justice (1994). *Social Justice: Strategies for National Renewal*. London: Vintage.

Community Service Volunteers (1987). *Learning in the Community: A Teachers' Handbook*. London: CSV.

Confederation of British Industry (1989a). *Towards a Skills Revolution - a Youth Charter* (Interim Report of the Vocational Education and Training Task Force). London: CBI.

Confederation of British Industry (1989b). *Towards a Skills Revolution* (Report of the Vocational Education and Training Task Force). London: CBI.

Connor, H., Burton, R., Pearson, R., Pollard, E. & Regan, J. (1999). *Making the Right Choice: How Students Choose Universities and Colleges*. London: Committee of Vice-Chancellors and Principals.

Consumers Association (1977). How You Rate Your Job. *Money Which?* September.

Coopers & Lybrand Deloitte (1990). *Surrey County Council - Review of Careers Service: Report*. London: Coopers & Lybrand Deloitte.

Courtenay, G. (1988). *England and Wales Youth Cohort Study: Report on Cohort 1 Sweep 1*. Sheffield: Manpower Services Commission.

Cox, S. & Golden, R. (1977). *Down the Road*. London: Writers and Readers Publishing Co-operative.

Craine, S. (1997). The `Black Magic Roundabout' : cyclical transitions, social exclusion and alternative careers. In MacDonald, R. (ed.) *Youth, the `Underclass' and Social Exclusion*. London: Routledge.

Crawford, I. & Thompson, A. (1994). Driving change: politics and administration. In Barr, N. (ed.) *Labour Markets and Social Policy in Central and Eastern Europe: the Transition and Beyond*. Oxford: Oxford University Press.

Cross, M., Wrench, J. & Barnett, S. (1990). *Ethnic Minorities and the Careers Service: An Investigation into Processes of Assessment and Placement* (Research Paper No. 73). Sheffield: Department of Employment.

Cunningham, P. & Fröschl, F. (1999). *Electronic Business Revolution*. Berlin: Springer.

Curran, J. & Stanworth, J. (1979a). Worker involvement and social relations in the small firm. *Sociological Review*, 27(2), 316-341.

Curran, J. & Stanworth, J. (1979b). Self-selection and the small firm worker – a critique and an alternative view. *Sociology*, 13(3), 427-444.

D'Amico, R. (1984). Does employment during high school impair academic progress? *Sociology of Education*, 57(3).

Davies, E. (1972). Work out of school. *Education*, 140(19), 10 November.

Daws, P. P. (1968). *A Good Start in Life*. Cambridge: Careers Research and Advisory Centre.

Daws, P.P. (1972). The role of the careers teacher. In Hayes, J. & Hopson, B. (eds.) *Careers Guidance: The Role of the School in Vocational Development*. London: Heinemann.

Daws, P.P. (1977). Are careers education programmes in schools a waste of time? – A reply to Roberts. *British Journal of Guidance and Counselling*, 5(1), 10-18.

Daws, P.P. (1981). The socialization/opportunity-structure theory of the occupational location of school leaver: a critical appraisal. In Watts, A.G., Super, D.E. & Kidd, J.M. (eds.) *Career Development in Britain*. Cambridge: CRAC/Hobsons.

de Grazia, R. (1980). Clandestine employment: a problem of our times. *International Labour Review*, 119 (5), September-October.

Department for Education and Employment (DfEE) (1997). *Careers Education and Guidance in Schools: Effective Partnerships with Careers Services*. Circular 5/97. London: DfEE.

Department for Education and Employment (DfEE) (1998a). *Final Careers Service Planning Guidance 1998-99*. London: DfEE (mimeo).

Department for Education and Employment (DfEE) (1998b). *Local Information, Advice and Guidance for Adults in England: Towards a National Framework*. Sheffield: DfEE.

Department for Education and Employment (DfEE) (1999a). *Learning to Succeed: a New Framework for Post-16 Learning*. London: Stationery Office.

Department for Education and Employment (DfEE) (1999b). *Planning Guidance for LEAs on Learning Mentors*. London: DfEE.

Department for Education and Employment (DfEE) (2000a). *Connexions: the Best Start in Life for Every Young Person*. London: DfEE.

Department for Education and Employment (DfEE) (2000b). *The Connexions Service and Schools*. Circular 0078/2000. London: DfEE.

Department for Education and Employment (DfEE) (2000c). *The Connexions Service: Prospectus and Specification*. London: DfEE.

Department for Education and Employment (DfEE) (2000d). *The Connexions Service: Professional Framework for Personal Advisers: Proposals for Consultation*. London: DfEE.

Department for Education and Employment (DfEE) (2000e). *Connexions Service Planning Guidance*. London: DfEE.

Department for Education and Skills (2003). *Challenging Age: Information, Advice and Guidance for Older Age Groups*. London: DES.

Department of Education and Science (DES) (1973). *Careers Education in Secondary Schools* (Education Survey 18). London: HMSO.

Department of Education and Science (1979). *Aspects of Secondary Education in England: A Survey by HM Inspectors of Schools*. London: HMSO.

Department of Education and Science (1987). *The National Curriculum: A Consultation Document*. London: DES.

Department of Education and Science (1988a). *Education at Work: A Guide for Schools*. London: HMSO.

Department of Education and Science/Department of Employment (1987). *Working Together for a Better Future*. London: DES/DE.

Department of Education and Science/Department of Employment (1991). *Education and Training for the 21st Century* (Volume 1). London: HMSO.

Department of Employment (1977). Statistical series. *Department of Employment Gazette*, 85(8), 812-863.

Department of Employment (1980a). Statistical series. *Employment Gazette*, 88(4).

Department of Employment (1980b). *The Careers Service: Guidance to Local Authorities in England and Wales* (1980 Revision). London: HMSO.

Department of Employment (1983). How many self-employed? *Employment Gazette*, 91(2), February.

Department of Employment (1990a). *The Careers Service: Annual Report 1989.* London: HMSO.

Department of Employment (1990b). *Training Credits for Young People: A Prospectus.* London: DE.

Devine, F. (1993). Gender segregation and labour supply: On "choosing" gender-atypical jobs. *British Journal of Education and Work*, 6(3), 61-74.

Dewey, J. (1963). *Experience and Education.* New York: Collier.

Doeringer, P.B. & Piore, M. (1971). *Internal Labour Markets and Manpower Analysis.* Lexington, MA: Heath.

Dore, R. (1976). *The Diploma Disease.* London: Allen & Unwin.

Dovey, K. & Mason, M. (1984). Guidance for submission: social control and guidance in schools for black pupils in South Africa. *British Journal of Guidance and Counselling* 12(1), 15-24.

Drapela, V. (ed.) (1979). *Guidance and Counselling around the World.* Washington, DC: University Press of America.

Drucker, P. (1969). *The Age of Discontinuity.* London: Heinemann.

Dubin, R. (1956). Industrial workers' worlds: A study of the "central life interests" of industrial workers. *Social Problems*, 3, 131-142.

Duffner Committee (2000). *Careers Service Review Committee Report.* Edinburgh: Scottish Executive.

Economist Intelligence Unit (1982). *Coping with Unemployment: the Effects on the Unemployed Themselves.* London: EIU.

Edgley, R. (1977). Education for industry. *Educational Research*, 20(1), 26-32.

Education and Training Action Group for Wales (1999). *An Education and Training Action Plan for Wales.* Cardiff: ETAGW.

Eisenstein, Z.R. (1982). The sexual politics of the new right: understanding the "crisis of liberalism" for the 1980s. In Keohane, N.O., Rosaldo, M.Z. & Gelpi, B.C. (eds.) *Feminist Theory: a Critique of Ideology.* Brighton: Harvester.

Erickson, F. (1975). Gatekeeping and the melting pot: Interactions in counseling encounters. *Harvard Educational Review*, 45(1), 44-70.

Esen, A. (1972). A view of guidance from Africa. *Personnel and Guidance Journal,* 50(10), 792-98.

Espin, O. M. (1979). A changing continent. In Drapela, V. (ed.) *Guidance and Counseling Around the World.* Washington, DC: University Press of America.

Esping-Andersen, G. (1994). Equality and work in the post-industrial life-cycle. In Miliband, D. (ed.) *Reinventing the Left.* Cambridge: Polity Press.

European Commission (1994). *Growth, Competitiveness, Employment: the Challenges and Ways Forward into the 21st Century.* Luxembourg: Office for Official Publications of the European Communities.

European Commission (1998). *From Guidelines to Action.* National Action Plans for Employment, D/98/6, Brussels.

European Foundation for the Improvement of Living and Working Conditions (1996). *The Role of Adult Guidance and Employment Counselling in a Changing Labour Market.* Loughlinstown, Co. Dublin: EFILWC.

Evans, J.H. & Burck, H.D. (1992). The effects of career education interventions on academic achievement: a meta-analysis. *Journal of Counseling and Development,* 71, 63-68.

Feige, E. (1981). The UK's unobserved economy: a preliminary assessment. *Journal of Economic Affairs*, 1(4), July.

Finn, D. (1984). Leaving school and growing up: work experience in the juvenile labour market. In Bates, I., Clarke, J., Cohen, P., Finn, D., Moore, R. & Willis, P. *Schooling for the Dole?: The New Vocationalism*. London: Macmillan.

Fleming, D. & Lavercombe, S. (1982). Talking about unemployment with school-leavers. *British Journal of Guidance and Counselling*, 10(1), 22-33.

Floud, J., Halsey, A.H. & Martin, F.M. (1976). *Social Class and Educational Opportunity*. London: Heinemann.

Flude, R. & Patron, A. (1979). *Education and the Challenge of Change*. Milton Keynes: Open University Press.

Folsom, B. & Reardon, R. (2003). College career courses: design and accountability. *Journal of Career Assessment*, 11, 421-450.

Forbes, I. & Mead, G. (1992). *Measure for Measure: A Comparative Analysis of Measures to Combat Racial Discrimination in the Member Countries of the European Community*. Sheffield: Employment Department.

Ford, G. (1998). *Career Guidance Mentoring for Disengaged Young People*. Stourbridge: Institute of Careers Guidance.

Ford, G. (2000a). *Youthstart 'Stepping Stones' Evaluation Report*. Stourbridge: Institute of Careers Guidance.

Ford, G. (2000b). *The Connexions Strategy and All-Age Guidance*. CeGS Occasional Paper. Derby: Centre for Guidance Studies, University of Derby.

Ford, G. (n.d.). *Youthstart Mentoring Action Project: Project and Evaluation Report*. Stourbridge: Institute of Careers Guidance.

Ford, G. & Watts, A.G. (1998). *Trade Unions and Lifelong Guidance* (NICEC Briefing). Cambridge: Careers Research and Advisory Centre.

Ford, J., Kempson, E. & Wilson, M. (1995). *Mortgage Arrears and Possessions: Perspectives from Borrowers, Lenders and the Courts*. London: HMSO.

Fortune, J., Jamieson, I.M. & Street, H. (1983). Relating work experience to the curriculum. In Watts, A.G. (ed.) *Work Experience and Schools*. London: Heinemann.

Frith, S. (1981). Dancing in the streets. *Time Out*, 20 March.

Full Employment UK (1991). *Investing in Skills: Part Four*. London: Full Employment UK.

Fuller, A. (1987). *Post-16 Work Experience in TVEI*. Lancaster: Institute for Research and Development in Post-Compulsory Education, University of Lancaster (mimeo).

Further Education Unit (1985). *CPVE in Action*. London: FEU.

Gabor, D. (1964). *Inventing the Future*. Harmondsworth: Penguin.

Galbraith, J.K. (1974). *The New Industrial State* (2nd edn). London: Penguin.

Gallagher, T. (1995). *Romania after Ceausescu*. Edinburgh: Edinburgh University Press.

Gamble, A. (1988). *The Free Economy and the Strong State: the Politics of Thatcherism*. London: Macmillan.

Garraty, J. A. (1978). *Unemployment in History*. New York: Harper and Row.

Gaullier, X. (1992). The changing ages of man. *Geneva Papers on Risk and Insurance*, 17, 3-25.

Gazier, B. (ed.) (1999). *Employability: Concepts and Policies: Report 1998.* Berlin: Institute for Applied Socio-Economics.

Gelatt, H.B. (1989). Positive uncertainty: A new decision-making framework for counseling. *Journal of Counseling Psychology*, 36(2), 252-256.

Gershuny, J.I. (1978). *After Industrial Society? The Emerging Self-Service Economy.* London: Macmillan.

Gershuny, J.I. (1979). The informal economy: Its role in post-industrial society. *Futures*, 11(1), 3-15.

Gershuny, J.I. & Pahl, R.E. (1979/80). Work outside employment: Some preliminary speculations. *New Universities Quarterly*, 34(1), 120-135.

Gershuny, J.I. & Pahl, RE. (1980). Britain in the decade of the three economies. *New Society, 900*, 7-9.

GHK Economics and Management (2000). *The Early Implementation of the Learning Gateway by the Careers Service* (Research Report RR203). London: Department for Education and Employment.

Gibb, A.A. (1987). Enterprise culture – its meaning and implications for education and training. *Journal of European Industrial Training*, 11(2), 2-38.

Giddens, A. (1991). *Modernity and Self-Identity*. Cambridge: Polity Press.

Giddens, A. (1993). *New Rules of Sociological Method* (2nd edn.). Cambridge: Polity Press.

Giddens, A. (1998). *The Third Way: the Renewal of Social Democracy.* Cambridge: Polity Press.

Gilmour, I. (1992). *Dancing with Dogma.* London: Simon & Schuster.

Goldthorpe, J.H., Lockwood, D., Bechhofer, F. & Platt, J. (1968). *The Affluent Worker: Industrial Attitudes and Behaviour.* Cambridge: Cambridge University Press.

Goodin, R.E. (1982). Freedom and the welfare state: Theoretical foundations. *Journal of Social Policy*, 11(2),149-176.

Goodman, J. (1992). The key to pain prevention: The dental model for counseling. *American Counselor,* 1(3), 27-29.

Goodnow, J.J. (1988). Children's household work: its nature and functions. *Psychological Bulletin*, 103 (1), 5-26.

Goodson, I.F. (1983). *School Subjects and Curriculum Change.* London: Croom Helm.

Gorz, A. (1982). *Farewell to the Working Class.* London: Pluto Press.

Gottfredson, L. S. (1981). Circumscription and compromise: A developmental theory of occupational aspirations. *Journal of Counseling Psychology*, 28(6): 545-79.

Graduate Prospects (2005/6). Prospects Directory salary and vacancy survey. *Graduate Market Trends,* Winter, 11-17.

Graham, D. & Tytler, D. (1993). *A Lesson for Us All: the Making of the National Curriculum*. London: Routledge.

Gray, A. (1982). *Trial by Restart.* London: Unemployment Unit, 1987.

Gray, J. (1996). *After Social Democracy.* London: Demos.

Gray, J., McPherson, A.F. & Raffe, D. (1983). *Reconstructions of Secondary Education*. London: Routledge & Kegan Paul.

Greenblat, C.S. (1981). Gaming-simulations for teaching and training: an overview. In Greenblat. C.S. & Duke, R.D. (eds.) *Principles and Practices of Gaming-Simulation.* Beverly Hills, CA: Sage.

Griffin, C. (1985). *Typical Girls?: Young Women from School to the Job Market.* London: Routledge & Kegan Paul.

Grubb, W. N. & Lazerson, M. (1975). Rally round the workplace: Continuities and fallacies in career education. *Harvard Educational Review*, 45(4), 451-74.

Grubb, W.N. & Lazerson, M. (1981). Vocational solutions to youth problems: The persistent frustrations of the American experience. *Educational Analysis*, 3(2), 91-103.

Guidance Council (2000). *Quality Standards for Learning and Work.* Winchester: Guidance Council.

Hague, D. (1991). *Beyond Universities: A New Republic of the Intellect* (Hobart Paper 115). London: Institute of Economic Affairs.

Halls, W. D. (ed.) (1990) *Comparative Education: Contemporary Issues and Trends.* London: Jessica Kingsley / UNESCO.

Halmos, P. (1974). The personal and the political. *British Journal of Guidance and Counselling*, 2(2), 130-48.

Halsey, A.H. (1975). Sociology and the equality debate. *Oxford Review of Education*, 1(1), 9-23.

Handy, C. (1997). *The Hungry Spirit.* London: Hutchinson.

Handy, C. (1989). *The Age of Unreason.* London: Business Books.

Hansen, J. (1979). The real black economy. *New Society*, 884.

Harding, G. (1994). *From Global to Local: Issues and Challenges Facing NGOs.* Durban: Olive.

Hargreaves, D. (1994). *The Mosaic of Learning.* London: Demos.

Harris Committee (2001). *Developing Modern Higher Education Careers Services.* Review chaired by Sir Martin Harris. London: Department for Education and Employment.

Harrison, R. (1976). The demoralising experience of prolonged unemployment. *Department of Employment Gazette,* 84(4).

Harvey, L. (2001). Defining and measuring employability. *Quality in Higher Education, 7(2),* 97-109.

Harvey, L., Geall, V. & Moon, S. (1998). *Work Experience: Expanding Opportunities for Undergraduates.* Birmingham: Centre for Research into Quality, University of Central England in Birmingham.

Harvey, L., Locke, W. & Morey, A. (2002). *Enhancing Employability, Recognising Diversity: Making Links between Higher Education and the World of Work.* London: Universities UK/Careers Services Unit.

Harvey, L., Moon, S., Geall, V. & Bower, R. (1997). *Graduates' Work: Organisational Change and Students' Attributes.* Birmingham: Centre for Research into Quality, University of Central England in Birmingham & Association of Graduate Recruiters.

Hashizume, L. & Crozier, S. (1994). A feminine definition of career achievement. In Crozier, S., Gallivan, J. & Lalande, V. (eds.) *Women, Girls and Achievement.* North York, ON: Captus Press.

Hatch, S. (1972). Change and dissent in the universities: an examination of the sources of protest. In Butcher, H.J. & Rudd, E. (eds.) *Contemporary Problems in Higher Education.* London: McGraw-Hill.

Havel, V. (1994). Foreword. In Barr, N. (ed.) *Labor Markets and Social Policy in Central and Eastern Europe: the Transition and Beyond.* Oxford: Oxford University Press.

Hawkins, P. & Winter, J. (1995). *Skills for Graduates in the 21st Century.* Cambridge: Association of Graduate Recruiters.

Hawthorn, R. (1995). *First Steps: A Quality Standards Framework for Guidance Across All Sectors.* London: RSA/National Advisory Council for Careers and Educational Guidance.

Hayek, F.A. (1944). *The Road to Serfdom.* London: Routledge.

Hayes, J. & Nutmann, P. (1981). *Understanding the Unemployed.* London: Tavistock.

Hayes, R. (1986). Men's decisions to enter or avoid nontraditional occupations. *Career Development Quarterly*, 35(2), 89-101.

Hayt, D.P. (1965). *The Relationship Between College Grades and Adult Achievement: A Review of the Literature.* Iowa City: American College Testing Program.

Hedges, A.(1978). *Employment and the Small Firm: A Survey of Covent Garden.* London: Social and Community Planning Research.

Heginbotham, H. (1951). *The Youth Employment Service.* London: Methuen.

Henry, F. (1978). *The Hidden Economy: the Context and Control of Borderline Crime.* London: Robertson.

Her Majesty's Inspectorate (1983). *A Survey of Work Experience for Year V Pupils.* Cardiff: Welsh Office.

Her Majesty's Inspectorate (1988a). *Careers Education and Guidance from 5 to 16.* Curriculum Matters 10. London: HMSO.

Her Majesty's Inspectorate (1990). *Work Experience and Work Shadowing for 14-19 Students: Some Aspects of Good Practice 1988/1989.* London: Department of Education and Science.

Her Majesty's Inspectorate (1992). *The Preparation of Girls for Adult and Working Life.* London: Department for Education.

Herriot, P. & Pemberton, C. (1995). *New Deals: The Revolution in Managerial Careers.* Chichester: John Wiley & Sons.

Herriot, P. & Pemberton, C. (1996). Contracting careers. *Human Relations*, 49, 757-790.

Herriot, P. (1992). *The Career Management Challenge.* London: Sage.

Hesketh, B. & Kennedy, L. (1991). Changes and responsibilities: Confronting careers guidance in New Zealand. *British Journal of Guidance and Counselling*, 19(3), 246-257.

Hiebert, B. & Bezanson, L. (eds.) (2000). *Making Waves: Career Development and Public Policy.* Ottawa: Canadian Career Development Foundation.

Higher Education Funding Council for England (2001). *Indicators of Employment.* Bristol: HEFCE.

Hillage, J. & Pollard, E. (1998). *Employability: Developing a Framework for Policy Analysis.* Research Report RR85. London: Department for Education and Employment.

Hirsch, F. (1977). *Social Limits to Growth.* London: Routledge & Kegan Paul.

Hirsh, W. & Jackson, C. (1996). *Strategies for Career Development: Promise, Practice and Pretence* (IES Report 305). Brighton: Institute for Employment Studies.

Hirsh, W., Kidd, J.M. & Watts, A.G. (1998). *Constructs of Work Used in Career Guidance* (NICEC Project Report). Cambridge: Careers Research & Advisory Centre.

HM Government (2013). *Inspiration Vision Statement.* London: HM Government.

Hodge, S. (1987). *Work Experience – Employer's Viewpoints*. Unpublished paper, Department of Education, University of Warwick (mimeo).

Hodgson, A. (1999). Analysing education and training policies for tackling social exclusion. In A. Hayton (ed.) *Tackling Disaffection and Social Exclusion: Education Perspectives and Policies*. London: Kogan Page.

Hodkinson, P. & Issitt, M. (eds.) (1995). *The Challenge of Competence: Professionalism Through Vocational Education and Training*. London: Cassell.

Hodkinson, P., Sparkes, A.C. & Hodkinson, H. (1996). *Triumphs and Tears: Young People, Markets and the Transition from School to Work*. London: Fulton.

Hofstede, G. (1984). *Culture's Consequences*. Beverly Hills, CA: Sage.

Holland, J. (1997). *Making Vocational Choices: A Theory of Vocational Personalities and Work Environments*, 3rd edn. Odessa, FL: Psychological Assessment Resources, Inc.

Holland, J. L. (1973). *Making Vocational Choices: A Theory of Careers*. Englewood Cliffs, NJ: Prentice-Hall.

Holmes, L. (2001). Reconsidering graduate employability: the 'graduate identity' approach. *Quality in Higher Education, 7(2)*, 111-119.

Holmes, S., Jamieson, I. & Perry, J. (1983). *Work Experience in the School Curriculum*. London: Schools Council/Trident Trust.

Hooley, T. (2014). 'We wanted to change that particular part of the world': the role of academics in the career development field, learning from the career of Tony Watts. *Journal of the National Institute for Career Education and Counselling*, 33, 37-43.

House of Commons Education Committee (2013). *Careers Guidance for Young People: the Impact of the New Duty on Schools.* HC 632-1. London: Stationery Office.

Hustler, D., Ball, B., Carter, K., Halsall, R., Ward, R. & Watts, A.G. (1998). *Developing Career Management Skills in Higher Education*. NICEC Project Report. Cambridge: Careers Research and Advisory Centre.

Hutton, W. (1995). *The State We're In*. London: Cape.

Hyde, C. (2014). *A Beacon for Guidance.* Derby: International Centre for Guidance Studies, University of Derby.

Ianni, F.A.J. (1989). *The Search for Structure: a Report on American Youth Today*. New York: Free Press.

Illich, I. (1971). *Deschooling Society*. London: Calder & Boyars.

Illich, I. (1977). *Disabling Professions*. London: Boyars.

Incomes Data Services (1982). *Cutting the Working Week*. Study 264. London: IDS.

Institute of Careers Guidance (ICG) (n.d.). *The Best Start in Life for Every Young Person*. Stourbridge: ICG.

Institute of Careers Officers (1972). *About Unemployed Young People*. Bromsgrove: Institute of Careers Officers.

Institute of Personnel Management (1988). *Improving Work Experience: A Statement of Principles*. London: IPM.

International Labour Organisation (1972). *Employment, Incomes and Equality: a Strategy for Increasing Productive Employment in Kenya*. Geneva: ILO.

Ipaye, B. (1989). Vocational guidance in Nigeria. *Prospects,* 69, 65-73.

Ishiyama, F. I. & Kitayama, A. (1994). Overworked and career-centered. Self-validation among the Japanese: Psychosocial issues and counselling implications. *International Journal for the Advancement of Counselling,* 17(3), 167-82.

Jackson, B. & Marsden, D. (1962). *Education and the Working Class.* London: Routledge & Kegan Paul.

Jackson, C. (1993). The case for diversity in computer-aided careers guidance systems: a response to Watts. *British Journal of Guidance and Counselling,* 21(2), 189–195.

Jahoda, G. & Chalmers, A.D. (1963). The Youth Employment Service: a consumer perspective. *Occupational Psychology,* 37 (1), 165-174.

Jahoda, M., Lazarsfeld, P. F. & Zeisel, H. (1972; first pub. 1933). *Marienthal: the Sociography of an Unemployed Community.* London: Tavistock.

Jamieson, I. & Lightfoot, M. (1982). *Schools and Industry.* London: Methuen.

Jamieson, I., Miller, A. & Watts, A.G. (1988). *Mirrors of Work: Work Simulations in Schools.* Lewes: Falmer.

Jessup, G. (1991). *Outcomes: NVQs and the Emerging Model of Education and Training.* London: Falmer.

Joint Board for Pre-Vocational Education (1985). *The Certificate of Pre-Vocational Education Handbook.* London: JBPVE.

Jones, K. (1989). *Right Turn: the Conservative Revolution in Education.* London: Hutchinson Radius.

Johnston, L., MacDonald, R., Mason, P., Ridley, L. & Webster, C. (2000). *Snakes and Ladders: Young People, Transitions and Social Exclusion.* Bristol: Policy Press.

Kanter, R.M. (1989). *When Giants Learn to Dance.* New York: Simon & Schuster.

Katz, M. (1963). *Decisions and Values.* New York: College Entrance Examination Board.

Katz, M. R. (1969). Can computers make guidance decisions for students? *College Board Review,* 72, Summer.

Katz, M. (1993). *Computer-Assisted Career Decision Making: The Guide in the Machine.* Hillsdale, NI: Erlbaum.

Keller, F.J. & Viteles, M.S. (1937). *Vocational Guidance throughout the World.* London: Cape.

Kelly, P. (2000). The dangerousness of youth-at-risk: the possibilities of surveillance and intervention in uncertain times. *Journal of Adolescence,* 23(4), 463-476.

Kidd, J. M. (1996). Career planning within work organisations. In Watts, A.G., Law, B., Killeen, J., Kidd, J.M. & Hawthorn, R. *Rethinking Careers Education and Guidance: Theory, Policy and Practice.* London: Routledge.

Killeen, J. (1996a). Career theory. In Watts, A.G., Law, B., Killeen, J., Kidd, J.M. & Hawthorn, R. *Rethinking Careers Education and Guidance: Theory, Policy and Practice.* London: Routledge.

Killeen, J. (1996b). The learning and economic outcomes of guidance. In Watts, A.G., Law, B., Killeen, J., Kidd, J.M. & Hawthorn, R. *Rethinking Careers Education and Guidance: Theory, Policy and Practice.* London: Routledge.

Killeen, J. (1996c). The social context of guidance. In Watts, A.G., Law, B., Killeen, J., Kidd, J.M. & Hawthorn, R. *Rethinking Careers Education and Guidance: Theory, Policy and Practice.* London: Routledge.

Killeen, J. & Kidd, J.M. (1991). *Learning Outcomes of Guidance: a Review of Research* (Research Paper No. 85). Sheffield: Employment Department.

Killeen, J., Sammons, P. & Watts, A.G. (1999). *The Effects of Careers Education and Guidance on Attainment and Associated Behaviour.* Cambridge: National Institute for Careers Education and Counselling.

Killeen, J., Watts, A.G. & Kidd, J.M. (1998). *The Social Benefits of Guidance: a Preliminary Exploration.* Cambridge: National Institute for Careers Education and Counselling.

Killeen, J., Watts, A.G. & Kidd, J. (1999). *Social Benefits of Career Guidance* (NICEC Briefing). Cambridge: Careers Research and Advisory Centre.

Killeen, J., White, M. & Watts, A.G. (1992). *The Economic Value of Careers Guidance.* London: Policy Studies Institute.

Kim, Y. M. (1987). Student guidance in secondary education in Latin America. *Prospects,* 17(1), 107-14.

King, D.S. (1987). *The New Right: Politics, Markets and Citizenship.* London: Macmillan.

King, Z. (2004). Career self-management: its nature, causes and consequences. *Journal of Vocational Behavior,* 65, 112-133.

Knight, P. & Yorke, M. (2003). *Assessment, Learning and Employability.* Maidenhead: Society for Research into Higher Education/Open University Press.

Knight, P. & Yorke, M. (2004). *Learning, Curriculum and Employability in Higher Education.* London: RoutledgeFalmer.

Kolb, D. A. (1984). *Experiential Learning.* Englewood Cliffs, NJ: Prentice-Hall.

Krumboltz, J. D. (1994). Improving career development from a social learning perspective. In Savickas, M. L. & Lent, R. W. (eds.) *Convergence in Career Development Theories: Implications for Science and Practice.* Palo Alto, CA: Consulting Psychologists Press.

Krumboltz, J.D. & Sheppard, L.D. (1969). Vocational problem-solving experiences. In Krumboltz, J.D. & Thoresen, C.E. (eds.): *Behavioral Counseling: Cases and Techniques.* New York: Holt, Rinehart & Winston.

Kuder, F. (1977). *Activity Interests and Occupational Choice.* Chicago: Science Research Associates.

Labour Party (1997). *A Successful Career: the Careers Service in the 21st Century.* Unapproved draft policy statement. London: Labour Party.

Lapan, R.T., Gysbers, N.C. & Sun, Y. (1997). The impact of more fully implemented guidance programs on the school experiences of high school students: a statewide evaluation study. *Journal of Counseling and Development,* 75, 292-301.

Law, B. (1981a). Careers theory: a third dimension? In Watts, A.G., Super, D.E. & Kidd, J.M. (eds.) *Career Development in Britain.* Cambridge: CRAC/Hobsons.

Law, B. (1981b). Community Interaction: a "mid-range" focus for theories of career development in young adults. *British Journal of Guidance and Counselling,* 9(2), 142-158.

Law, B. (1996). A career-learning theory. In Watts, A.G., Law, B., Killeen, J., Kidd, J.M. & Hawthorn, R. *Rethinking Careers Education and Guidance: Theory, Policy and Practice.* London: Routledge.

Law, B. (2000). As Peter was saying before he was so rudely interrupted. *Career Research and Development,* 1, 25-27.

Law, B. & Watts, A.G. (1977). *Schools, Careers and Community.* London: Church Information Office.

Lee, C. (2000). Cybercounseling and empowerment: bridging the digital divide. In Bloom, J.W. & Walz, G.R. (eds.) *Cybercounseling and Cyberlearning: Strategies and Resources for the Millennium* (pp. 85–93). Alexandria, VA: American Counseling Association/CAPS.

Lee, D., Marsden, D., Richman, P. & Duncombe, J. (1990). *Scheming for Youth: a Study of YTS in the Enterprise Culture.* Milton Keynes: Open University Press.

Lee, G. & Wrench, J. (1983). *Skill Seekers: Black Youth, Apprenticeships and Disadvantage.* Leicester: National Youth Bureau.

Le Fanu, J. (2000). Proud to be ignorant. *New Statesman*, 7 February.

Le Grand, J. (1989). Markets, welfare, and equality. In Le Grand, J. & Estrin, S. (eds.) *Market Socialism.* Oxford: Clarendon.

Le Grand, J. & Estrin, S. (eds.) (1989). *Market Socialism.* Oxford: Clarendon.

Levitan, S. & Johnston, W.B. (1973). *Work is Here to Stay, Alas.* Utah: Olympus

Levitas, R. (1998). *The Inclusive Society?: Social Exclusion and New Labour.* Basingstoke: Macmillan.

Lewin, K. (1951). *Field Theory in Social Sciences.* New York: Harper & Row.

Little, B. & ESECT colleagues (2005). *Part-Time Students and Employability.* Learning and Employability Series Two. York: Higher Education Academy.

Little, B. & ESECT colleagues (2006). *Employability and Work-Based Learning.* Learning and Employability Series. York: Higher Education Academy.

Little, B., Harvey, L., Brennan, J., Moon, S., Pierce, D. & Marlow-Hayne, N. (2002). *Nature and Extent of Undergraduates' Work Experience.* Bristol: Higher Education Funding Council for England.

Loughary, J.W. & Ripley, T.M. (1974). *This Isn't Quite What I Had in Mind*. Eugene, OR: United Learning Corporation.

Lutz, B., Meriaux, B., Mukherjee, S. & Rehn, G. (1976). *Outlook for Employment in the European Community to 1980*. Brussels: Commission of the European Communities.

Macafee, K. (1980). A glimpse of the hidden economy in the national accounts. *Economic Trends*, 316, 147-161.

Machula, C.S. (1989). The Soviet school reforms of 1984: making career development a matter of state control. *Career Development Quarterly*, 38(1), 39-56.

MacLennan, E., Fitz, J. & Sullivan, J. (1985). *Working Children*. London: Low Pay Unit.

Madahar, L. & Offer, M. (2004). *Managing E-Guidance: Interventions within HE Careers Services.* Manchester: Graduate Prospects/Higher Education Careers Services Unit.

Madsen, B. (1986). Occupational guidance and social change. *International Journal for the Advancement of Counselling*, 9(1), 97-112.

Maguire, M. (2005). *Delivering Quality.* London: Department for Education and Skills.

Maguire, M.J. & Ashton, D.N. (1981). Employers' perceptions and use of educational qualifications. *Educational Analysis*, 3(2), 25-36.

Maizels, J. (1970). *Adolescent Needs and the Transition from School to Work*. London: Athlone.

Manpower Services Commission (MSC) (1976). *Towards a Comprehensive Manpower Policy.* London: MSC.

Manpower Services Commission (MSC) (1977a). *Young People and Work.* London: MSC.

Manpower Services Commission (MSC) (1977b). *The New Special Programmes for Unemployed People: The Next Steps.* London: MSC.

Manpower Services Commission (1978). *Review* of *Occupational Guidance.* London: MSC.

Manpower Services Commission (1985). *Work-Based Projects in YTS.* Sheffield: MSC.

Manpower Services Commission (1988). *The Human Impact of Restart Courses* (Psychological Services Report 260/S). Sheffield: MSC.

Mari, S. K. (1982). Cultural and socio-political influences on counseling and career guidance: the case of Arabs in the Jewish state. *International Journal for the Advancement of Counselling,* 5(4), 247-63.

Marsden, D. (1975). *Workless.* Harmondsworth: Penguin.

Martin, J. & Roberts, C. (1984). *Women and Employment: A Lifetime Perspective.* London: HMSO.

Marx, K. (1963 edn.). *Selected Writings In Sociology and Social Philosophy* (ed. T. B. Bottomore & M. Rubel). Harmondsworth: Penguin.

McCash, P. (2006). We're all career researchers now: breaking open careers education and DOTS. *British Journal of Guidance and Counselling, 43(4),* 429-449.

McKinlay, B. (1989). Information systems in career development: history and prospects. In Watts, A.G. (ed.) *Computers in Careers Guidance.* Cambridge: Careers Research and Advisory Centre.

McLennan, N. (1999). NHS Direct: here and now. *Archives of Disease in Childhood,* 81, 376–378.

McNair, S. (1990). Guidance and the education and training market. In Watts, A.G. (ed.) *Guidance and Educational Change.* Cambridge: CRAC/Hobsons.

Merton, B. (1998). *Finding the Missing.* Leicester: Youth Work Press.

Merton, B. & Parrott, A. (1999). *Only Connect.* Leicester: National Institute of Adult Continuing Education.

Metcalf, D. (1976). *Youth unemployment in Britain.* Paper prepared for the Ditchley Park Conference on Young People in Contemporary Industrial Society (October).

Metcalf, H., Walling, A. & Fogarty, M. (1994). *Individual Commitment to Learning: Employers' Attitudes* (Research Series No. 40). London: Employment Department.

Milburn, A. (2009). *Unleashing Aspiration: The Final Report of the Panel on Fair Access to the Professions.* London: Cabinet Office.

Miller, A., Watts, A.G. & Jamieson, I. (1991). *Rethinking Work Experience.* London: Falmer.

Miller, J., Taylor, B. & Watts, A.G. (1983). *Towards a Personal Guidance Base.* London: Further Education Unit.

Ministry of Education (1964). *Statistics of Education 1962, Part Three.* London: HMSO.

Mishan, E. J. (1977). *The Economic Growth Debate: an Assessment.* London: Allen & Unwin.

Mitchell, K.E., Levin, A.S. & Krumboltz, J.D. (1999). Planned happenstance: Constructing unexpected career opportunities. *Journal of Counseling and Development,* 77(2), 115-124.

Moon, J. (2004). *Reflection and Employability.* Learning and Employability Series No.4. York: Learning and Teaching Support Network.

Moon, J.A. (1999). *Reflection in Learning and Professional Development: Theory and Practice.* London: Kogan Page.

Morocco, J. (1979). Arab countries. In Drapela, V. (ed.) *Guidance and Counselling Around the World.* Washington, DC: University Press of America.

Moreland, N. (2006). *Entrepreneurship and Higher Education: an Employability Perspective.* Learning and

Employability Series. York: Higher Education Academy.

Morey, A., Harvey, L., Williams, J., Saldana, A. & Mena, P. (2003). *HE Careers Services and Diversity*. Manchester: Careers Services Unit.

Morgan, S. & Hughes, D. (1999). *New Start Paving the Way for the Learning Gateway: an Evaluation of Second Round Projects*. London: Department for Education and Employment.

Morris, B. (1955). Guidance as a concept in educational philosophy. In *The Year Book of Education 1955*. London: Evans.

Morris, M. (1996). *Careers Education and Guidance Provision for 13 and 14 Year Olds* (QADU/RD10). London: Department for Education and Employment.

Morrison, P. (1983). Parting clouds – or all our futures? *Careers Journal*, 4(2), 6-11.

Morton-Williams, R. & Finch, S. (1968). *Young School Leavers* (Schools Council Enquiry One). London: HMSO.

Mukherjee, S. (1974). *There's Work To Be Done*. London: HMSO.

Mukherjee, S. (1976). *Unemployment Costs*. London: PEP.

Murray, C. (1990). *The Emerging British Underclass*. London: Institute of Economic Affairs.

National Assembly for Wales Policy Unit (2000). *Extending Entitlement: Supporting Young People in Wales*. Cardiff: National Assembly for Wales.

National Association of Citizens Advice Bureaux (1997). *Flexibility Abused*. London: NACAB.

National Audit Office (1997). *Contracting Out of Careers Services in England*. London: NAO.

National Career Development Association (1997). *NCDA Guidelines for the Use of the Internet for Provision of Career Information and Planning Services*. Columbus, OH: NCDA.

National Careers Council (2013). *An Aspirational Nation: Creating a Culture Change in Careers Provision*. London: NCC.

National Committee of Inquiry into Higher Education (1997). *Higher Education in the Learning Society* (Dearing Report). London: NCIHE.

National Curriculum Council (1990). *Curriculum Guidance 6: Careers Education and Guidance*. York: NCC.

National Educational Guidance Initiative (1990). *Educational Guidance for Adults in 1989*. Leicester: Unit for the Development of Adult Continuing Education.

National Joint Advisory Council (1958). *Training for Skill* (Carr Report). London: HMSO.

National Youth Bureau (1977). Comment. *Youth in Society*, 20.

National Youth Employment Council (1974). *Unqualified, Untrained and Unemployed* (Report of a Working Party). London: HMSO.

Nicholas, E. J. (1983). *Issues in Education: a Comparative Analysis*. London: Harper & Row.

Niskanen, W.A. (1971). *Bureaucracy and Representative Government*. Chicago, IL: Aldine-Atherton.

Nowikova, T. (1991). Problems of vocational orientation in the USSR. *Educational and Vocational Guidance*, 52, 8-15.

Oakeshott, M. (1990). *Educational Guidance and Curriculum Change*. London: Further Education Unit/Unit for the Development of Adult Continuing Education.

Offer, M. (1997). *A Review of the Use of Computer-Assisted Guidance and the Internet in Europe*. Dublin: National Centre for Guidance in Education.

Offer, M. (1998). "Guidance" websites: we're here, because we're here, because we're here? *Newscheck*, 9(4), 13-14.

Offer, M. (2003). *Report on the CSU/NICEC Careers Service Web Site Design Project 2001-2003*. Manchester: Higher Education Careers Services Unit .

Offer, M. & Sampson, J. P. (1999). Quality in the content and use of information and communications technology in guidance. *British Journal of Guidance and Counselling*, 27(4), 501–516.

Offer, M., Sampson, J.P. & Watts, A.G. (2001). *Careers Services: Technology and the Future*. Manchester: Higher Education Careers Services Unit.

Offer, M. & Watts, A.G. (2000). *The Use of Information and Communications Technologies in the Connexions Service* (CRAC/NICEC Conference Briefing). Cambridge: Careers Research and Advisory Centre.

Office for Standards in Education (Ofsted) (1998). *National Survey of Careers Education and Guidance*. London: Ofsted.

O'Keefe, D.J. (1994). *Truancy in English Secondary Schools*. London: HMSO.

Oliver, L. W. & Zack, J. S. (1999). Career assessment on the Internet: an exploratory study. *Journal of Career Assessment*, 7(4), 323–356.

Oliver, L.W. & Spokane, A.R. (1988). Career intervention outcomes: What contributes to client gain? *Journal of Counseling Psychology*, 35, 447-462.

Organisation for Economic Co-operation and Development (1998). *Maintaining Prosperity in an Ageing Society*. Paris: OECD

Organisation for Economic Co-operation and Development (2000a). *Learning to Bridge the Digital Divide*. Paris: OECD.

Organisation for Economic Co-operation and Development (2000b). *From Initial Education to Working Life: Making the Transition Work*. Paris: OECD

Organisation for Economic Co-operation and Development (2000c). *Reforms for an Ageing Society*. Paris: OECD.

Organisation for Economic Co-operation and Development (2001a). *E-learning: the Partnership Challenge*. Paris: OECD.

Organisation for Economic Co-operation and Development (2001b). Lifelong learning for all: Policy challenges. In *Education Policy Analysis*. Paris: OECD.

Organisation for Economic Co-operation and Development (2002). Rethinking human capital. In *Education Policy Analysis* (pp. 117–131). Paris: OECD.

Organisation for Economic Co-operation and Development (2003). *Beyond Rhetoric: Adult Learning Policies and Practice*. Paris: OECD.

Organisation for Economic Co-operation and Development (2004). *Career Guidance and Public Policy: Bridging the Gap*. Paris: OECD.

Orwell, G. (1962 [first published 1937]). *The Road to Wigan Pier*. London: Penguin.

O'Toole, J. (principal author) (1973). *Work in America*. Cambridge, MA: MIT Press.

Outer Policy Research Circle (1979). *Policing the Hidden Economy*. London: OPRC.

Pahl, R.E. (1980). Employment, work and the domestic division of labour. *International Journal of Urban and Regional Research*, 4(1), 1-20.

Pahl, R. E. (1984). *Divisions of Labour.* Oxford: Blackwell.

Panel on Fair Access to the Professions (2009). *Unleashing Aspiration: the Final Report of the Panel on Fair Access to the Professions.* London: Panel on Fair Access to the Professions.

Parker, H. (1989). *Instead of the Dole*. London: Routledge.

Parker, S. (1976). *The Sociology of Leisure.* London: Allen & Unwin.

Parsons, C. (1999). *Education, Exclusion and Citizenship*. London: Routledge.

Parsons, F. (1909). *Choosing a Vocation.* Boston: Houghton Mifflin.

Patterson, C. H. (1978). Cross-cultural or intercultural counseling or psychotherapy. *International Journal for the Advancement of Counselling,* 1(3), 231-47.

Patton, W. & McMahon, M. (1999). *Career Development and Systems Theory: a New Relationship.* Pacific Grove, CA: Brooks/Cole.

Payne, J. (2000). *Young People Not in Education, Employment or Training* (Research Report RR201). London: Department for Education and Employment.

Pearce, N. & Hillman, J. (1998). *Wasted Youth: Raising Achievement and Tackling Social Exclusion*. London: Institute for Public Policy Research.

Pedagogy for Employability Group (2006). *Pedagogy for Employability.* Learning and Employability Series. York: Higher Education Academy.

Percival, F. & Ellington, H.I. (1980). The Place of Case Studies in the Simulation/ Gaming Field. In Race, P. & Brook, D. (eds.) *Perspectives on Academic Gaming and Simulation 5: Simulation and Gaming for the 1980s.* London: Kogan Page.

Perkin, H. (1989). *The Rise of Professional Society: England Since 1880.* London: Routledge.

Peterson, A.D.C. (1975). Education for Work or for Leisure? In Haworth, J.T. & Smith, M.A. (eds.) *Work and Leisure*. London: Lepus.

Peterson, G.W., Sampson, J.P. & Reardon, R.C. (1991). *Career Development and Services: a Cognitive Approach.* Pacific Grove, CA: Brooks/Cole.

Phillips, D. (1973). Young and unemployed in a Northern city. In Weir, D. (ed.) *Men and Work in Modern Britain*. London: Fontana.

Pierce, D. (2002). *Employability: higher education and careers services*. Paper prepared for the Association of Graduate Careers Advisory Services.

Piper, H. & Piper, J. (1998/99). `Disaffected youth': A wicked issue: a worse label. *Youth and Policy*, 62, 32-43.

Plant, P. (1990). *Transnational Vocational Guidance and Training for Young People and Adults*. Berlin: CEDEFOP.

Plant, P. (1997). The evolving role of the guidance counsellor. *Educational and Vocational Guidance Bulletin*, 59, 30-34.

Porter, M. (1990). *The Competitive Advantage of Nations*. London: Macmillan.

Pratt, J., Broomfield, J. & Seale, C. (1984). *Option Choice: A Question of Equal Opportunity*. Windsor:

NFER-Nelson.

Prout, G. (1983). Careers. In Whyld, J. (ed.). *Sexism in the Secondary Curriculum*. London: Harper & Row.

Pryor, R. G. L. (1991). When the luck runs out: Policy challenges confronting careers guidance in Australia. *British Journal of Guidance and Counselling,* 19(3), 283-97.

Pulay, G. (1994). The role of counselling in occupational policy. *Educational and Vocational Guidance Bulletin*, 56, 4-6.

QAA (2001a). *Code of Practice for the Assurance of Academic Quality and Standards in Higher Education: Career Education, Information and Guidance*. Gloucester: Quality Assurance Agency for Higher Education.

QAA (2001b). *Guidelines for HE Progress Files.* Gloucester: Quality Assurance Agency for Higher Education.

Ranson, S. & Ribbins, P. (1988). *Servicing Careers in the Post-Employment Society*. Lewes: Falmer.

Rapaport, A. & Channah, A. (1970). *Prisoners Dilemma: a Study in Conflict or Co-operation*. Michigan: University of Michigan Press.

Raven, J. (1977). *Education, Values and Society.* London: Lewis.

Rawls, J. (1972). *A Theory of Justice*. Oxford: Oxford University Press.

Rees, G., Williamson, H. & Istance, D. (1996). `Status zero' : A study of jobless school-leavers in South Wales. *Research Papers in Education*, 11(2), 219-235.

Rees, T. (1988). Education for enterprise: the state and alternative employment for young people. *Journal of Education Policy*, 3(1), 9-22.

Rees, T. (1992). *Women and the Labour Market*. London: Routledge.

Rees, T., Bartlett, W. & Watts, A.G. (1996). *The marketisation of guidance services in the UK, France and Germany*. Paper delivered to a conference on "Research on Lifelong Learning: Implications for Policy and Practice" held at the University of Newcastle, November.

Rehn, G. (1974). Towards flexibility in working life. *Universities Quarterly*, 28 (3), 276-286.

Reich, R. B. (1991). *The Work of Nations*. London: Simon and Schuster.

Rennie, J., Lunzer, E.A. & Williams, W.T. (1974). *Social Education: an Experiment in Four Secondary Schools*. Schools Council Working Paper 51. London: Evans/Methuen.

Reubens, B. (1977). *Bridges to Work: International Comparisons of Transition Services*. Montclair, NJ: Allanheld, Osmun.

Reuchlin, M. (1964). *Pupil Guidance: Facts and Problems*. Strasbourg: Council for Cultural Co-operation of the Council of Europe.

Rifkin, J. (1995). *The End of Work.* New York: Tarcher & Putnam.

Ritook, M. (1993). Career development in Hungary at the beginning of the 90s. *Journal of Career Development*, 20(1), 33-40.

Roberts, K. (1967). The incidence and effects of spare-time employment amongst school-children. *Vocational Aspect of Education,* 19(43), 129-136.

Roberts, K. (1971). *From School to Work: a Study of the Youth Employment Service*. Newton Abbot: David and Charles.

Roberts, K. (1977). The social conditions, consequences and limitations of careers guidance. *British Journal* of Guidance and Counselling, 5(1), 1-9.

Roberts, K. (1981). The sociology of work entry and occupational choice. In Watts, A.G., Super, D.E., & Kidd, J.M. (eds.) *Career Development in Britain*. Cambridge: CRAC/Hobson.

Roberts, K, (1982). *Automation, Unemployment and the Distribution of Income.* Maastricht, Netherlands: European Centre for Work and Society.

Roberts, K. (2000). Cause for optimism. *Careers Guidance Today*, 8(5), 25-27.

Roberts, K., Dench, S. & Richardson, D. (1987). *The Changing Structure of Youth Labour Markets* (Research Paper No. 59). London: Department of Employment.

Roberts, K., Duggan, J. & Noble, M. (1981). *Unregistered Youth Unemployment and Outreach Careers Work* (Research Paper No. 3). London: Department of Employment.

Roberts, K., Noble, M. & Duggan, J. (1982). Youth unemployment: an old problem or a new life-style? *Leisure Studies*, 1, 171-182.

Robertson, D. (1994). *Choosing to Change*. London: Higher Education Quality Council.

Robinson, P. (1999). Education, training and the youth labour market. In Gregg, P. & Wadsworth, J. (eds.), *The State of Working Britain*. Manchester: Manchester University Press.

Rogers, C. (1961). *On Becoming a Person*. London: Constable.

Room, G. (1995). *Beyond the Threshold: the Measurement and Analysis of Social Exclusion*. Bristol: Policy Press.

Rose, N. & Miller, P. (1992). Political power beyond the state: Problematics of government. *British Journal of Sociology*, 43, 173-205.

Rothbard, M. (1977). *Power and Market.* Kansas City: Sheed Andrews & McMeel.

Rousseau, D.M. (1995). *Psychological Contracts in Organizations*. Beverly Hills, CA: Sage.

Rowley, G. & Purcell, K. (2001). Up to the job? Graduates' perceptions of the UK higher education careers service. *Higher Education Quarterly, 55(4),* 416-435.

Rubber and Plastics Processing Industry Training Board (1976). *School Curricula for a Changing World.* Brentford, Middlesex: Rubber and Plastics Processing Industry Training Board.

Ruben, B.D. (1973) *The When and Why of Gaming: a Taxonomy of Experience Based Learning Systems*. Paper presented at the 12th Annual Meeting of the National Gaming Council and the 4th Annual Meeting of the International Simulation and Gaming Association (mimeo).

Runciman, W. G. (1966). *Relative Deprivation and Social Justice*. London: Routledge & Kegan Paul.

Russell, B. (1935). *In Place of Idleness, and Other Essays.* London: Allen & Unwin.

Sampson, J. P. (1999a). Integrating Internet-based distance guidance with services provided in career centers. *Career Development Quarterly*, 47(3), 243–254.

Sampson, J. P. (1999b). *Effective design and use of Internet-based career resources and services: a North American perspective.* Paper presented at the International Association for Educational and Vocational Guidance Conference, Wellington, New Zealand, January.

Sampson, J. P., Palmer, M. & Watts, A.G. (1999b). *Who Needs Guidance?* Derby: Centre for Guidance Studies, University of Derby.

Sampson, J. P., Peterson, G. W., Reardon, R. C. & Lenz, J. G. (1999a). *Improving career services through readiness assessment: a cognitive information processing approach.* Unpublished manuscript, Center for the Study of Technology in Counseling and Career Development, Florida State University, Tallahassee, FL.

Saner-Yui, R. & Saner-Yui, L. (1985). Value dimensions in American counseling theory: a Taiwanese-American comparison. *International Journal for the Advancement of Counselling,* 8(2), 137-46.

Saunders, M. (1987). At work in TVEI: students' perceptions of their work experience. In Gleeson, D. (ed.) *TVEI and Secondary Education: A Critical Appraisal*. Milton Keynes: Open University Press.

Saunders, M. (1993). TVEI and the National Curriculum: Culture clash between use and exchange value. *Evaluation and Research in Education*, 7, 107-115.

Savas, E.S. (1987). *Privatisation: the Key to Better Government.* Chatham, NJ: Chatham House.

Savickas, M. (1993). Career counseling in the postmodern era. *Journal of Cognitive Psychotherapy,* 7, 205-215.

Sawdon, A., Pelican, J., Tucker, S. & Rose, C. (1980). *Study of the Transition from School to Working Life* (Second Main Report). London: Youthaid.

Scaff, M. K. & Ting, M. G. (1972). Fu Tao: Guidance in Taiwan Seeks a Value Orientation. *Personnel and Guidance Journal,* 50(8), 645-53.

Scharff, D.E. (1976). Aspects of the transition from school to work. In Hill, J.M.M. & Scharff, D.E. *Between Two Worlds*. London: Careers Consultants.

Schools Council (1972). *Careers Education in the 1970s.* Working Paper 40. London: Schools Council.

Schools Council (1981). *The Practical Curriculum.* Working Paper 70. London: Methuen.

Schulz, R. L. & Sullivan, E. M. (1972). Developments in simulation in social and administrative science. In Guetzcow, H., Kotler, P. & Schulz, R.L. *Simulation in Social and Administrative Science.* Englewood Cliffs, NJ: Prentice-Hall.

Schumacher, E. F. (1973). *Small Is Beautiful.* London: Blond & Briggs.

Scottish Education Department (1961). *From School to Further Education* (Brunton Report). Edinburgh: HMSO.

Sessions, J. A. (1975). Misdirecting career education: a union view. *Vocational Guidance Quarterly*, 23(4), 311-16.

Sharp, J. (1988). Restart and youth unemployment: A chance to begin again?' *Youth and Policy*, 25, Summer.

Shaw, M.E., Corsini, R.J., Blake, R.R. & Mouton, J.S. (1980). *Role Playing: a Practical Manual for Group Facilitators*. San Diego, California: University Associates.

Shilling, C. (1987). Work-experience as a contradictory practice. *British Journal of Sociology of Education,* 8(4).

Sillitoe, K. & Meltzer, H. (1985). *The West Indian School Leaver, Volume 1: Starting Work.* London: HMSO.

Silver, H. (1965). Salaries for students. *Universities Quarterly*, 19(4), 409-413.

Silver, H. (1994). Social exclusion and social solidarity: three paradigms. *International Labour Review, 133*(5-6), 531-578.

Simon, B. (1960). *Studies in the History of Education 1780-1870*. London: Lawrence & Wishart.

Sims, D. (1987). Work experience In TVEI: student views and reactions – a preliminary study. In Hinckley,

S.M., Pole, C.J., Sims, D. & Stoney, S.M. (eds) *The TVEI Experience: Views from Teachers and Students*. Sheffield: Manpower Services Commission.

Skorikov, V. & Vondracek, F.W. (1993). Career development in the Commonwealth of Independent States. *Career Development Quarterly*, 41(4), 314-329.

Sleigh, J. & Boatwright, B. (1979). New technology: the Japanese approach. *Department of Employment Gazette*, 87(7), July.

Smith, A. (1776). *An Enquiry into the Nature and Causes of the Wealth of Nations*. Edinburgh: Black.

Smith, D. (1988). *Industry in the Primary School Curriculum*. London: Falmer Press.

Smith, D. (2010). *Some Sort of Bridge*. Cambridge: Granta Editions.

Smith, D. & Storey, J. (1988). Is it working?: The Wider Concepts of Work project. In Smith, D. (ed.) *Partners in Change: Education-Industry Collaboration*. York: Longman for the School Curriculum Development Committee.

Social Exclusion Unit (SEU) (1999). *Bridging the Gap: New Opportunities for 16-18 Year Olds Not in Education, Employment or Training*. London: Stationery Office.

Sorrentino, C. (1992). Analyzing labor markets in central and eastern Europe. *Monthly Labor Review*, 115(11),43-46.

Spokane, A.R. & Oliver, L.W. (1983). The outcomes of vocational intervention. In Walsh, W.B. & Osipow, S.H. (eds.) *Handbook of Vocational Psychology* (Volume 2). Hillsdale, NJ: Erlbaum.

Steinberg, L.D. (1984). The varieties and effects of work during adolescence. In Lamb, M.E., Brown, A.L. & Rogoff, B. (eds) *Advances in Developmental Psychology*, Volume 3. Hillsdale, NJ: Erlbaum.

Steinberg, L.D., Greenberger, E., Jacobi, M. & Garduque, L. (1981). Early work experience: a partial antidote for adolescent egocentrism. *Journal of Youth and Adolescence*, 10(2).

Steptoe, B. (1990). Fortune favours the solvent! *Phoenix*, 51.

Stone, V., Cotton, D. & Thomas, A. (2000). *Mapping Troubled Lives: Young People Not in Education, Training or Employment* (Research Report RR181). London: Department for Education and Employment.

Stonier, T. (1983). *The Wealth of Information*. London: Methuen.

Streeck, W. (1989). Skills and the limit of neo-liberalism: the enterprise of the future as a place of learning. *Work, Employment and Society*, 3, 89-104.

Streeck, W. (1992). *Social Institutions and Economic Performance*. London: Sage.

Stephens, W. R. (1970). *Social Reform and the Origins of Vocational Guidance*. Washington, DC: National Vocational Guidance Association.

Stronach, I. (1984). Work experience: the sacred anvil. In Varlaam,C. (ed.) *Rethinking Transition: Educational Innovation and the Transition to Adult Life*. London: Falmer Press.

Sultana, R. (1990). Gender, schooling and transformation; evaluating liberal feminist action in education. *New Zealand Journal of Educational Studies*, 25(1), 5-25.

Sultana, R. G. (2003). *Review of Career Guidance Policies in 11 Acceding and Candidate Countries: A Synthesis Report*. Turin: European Training Foundation.

Sultana, R. G. (2004). *Guidance Policies in the Knowledge Society: Trends, Challenges and Responses across Europe*. Thessaloniki: CEDEFOP.

Sultana, R.G. (2014). Pessimism of the intellect, optimism of the will? Troubling the relationship between career guidance and social justice. *International Journal for Educational and Vocational Guidance,* 14(1), 5-19.

Super, D. E. (1954). Guidance: manpower utilization or human development? *Personnel and Guidance Journal,* 33, 8-14.

Super, D.E. (1957). *The Psychology of Careers.* New York: Harper & Row.

Super, D. E. (1974). The broader context of career development and vocational guidance: American trends in world perspective. In Herr, E. L. (ed.) *Vocational Guidance and Human Development.* Boston, MA: Houghton Mifflin.

Super, D. E. (1981). Approaches to occupational choice and career development. In Watts, A.G., Super, D. E. & Kidd, J. M. (eds.) *Career Development In Britain.* Cambridge: CRAC/Hobsons.

Super, D. E. (1985). Guidance and mobility in the educational systems of developing and developed countries. *Educational and Vocational Bulletin,* 44, 24-28.

Swift, B. (1973). Job orientations and the transition from school to work: A longitudinal study. *British Journal of Guidance and Counselling,* 1(1), 62-78.

Tait, A. (1999). Face-to-face and at a distance: the mediation of guidance and counselling through the new technologies. *British Journal of Guidance and Counselling,* 27(1), 113– 122.

Tansey, P.J. & Unwin, D. (1968). *Simulation and Academic Gaming: Highly Motivated Teaching Techniques.* Paper presented to the Conference on Programmed Learning and Educational Technology, University of Glasgow, April.

Theobald, R. (1963). *Free Men and Free Markets.* New York: Potter.

Thomas, H. (1979). Schools, teacher training and the working world: Reflections on case studies. *European Journal of Education,* 14(4), 313-321.

Thompson, E.P. (1967). Time, work-discipline and industrial capitalism. *Past and Present,* 38, 56-97.

Toffler, A. (1980). *The Third Wave.* London: Collins.

Tönnies, F. (1957 edn). *Community and Society* (trans. C. P. Loomis) (first pub. 1887). New York: Harper & Row.

Trades Union Congress (n.d.). *Work Experience Guidelines.* London: TUC.

Turner, F. J. (1921). *The Frontier in American History.* New York: Holt.

Turner, G. (1983). *The Social World of the Comprehensive School.* London: Croom Helm.

Turner, R.H.: (1960). Sponsored and contest mobility and the school system. *American Sociological Review,* 25(5), 855-867.

UNESCO (1980). *Sub-Regional Seminar on the Promotion of Educational and Vocational Guidance in the Arab States: Final Report.* Beirut: UNESCO (mimeo).

Universities UK (2002). *Modernising HE Careers Education: a Framework for Good Practice.* London: Universities UK.

University Grants Committee (1964). *University Appointments Boards* (Heyworth Report). London: HMSO.

Van Dyke, R. (1981). Patriarchy and careers education. *Schooling and Culture,* 10, 16-24.

van Ments, M. (1983). *The Effective Use of Role-Play: a Handbook for Teachers and Trainers.* London: Kogan Page.

Varlaam, C. (1983). Making use of part-time job experience. In Watts, A.G. (ed.) *Work Experience and Schools*. London: Heinemann.

Verma, G.K. & Darby, D.S. (1987). *Race, Training and Employment.* Lewes: Falmer.

Walker, P. (1978). *The Middle Way Forty Years On.* Iain Macleod Memorial Lecture. London: Greater London Young Conservatives.

Wallace, C. (1980). Adapting to unemployment. *Youth in Society*, 40, 6-8.

Wallace, C. (1987). *For Richer, for Poorer: Growing Up In and Out of Work*. London: Tavistock.

Walters, S. (1989). *Education for Democratic Participation*. Cape Town: Centre for Adult and Continuing Education, University of the Western Cape.

Walton, P. (1977). *A Survey of Work Experience in British Secondary Schools*. Stourbridge: Institute of Careers Officers.

Ward, C. & Fyson, A. (1973). *Streetwork*. London: Routledge & Kegan Paul.

Ward, R., Jackson, N. & Strivens, J. (2005). *Progress Files: Are We Achieving Our Goal?* Wigan: Centre for Recording Achievement.

Waterman, R.H.Jr., Waterman, J.A. & Collard, B.A. (1994). Towards a career-resilient workforce. *Harvard Business Review*, 72 (4), 87-95.

Watts, A.G. (1972). *Diversity and Choice in Higher Education*. London: Routledge & Kegan Paul.

Watts, A.G. (1973a). A structure for careers education. In Jackson, R. (ed.) *Careers Guidance: Practice and Problems*. London: Arnold.

Watts, A.G. (1973b). The qualifications spiral. *Sunday Times Magazine,* 7 October.

Watts, A.G. (1977a). Careers education in higher education: Principles and practice. *British Journal of Guidance and Counselling*, 5(2), 167-184.

Watts, A.G. (1977b). A policy for youth? *The Ditchley Journal,* 4(1), 35-50.

Watts, A.G. (1978a). The implications of school-leaver unemployment for careers education in schools. *Journal of Curriculum Studies*, 10(3), 233-250.

Watts, A.G. (1978b). Careers guidance in a developing country: Malaysia. *International Journal for the Advancement of Counselling* 1(2), 97-105.

Watts, A.G. (1980a). Educational and careers guidance services for adults: A review of current provision. *British Journal of Guidance and Counselling,* 8(2), 188-202.

Watts, A.G. (1980b). Careers guidance under apartheid. *International Journal for the Advancement of Counselling*, 3(1), 3-27.

Watts, A.G. (1980c). Careers guidance and public policy. *Careers Journal*, 1(2).

Watts, A.G. (1981a). Careers guidance in Sweden: a British perspective. *International Journal for the Advancement of Counselling* 4(3), 187-207.

Watts, A.G. (1981b). Introduction. In Watts, A.G., Super, D. E. & Kidd, J. M. (eds) *Career Development in Britain*. Cambridge: Careers Research and Advisory Centre/ Hobsons.

Watts, A G. (1981c). Careers education and the informal economies. *British Journal of Guidance and Counselling,* 9(1).

Watts, A.G. (1983a). *Education, Unemployment and the Future of Work.* Milton Keynes: Open University Press.

Watts, A.G. (1983b). Unemployment and "political education" in the Youth Training Scheme. *Liberal Education*, 50, Autumn.

Watts, A.G. (ed.). (1983c). *Work Experience and Schools*. London: Heinemann.

Watts, A.G. (1985). The Japanese "lifetime employment system" and its Implications for careers guidance. *International Journal for the Advancement of Counselling*, 8(2), 91-114.

Watts, A.G. (1986a). *Work Shadowing.* York: Longman for the School Curriculum Development Committee.

Watts, A.G. (1986b). The role of the computer in careers guidance. *International Journal for the Advancement of Counselling*, 9(2), 145–158.

Watts, A.G. (1988a). The changing place of careers guidance in schools. *Prospects,* 18(4), 473-82.

Watts, A.G. (1988b). Changing conceptions of careers guidance and a proposed model for Singapore schools. *Singapore Journal of Education*, 9(1), 28-36.

Watts, A.G. (1992). *Occupational Profiles of Vocational Counsellors in the European Community*. Berlin: CEDEFOP.

Watts, A.G. (1993). The politics and economics of computer-aided careers guidance systems. *British Journal of Guidance and Counselling*, 21(2), 175–188.

Watts, A.G. (1994a). *Lifelong Career Development: Towards a National Strategy for Careers Education and Guidance.* CRAC Occasional Paper. Cambridge: Careers Research and Advisory Centre/Hobsons.

Watts, A.G. (1994b). *A Strategy for Developing Careers Guidance Services for Adults*. Cambridge: Careers Research and Advisory Centre.

Watts, A.G. (1995). Applying market principles to the delivery of careers guidance services: a critical review. *British Journal of Guidance and Counselling*, 23(1), 69-81.

Watts, A.G. (1996a). Computers in guidance. In Watts, A.G., Law, B., Killeen, J., Kidd, J.M. & Hawthorn, R. *Rethinking Careers Education and Guidance: Theory, Policy and Practice.* London: Routledge.

Watts, A.G. (1996b). Careers guidance and public policy. In Watts, A.G., Law, B., Killeen, J., Kidd, J.M. & Hawthorn, R. *Rethinking Careers Education and Guidance: Theory, Policy and Practice.* London: Routledge.

Watts, A.G. (1996c). A framework for comparing careers guidance systems in different countries. *Educational and Vocational Guidance Bulletin*, 58, 53-63.

Watts, A.G. (1996d). *Careerquake.* London: Demos.

Watts, A.G. (1996e). International perspectives. In Watts, A.G., Law, B., Killeen, J., Kidd, J.M. & Hawthorn, R. *Rethinking Careers and Guidance: Theory, Policy and Practice.* London: Routledge.

Watts, A.G. (1996f). Towards a policy for lifelong career development: a trans-Atlantic perspective. *Career Development Quarterly*, 45(1), 41-53.

Watts, A.G. (1997). *Strategic Directions for Careers Services in Higher Education.* Cambridge: Careers Research and Advisory Centre/Association of Graduate Careers Advisory Services.

Watts, A.G. (1999a). *Reshaping Career Development for the 21st Century.* Derby: Centre for Guidance Studies, University of Derby.

Watts, A.G. (1999b). *The Role of the Personal Adviser: Concepts and Issues*. CeGS Occasional Paper. Derby: Centre for Guidance Studies, University of Derby.

Watts, A.G. (2000a). Synthesis. In B. Hiebert & L. Bezanson (eds.), *Making Waves: Career Development and Public Policy* (pp. 278–292). Ottawa: Canadian Career Development Foundation.

Watts, A.G. (2000b). The role of guidance within innovative training structures for young people at risk. In *Constructing the Future*. Stourbridge: Institute of Career Guidance/Trotman.

Watts, A.G. (2001a). *Second international symposium on career development and public policy: rapporteur's report*. Unpublished manuscript, Canadian Career Development Foundation, Ottawa, Canada.

Watts, A.G. (2001b). Career guidance and social exclusion: a cautionary tale. *British Journal of Guidance and Counselling*, 29(2), 157-176.

Watts, A.G. (2013). False dawns, bleak sunset: the Coalition Government's policies on career guidance. *British Journal of Guidance and Counselling*, 41(4), 442-453.

Watts, A.G. (2014a). Forty years of the BJGC: a personal review. *British Journal of Guidance and Counselling*, 42(1), 2-8.

Watts, A.G. (2014b). Cross-national reviews of career guidance systems: overview and reflections. *Journal of the National Institute for Career Education and Counselling*, 32, 4-14.

Watts, A.G. (2014c). The evolution of NICEC: a historical review. *Journal of the National Institute for Career Education and Counselling*, 33, 4-14.

Watts, A.G., Bezanson, L. & McCarthy, J. (2014). The international symposia on career development and public policy: retrospect and prospect. *Australian Journal of Career Development*, 23(3), 108-118.

Watts, A.G., Dartois, C. & Plant, P. (1988). *Educational and Vocational Guidance Services for the 14-25 Age Group in tlte European Community*. Maastricht: Presses Interuniversitaires Europeennes.

Watts, A.G. & Dent, G. (2002). "Let your fingers do the walking": the use of telephone helplines in career information and guidance. *British Journal of Guidance and Counselling*, 30(1), 17–35.

Watts, A.G. & Ferreira Marques, J.H. (1979). *Guidance and the School Curriculum*. Paris: UNESCO.

Watts, A.G. & Fretwell, D. (2004). *Public Policies for Career Development: Policy Strategies for Designing Career Information and Guidance Systems in Middle-Income and Transition Economies*. Washington, DC: World Bank.

Watts, A.G., Guichard, J., Plant, P. & Rodriguez, M. L. (1994). *Educational and Vocational Guidance in the European Community*. Luxembourg: Office for Official Publications of the European Communities.

Watts, A.G. & Hawthorn, R. (1992). *Careers Education and the Curriculum in Higher Education*. NICEC Project Report. Cambridge: Careers Research and Advisory Centre.

Watts, A.G., Hawthorn, R., Hoffbrand, J., Jackson, H., & Spurling, A. (1997). Developing local lifelong guidance strategies. *British Journal of Guidance and Counselling*, 25, 217-227.

Watts, A.G. & Herr, E.L. (1976). Career(s) education in Britain and the USA: Contrasts and common problems. *British Journal of Guidance and Counselling*, 4(2), 129-142.

Watts, A.G. & Kant, L. (1986). *A Working Start: Guidance Strategies for Girls and Young Women*. York: Longman/School Curriculum Development Committee.

Watts, A.G. & Kidd, J.M. (1978). Evaluating the effectiveness of careers guidance: A review of the British research. *Journal of Occupational Psychology*, 51, 235-248.

Watts, A.G. & Knasel, E.G. (1985). *Adult Unemployment and the Curriculum*. London: Further Education Unit.

Watts, A.G. & Law, B. (1985). Issues for careers education in the multi-ethnic classroom. *Pastoral Care in Education*, 3(2), 119-27.

Watts, A.G., Law, B., Killeen, J., Kidd, J. M., & Hawthorn, R. (1996). *Rethinking Careers Education and Guidance: Theory, Policy and Practice*. London: Routledge.

Watts, A.G. & McCarthy, J. (1996). *Non-Formal Guidance for Young People at Risk.* Dublin: National Centre for Guidance in Education.

Watts, A.G. & McCarthy, J. (1998). *Training in Community Based Guidance*. Dublin: National Centre for Guidance in Education.

Watts, A.G. & Moran, P. (eds.) (1984). *Education for Enterprise.* Cambridge: CRAC/Hobsons.

Watts, A.G. & Stevens, B. (1999). The relationship between career guidance and financial guidance. *Widening Participation and Lifelong Learning*, 1(3), 11-19.

Watts, A.G., Super, D.E. & Kidd, J. (eds.) (1981). *Career Development in Britain.* Cambridge: CRAC/Hobsons.

Watts, A.G. & Young, M. (1997). Models of student guidance in a changing 14-19 education and training system. In Hodgson, A. & Spours, K. (eds.), *Dearing and Beyond: 14-19 Qualifications, Frameworks and Systems*. London: Kogan Page.

Weiner, G. (ed.) (1985). *Just a Bunch of Girls: Feminist Approaches to Schooling*. Buckingham: Open University Press.

Weiyuan, Z. (1994). The history and current state of careers guidance in China. *Educational and Vocational Guidance Bulletin*, 55, 1-7.

Weinstock, A. (2000). Developing Connexions. *Careers Guidance Today*, 8(5), 14-16.

Wellman, B., Carrington, P. J. & Hall, A. (1988). Networks as personal communities. In Wellman, B. & Berkowitz, S.D. (eds.). *Social structures: A Network Approach*. Cambridge: Cambridge University Press.

Westergaard, J. & Resler, H. (1975). *Class in a Capitalist Society*. London: Heinemann.

White, M. (1980). *Shorter Working Time.* London: Policy Studies Institute.

Wiener, M.J. (1981). *English Culture and the Decline of the Industrial Spirit, 1850-1980*. Cambridge: Cambridge University Press.

Wilensky, H. L. (1961). Orderly careers and social participation: The impact of work history on social integration in the middle mass. *American Sociological Review*, 26, 521-539.

Williams, R. (1961). *The Long Revolution*. London: Chatto & Windus.

Williamson, E. G. (1965). *Vocational Counseling: Some Historical, Philosophical, and Theoretical Perspectives.* New York: McGraw-Hill.

Williamson, H. (2000). Status zero: From research to policy and practice in the United Kingdom. In Walvaren, G., Parsons, C., Van Veen, D. & Day, C. (eds.) *Combating Social Exclusion through Education*. Leuven: Apeldoorn-Garant.

Willis, P. (1977). *Learning to Labour*. Farnborough: Saxon House.

Wilson, J. & Jackson, H. (1998). *What Are Adults' Expectations and Requirements of Guidance? A Millennium Agenda*. Winchester: National Advisory Council for Careers and Educational Guidance.

Wolf, A., Fotheringhame, J. & Grey, A. (1990). *Learning in Context: Patterns of Skills Transfer and Training Implications*. Research and Development Report No.58. Sheffield: Training Agency.

Woods, P. (1979). *The Divided School*. London: Routledge & Kegan Paul.

Wrench, J. (1991). Gatekeepers in the urban labour market: Constraining or constrained? In Cross, M. and

Payne, G. (eds.), *Work and the Enterprise Culture*. London: Falmer.

Yorke, M. & Knight, P. (2006). *Embedding Employability in the Curriculum.* Learning and Employability Series. York: Higher Education Academy.

Yorke, M. (2006). *Employability in Higher Education: What It Is – What It Is Not.* Learning and Employability Series. York: Higher Education Academy.

Young, S. & Hood, N. (1977). *Chrysler UK: a Corporation in Transition*. New York: Praeger.

Zajda, J. (1979). Education for labour in the USSR. *Comparative Education*, 15(3), 287-299.

Zelizer, V.A. (1985). *Pricing the Priceless Child*. New York: Basic Books.

Table showing original copyright

Chapter/article title	Original publication	Original copyright
1. Education and Employment: the Traditional Bonds	A.G. Watts, Education, Unemployment and the Future of Work (1983). Milton Keynes: Open University Press	Rights reverted to author
2. Reshaping Career Development for the 21st Century	CeGS Occasional Paper. Derby: Centre for Guidance Studies, University of Derby, 1999.	iCEGS holds copyright
3. Careers Education and the Informal Economies	British Journal of Guidance and Counselling, Volume 9 No. 1, January 1981.	Taylor and Francis
4. The Economic and Social Benefits of Career Guidance	Educational and Vocational Guidance Bulletin, No. 63, 1999.	IAEVG Board
5. Careers Education	Law, B. & Watts, A.G.: Schools, Careers and Community. London: Church Information Office, 1977	Church Information Office
6. Power in Careers Guidance Work	As above	Church Information Office
7. The Concept of Work Experience	in Miller, A., Watts, A.G. & Jamieson, I.: Rethinking Work Experience. London: Falmer, 1991.	Taylor and Francis
8. Work Simulations in Schools: a Conceptual Framework	in Jamieson, I., Miller, A. & Watts, A.G.: Mirrors of Work: Work Simulations in Schools. Lewes, Sussex: Falmer, 1988.	Taylor and Francis
9. Career Development Learning and Employability	Learning and Employability Series Two No.5. York: Higher Education Academy, 2006.	Higher Education Academy
10. The Role of Information and Communication Technologies in Integrated Career Information and Guidance Systems: a Policy Perspective	International Journal for Educational and Vocational Guidance, Volume 2 No.3, 2002.	Springer Science+Business Media
11. Socio-political ideologies in guidance	in Watts, A.G., Law, B., Killeen, J., Kidd, J.M. & Hawthorn, R. (eds): Rethinking Careers Education and Guidance: Theory, Policy and Practice. London: Routledge. 1996	Taylor and Francis
12. The Implications of School-Leaver Unemployment for Careers Education in Schools	Journal of Curriculum Studies, Volume 10 No. 3, September 1978.	Taylor and Francis
13. The Impact of the 'New Right': Policy Challenges Confronting Careers Guidance in England and Wales	British Journal of Guidance and Counselling, Volume 19 No. 3, September 1991.	Taylor and Francis

14. Career Guidance and Social Exclusion: a Cautionary Tale	British Journal of Guidance and Counselling, Volume 29 No. 2, May 2001.	Taylor and Francis
15. The New Career and Public Policy	In Collin, A. & Young, R.A. (eds.): The Future of Career. Cambridge: Cambridge University Press, 2000.	Cambridge University Press
16. The Role of Career Guidance in Societies in Transition	Educational and Vocational Guidance, No. 61, 1998.	IAEVG Board
17. Career guidance: an international perspective	in Watts, A.G., Law, B., Killeen, J., Kidd, J.M. & Hawthorn, R. (eds): Rethinking Careers Education and Guidance: Theory, Policy and Practice. London: Routledge. 1996	Taylor and Francis
18. Policy Challenges for Career Guidance	Organisation for Economic Co-operation and Development: Career Guidance and Public Policy: Bridging the Gap. Paris: OECD, 2004. (Written by Sweet, R. & Watts, A.G.)	OECD
19. Career Guidance Policies in 37 Countries: Contrasts and Common Themes	Co-author Ronald Sultana. International Journal for Educational and Vocational Guidance, Volume 4 Nos.2-3, 2004.	Springer Science+Business Media
20. Unemployment and the Future of Work	Educational and Vocational Guidance Bulletin, No. 43, 1985.	IAEVG Board
21. Career development: Looking back, moving forward?	iCeGS, 2014	iCEGS

Index

11+ 74
21st Century 12, 229, 320

A

A level 74, 85, 98
Academic empathy 148
Academic subjects 23, 91, 251
    Business studies 98
    English 8, 15, 31, 34, 76, 86, 112, 241, 330,
    History 2, 147, 299, 337,
    Mathematics 74, 86,
    Science 16, 71, 74
Adaptability 192
Adolescence 105, 180
Adviser, career
    At-risk youth 227
    Delivery of learning 148
    Employment 233
    General 29-30, 37, 72, 158, 331, 333
    Policy 333, 335
    Professional activities 32-33, 233-234
    Socio-political dimension 179-183
Adviser, personal 231, 233-235
African National Congress 266
Agency, human 4, 7, 12, 224-225, 280
AimHigher 333
Alienation 48, 178, 184, 191
All-age services/strategies 158, 229, 237-238, 332-333
Andrews, David 4, 58, 238,
Apartheid 266-267, 274-275, 297
Apprenticeship 90, 226, 279, 282
Approaches to careers education
    Conservative 168, 173-175, 179, 181, 183-184, 273, 275
    Liberal 168, 173-184, 207, 236, 275, 279
    Progressive 168, 173-184, 212, 247, 275, 285
    Radical 168, 173-176, 178, 180-181, 183-184, 244, 269, 275-276, 293, 323
Aptitudes 15, 18, 23, 26, 75
Aristocracy 242
Ashton, David 18, 20, 22-23, 44-45, 188, 194
Aspiration 26, 50, 75, 159, 171, 173-174, 179, 182, 184, 203, 250, 263
Assessment
    Career 123, 153, 155, 158, 163, 296
    Centre 36
    Learning 120, 143, 250, 290
Association of Graduate Careers Advisory Services (AGCAS) 131-133, 136, 138, 140, 143, 207, 216, 339
Austerity 333
Australia 277, 287-289, 295, 303, 305
Austria 287-289, 295, 302
Autonomy, school 333, 336
Awareness
    Opportunity 24, 61, 75-77, 132, 133, 153
    Self 24, 57, 75-77, 80, 130, 132, 133, 135, 153

B

Bargaining, collective 36, 124-125, 253
Bataiawo 278
Behaviours
    Boundary management see Boundary management
    Influence 134
    Positioning 134
Belgium 281, 295
Beliefs, efficacy 34, 130, 194
Bentley, Tom 36, 231
Black economy see Economy, black/hidden
Blair, Tony 63, 221
Blue-collar 17
Blueprint for Life-Work Design 307
Blunkett, David 230, 332
Boundary management 134
Boundaryless career 40
Bridgewater, Adrian 2, 329
Bridging the Gap 230-231, 234-235
British Journal of Guidance and Counselling 3
British Youth Council 188, 198, 200
Brokerage 37, 148, 231-233, 253, 263
Brunton Report 26
Budgetary skills see Financial education
Bulgaria 295
Bureaucracy 32, 210
Business studies see Academic subjects
Byers/Gee document 229, 237

C

Canada 153, 158, 164, 203, 281, 287-289, 295, 297, 304-305, 307
Capital
   Cultural 20, 35, 182
   Human 60, 127, 134, 299-300
Capitalism 7, 324
Career Development Institute (CDI) 336, 339
Career
   Adviser see Adviser, career
   Coach 39, 174
   Co-ordinator 80, 84, 248
   Counsellor 7, 29, 34, 38-39, 57, 154-156, 159-160, 172, 274, 276-278, 280-282, 301, 303-304
   Education 1, 3, 7, 12, 58-60, 68, 235, 251, 296, 300-301, 307
   Exploration 122, 300
   Fair 139
   Ladder 30
   Modules 138
   Officers 81, 91, 176-177, 179, 182, 187, 207, 213, 238, 282
   Planning 36-37, 68, 87, 89, 92, 130, 140-141, 143, 251, 299-302, 308
   Professional 331, 334-336
   Rainbow 328
   Self-management 59, 131, 134, 137, 251, 308
   Teacher 63, 174, 177, 181, 206, 215, 281-282, 331
Career learning theory 34
Career management skills (CMS) see Skills
Career resource centre 36, 251
Careering about 31, 330
Careerism 262, 273
Careerquake 30, 241, 268
Careers Education in the 1970s 71
Careers England 4, 349
'Careers for all' 32, 35, 243, 332
Careers Research and Advisory Centre (CRAC) 2, 63, 329
Careers Service 45, 77, 81, 173, 179, 206, 211, 213, 215-217, 221, 229-233, 236-237, 331-333
Careership 215, 218
Carr Committee 26
Case-managed services 155
Case-studies 111-112, 121
Catchment areas 18
Centre for Career Management Skills 144
Centre for Guidance Studies see International Centre for Guidance Studies 3
Certificate of Pre-Vocational Education (CPVE) 101
China 262, 273
Chrysler UK 198
Chubb, Paul 332
Citizenship 244
Civil society 254, 263, 265
Class systems 277
Coalition Government 3, 333
Cohesion, social 222, 242, 326
Colleges 20, 25, 36, 85, 191, 206, 211, 214, 216, 230, 234, 235, 246, 295, 331
Collin, Audrey 31
Commercial agents 253
Communist Party 262, 273
Community placements 101
Community 77-78, 80-82, 101-103, 105-108, 135, 142, 152, 178, 189-190, 192-193, 202, 203, 226-228, 231, 242-243, 247-249, 262, 266, 273, 275, 297, 303, 305-306, 330-331
Competencies 40, 235, 247, 251, 303-304, 307, 310
Computers 152-153, 337
Confederation of British Industry (CBI) 25, 215, 243
Connexions 3, 221, 231-239, 332-333
Conservative Government 3, 62, 221, 229, 237, 334
Constructivist theory 34
Control, social 172, 175, 177, 179, 183, 195-196, 212-213, 217, 236, 273, 275
Cornmarket Press 2, 329
Cost-effective models 258, 310
Counselling
   One-to-one 154, 178
   Group 155
   Non-directive 173
Course tasters 300
Credentialism 19-20, 44, 227
Credit accumulation and transfer system (CATS) 249

Crime 31, 188, 199, 222, 224, 226, 241, 263, 319
Cultural capital see Capital, cultural
Curriculum
National 17-18, 21, 24-27, 33
CV 140-141, 143
Cyprus 295
Czech Republic 263, 295

D

Data collection 75
Daws, Peter 2, 24, 173, 206-207, 279, 317
Dearing Report 139, 142
Decision making, process of 34, 57, 61, 72, 76, 114, 118, 153-154, 168, 181, 275, 278, 286, 292, 303
Delinquency 199, 222, 319
Democracy 202, 209, 263
Demos 231-232, 243
Denmark 52, 279, 286, 288-289, 295, 301, 306
Department for Business, Innovation and Skills (BIS) see Government departments
Deployment 83, 129-130
Developing country 8, 156, 272
Development
Economic 241, 258, 261, 264, 272, 297
Professional 135, 207, 219, 250, 253
Diagnostic approach 154
Digital phase 152
Discrimination
Gender 180
Race 182-183
Division of labour 103, 114, 261, 272
DOTS model 132, 134, 152
Dual-labour market theory 199-200
Duffner Committee 237
Durkheim, Emile 222

E

Economic benefits 56-57, 60, 62, 64
Economic floor 49, 200
Economy
Black/hidden 46-48, 107-108, 112, 177, 225, 244, 265, 324-325
Command 264, 297
Communal 46-47, 107-108, 225, 325
Formal 43, 45-50, 52, 107-108, 112, 214, 225, 227, 319, 324-325
Household 47, 107-108, 225, 325
Informal 7, 46-48, 108, 214, 226, 296, 315
Planned 32
Subsistence 261, 272, 317
Education
Adult 282, 302
Comparative 271
Enterprise 138, 177
Financial 37, 76, 253
Further 25, 85, 191, 193, 214, 243, 290
Higher 2-3, 7, 24, 40, 68, 85, 127-132, 134, 136-138, 141-149, 206, 216, 229, 247, 249, 251, 272, 301, 331
Post-compulsory 40, 249, 357
Secondary 17, 74
Vocational 26, 59, 86, 101, 123, 211, 272, 279
Education Act 1997 234
Education Reform Act 1988 212
Education-Business Partnerships 333
Educators, public 17
Egalitarian 73, 103, 218, 244
E-guidance 145
Employability
General 40, 64, 176-177, 183, 222, 242, 245, 249, 253, 268, 285, 291-292, 298-299, 302, 309
Graduate 68, 127-149
Schools 192, 194
Employer liaison 144
Employers 153
Employment
Paid 47, 49-50, 100-101, 103, 105-108, 112, 190, 201, 222, 243-244, 326, 330
Under 320
Employment and Training Act 1973 221
English see Academic subjects
Enhancing Employability, Recognising Diversity 130
Enterprise
Social 329
Mini 95, 101, 107, 114-118, 126
Equal-opportunities 89, 179
Equity, Social 12, 35, 49, 127, 161, 208, 242, 244, 262-263, 268, 285-286,

289, 298, 330, 337
Estonia 295
Ethnic-minority 182-183
Europe
    Central 261, 263, 265-266, 297-298
    Eastern 219, 261, 263, 265-266, 297
    Western 277, 283, 296, 318, 320, 322
European classicism 279
European Commission 4, 151, 222, 229, 265, 288, 291, 295, 298, 338
European Employment Strategy 291
European Lifelong Guidance Policy Network (ELGPN) 4, 338, 339
European Union 221, 222, 295
Examination 18, 21-22, 27, 44, 52, 58-59, 73-74, 88, 91, 129, 143, 190, 247-248
Exclusion, social 8, 31, 32, 63-64, 168, 221-225, 227-228, 230-232, 239, 244, 332-333, 336
Extended careers 22
Experiential learning see Learning, experiential
Extra-curricular activities 128, 139

F

Family 4, 12, 37, 50, 63, 75, 77, 103-107, 182, 190, 203, 210, 224, 243, 261, 271-272, 274, 277-278
Father 4, 278
Finland 287-289, 295
France 222, 241, 268, 269, 279, 281, 295
Free sector see Informal economy
Further education see Education
Future of work 113, 315, 317, 326, 328

G

Games 95, 112-122
Gatekeepers 33, 134, 173
Gemeinschaft 278
Gender 103, 155, 173, 178-184, 289
Germany 4, 38, 241, 250, 268-269, 274, 279, 281-282, 284, 287-289, 295, 301-302, 305
Gesellschaft 278
Giddens, Anthony 32, 224, 270, 273
Ginzberg, Eli 207
Globalisation 30, 267, 296
Goodman, Jane 35-36, 252
Gove, Michael 335-336

Government departments
    Department for Business, Innovation and Skills 335
    Department for Education and Employment 221, 232
    Department for Education and Skills 292
    Department of Education and Science 71
Greece 281, 295
Guidance
    Adult 39, 219, 237, 269-270, 307
    Client-centred 215
    Counsellor see Career, counsellor
    Distance 155
    Green 270
    Interview 130, 141, 192, 233
    Lifelong 4, 285, 293, 300, 302, 307-308, 338
    Programmes 58-60, 177, 227, 265-266, 306-307
    Systems 4, 33, 68, 81, 83, 151-153, 156, 162, 262, 266, 271-272, 279, 282-293, 285, 293, 296-297, 307-309
    Targeting of 63, 145, 229-230
    Vocational 29, 55, 151, 172, 233, 261-262, 269, 272, 274, 276, 279, 281, 283, 286, 295, 301, 305, 307, 315, 317
Guidance Council 38, 164, 307, 332, 338, 344, 349

H

Hancock, Matthew 334
Hansard 221, 232, 233
Harris Committee 145-146
Hayes, John 2, 180, 319, 333, 334
Headteacher 58, 124, 234
Higher education see Education
History see Academic subjects
Holland Report 188, 198
Hooley, Tristram 2, 152, 338-339
Hopson, Barrie 2
Hughes, Deirdre 225, 228, 236, 339
Humanists 16-17, 21
Hungary 295

I

Iceland 295

Identity, professional 280-281
Impartiality 36, 162, 234-235, 301-302
Individual Learning Accounts (ILA) 39-40, 246, 252
Individualism 9, 64, 209, 258, 262, 273, 277, 283-284, 297
Industrial revolution 16, 25, 327
Informal economy 7, 46-48, 108, 214, 226, 296, 315
Information age 29
Information and communication technology (ICT) 30, 38, 68, 139, 145, 151- 164, 238, 296, 303-304, 308
Inspiration Vision Statement 334
Institute of Careers Officers 187, 207, 213
Interdisciplinary 6, 13
International Association of Educational and Vocational Guidance (IAEVG) 315, 317
International Centre for Guidance Studies (iCEGS) 3, 329
International Labour Organisation (ILO) 4, 46
International Round Table for the Advancement of Counselling (IRTAC) 283
International standards 305
Internationalisation 289, 338
Intervention
    Asynchronous 158-160
    Directive 181, 262, 273, 278-279
    Non-directive 173, 175, 179, 184, 195-197, 275
    Synchronous 158, 160
Interview
    Guidance 65, 77, 145, 154, 156, 160, 178, 213-214, 230, 233, 252, 281-282, 285, 287, 293, 296, 298, 304, 336
    Mock 122, 133, 140, 143
    Recruitment 153, 176, 192
Investors in People (IiP) 36
Ireland 20, 281, 287-289, 295
Israel 274

J
Jackson, Heather 38, 154, 174, 246, 252, 334
Jamieson, Ian 25-26, 85-109, 111-125, 212, 248, 338
Japan 241, 280, 282-283
Job
    Club 62
    Creation 45, 199-200, 203, 323
    Higher-status 26, 142
    Maintenance 64, 134, 162, 198-199, 323
    Sampling 86-87, 89-91, 96, 122
    Satisfaction 19, 23, 45, 50, 55, 62, 77, 97, 144, 173, 184, 236, 276, 286, 299-300, 309, 324-325
Job search see Skills, jobsearch
Jobcentre/Job Centre 213
Juvenile Employment Service 206

K
Katz, Martin 2, 71, 175
Kidd, Jennifer 40, 56-57, 62-63, 65, 171, 207, 225, 250-251, 271
Killeen, John 56, 57, 59-63, 65, 171, 172, 178, 225, 250, 262, 271, 277
Kolb, David 92-93
Korea 288-289, 295-296
Krumboltz, John 34, 122

L
Labour Force Survey 236
Labour Government 3, 32, 210, 221-222, 226, 269, 333, 336
Labour market
    Bureaux 205
    General 12, 26, 29, 35, 40-45, 60-63, 81-83, 127, 129-130, 173-174, 178, 182-183, 199-201, 206, 208, 211, 218, 225, 238, 250, 258, 262, 264-265, 258, 268, 275-276, 279-281, 301-303, 309-310, 335, 337
    Flexibility 31, 40, 64, 241-243, 245-246, 253-254, 285-293, 296, 298, 308-310, 319-320, 323, 327, 332-333
    Information 153, 227, 301, 306, 308
Latin America 278
Latvia 295
Law, Bill 2, 24, 34, 68, 71, 79, 131-132, 153, 181, 183, 189-190, 283, 338
Learndirect see Telephone counselling
Learning

Decision 24, 57, 75-77, 132, 153
Experiential 92-93, 212, 248, 300
Flexible 248-249
Gateway 236
Lifelong 7, 32, 40, 136, 230, 247-249, 251, 285, 288, 290, 298, 300, 302, 309-310
Mentor 235
Outcomes 56-59, 132-134, 144, 219, 299
Transition 24, 57, 75-77, 132-133, 153
Work-related 95, 247, 249, 333
Learning and Skills Bill 232
Learning model (of career development) 2, 34
Leisure class see Society, leisure
Liberal Democrats 334
Life chances 72-73, 171
Lifelong career development see Guidance
Linnecar, Robert 30
Lithuania 295
Local Authorities 205
Local Education Authority (LEA) 211, 213, 216
Luxembourg 289, 295

M

Mainframe phase 151
Malta 295
Mandela, Nelson 266
Manpower Services Commission 188
Marginalised groups 189
Market
 Labour see Labour market
 Economic 30-32, 48, 55, 200, 205, 209-215, 219, 241, 245-246, 262-264, 275, 277, 290, 297, 318, 323, 325-326
 Failure 39, 56, 61, 161-163, 246, 264, 305
 Guidance 38-39, 161, 214-218, 221, 269-270, 305, 332
Marx, Karl 324, 330
Marxist-Leninism 279
Matching model 62, 265
Mathematics see Academic subjects
Matrix quality standards 145
Maxi systems 153-154, 163

Medical model (of career development) 2, 331
Mentor 231, 235-236, 248
Mentoring 1, 36, 229, 236, 251
Mentoring Action Project 229, 236
Meritocracy 18, 30, 182
Meta-ability 137
Metacognition 130, 137
Meta-skills see Skills
Microcomputer phase 151
Middle ages 15
Middle-income countries 295-296, 304, 307
Migration 289
Milburn, Alan 238, 333
Miller, Andy 85-109, 111-125, 248, 338
Mini-enterprise see Enterprise, mini
Mixed-economy 305
Mobility
 Contest 18, 73, 279
 Social 9, 20, 27, 64, 277, 279, 284, 330, 333
 Sponsored 17-18, 73, 279
Monetarism 318
Moral underclass 222
Morgan, Nicky 336
Motivation 27, 33, 59-60, 87, 92, 122, 137, 191, 193, 196, 248, 276, 286, 288, 290, 339
Motivation theory 60

N

Narrative, career 34-35
National Careers Service 333-334
National IAG Board 307
National Institute for Career Education and Counselling (NICEC) 1, 3, 36, 40, 56-58, 62-63, 338-339
National Institute for Economic and Social Research 198
National Occupational Information Coordinating Committee 162
National Qualifications Framework 249
National telephone helpline see Telephone guidance
National Youth Bureau 189
National Youth Employment Council 188
Negotiation 98, 124-126, 135, 155, 175, 184

Neo-Marxism 173
Netherlands 277, 279, 281, 287-289, 295, 302, 305
Network 37, 47, 64, 135, 183, 226, 253-254, 277, 283, 325, 338-338
New Deal 223
New Labour see Labour Party
New Right 3, 8, 32, 168, 205, 208-215, 218-219, 276
New Start 236
New technologies see Information and communication technology and Telephone guidance
Next Step 333
Nigeria 278
North America 163, 296
Norway 286, 288-289, 295, 301-302
Not in education, employment or training (NEET) 223, 230, 368

O
Occupational Guidance Service 206, 211
Occupational Preparation Systems 123
Occupations
 Careerless 23
 Knowledge 273
Ofsted 234-235
Opportunity
 Awareness 24, 57-58, 77, 132-133, 153, 193
 Creation 177, 193
 Structures 35, 226
Organisation for Economic Co-operation and Development (OECD) 4, 151, 58, 285-286, 290-293, 295-310
Ori 278
Orientation 19, 24-25, 27, 140, 176, 262, 272, 274, 279
Outplacement 39, 162, 269, 305
Outreach 228-229, 301

P
Parsons, Frank 29, 223, 286
Partnership model 333-334
Pastoral-care 233, 282
Pedagogy for Employability Group 128, 140
Peer review 140
Pensions 37, 244-245, 269

Performance management 246
Personal development planning 139, 146
Personality 75, 77, 133, 155, 224
Philippines 281, 295
Planful serendipity see Serendipity
Planned happenstance 34
Planning Guidance 234, 237
Poland 295, 301, 307
Policy borrowing 8, 271, 297
Portfolios 143, 306
Portugal 295
Post-16 89, 215, 234-235
Power 32-33, 48, 68, 73, 79-84, 136, 159, 178, 180, 183, 242, 258, 264, 299, 321, 326, 336
Prisoners Dilemma 125
Productivity 19, 48, 61, 188, 197, 201, 318
Professionalisation 81
Progress file 139, 146
Progression 7, 30-32, 101-102, 130, 137, 146, 211, 239, 243, 245, 268, 273, 330
Psychology 2, 6, 12, 83, 147, 168, 287, 304, 335, 337
Psychometrics 62, 153, 163, 252, 269, 278, 281, 298, 331
Public policy 4, 8, 12-13, 32, 152, 159-160, 168, 205, 207-208, 210, 218, 221, 226, 242-244, 254, 285-286, 288, 295, 298, 302, 309-310, 338
Pupil Referral Units 234

Q
Qualifications
 Formal 20, 44
 Over-qualification 19
 Vocational 15-16, 21, 25-26, 29, 35, 55, 59, 77, 85-87, 89, 91-92, 100-101, 120, 123, 127
Quality Assurance Agency 131
Quality in Careers Standard 339
Quality of life 31, 64, 244, 317, 326

R
Race 18, 27, 191
Realism 141, 168, 171, 174, 182, 187
Recruitment 44, 58, 90, 133, 140-141,

161-163, 183, 199, 213
Reflection 5, 49, 137, 139-140, 337
Reform, social 172, 184
Reich, Robert 29, 242
Relationship-centred models 159
Resilience 84, 246
Restart programme 213-214
Retirement 4, 201, 289, 292, 303, 349
Right to work 49, 200, 222, 321, 322, 324
Rogers, Carl 173, 207
Role
   Play 112, 121-123, 126, 140, 298
   Tension 85
   Transition 134
Role-deployment 83
Romania 261, 263, 295
Russia 263, 295

S

Sampson, Jim 154-157, 161-163, 338
Sandwich courses 85, 142
Saudi Arabia 4
Scandinavia 277
School
   Curriculum 17, 21, 26, 86-87, 189, 192
   Effectiveness 56, 58-59, 64
Schooling
   Compulsory 17, 95, 221, 223, 251
   Selective 18
School-leaver 18
Schools
   Comprehensive 18
   Primary 33, 97, 300
   Public/private 18
   Secondary 23, 33, 71-78, 79-84, 85-109, 111-125, 187-203, 206, 211-212, 223, 227, 230, 232-236, 238, 248, 250-252, 262, 265, 281-282, 292-293, 300-302, 331-335
Schools Council Careers Education and Guidance Project 71, 175
Science see Academic subjects
Scotland 26, 139, 233, 236-237
Sector, 'free' 44
Segregation, gender 103, 178
Self
   Actualisation 202-203, 278, 283-284
   Awareness 24, 57, 75-77, 80, 130, 132-133, 135, 153
   Employment 31, 45, 50, 106-108, 112, 132, 136, 193, 214, 225, 227, 242-243, 263, 292, 319
   Interest 55, 205, 209, 246, 254, 335
   Presentation 132-133, 139
Serendipity, planful 34
Seven Point Plan 331
Shadowing 94-97, 108, 142, 156, 179, 300
Silver, Ruth 200, 222, 333
Singapore 282
Sixth form 74, 85, 208
Skilled
   Highly skilled 18, 95
   Semi-skilled 16, 23
   Unskilled 23, 95, 97, 301, 319
Skills
   Budgetary 76
   Career management 4, 7, 33, 130-131, 134, 136, 138-141, 144-147, 157, 253, 293, 296, 299-300, 302, 308
   Certificates 138, 248
   Clerical 124
   Communication 30, 38, 68, 76, 77, 82, 151, 207, 236, 238
   Coping 77, 136, 177, 192, 245, 265
   Core 129, 135, 249
   Decision-making 24, 34, 80, 114, 132-133, 135, 143
   Group-dynamic 122
   Interpersonal 76, 122
   Job search 130, 176, 192
   Key 129
   Meta 137
   Negotiation 98, 124-126, 135, 155, 175, 184
   Organisation 80
   Revolution 31, 229, 243, 332
   Shortages 199, 289
   Social 19, 88, 192
   Transferable 129, 133, 136, 162
Slavery 317, 320
Slovakia 295
Slovenia 295
Smith, Adam 2, 95, 100, 210, 215, 264, 310, 338
Social benefits (of guidance) 56, 63, 239
Social Exclusion Unit 221, 230-231

Social learning theory 34
Social networks see Networks
Socialisation 18-19, 22-24, 27
Society
- Ageing 289
- Agrarian-based 261, 272
- Civil 254, 263, 265
- Democratic 8, 64
- Leisure 49, 315, 320
- Post-industrial 254

Sociology 3, 6, 12, 83, 287, 337
Socrates 330
South Africa 4, 261, 266, 274-275, 295, 297
Spain 288-289, 295
Statutory Guidance 333-336
Stepping Stones project 236
Stigma 26, 302, 321
Stuart, Graham 334
Sultana, Ronald 180. 258, 295-310, 330, 338
Super, Donald 2, 76, 207, 270-271, 273, 287, 328
Support services 192, 214, 237
Sweden 275, 281, 295, 303
Sweet, Richard 258, 285, 336, 338
Symbolic analysts 242

T

Targeting see Guidance, targeting of
Taxation 46, 49, 107, 210, 225
Teachers 15, 17, 20, 22-23, 25-26, 29-30, 45, 51, 63, 73-73, 78, 80-81, 83-84, 90, 95, 104-105, 116, 119-122, 124, 128, 148, 174-175, 177, 178-180, 182, 190-191, 194, 196-197, 205-207, 209, 215, 231, 234, 248, 262, 274, 280-282, 304, 321, 326, 331
Technical and Vocational Education Initiative (TVEI) 86, 123, 211
Technology 33, 83, 84, 113, 121, 160, 246-248, 266-267, 320, 337
Temporary Employment Subsidy 198
Thatcher, Margaret 62, 205, 210, 213-214, 219, 238, 332
Third way 32, 241
Third world countries see Developing countries
Third-sector 39, 265, 267, 269

Trade union 43, 117, 122, 124, 126, 276
Trade Union Congress (TUC) 88-90
Trainer, industrial 17
Training
- General 15, 19, 22, 31 35, 40, 58, 60-61, 63, 73-74, 78, 81, 86, 89, 94, 96, 98-99, 123-124, 129, 134, 147, 153, 160, 172, 174, 176, 189, 191-192, 195, 198-199, 203, 207, 211-212, 215-216, 221-223, 225-227, 229-231, 233, 236-237, 242-243, 245-247, 262, 271-273, 279, 287, 290-291, 295, 297-298, 303-304, 306, 330,
- Careers professionals 158, 160, 172, 183, 228, 280-281, 301-302, 304, 309, 339
- Credits 217-218
- Vocational see Education, vocational

Training and Enterprise Councils (TECs) 215, 216
Turkey 295

U

Unemployment 3, 8, 27, 37, 43, 48-49, 52, 61, 73, 83, 100-101, 168, 173, 176-178, 187-203, 212-214, 223, 241-242, 244-245, 253, 263, 265, 286, 289, 291-292, 297, 301, 315, 317-321, 323, 325, 327-328, 332
United Nations 322
United States of America (USA) 19, 22, 26, 29, 35, 37, 44, 47, 62, 122, 132, 138, 143, 153, 156, 162-164, 172, 241-242, 262, 272, 277, 279, 281-283, 307, 325, 337
Universal Declaration of Human Rights 322
Universities UK 130, 146
University see Education, higher
USSR 262, 273

V

Vacation jobs 145
Venezuela 282
Victorian era 16
Vocational education see Education, vocational
Vocational impulse 26

W

Wales 18, 91, 168, 205, 233, 236-237, 282
Wales Policy Unit 237
Wealth 25, 50, 112-113, 201, 321, 326-327
Web phase 152
Web-based services 156, 296, 303
Weinstock, Anne 238, 333, 336
Welfare state 32, 48, 55, 198, 205, 209, 226, 243-244, 325-326
Welfare to Work 223
White Paper 217-218, 230-231
White-collar 17-18, 21, 26
Work
    Ethic 49, 190, 197, 200, 322
    Experience 7, 25, 68, 85-96, 98-103, 105-109, 122, 137, 142, 146, 156, 188, 193, 211, 300, 302
    Household 103, 107-108, 113
    Observation 93-95
    Part-time 292
    Shadowing 94-97, 108, 142, 156, 179, 300
    Simulation 7, 25, 93, 95, 113-114, 118-121, 126
    Voluntary 101, 103, 107-108, 113, 142, 153, 177, 194, 245, 292, 303
    World of 15, 22-24, 33, 73, 87-88, 91-92, 122, 140-141, 175, 181, 188, 213, 247-248, 280, 300, 331
Workers
    Migrant 274
    Older 244
Working-class 26, 45, 174
World Bank 4, 265, 295-298, 307, 338
Writing 168, 173, 329, 338

Y

Youth Cohort Study 103, 223
Youth Opportunity Guarantee 189
Youth Service 193, 221, 230-231, 233, 333
Youth Training Guarantee 223
Youth Training Scheme (YTS) 86, 98, 123, 213

www.ingramcontent.com/pod-product-compliance
Lightning Source LLC
Chambersburg PA
CBHW080540230426
43663CB00015B/2654